Personal Archives and a New Archival Calling

Readings, Reflections and Ruminations

D1295802

Personal Archives
and a New Archival Calling

Readings, Reflections and Ruminations

By

Richard J. Cox

Litwin Books, LLC
Duluth, Minnesota

Copyright 2008 Richard J. Cox

Published in 2008

Litwin Books, LLC
PO Box 3320
Duluth, MN 55803

http://litwinbooks.com/

Printed on acid-free paper

ISBN 978-0-9802004-7-8

Library of Congress Cataloging-in-Publication Data

Cox, Richard J.
 Personal archives and a new archival calling : readings, reflections and
ruminations / by Richard J. Cox.
     p. cm.
 Includes bibliographical references and index.
 Summary: "Examines issues affecting the future of personal and family
archives, from the point of view of archival science"--Provided by
publisher.
 ISBN 978-0-9802004-7-8 (alk. paper)
 1. Personal archives--Management. 2. Family archives--Management.
 3. Records--Management. 4. Electronic records--Management. 5.
 Archives--Philosophy. 6. Archives--Social aspects. I. Title.
 CD977.C68 2008
 025.1'97--dc22
                                 2008045503

Table of Contents

Introduction

As this book argues, personal archives might be assuming a new importance in society as the technical means for creating, maintaining, and using documents improve and become more cost-effective, and, as individuals and families also seek to preserve their old documents, especially traditional paper forms, as a connection to a past that may seem to be in risk of being swallowed up in the immense digital gadgetry in our Internet Age. There is a reversal to older technologies as well, such as leather bound journals and fountain pens, by some individuals resisting or protesting the increasingly digital world they reside in. Behind these very different approaches are similar impulses, and, these divergent paths raise identical questions about the role and purpose of traditional archives dating back two centuries and more. Personal recordkeeping raises a remarkable array of issues and concerns about records and their preservation, public or collective memory, the mission of professional records managers and archivists, the nature of the role of the institutional archives, and the function of the individual citizen as their own archivist. Archivists need to develop a new partnership with the public, and the public needs to learn from archivists the essentials of preserving documentary materials. We are on the cusp of seeing a new kind of archival future, and whether this is good or bad depends on how well archivists equip citizen archivists.

What follows are a heavily revised and expanded set of essays originally written over the past few years about personal recordkeeping for the *Records & Information Management Report*, as well as reviews of relevant studies and reports originally posted on my blog, "Reading Archives." In these essays I try to capture something of the changes underway in how individuals create personal and family records, and I provide some assessment of whether these changes are so substantial that they require the archival profession to re-examine how they approach the preservation and promote the use of such historical documents. Christine Harold argues that our lives are shaped by the intensive hyperactive media surrounding us, believing that

> our public rhythms are shaped and punctuated by an endless systolic and diastolic *pulsing* of newspapers, Hollywood films, twenty-four news channels, sitcoms, movies of the week, banner ads, billboards, reality television, presidential debates, novels, fashion magazines, hip-hop

videos, porn, blogs, talk radio, bumper stickers, anime, political smear campaigns – the texts of everyday life that constitute the teeming and multicitational field in which publics are made.[1]

Some of these, such as blogs, also relate to how people can produce new documentary forms, but most of these are documentary forms that might be collected in order to help us mark our own lives. In a discussion about the new nature of memory, Joshua Foer states that

> Over the past millennium, many of us have undergone a profound shift. We've gradually replaced our internal memory with what psychologists refer to as external memory, a vast superstructure of technological crutches that we've invented so that we don't have to store information in our brains. We've gone, you might say, from remembering everything to remembering awfully little. We have photographs to record our experiences, calendars to keep track of our schedules, books (and now the Internet) to store our collective knowledge, and Post-It notes for our scribbles. What have the implications of this outsourcing of memory been for ourselves and for our society? Has something been lost?[2]

When one reads a description such as this, it is relatively easy to envision archives (along with museums and libraries) and the roles these institutions play to preserve such materials so that there can be a societal memory. However, the new challenge may be that many of the newer digital versions of such documents may be impossible to maintain in an archives, at least as has been traditionally thought of, and may be shifting more and more to be the responsibility of the records creator – and these records creators need a new kind of assistance. Archivists need to help individuals maintain personal and family archives, only collecting those of special or extraordinary significance when they are endangered.

In the first chapter, "Posting Notes and Then Saving Them," I set the stage for why we may need to think about the preservation of family and personal archives in new ways. Although a visit to any bookstore will suggest that Americans are a people addicted to self-help publications, we will find few such volumes that provide reasonable advice about personal archiving or recordkeeping. Why is this when we know that we follow many impulses to save old documents, especially those connected with ourselves or our families. Some of these impulses have been altered, even enhanced, by elements of our own digital era. More important, however, might be the contrast between old style

institutional collectors (like historical societies) and the changing nature
of what can be collected (or maybe not collected) in our own increasing
reliance on digital documents and objects. Many of the records being
acquired by these institutions are actually the product of personal and
family efforts to gather, organize, and maintain their documents.
Individuals, in whatever era, have nonetheless administered their own
records in interesting and sometime creative ways, as the life of the
eighteenth century figure Jonathan Edwards and Ben Schneiderman's
use of Leonardo da Vinci as an inspiration for administering digital
documents demonstrate. Indeed, one thing that has not changed is the
interest in maintaining one's place in the world by remembering,
through archives and artifacts, where one has come from. Some have
characterized our present information era as also an age of forgetfulness
because there is far too much information for us to handle and digest.
The value of personal and family archives may be on the rise – but how
will we be able to save them?

The second chapter, describing recent research and reflection about
certain personal documents – the journal, letter, oral messages, and the
Web page – suggests that there is a romanticized notion about each of
these documentary forms that continues to pull us into using them; the
heart of this chapter was originally published as "The Romance of the
Document," *Records & Information Management Report* 22 (January 2006):
1-13. While predictions about Americans' loss of interest in the past and
their general rootlessness grow, they continue to scour flea markets,
antique stores, museums, libraries, and historic sites. And, while on their
quests, these individuals are often searching for letters, diaries, and
other such documents, all while they are continuing to generate these
traditional forms of records. People are interested in touching the past
and, it seems, contributing to it in the form of generating new
documents. They like the stories they extract from old family records,
and they are utilizing Web sites to create new personal and family
albums in ways far more public than anything we have seen before.
Whether on aging paper or the most sophisticated digital repository,
there continues to be a lure of the document. It is the romance of the
document that encourages individuals to maintain personal and family
archives, and, in some instances, to turn these over to archival
repositories. Of course, in these repositories, many archivists are there
because they long ago heard the call of the document.

The third chapter considers how people acquire information, and it
is based on a lengthy review essay considering the three-volume work of

linguist Stephen Roger Fischer on the history of language, writing, and reading – all basic human attributes centering around the notion of the document and with particular importance for the idea of the personal archives (this essay was originally published as "Back to Basics: Speaking, Writing, Reading—and Records," *Records & Information Management Report* 20 [May 2004]: 1-13 and an earlier essay – "Information 'Documents': How People and Organizations Acquire Information," *Records and Information Management Report* 17 (January 2001): 1-16 – building off my reading and study for a graduate course I was then teaching, Understanding Information, where I sought to motivate students to consider how diverse is the array of information sources used by most people.

Speaking, writing, reading, and recordkeeping are all part of the most fundamental human activities. This has been the case for a few thousand years, and it continues to be the case even in the digital era, where the characteristics of these activities are changing rapidly. In one sense, there has been part of a shift from the notion of experts to the empowerment of all people, at least those with enough education and resources to cope with the new technologies. The pace and nature of new digital technologies may be prompting people to be more conscious of the act of creating documents and the need to provide new levels of care for their personal and family archives, constituting both traditional and new forms of documentation. These societal transformations have brought with them a broadening of the definition of records and documents, as well as placing the main center for conceiving of such documents in the communities that the documents support. Likewise, individuals may be considering their personal and family archives in different ways that they did a generation or two ago. For generations, we have relied on printed books, newspapers, maps, and photographs as chief sources of information, all sources that can knit us into functional communities. We also rely on other information sources such as movies, artifacts (such as buildings, household objects, and monuments), landscapes and cityscapes – many of these and others providing the necessary context of a document (an architectural drawing is only a representation of a building, but a building is only a representation of the architectural rendering as well). Artifacts, buildings, and landscapes all serve as additional witnesses to the past, supplementing and complementing traditional textual sources.

Chapter four, a "'Therapeutic Function': Personal Recordkeeping," along with the next two chapters, originally published as a triptych of essays on personal recordkeeping in the February, March, and April 2006 issues of the *Records & Information Management Report*, represent the heart of what this book concerns. This chapter considers the manner in which people have relied on various documents, from the letter to the property record, as a kind of supporting function for personal identity and purpose; it was originally published as "A 'Therapeutic Function': Personal Recordkeeping," *Records & Information Management Report* 22 (February 2006), 1-13. We hear of more and more stories about the misuse of personal records or government efforts to intrude upon documents closely related to our activities – embedding passports with chips, the rising loss of laptops and the growing problem of identity theft, and laws to protect personal information generated in medical records. Yet, people still continue to create personal documents and to use every means, no matter how insecure, to create, store, and use these records. Archives are full of documents providing testimonies of lives lived and stories yearning to be heard. They are a cloud of witnesses about our society. Many would argue that we are driven to think about personal and family archives because of the nature and challenges of cyberspace. The notion that we are immersed in cyberspace is only an extension of the much older notion of being immersed in a documentary universe. Creating and maintaining records is an old, even ancient, impulse, manifested by the oldest forms of recordkeeping, keeping track of property and finances, and continues to be a dominant part of personal recordkeeping today. Letter writing is also an ancient form of personal document. With the advent of the modern postal system in the nineteenth century we know that the act of delivering mail was an important social activity and letter writing itself had become a symbol of connection; even with the advent of telecommunications, the letter remains and with it has come a resurgence of interest in fine writing materials and instruments. The rite of personal recordkeeping is also evident in the creating and maintaining of property records. When we buy a house we sign lots of documents, many of these ancient in form and purpose. The 900 hundred year Domesday Book is the exemplary symbol of this personal and governmental function, and the old metal document boxes stacked up in flea markets and antique shops are the residue of the more modern versions of such recordkeeping.

The second part of the original series of essays, now chapter five, examines the idea that very basic human impulses drive the creation and maintenance of personal records. Individuals hang onto records, such as birth certificates and photographs, for reasons that cannot just be explained in a rational way; the core section of this essay was originally published as "Human Impulses and Personal Archives," *Records & Information Management Report* 22 (March 2006): 1-13. This chapter plays with the situation of trying to live without records. We create regularly, and often systematically, personal records because of legal, regulatory, best practices, and societal customs and traditions. Etiquette manuals abound guiding us about how to create certain kinds of records. Every record created possesses a specific reason both for its creation and for how it needs to be maintained. We are surrounded by documents which we associate both with our connections with government and other institutions – the vital records of death, marriage, birth, and baptisms – hanging on our walls, pasted in our scrapbooks, and linked to our genealogies. Government demonstrates its pervasive influence in our lives with our extensive licensing and other documents such as passports; of course, the meaning of these documents has changed since the tragic events of September 11, 2001. We dribble evidence of our activities, every time we swipe an ATM card or go online. We understand the issues of privacy such activities may cause, but the human impulses to create records as well as the need to conduct business efficiently and effortlessly cause us to work in this way.

These human impulses are especially evident as millions move from their personal scribbling in diaries, with diary writing on the rise as the sales of blank books soar, to blogging directly online. We document ourselves, and we invite others to be our witnesses to our activities. The penultimate expression of building a family archives may be the act of creating and displaying photographs. Photographs are literally the visualization of the past, stirring up more emotions than most documents. With photography functioning as a ubiquitous, low-cost technology, everyone gets to play both archivist and historian. People often assemble personal and family archives because of the deep symbolic meaning these documents hold for them, explaining the scrapbooking craze in our digital age. Most of us like the ease of playing with digital documents, but we also crave the touch and smell of the document as real artifact.

And the final part of the original series, chapter six, concerns how personal archives create material traces, traces that now may be threatened by the virtual world of the digital; the backbone of this chapter was originally published as "Traces of Ourselves: Concluding Thoughts on Personal Recordkeeping," *Records & Information Management Report* 22 (April 2006), 1-14. The symbolic role of archives looms large for us, and this is an essential reason individuals and families cling to old documents and artifacts. The documents surrounding us provide comfort, security, and testimony to our lives. More and more novels and mysteries feature archivists, additional evidence to the growing fascination we have for old documents and the stories they spin. The material world, in the form of briefcases and desks and other document containers, has reflected the continuing and growing importance of personal recordkeeping. Laptops and other portable data devices, also growing in capacity, are, in some ways, merely an extension of other older carrying and storing devices.

There are, however, also many forces working against the creation and maintenance of personal and family archives. The networking era we live in, with its array of wireless devices such as cell phones and PDA's with multiple functions, certainly is generating some difficult challenges. However, the World Wide Web also has created a new kind of space for personal archiving that may counteract the negative issues. Literary and historical scholars, especially those with a postmodernist bent, have devoted considerable time to understanding texts and the nature of the archive. These scholars provide a theoretical, but nonetheless, engaging framework for us to approach and understand personal and family archives. All of this is made difficult by the fact that archives and archivists are not fully understood in society. Shifting notions of the archive by scholars and reinforcements in the popular perception of what archives represent make this a continuingly difficult task to deal with. Self-help books and vendors pitching products to help individuals care for personal papers, write family histories and memoirs, and conduct other similar tasks suggest some new possibilities, assuming that archivists become involved (either in writing some of these guides or in advising their authors). In order to deal effectively with personal and family archives, archivists need to explore new ways to connect with the public. Archivists, rather than protecting and policing their guild, need to work to make a better group of informed amateur archivists. They need to transform their own culture from one of collecting and acquiring to one of collaborating and assisting. Doing this should also open up new possibilities for promoting, in a more understandable fashion, the archival mission. Specifically, archivists need to build off of other new research areas, such as personal information management and the scholarly research on the history of personal and communitarian recordkeeping, and open their own horizons for work and collaboration. There are great opportunities and possibilities in both the present and the future.

The next two chapters examine two of the most prominent technology changes transforming personal archiving, electronic mail and blogging, originally written as a series of essays at the end of 2007 for the *Records & Information Management Report.* Chapter Seven, "Electronic Mail and Personal Recordkeeping," explores the nature of this communications system on personal archiving. E-mail is common because it is so easy to use, and because we have become so dependent on it. Nevertheless, records professionals have developed extremely different notions about e-mail – records managers see it as dangerous potential liabilities and want to destroy it, while archivists understand e-mail as the replacement of traditional letter writing and want to preserve it, at least selectively. People have become so dependent on e-mail that they willingly accept having it regulated while at work, putting up with spam mail, or facing the various challenges of managing e-mail (especially figuring out how to preserve selected portions of it). E-mail also generates considerable risks, such as security and compliance problems – reflecting a records creating entity that is the antithesis of control records professionals strive to assist their organizations to achieve. Most of these problems have been documented by considering landmark court cases affecting government or large businesses, but these problems extend to individuals as well. Records professionals have also shifted a good deal of their attention to dealing with the fact that their organizations have become far more porous, as laptops are stolen, firewalls breached, and hackers break in; private individuals also have just as many issues to contend with in their own digital archives.

Such issues, as we can see in organizations, have brought new attention to archives and records management, and there is no reason that we won't see similar kinds of interest among private citizens as well. While some fear the loss of control by records professionals in administering records in their organizations as the technologies equip everyone to function as an archivist, perhaps we need to embrace such a concept and work to make each person a better records manager. After all, we have many standards and policies or procedures we can use as a beginning point for such work. Report after report, study after study, reveals how poorly we are doing with digital documents, especially as we increase our use of portable devices. What the public might ask, when it gets around to doing so, are what it is supposed to do with the information and evidence they generate on such devices if the experts can't figure what to do? We have time before such questions are asked, but not much. Meanwhile, some are predicting in the near future the disappearance of the distinction between organizational and personal recordkeeping. While records managers want to destroy e-mail as a liability, archivists see e-mail as a threat to a prime and cherished historical document. However, archivists worry about the greater potential loss of e-mail, and its threat to older documentary forms; it is fairly obvious that even if the older documentary forms continue to be used in various ways, they will not be the prevalent or richest sources in the future.

We can see evidence that some archivists and records professionals are rolling up their sleeves to develop practical in-house solutions to their e-mail problems, but we also need to begin anew efforts to work with the public on their personal and family archives. Archivists initially thought of e-mail as a mechanism for their reference services, assuming that more and more of their actual (and potential) users were becoming computer savvy; this ought to have reminded archivists that this also meant that more of their potential acquisitions of personal and family archives might arrive in digital form. Some archivists believe that e-mail has already replaced the personal letter, noting that individuals are producing far more e-mail than they ever created in paper and posted letters while saving far less. The search for a middle ground between archivists and records managers leads to some basic, common characteristics in the necessary features of functioning e-mail systems; however, the more important role for archivists might be to scale down organizational systems to accommodate the needs of individuals and families. While it is important for records professionals working in their organizations to manage effectively records and information resources, this cannot be done at the expense of another important component of the documentary universe – the records created and maintained as personal and family archives. Without some rethinking and some aggressive new action on the part of archivists, the present digital era may become known in the future as the time when the documentary heritage collapsed. This may happen unless we recreate the modern equivalent of ancient scribes who assisted the public in generating documents needed for their normal lives, except in this case the modern version is advising in the management of personal and family archives.

Chapter Eight, "The Web of Records: The World Wide Web, the Records Professions, and Personal Archiving," moves from e-mail to the Web, more specifically blogging, as another way of understanding new incentives and challenges for personal and family archives. We cannot think about information now without thinking about the World Wide Web. However, the Web is a constantly shifting realm, different from the notion of fixity accompanying, first, writing, and, then, printing. It is hard to imagine the Web being like a library or archives when it has no inherent preservation function. As our documentary heritage spreads out from institutions such as libraries and archives into private homes with their personal and family archives, the preservation challenges grow. And so do concerns about the loss of things that define us, since real things – written manuscripts or bound diaries – reassure us about their ability to last over time. The difficulty is trying to develop practical solutions for long-term maintenance of digital artifacts, although some would argue that the term digital artifact is an oxymoron. Americans, and others, are utilizing the growing number of Web applications, such as blogs and YouTube, to express and document themselves. We can think of Web sites as a kind of museum catalog or archival finding aid, except that the sites have a much greater potential for interaction and, obviously, greater potential in enhancements for linkage to other information sources. The more we live and work in the digital realm, the more comfortable we become with navigating through this life with digital surrogates of artifacts.

Archives – both the concept and the actual documents— might be continuously changing, even as archivists seek to fix certain key documents; a substantial portion of future work might be the effort to identify personal and family archives (certain kinds of organizational records as well) on the Web and to try to follow them as they are moved and removed. There is still confusion about who is responsible for records and archives on the Web, and how these materials will be maintained for the long-term. For as difficult as the Web records are in organizations, the challenges of preserving sources of long-term value created by the public are many times more complicated. Archivists and records managers have been involved in a variety of experiments and research projects in order to determine how best to administer archival materials located on the Web, but there is a long way to go before candid, practical advice is being offered that individuals can harness for their personal and family archives.

We used to believe that the documents we created would outlast us, but now, when we use technologies such as the Web, we have to contemplate much more carefully just what might lie in store for us, and our personal and family archives. How do we characterize the Web and the sites on it, so that archivists will develop workable solutions to it? Although many archives have accessioned scrapbooks, for example, and scrapbooks are close to being the paper version of Websites in purpose, these documentary genres present major preservation and sometimes other challenges (such as representing their content) as well. Some commentators have argued that the traditional missions, functions, knowledge, and skills of archivists and librarians will be enhanced as the digital era evolves and individuals and institutions grow ever more dependent on the World Wide Web, its spin-offs, and its successor. Yet, we must recognize that this will not happen unless the records and information professionals re-evaluate how they carry out their work.

Some newer digital forms, such as blogs, now numbering in the millions and growing rapidly, are new versions of older document forms, such as diaries, except that they won't be physically collected by archives as their predecessor documentary sources have been. In many ways, blogs and other new digital documents replace older record forms, but it is not certain whether these documents can be collected in the same way as older sources once used to be. Few archives, of any type, are actually dealing with document forms such as blogs; they are generally left to their creators, and maybe in the face of a documentary universe far larger than anyone ever anticipated this may be an acceptable approach. Even with older technologies, we have seen earlier foretelling of blogging, such as in diaries created, hidden, maintained, and passed around by victims of the Holocaust and their descendants. If we have been eager to identify and preserve such diaries, won't we want to grab and maintain the present blogs of military personnel in war zones, genocide chroniclers and victims, and insider political commentators?

A concluding essay strives to bring together all the various strains and themes from the various chapters, seeking to answer a basic question—what is the future of the personal archives and, as well, what is the future of the archival profession in ensuring that personal and family archives are preserved? As I suggest, the prognosis is good, but it is very different from how we, archivists and private individuals alike, have tended to view the importance, role, and use of personal records. At one time, personal archives were the backbone of public archives, the most prized acquisition by archivists, manuscripts curators, and special collections librarians because of the quality of the documentary evidence they provide and, often, their association with important events or famous people. Now they may be valued more by the individuals and families keeping them for highly personal reasons of identity, memory, sentimentality, or whatever. In my opinion, the archival mission is in the midst of great change, and it is a change that needs to be embraced and nurtured.

Chapter One

Posting Notes and, Then, Saving Them

Introduction.

If you wander into any bookstore's self-help section, you will discover a lot of books about managing one's life, with some about organizing and maintaining personal papers. Some of the authors have professional backgrounds, or day-jobs, that seem particularly attuned to contending with such matters. Librarians, for example, have written some of these self-help guides. Denise Dale, in a brief article building on her own contribution to this publication genre, offers tips on sorting out personal papers and deciding what should be kept and what should be tossed. She argues that you should classify such documents into categories such as "household files, permanent files, and reference files. Storing documents within one of these categories facilitates quick access and retrieval and may help you determine how long to keep information."[1] Yes, commonsense is the hallmark of such publications.

Surprisingly, there have been no archivists involved in contributing to or authoring such mass-market self-help books. My aim is not to rectify this situation. One purpose of this book is to explore why individuals and families, sometimes over many generations, have sought to manage personal and family archives, reflecting an intense human impulse. Another purpose is to argue that, partly because of new technologies and partly because of a rapidly expanding documentary universe, archivists need to shift their mission from one of evaluating, identifying, and acquiring such archives for their own repositories to equipping individuals to maintain these archives in a manner appropriate to the needs and interests not just of these individuals and families but of scholarly disciplines who might need access to such documents. My point is that the instinct to preserve personal and family papers is so strong that those professionals committed to maintaining our documentary heritage need to re-imagine how they use this desire to build greater understanding of the archival mission while helping individuals achieve their personal archival agendas. Archivists need to add to their professional agenda the making of citizens who have some basic understanding of how to care for their own historical records.

While my intended audience is professionally educated archivists, I also acknowledge that we need not just librarians but archivists contributing to the self-help literature (but I am not the person for the job).

Those who know my writings will recognize that these purposes are not especially new for me. In my book on institutional archives, back in 1992, I posited that archivists needed to ramp up their efforts to work with organizations of all types to establish and maintain archival programs rather than depositing them in established archival repositories; such acquisitions should happen only as a last resort when an institution was dying and the archival records were threatened or when there was a real working partnership between an archives and an organization for an already existing repository to function as the institutional archives.[2] In one sense, I am extending this argument to personal and family papers, although I didn't foresee this in the early 1990s. Much has transpired with personal information technologies in the past two decades suggesting that personal archiving, from websites and blogs to digital photograph albums and scrapbooks, is already a prominent feature of our society (or that these technologies, with their more dramatic inbred fragility, drive individuals to be more mindful about preservation issues). Archivists need to recognize that such developments may be changing how and what they do.

Another theme in my own writings has been about the need for archivists to advocate more effectively about their mission in society and with policymakers. My books on documenting localities, records as evidence and information, and ethics and accountability in recordkeeping include such emphases,[3] but I am not the only one or hardly the first, of course, to consider such matters. For more than three decades archivists have been writing about their experiences in mounting exhibitions, making audio-visual productions, lobbying for resources, and developing public relations campaigns, but it is difficult to know whether archivists, their work, and their mission are really understood or not. For one thing, archivists have tended to address such matters mostly among themselves, and I plead guilty to this as well. For another, archivists have tended to take more conceptual views of their role in society, to the extent that the average person has little ability to connect in any meaningful fashion with the archival mission.

The present interest in personal archiving represents a major new opportunity for archivists to re-imagine and better communicate their mission in society by aiding individuals who have already developed some interest in the archival enterprise. We need some archivists to develop publications, Web sites, and other training materials to assist this part of the public (but again, I am not the person for this assignment). Instead of trying to grab the attention of a public distracted by a million other things, archivists now have the opportunity to connect with a growing number of individuals who are looking for advice about selecting, organizing, and preserving documents with long-term value. Archivists, in order to do this, need to alter their mission and their practical priorities, but the possible results may be unprecedented in terms of gaining public support and building a better professional profile.

The purposes of this first chapter are to suggest something about the instinctive sense to care for personal and family archives. This aspect of our human nature can be seen in the collecting that seems to be inbred into us, perhaps as basic a human need as eating, drinking, seeking shelter, and sleeping. In other words, collecting may somehow extend from our desires to survive, connected to the hunting of other essential necessities for sustaining life. The memoir of Susan Sontag's last battle against cancer, written by her son David Rieff, suggests something of this intimate connection between surviving and archiving. Rieff writes, for example, "In a strange way, she lived her life as if stocking a library, or materializing her longings ... She never said this, but I wonder if her sense of herself was not inextricably bound up in this collecting – the subject of so much of her best writing." She kept at such efforts right to the end: "She would not contemplate extinction until the last month of her life. And even then ... Instead, throughout most of her illness, she was still interested in compiling lists of restaurants and books, quotations and facts, writing projects and travel schedules, all of which I understood to be her way of fighting to the end for another shard of the future."[4] Creating such documents was partly a means for Sontag's control and survival, and what we see is a glimpse into how personal recordkeeping is linked to the human impulse for resisting oblivion. As I discuss at the end of this chapter, gathering and maintaining the documents associated with our lives and families may be similar to our efforts to learn to speak, read, and write, all functions that have something profound to suggest about our innate desire to possess meaning about ourselves, to be able to communicate that meaning to others, and, above all, to survive by leaving something behind.

The Impulse to Save.

   Collecting is a basic human instinct and books and articles pour
forth about the history and meaning of collecting. Understand collecting
and you grasp something of both the mission of archivists and personal
recordkeeping most individuals engage in, sometimes because they have
to, but just as often because they want to preserve something of their
own lives or their family's history. The impulse to collect and to
preserve is quintessentially a personal one, so much so that even much
of what institutional repositories, such as archives, acquire has first been
filtered through an individual's hands. Institutional collections often
started life as various individual collections.
   Personal collecting can seem quirky or frivolous, but it always
reveals some deeper inner meaning to life's purpose. In the
Renaissance, ushering in a new interest in the world, many individuals
created cabinets of curiosities, eclectic displays revealing how people
lived, viewed their mortality, and evaluated their lot in life. Some
scholars, such as Valentin Groebner, have analyzed the growth of
government and religious recordkeeping systems – such as seals, badges,
coats of arms, notary signatures, correspondence, and other documents
-- in early modern Europe, suggesting that these systems were more the
result of institutional and societal needs for order and control and less
about any quest for personal meaning. However, it is difficult to not
believe that the increasing number of documents related to individuals,
requiring nearly everyone to carry and to be able to produce documents
when necessary, did not have some effect on how these individuals
associated these documents with personal meaning. One of the major
innovations was that these passports and letters of identification
transformed from being in the possession of the privileged to becoming
obligatory documents for everyone in society; this was part of a major
shift in how society and its organizations viewed and utilized
recordkeeping. Assessing an authentic identity becomes a process based
on "matching documents with internal registers, replete with
information supposedly readily on hand in official archives,"[5] meaning
that both individuals and governments and religious institutions were
mandated to maintain archives (no matter how primitive these may
seem to us today).
   Collecting was seen as part of a quest for personal meaning, and in
the hands of an expanding wealthy merchant class some of the cabinets
of curiosities, along with other documents individuals were made to

keep for legal, commercial, and other uses, formed the basis for the first public natural history, art, and history museums; private expressions of collecting became, in some case, public expressions. In these earlier, as well as later, eras much of what was collected was trash, as Phillippe Blom suggests, the "cast-offs of society, overtaken by technological advance, used and disposable, outmoded, disregarded, unfashionable." [6] It is not that much of a leap to see why today individuals hold onto cancelled checks, compile scrapbooks, and adorn their walls with family photographs and old family documents. The personal archive is like the old cabinet of curiosities, where the odd and unique markers of past activities are gathered. But the personal archive is also partly formed because of legal and government requirements (checks and other receipts accumulate partly because of our need to complete annual personal tax forms). Think how today a teenager might view an old typewriter or consider the stories of standing in line at a bank to deposit a paycheck or to seek the assistance of a teller; they may only comprehend such matters if they examine and touch old instruments, see candid photographs of such past activity, and read or hear the testimonies of individuals who worked in important, but now largely forgotten, positions.

Changing technologies of recordkeeping also have had some impact on how we see personal and family archives. In the Internet age, collecting has become a fixation for more people than ever. John Freyer gives us a kind of reverse image of the virtual process of collecting, as he documents the online selling off of his personal possessions, with ample detail about why people may want to buy the most ridiculous stuff (used socks, frozen and canned food, a partially used bottle of mouthwash). As Freyer relates, "I listed a few items a week on eBay, and was amazed when they sold. I started to photograph the objects and write descriptions, and as I did that I couldn't help but think about where each object came from, and why I even had it in the first place." [7] Freyer creates a web site, gets his friends to help inventory his possessions, and then he proceeds to gather data on who buys his stuff and where it goes. Each of Freyer's descriptions is a little homily about modern collecting, such as this one accompanying the picture of a Spa City Rockers t-shirt:

> The high bidder on this shirt asked me to send it to a friend of his. A week after I put it in the mail I received a handwritten note from its new owner, who said that upon opening the packaging he was overwhelmed by the 'musty old shirt' and decided to throw it in the trash. I really loved that shirt. But that's what happens when [you]

send your loved objects to total strangers. Eric Mast read about this
tragedy somewhere on my site and sent me a new Spa City Rockers
shirt when I returned from my trip. The new one is cleaner than the
old one, but since it is one of my only shirts it too will become old and
musty.[8]

Old and musty have long been hallmarks of collecting. And old and
musty are certainly characteristics for many personal archives, even
when these are not attributes anybody wants to associate with the family
records carefully stored in closets, file cabinets, and various storage
containers. Freyer's web site and the book are a kind of archival
collection that may never cross into a traditional or "real" archival
repository (and this is a feature of contemporary collecting archivists
need to re-examine).

Why do Americans (or anyone for that matter) collect things, or
hold onto stuff they have created? Leah Dilworth thinks, "collecting is a
narrative activity, a practice in which objects are signs for referents and
require a narrator (collector or curator) to make meaning. Thus
collections become sites of cultural memory and reproduction."[9]
Certainly, we can see how narratives play in the creation and
maintenance of personal and family archives. Or, in the debate about
what ought to be preserved or not, sometimes generated by the
discarding by libraries of worn or unused books, we watch unfold a
narrative, according to Nicholas A. Basbanes, of a "growing uneasiness
over the possibility that a discard might be the last copy of a particular
title still being held in any institutional collection, and that with its
banishment from its stacks, that work – regardless of its literary or
historical merit – is lost, not only to formal scholarship but to casual
discovery, which some people contend is just as egregious a cultural
offense."[10] If we are uneasy about the loss of such printed volumes,
objects that have a remarkable propensity to survive in some state under
the worst conditions, how uneasy should we be about e-books and the
increasing number of documents generated in a digital form?

Printed books are one thing, numbering only in the hundreds of
millions, but personal documents are quite another, probably
numbering in the hundreds of billions (or even trillions – who really
knows?). Basbanes believes that the "great paradox of our age is that for
all the wonders of modern technology, there is a real possibility that
enormous chunks of our common legacy are at immediate risk of
disappearing forever, in many instances without a trace."[11] It is precisely
what might drive individuals to take a greater interest in preserving our

documentary heritage, as their own awareness of the potential loss of records of great personal meaning are threatened with disappearing (especially as vendors market all digital systems as supporting archival permanence, which is, obviously, not true). And this is not lost on Basbanes, who enables the reader to imagine his or her own use of information technologies in light of what librarians and archivists face: "Anyone whose first computer used 5.25-inch floppy disks, anyone who wrote correspondence, reports, or journalism on WordStar or kept business records on VisiCalc, anyone whose attempt to access a website is greeted by an 'Error 404' response – an indication that the site has been abandoned and is inaccessible – has a sense of the crisis being faced on a far more massive scale by librarians, archivists, and curators all over the world."[12] As more and more individuals copy or create their personal records into digital form, the greater the likelihood that they will gain an appreciation of the challenges of the archival mission, assuming if archivists are there to assist them comprehend the complexities of digital preservation. Basbanes sees that the "ultimate challenge lies in deciding what information will be saved, and what is allowed to disappear."[13] No one involved in trying to save their family's scrapbooks, photographic albums, grandparents' birth and marriage certificates, and ancestral letters and other documents will need to be told about the artifactural or any other value of such items. They want to preserve not just information (oh, how deceptively easy that is) but the feel, smell, and look of the old items (and that may be a harder task).

The Internet age is full of surprises. Much of the Basbanes book is about surprises. Basbanes is surprised about what survives and what doesn't, striking at the serendipitous nature of survival that is the far extreme of the planned and deliberative selection process that has generated much of the intellectual discussion about appraisal or selection of humanity's documents (and, it seems, in recent decades, that has also stimulated much of the debate about the idea of preservation). There are numerous references to fragments of literary texts and other documents that survive because they were re-used in the production of a later book or document. He is also surprised about the purposeful destruction of books and archives, libraries and museums that has characterized many wars and that has become more noticeable in our modern age of rapid telecommunications (although one of the surprises for Basbanes is how often such documentary destructions have not gained much media attention). He discusses the irony of governments and peoples purposing to destroy another people and who maintain meticulous documentation of their activities. Need I say that this happens in families as well? In my own case, my crazy grandmother systematically destroyed old family photographs because she thought them possessed by demonic spirits, while we knew she was mainly seeking to eradicate the memory of certain family members. Mad or not, her activities are by no means rare.

One issue that particularly angers and perplexes Basbanes, as it does many, is when libraries and other repositories sell off collections in order to generate funds for the purchase of information technology. The author includes a number of examples where this has happened, with ample quotations about the demise of the library and the emergence of an anti-book mentality. Ironically, the effort to acquire the new technologies, or to update them as is often needed, is done as part of an effort to have access to current information while the process often has led to the loss of information via the discarding of books and other materials. Basbanes speculates that the collectors who generally acquire the discards for personal collections often serve as a "final line of defense against the loss of important material."[14] Of course, this has always been the case, even before the emergence of an era where impermanence seems a fact of life. Many of the famous and most significant repositories started out through the work of private collectors.

When we reflect on collecting today, much of our attention is directed to the mercenary aspects of collecting. In late 2006 a *New York Times* reporter wrote an essay about how the archives (consisting of 3500 clothing design illustrations) of Jacques Fath, a French fashion designer of the mid-twentieth century, could be purchased for $3.5 million. As the *Times* essay reports, the Fath collection was sold by the owner of a Beverley Hills store who had purchased the archives nine years before, with a "caveat. The new owner must keep the collection together, ideally as a donation to a museum or the basis for a research center."[15] Half a year later the *New Yorker* magazine featured an essay on the frenetic collecting of literary manuscripts and archives by the Harry Ransom Humanities Research Center at the University of Texas at Austin and its director, Tom Staley. D. T. Max chronicles Staley's energetic quest for literary manuscripts and archival collections, noting how the Center is outwitting Yale, Harvard, and the British Library in its acquisition efforts. As Max suggests, the Ransom Center "operates more like a college sports team, with Staley as the coach – an approach that fits the temperament of Texas."[16] And the sense one gains from this essay is the fun and profit from building great pots of money in order to wheel and deal for the literary manuscript treasures. Max says that to Staley the "world is a map of treasures whose locations he already knows."[17] There are references to putting individuals on the Center's advisory board because the individual might have sway to acquire a particular writer's papers. Large sums of money, $5 million for the Bob Woodward and Carl Bernstein Watergate papers and $2.5 million for the Norman Mailer archives, are mentioned in the essay. Competition seems to be the key factor, as well as the thrill of the quest for a new treasure (vaguely reminiscent of the antics of the treasure hunters in the *National Treasure* movies). Present director Staley is described as a "natural collector."[18] Max contrasts Staley with his predecessor, Decherd Turner, who made a "mistake" because he was only "focused on the preservation of manuscripts," rather than hunting down and acquiring collections.[19]

Historical value these days seems to be measured by financial values rather than the evidence and information provided by the documents (just watch the *Antiques Roadshow* for a few weeks), and the result is that much of the media attention seems focused on the monetary aspects of collecting. The large dollar amounts connected with sports memorabilia has generated some interesting trends paralleling what we see in the general autograph and manuscripts market. If you want to get some publicity about your program or about the profession, just acquire something worth a lot of money. Michael O'Keefe and Teri Thompson, tracking the story of one of the rarest and most valuable of sports memorabilia, the 1909 Honus Wagner tobacco card, offer a view into the collectables marketplace, describing the sports memorabilia marketplace as an "unregulated and often cutthroat industry rife with fraud and corruption,"[20] a far different activity than what we see in the joy associated with keeping score at a baseball game (although scorecards from far distant games or games in which landmark events occurred can become financially valuable collectibles).[21] The sports memorabilia marketplace parallels in some ways the rampant illegal trade in antiquities.[22] In these cases, everything is boiled down to having a price, and value is mostly or even exclusively associated with a monetary value. The point I want to make is that personal and family archiving is not about such crass ends (except when some distant descendant of a famous or infamous historical figure decides it is time to make a little money by putting up the documents for sale). Individuals working on maintaining their own and their family archives are motivated by other and higher values, and it is these that archivists want to connect with as they advocate their mission in preserving our documentary heritage.

We can generally detect such a mix of values in the origins of the pioneering historical records repositories, although the financial aspects of historic documents did not emerge as an issue until many decades later when autograph and auction firms emerged, endowment funds were established, and financial problems became prevalent. Despite our assumption today of the existence of archival repositories, these institutions have been around for a relatively modest amount of time; although we can find evidence of them back in the ancient world, archives and historical manuscripts repositories have mostly emerged in a serious way only about a century or two ago. Besides, this might not be the point anyway.

Collecting is a very personal expression, and personal collectors both predate and outnumber their institutional rivals. Art professor Marilynn Gelfman Karp defines collecting as "an act of very personalized commitment. It's about erecting a bond between yourself and object; it's all about what you choose to be responsible for. Whoever collects understands this. Humanity can be divided into two parts: those who collect and the others."[23] Her focus is on the most common and seemingly uncollectible objects. Archivists are among those, along with museum and art curators and other similar professionals, who have chosen to make their livelihood what others have deemed to be a hobby. No matter how we intellectualize what professionals like archivists do, there will always be an aspect of their work that involves an activity that contains a recreational or deeply psychological aspect – the hunting and gathering of that portion of the documentary universe that seems to possess some sort of long-term value. And, moreover, there will be private collectors, following their impulses, carrying out serious archival tasks. Some of the traits Karp identifies are similar to some of the functions archivists carry out, such as when she asserts that there is "deep satisfaction in organizing, inventorying, embracing, handling, and communing" with what we have acquired.[24] Karp connects with what motivates seemingly normal individuals to become compulsive acquirers, discerning how even broken or tasteless and socially objectionable objects speak to us to possess them and how difficult it is to resist their message. Archivists, with their practical and theoretical emphasis on provenance and the institutional and societal context of documents, also need to comprehend the implications of this world of collectors and acquirers, rational or not, for what they do.

Crazy Families, Crazy Institutional Collectors.

In America, organized institutional approaches to acquiring and preserving personal and family papers have been around since the late eighteenth century and the founding of the Massachusetts Historical Society. Close studies of these historical societies and other archival repositories reveal that they have often been plagued, especially in later years of their existence, by difficult problems that ought to suggest to the archival community the limitations they bring in documenting society and what the world of private archival enterprises might mean in such circumstances. While they may be the best we have for the maintenance of many documentary collections that might otherwise have been lost by the ravages of time and neglect, we must also realize that these institutions are not the only players in acquiring and preserving historical sources.

Studies of pioneering historical societies such as the Historical Society of Pennsylvania (HSP) reveal intense wrestling with their identity, relevance, and future. Such repositories often possess a public persona that suggests that they are affluent, acquire and preserve everything, and possess limitless space, financial, and staff resources allowing them to do pretty much as they want. The reality is that these organizations are often strapped for cash and beset by other problems. They proved their worth from their earliest years as great collecting forces, but they have faced a much harder road in proving their mettle in managing what they acquired – often beset by cantankerous internal debates, public relations nightmares, and intense planning processes.[25]

In the case of the HSP, it became so absorbed by collecting with modest parameters that it began, in the early twentieth century, to try to divest itself of documents and artifacts that seemed out of the scope of the HSP's primary mission, discovering quickly that it is difficult to do this without offending members, donors, and the general public. As early as the 1940s the organization started de-accessioning, and it began to be more selective in what it acquired. The de-accessioning efforts led to heated debates, along with legal and ethical problems about how to handle such matters, especially about items that might be sold and how the proceeds could be used. Even then it was obvious that any efforts at trimming back would have a minor impact on the scale of the holdings, especially as the HSP shifted from collecting rare, individual documents and more modest (in volume) personal or family papers to acquiring "large masses of documents" reflecting more modern organizations.[26]

Some of the aspects of managing the constantly growing collections provide interesting commentary on the manner in which an organization like the HSP works, reflecting that sometimes there may seem to be little difference between the idiosyncratic collecting behaviors of individuals and institutions (or that such institutions such as the HSP were mostly vehicles for individual collectors and their personal agendas). Some of this relates directly to the lack of staff and the reluctance of the HSP to systematize its work practices (harking back to a kind of connoisseurship mentality) or to adopt professional standards available to it. Just as the HSP was possessed by its holdings, the institution often was stymied by the large backlogs of unprocessed materials, the lack of staff to deal with these holdings, and a lack of other resources (including access to newly emerging professional approaches) that could resolve these problems, most consistently reflected in problems with hiring and maintaining the right kind and number of professional staff. Staff identified with the institution not a professional community and with the HSP's own traditional, rather than standardized professional, practices, revealing an "ever-widening gap between material means and professional norms,"[27] a common concern for most museums, archives, libraries, and other similar institutions.

Why discuss the history and present administration of such venerable archival repositories in a book focusing on personal archiving? The general perception is that these repositories have preserved countless individual and personal papers that would otherwise have been lost (and this is true) and that these institutions are a superior solution to any other approach for safeguarding our documentary heritage (and a strong case can be made for this). However, the reality is that these institutions also have suffered immensely, typified by the specter of the HSP in the late 1980s trying to serve so "many demanding constituencies" that it was at the "brink of financial disaster," and its own rationale of broad and aggressive collecting had come to an abrupt end.[28] It is even more complicated than that, as historian Gary Nash reminds us in his study of the HSP and historical memory in Philadelphia, arguing that such organizations are "not dispassionate and impartial venues but rather institutions that carry out, however subtly, ideological, cultural, and politically informed agendas."[29] Institutional collectors like the Historical Society of Pennsylvania, Nash argues, seem to be participating in an "exercise in stabilizing society and legitimating order, authority, and status."[30] Nash emphasizes the roles of these repositories in telling stories, creating meaningful myths, generating "useful" knowledge, fashioning order and unity in society, perpetuating the frauds of bogus artifacts in order to shape a particular cultural memory, and sustaining legends as a means of getting at the truths of the past. And although Nash demonstrates that he doesn't understand fully the nature of archival work,[31] he provides an important framework for understanding that such archival programs did not operate minus biases or social or political agendas influencing their historical endeavors.

What partly emerges from such studies by scholars such as Griffith and Nash is that the pioneering historical records repositories often established their legacy of collecting and preserving individual and family archives for reasons far removed from professional or altruistic motives. The historical societies primarily sought to preserve the documents of prominent families and individuals, and they often carried out such activities in hopes of bringing order and stability to the unrest they imagined was evident in society not in generating a representative or comprehensive documentation of American society that would support serious inquiry into understanding this society. These repositories revealed little interest in the records of individuals and families they saw as socially inferior or of little use to their own objectives, and it was only much later, in the last third of the twentieth century, that these kinds of archival programs turned to broader social documentation projects and initiatives, following historical trends reflecting concern for a more inclusive social history.

New immigrant groups and lower socio-economic classes were, for a long time, ignored by anything seeming remotely like a professional archives, and these groups, recognizing this, also discovered in their own ways the power of personal recordkeeping. Chinese entering the United States in the late nineteenth to early twentieth century created an elaborate fictional world, inventing descriptions of Chinese locales, family relationships, and even names in order to meet the evolving U.S. immigration laws and procedures, especially after the 1906 San Francisco earthquake destroyed the Chinese public records and made it more difficult for the U.S. to counter claims about citizenship and family relationships. While the American officials developed more detailed case files on these immigrants with applications, questionnaires, fingerprints, photographs, the Bertillon system, and physical descriptions, the immigrants developed equally elaborate fictions, in terms of false identities and communities, ensuring that they would be able to gain entry to the United States. As Estelle Lau indicates, the Chinese "crafted and maintained their personal stories and family narratives carefully,"[32] developing coaching papers (some of which turned up in the immigration service records). As immigration officials asked increasingly more detailed questions, the Chinese generated more detailed responses, and the result was a change in the nature of their family structure and identity, altering family histories and creating new fictions of individual and community memory. Lau argues, "The creation of paper families ... has impacted not only how Chinese perceive their history in the United States but it has also directly impacted their history, structuring Chinese family, economic, and social relations by forcing the Chinese to accept a fiction at the heart of their community."[33] Such immigrant groups not only needed to generate new kinds of personal archives, but they also usually needed to form their own historical societies and archives as the mainstream, traditional archival programs avoided or ignored their presence in their communities. The point here, however, is that we can discern many instances where individuals, families, and other groups have generated their own archiving systems because they recognized the importance and power of such documents for sustaining them, especially when under stress or duress of some kind. Ultimately, years later, such ethnic groups (and other groups which felt disenfranchised in the mainstream historical records repositories) established their own independent archival programs.

Americans, however long they have been in this country or whatever social status they have enjoyed, have understood the power of personal archiving, as we can see in the documents they have left behind. The eighteenth century American puritan divine, revivalist, theologian, educator, and philosopher, Jonathan Edwards, provides a case in point.

Personal Archives, Eighteenth Century Style.

Today, Jonathan Edwards's papers are safely housed in an archival repository, the inevitable result of his assiduous sense of importance of his own place in history and remarkable attention to maintenance of his personal papers. Edwards was obsessed with note taking and the maintenance of his own personal archives. Edwards deliberately and laboriously recorded his struggles, victories and defeats, in a range of personal documents that are truly remarkable both for their detail and the ways in which he created and maintained them. Edwards's struggles with his spiritual well-being, including constant wrestling about his own salvation, might have led him to write down so much, marking his progress and providing a pathway to understanding where he was spiritually at in a particular time and place (not unlike the task of many diarists, although Edwards only maintained a spiritual diary for a particular period, prior to his move to the Northampton church).[34] As Edwards's biographer George Marsden contends, "Edwards was a man of Scripture and a man of rules," so it should not be surprising to us that Edwards was so meticulous in maintaining his papers.[35] Archivists and records managers are about a rules-oriented group as anyone could find, and Edwards would have enjoyed conversations with such professionals in order to seek advice on how to administer his personal papers. Likewise, in our society's present fascination with how-to manuals and self-help guides, from everything about how to lose weight to constructing a winning Web site, many among us, like what we could assume Edwards would be interested in, also would appreciate some discussion with a records professional to get some practical tips on managing a personal archives.

Edwards rose at 4 or 5 each morning to work 13 hours in his study, modeling himself after Christ's rising from the dead early in the morning.[36] Despite his intense involvement with church, family, community, and politics, the wide-ranging affairs and their intensity Edwards was always drawn to his study, library, scholarship, and growing accumulation of notes. Marsden indicates "his heart was most often in his work as a writer" and his "studying was another kind of worship."[37] While we might at first surmise that only scholars, like Edwards, will have this draw back to their study and the papers there, we also can detect that many individuals feel a similar attraction to where personal and family papers are maintained. Working through these papers brings us closer to our origins and our place in the world, as many have written about,[38] just as Edwards sought a connection to God and the spiritual realm.

Given the level of devotion to such scholarship, and Edwards' orientation to order and rules, it is not hard to imagine that Edwards spent considerable time in organizing and maintaining his personal papers. Indeed, some of this was typical of those involved in the early eighteenth century religious awakenings. John Fea, describing how the revivalists and other spiritual leaders communicated in this era, indicates that "correspondence served as an agent in the creation, preservation, definition, and redefinition of a revival community." Fea believes that "a letter signed by an ordained minister brought instant credibility to such news and confirmed the authenticity of revival reports... Letters were important agents for quantifying and qualifying the spiritual excitement."[39] Given Edwards's lifelong quest to convince him self and others that these revivals were genuine and a special outpouring of God's Spirit, it is not difficult to see how he coveted such reports and how he would carefully organize them for future reference and use in his own writings. Fundamental to his life's work, Edwards needed to manage his records, and given his range of responsibilities and scholarly activities, what he had to administer was certainly far greater than the normal American colonist and probably greater than most other clerics or scholars of his time. We can place ourselves in Edwards's shoes, reflecting on the care we might spend in writing a personal letter or remembering the joy when we receive and read a personal letter, literary forms that may seem to be declining in an age when people sit before television sets or in front of computer screens, either in reactive mode or carelessly writing email messages that posterity either does not want or won't understand.

If studying was done in a worshipful manner, it was still hard and serious labor for Edwards. Edwards struggled to read and keep up with scholarship, partly because he earnestly believed that he was playing a critical role in "bringing God's kingdom to earth."[40] Edwards, as a result, was not prone to waste time. Often sickly in nature, Edwards walked for his health and for rejuvenating his spirits: "His walks were in part for contemplation, prayer, and spiritual communion," Marsden writes, "but so that no time would be wasted, he also carried with him pen and ink to write down his thoughts along the way. For longer horseback rides, he used a memory device. For each insight he wished to remember, he would pin a small piece of paper on a particular part of his clothes, which he would associate with the thought. When he returned home he would unpin these and write down each idea. At the ends of trips of several days, his clothes might be covered with quite a few of these slips of paper. Fashionable appearance apparently was not a high priority."[41] Today, we would recognize Edwards as the compulsive type-A personality, daily compiling to-do lists, compiling notes at every moment in the day, and fretting about the organization of personal papers – precisely the kind of person whose papers archivists like to acquire.

The modern archivist and records manager, dealing with files often marked up with hundreds of Post-It notes, has a pretty good idea of what Edwards must have looked like when he came home from a walk. Henry Petroski provides a brief description of the origins of Post-It notes and the initial reluctance of 3M marketers to take on the product. However, as Petroski relates, "Though no prior need for the little sticky notes had been articulated, once they were in the hands of office workers all sorts of uses were found and suddenly people couldn't do without the things."[42] Edwards would have loved them. Today, we are used to such devices as these lightly glued markers, and we are surrounded by the sight of moderns constantly linked to their workplaces as they sit in coffee shops constantly fingering their laptops or walk with their personal data assistants (but Edwards provides a glimpse into how human such impulses are, despite whatever technological limitations may exist). Still, today's digital devices need to be evaluated by the impact they might be having on creating sustainable personal archives; at least, we can go back and remove the sticky notes, no friends for preserving paper documents, regardless of whatever convenience they may have offered us when we first used them.

Edwards was both an immense collector of information and a careful miser in the use of paper, presaging the efficiency and economy mantra sounded by twentieth century records managers. Once when returning from a trip, Edwards learned of his wife's period of spiritual awakening. "Always the eighteenth-century philosopher and collector of evidence," Marsden chronicles, "he wrote down her account of the entire episode as she dictated it."[43] Yet, it is in Edwards's quirky use of paper that we see some of his perspective concerning his personal papers. We can learn of a prescription written for Edwards' wife, Sarah, because the "always economizing Jonathan used the paper for a sermon preached in December 1742. Another sheet of paper used for the same sermon contains a prayer bid, one of the written requests for prayer that parishioners would give the pastor."[44] Wrapped up in a controversy in Northampton, Edwards defended himself and we know precisely what he based his arguments on since, "We still have his notes. (Ever frugal, Edwards wrote these notes on three pieces of fan paper, apparently scraps of the material Sarah and her daughters used for making fans)."[45]

Paper was often scarce at certain times and places, with paper being reused for personal purposes with often evidence of paper re-use found in personal collections or being re-used in binding books. When Marsden examines Edwards's notes for his unfinished work on the "History of Redemption," he provides a detailed glimpse into what these papers looked like:

> The extraordinary physical quality of the first of these notebooks is worth pausing to notice. It is 123 numbered pages of all sorts of scraps of paper of various shapes and sizes, sewn with a cover. Early pages are printer's proof from Joseph Bellamy's *True Religion Delineated*. Edwards then seems to have rummaged for any other paper he could get his hands on. A number of pages are copies of the official proclamation in Northampton of the marriage of Sarah Jr. and Elihu Parsons. One page is a draft of a prayer for ailing Deacon Clark. Others are from drafts of letters or a title page from his farewell sermon. Many of the irregularly shaped pages seem to be trimmings from the fans that his family was producing for sale in Boston."[46]

Records professionals, especially archivists, can relate to what this biographer found in using Edwards's papers, another reflection of the basic human resource to use any scrap of paper for scratching a note. In our highly technological society, with many still pursuing the idea of a paperless environment, paper continues to be an important presence.[47] Mostly, of course, the debate about the paperless society occurs within organizational settings, with people bombarded by advertising hype and vendors' pitches, rather than at home where people covet the old paper of their personal and family archives.

It is the condition of Edwards's papers and Edwards's "nearly illegible handwriting" that makes us understand why Marsden in his preface gives thanks to *The Works of Jonathan Edwards* project at Yale University, especially as the project brought together previously unpublished materials and deciphered the scribbling by the eighteenth century theologian and philosopher.[48] But it is with two pieces of furniture owned by Edwards that we get a glimpse of Edwards's own interest in being a personal record-keeper.

Featured in Marsden's book is a picture of Edwards' desk (the original desk is at Yale University Art Gallery) with increased space and compartments to hold his notebooks and papers.[49] For some reason Marsden decides not to discuss this remarkable artifact (although the Edwards editorial project logically uses an image of the desk on its Web site), the desk handsomely running alongside of *The Works of Jonathan*

Edwards mission statement, a reasonably simple, early eighteenth century writing desk that has been considerably expanded with later bookcases.[50] Jon Butler, in his study of eighteenth century America, provides a very elaborate description of the history and nature of the desk, starting with the simple premise that Edwards "needed a desk":

> Edwards indeed needed storage space for his many manuscripts, plus his pens, inks, blank paper, and books. Sometime between a stint as a Yale tutor in 1724 and his move to Northampton, Massachusetts, in 1726, Edwards acquired a handsome, if modest, desk, most likely made by a joiner in either New Haven or the upper Connecticut River valley. It was not long before Edwards or a woodworker constructed drawer dividers to fit precisely the duodecimo-, small octavo-, and quarto-sized papers that Edwards carefully trimmed from Flemish, Dutch, and English paper quires he proudly imported from Europe... Edwards also expanded his desk. At some unknown point he attached two cupboards for his mounting piles of manuscripts, one to each side. Perhaps after his arrival in Stockbridge, Massachusetts, in August 1751, where he ministered to Indians on a still dangerous frontier, he stacked three long, sliding-door bookcases above the desk and cupboards; these could double as book boxes if he had to move quickly. By now Edwards and his woodworkers had turned a small, handsome desk into a tinkerer's contraption that might have delighted Benjamin Franklin, if not a Philadelphia cabinetmaker. Yet whatever the loss in elegance, the desk, cupboards, and bookcases well served Edwards's pressing demand to shelter the extensive materials necessary to an intellectual life on the Massachusetts frontier.[51]

The desk is an amazing artifact, physically depicting how one would have organized personal papers more than two centuries ago. It is a crude harbinger of what developed a century and a half later with the "cabinet office secretary" or pigeonhole desks, with numerous compartments for storage, made by William S. Wooton, a landmark in the emergence of modern office furniture and technology. The motto of these desks was "a place for everything and everything in its place," certainly a statement Edwards could have used for his eighteenth-century version. These desks were part of a revolution in modern office furniture following the technologies of creating and administering records and reminding us of how closely connected office furniture is to office technology *and* the creation and maintenance of records. Stanley Abercrombie termed these desks as a "monster composed of three hinged parts," a piece of furniture that "virtually enveloped its user and offered dozens of shelves, pigeonholes, and drawers, not to mention a pediment and finials."[52] Thomas J. Schlereth places the Wooton desk in its historical context, indicating that the desk demarcated where a clerk was clearly responsible for all his work, representing a "small personal domain" before the office desk shifted to the so-called "modern efficiency desk" where office workers moved to an assembly line kind of activity.[53]

The other piece of furniture, Edwards's library desk, now located at the Stockbridge Library Association, is more typical of the desks of the period and, in fact, mimics the desks that we see depicted in woodcuts of scribes and scholars of the late medieval period and later Renaissance. Marsden only comments on it as being useful for Edwards working with his "massive" notebooks in which he laboriously and tenaciously copied notes for his various sermons, Scriptural studies, and philosophical writings.[54] The latter desk is also an interesting artifact. Butler uses the larger writing desk to portray Edwards as part of the transformation of a distinctive American society that was more modern in its sensibilities about the economy, politics, religion, and all aspects of society. When we look at the contrived, compartmented piece of furniture Edwards cobbled together over a couple of decades, especially in comparison to latter desks expanding to accommodate an increasing number of records generated by larger and larger bureaucracies, we can certainly think of him and his desk as symbolizing the "modern complication of secular life in the British mainland colonies between 1680 and 1770."[55]

The library table reveals something else, a closer tie to Erasmus in his Renaissance study or even the depictions of Jerome and Augustine (or, as one of my colleagues commented, closer to the desk of Bartleby the scrivener, a character featured in a short story written by Herman Melville in 1853 about an elderly copyist discouraged by his livelihood and a commentary on the bleakness of modern corporate America. A film version, directed by Jonathan Parker, set in the modern day, was released as *Bartleby* in 2001). Marsden, perhaps more correctly, tries not to engage in debate about whether Edwards was a modern, an ancient, or a transitional figure and simply tries to see him in the context of his time and his personal circumstances. If nothing else, Edwards, as reflects his furniture, was a practical engineer as depicted by Petroski where "engineering is the rearrangement of what is."[56] Edwards's desk certainly reflects this kind of creative tinkering, and, moreover, it reflects the synergy between technology and recordkeeping that continues to influence how we maintain personal archives. Today, it may be the case that more people are self-conscious about personal archives because of the greater use of computers and increasing software availability (think of digital cameras and how they have transformed the idea of family photograph albums), themes I will explore at various places in this book.

The Edwards desk is an important reminder of the nature of personal papers as a form of record. Archivists, as part of their ongoing efforts to contend with electronic records, have spent a considerable amount of resources defining the notion of a record and causing some to worry or to contend that personal papers were somehow different from records and recordkeeping systems. Archivists, often receiving personal accumulations of documents in a mixed or somewhat incoherent state, sometimes assume that personal papers are usually created and maintained in that fashion and, as a result, somehow different from records associated with organizational entities. Increasingly, evidence mounts that personal records often reveal careful organization and maintenance, mimicking what organizations have done with their records. Walter Benjamin, the great literary and cultural critic of the early twentieth century, as one example recently depicted in an exhibition of his writings, followed "strategic calculation" in preserving his archives through "which he deposited his manuscripts, notebooks, and printed papers in the custody of friends and acquaintances in various countries. His archives landed in the hands of others, so that their documents might be delivered to posterity. Those who received his work accepted the obligatory nature of their roles and faithfully conserved the papers." Benjamin, it seems, possessed the "ethos of an archivist" and the "passions of the collector." [57]

Records managers, on the other hand, have tended to focus almost exclusively on government and corporate records, quite naturally because that is who hire them. However, many records managers often have to deal with personal papers mixed in with organizational records or are employed by organizations where there is an active archives program charged with collecting personal papers associated with individuals who have played key roles in the institutions. Jonathan Edwards's desk, and his ruminations on the making and maintaining of his papers as portrayed in Marsden's biography, reminds us that personal papers have an inherent structure and purpose much as any other form of records system. And, this also remains us that the impulse to create and keep records is a very natural impulse, long pre-dating the emergence of associations of professional records managers and archivists or the array of digital information technologies now supporting new ways of creating and maintaining personal records and information systems.

Personal Archives, Digital Age Style.

One of the continuing promises of our present Information Age is the idea that individuals will be able to save every scrap of information about their lives and families and call them effortlessly and seamlessly whenever needed. No one will deny that this is an intriguing prospect, or that it is an engaging topic to reflect on, especially when we can identify in historical figures like Jonathan Edwards the same interest or desire. Designers and researchers exploring the MyLifeBits software, designed by Gordon Bell, certainly reveal why digital personal archives can be so captivating.[58] Reviewing the advances in cheap storage, desktop search tools, and metadata development, these software advocates describe a database supporting the range of personal documents each of us is likely to produce in our lifetime. The software designers have the notion of document type as a form of classification of information, and the document forms encompass much of what each of us create, use, and retain or dispose on a regular basis.

Records professionals might question some of the underlying assumptions of MyLifeBits. Gemmell, Bell, and Lueder, in discussing this innovative software, argue, "Since we can't predict when an old bill, conference announcement page, attendee list, or business card will be required, the easiest and safest thing is to simply keep it all."[59] They suggest that this provides a kind of security, especially as the software platform enables automatic copying and storing and builds on our sense that soon most of how we transact business will be carried out in the digital realm. They criticize the notion that we might save too much: "We never regret capturing; but we often regret not capturing more. Storage space is essentially free and we can always add software to filter out less interesting items."[60] Archivists know that a very small portion of documentary sources needs to be saved (or really can be effectively saved) over the long term. Records managers also realize the critical legal and other problems that storing vast amounts of information might generate for the organization or individual striving to do so.

An essay in *The New Yorker* provides a closer view into the origins of MyLifeBits, considering Gordon Bell's efforts to document electronically every aspect of his life. Bell, now at Microsoft, but known for his earlier work on networking at the Digital Equipment Corporation and with the National Science Foundation, is described as desiring his present project to document the "daily minutiae of his life," generating the "most extensive and unwieldy personal archive of its kind in the world."[61] Bell, discovering some time ago the utility of digitizing paper documents, has become involved in MyLifeBits, software for storing all this stuff, including video captured with a portable Cam recorder worn around the neck and capturing activity through his day. Consider the description of this strange archive:

> Bell's archive now also contains a hundred and twenty-two thousand e-mails; fifty-eight thousand photographs; thousands of recordings of phone calls he has made; every Web page he has visited and instant-messaging exchange he has conducted since 2003; all of the activity of his desktop (which windows, for example, he has opened); eight hundred pages of health records, including information on the life of the battery in his pacemaker; and a sprawling category he describes as 'ephemera,' which contains such things as books; the labels of bottles of wine he has enjoyed; and the record of a bicycle trip through Burgundy, where he tried to eat in as many starred restaurants as he could...[62]

This *New Yorker* profile is, of course, just one of many examples of using technology to solve particular problems, sometimes far extending beyond its original intended purpose. It reminds me, a little bit, of Ray Kurzweil's efforts to harness computer technology to achieve immortality, a human response for sure but one that can seem also misplaced or odd.[63] It also reminds me of many conversations with individuals suggesting that information technology with its corresponding relationship of increased storage and reduced costs eliminates one of the core archival premises that we need to appraise the documentary universe, selecting the portions with long-term or archival value. Not too many years ago, in response to Nicholson Baker's scathing indictment of library and archives preservation approaches, a report by a group of leading professionals asked, "With so much information produced, how do members of the research community—scholars and teachers, librarians and archivists, and academic officers who support their work—distinguish between what is of long-term value, what is ephemeral, and what of that ephemera is valuable for the preservation of a rich historical record?"[64] True believers in technology are, however, more prone to have faith that it can somehow eliminate the need to ask such questions, although clearly other questions emerge. In reality, the application of such technologies for managing documents such as diaries, correspondence, checking accounts, and other common forms of personal papers is more likely to raise serious questions about the nature of archiving, opening up new opportunities for promoting the importance of the archival function.

Thinking about a widespread adoption of software like MyLifeBits suggests wild futuristic scenarios we only can imagine in science fiction. Imagine, for example, if we passed legislation requiring elected officials to record all of their activities. Or, consider what might happen if CEO's were also pressured into the same use of MyLifeBits in order to affirm that they were engaged in ethical and legal behavior. The notion of accountability in an era where this topic seems to have generated lots of attention, as well as creative means of avoiding it, would be transformed. I am more interested here, though, in ruminating on the implications for archivists. Let's imagine that MyLifeBits becomes an ordinary system adopted by millions; does this mean that archival repositories will cease to acquire personal papers? Or, will archivists need to develop a new set of appraisal criteria by which they seek to preserve the new form of personal archives for individuals who assume significant roles in society or a variety of people who live rather ordinary lives (although isn't it difficult to imagine that anyone engaged in this extensive self-documentation could be classified as ordinary). Or, are we seeing another opportunity for the kind of citizen archivists espoused by Rick Prelinger?

What is interesting about the MyLifeBits effort are the issues that it neglects. For example, other researchers, commentators, and policy observers are focusing on the challenges that "social-networking sites" such as Facebook and MySpace are generating for privacy and socially deviant behavior (such as enabling sexual predators).[65] Other observers are commenting on the fact that more people are capturing more information about themselves with or without the support of software platforms. Neil Beagrie writes, "people are able to create, capture and store an ever-increasing amount of digital information about or for themselves, including emails, documents, portfolios of work, digital images, and audio and video recordings, and can edit, share, and distribute them easily over the net via blogs, personal webpages, peer to peer networks, or shared services." And such trends open up many new challenges: "As personal collections shift from paper and analogue formats to hybrid and increasingly digital formats, personal digital collections are emerging. These personal collections are often composites drawing material from the individual's private life, work, and education, as well as from external communities and content sources. Ownership and intellectual property rights in such collections are therefore often diverse and complex. These collections are often composed of materials intended solely for private reference and use, and/or materials intended to be shared with others at work, or with other communities including family, friends, and interest groups." And, Beagrie understands that "As digital content in personal collections continues to grow, particularly content that has been paid for such as digital music or video, it seems likely that individual and public consciousness of and concerns over digital continuity will also increase," precisely what archivists and other records professionals ought to hope happens, deepening society's comprehension of the archival mission and the need for solutions to the maintenance of digital documents.[66]

While at one time the focus of those writing about information technology seemed to be more about the costs, efficiency, effectiveness, and other attributes of computing in organizations, now there are scholars and technologists analyzing how the individual can harness these technologies. Ben Shneiderman seeks to "raise" the reader's "expectations of what you get from information and communication technologies. It preserves a vision of truly helpful technologies in harmony with human needs."[67] He discusses poorly designed software, unusable interfaces, and the waste of time spent by individuals trying to use their computers or in salvaging stuff when they crash. Shneiderman calls for a new computing, brought about not by a "technology breakthrough" but because of users' "change in expectations and willingness to ask for higher quality."[68]

Shneiderman's inspiration comes from Leonardo Da Vinci's penchant for personal recordkeeping: "He was an endless doodler, sketcher, and dreamer who tucked several notebooks of varying sizes into his waist belt to record his thoughts,"[69] reminding us of Jonathan Edwards. Shneiderman expands the modern meaning of Leonardo: "Inspired by Leonardo's penchant for portable notebooks, and larger sketchbooks, and by his frescoes, we as users and technology developers might imagine the need for a comprehensive line of computers from small but elegant wearable devices to ornate desktop machines and impressive wall-sized models."[70] While the inspiration may come from Leonardo's use of information, sometimes expressed in recordkeeping, one would be skeptical of how much attention Shneiderman might devote to the mechanics of records systems. However, in his four applications – e-learning, e-business, e-healthcare, and e-government – there are allusions to just such matters, if sometimes only in symbolic or general ways. For example, Shneiderman tries to demonstrate the potential power of computing when he compares the ability of the elite to establish archives and museums being rivaled by the new potential of computing sensitive to human needs: "Royalty and presidents have libraries of their archives with photos of their accomplishments but in the future more people will create museums on the Web and slide shows about their lives and ancestors."[71] However, with the increasing power of computing along with its lower costs, we now see a situation where the ability to create and maintain personal archives has passed from the elite to lower ranks in society, the subject of my chapters to follow.

From the perspective of an archivist or records manager many questions may arise about the relevance of such human sensitive computing for administering records systems. Given the continuing struggles to find practical solutions for electronic records management, one wonders whether the issue is creativity of the records professionals or the interest of systems designers or the fact that individuals and institutions still have not determined that the maintenance of digital records is a crucial matter. Perhaps when all those digital images of family and friends, vacations and travel begin to disappear, users' expectations for quality systems preventing this from happening will bring greater resources, talent, and creativity to bear on such matters. Yet, it may be that the solution to the challenges of maintaining digital records may come from the combined power and influence of the people, functioning as consumers and voters.

Personal and Family Remembrance in the Age of Forgetfulness.

Ours is, of course, not only an age seeking to remember, emboldened by remarkable new technologies enabling us to capture so much information. Ours is also an age where so many want to forget, or to control what we remember. The remarkable spate of scholarship in the last couple of decades on the topic of public memory may be a reaction to the sense that the twentieth century was an age of particular horror, with events such as the Holocaust and other acts of genocide, prompting some to want to forget and others to do everything so that they could not forget. The additional challenges presented by the potential destruction of more unstable digital records and information systems have compounded the problems of ensuring memory.

Daniel Mendelsohn's search to learn more about the family he lost in the Holocaust, depicting a moving story of loss and remembrance, is a poignant example of this tension between personal forgetting and remembering. The author tracks the events concerning the loss of six of his family members who lived in a small Ukrainian town and who were murdered by the Germans during World War Two. Mendelsohn discusses his examination of the family archives, the challenges posed by scattered and incomplete documentary materials, and the relating of various stories to what the documents seem to tell him. Mendelsohn describes how he had become the family's official historian by the age of 15, relating how one afternoon visit with his grandfather provided an opportunity to gain some knowledge of the family's documentation, indicating "he'd wanted my help in cleaning out a lot of old boxes of 'useless things,' as he called them, and I sat next to him for a few hours one day, tossing things he was handing me – packets of letters wrapped in rubber bands or string, old driver's licenses, articles from *Reader's Digest* that he'd thrown out – into a tall kitchen garbage pail lined with a white plastic bag."[72] Most of us can identify with this experience (a typical start to someone compiling a genealogy or beginning a scrapbook – leading to more formal efforts to establish a family archives), although few of us wind up becoming so absorbed as Mendelsohn ultimately does, traveling around the world to look at other sources and to talk with distant relatives and their friends and acquaintances.

Prompted by some disturbing revelations about the fate of these family members, the initial reluctance of eyewitnesses to discuss the tragic events, and some gaps in the evidence of the past, Mendelsohn "started to wonder, then, how many other traces she had left behind, how many other clues might be out there, floating in Internet postings and buried in archives that I wouldn't even know were relevant because I had so little to go on, that I wouldn't even know were relevant even when I saw them."[73] Indeed, one can read this book as if it is a mystery, with Mendelsohn as the sleuth searching for clues, many of which lead to absolute dead ends, and all relating to an entire village that essentially disappeared in the 1940s. The author discovers Shlomo Adler, an individual dedicated to keeping in touch with the whereabouts of the dispersed survivors of the village. Visiting Adler, Mendelsohn finds a bedroom transformed into an office:

Everywhere you look, papers spill from boxes crammed onto shelves, and loose-leaf notebooks are stacked one of top of another: dominating the room, sitting atop a smallish desk that it dwarfs, is a large beige computer monitor. It is from this room that Shlomo does his Internet research and Web browsing, and keeps track of the other Bolechowers, sending them e-mails and letters, occasionally sending out his *samizdat* newsletters and, most important, the yearly reminders that go out not only to the survivors themselves but to their relatives and friends and, indeed, anyone who might have anything to do with Bolechow, which is to say people like me, about the annual Bolechow memorial service that he organizes.[74]

What is very interesting about *The Lost* is Mendelsohn's painstaking efforts to go to where every possible shred of evidence might be and the manner in which he describes his experiences, such as when he ventures to Auschwitz: "One reason to go to Auschwitz is that the entire site is a gigantic piece of evidence, and in this respect seeing the piles of eyeglasses or shoes themselves, as opposed to merely knowing about them or seeing photographs or videos of the piles of eyeglasses or shoes or luggage, is more useful in conveying what happened." He notes that another reason has to do with sentimentality: "You go to Auschwitz" for the same reason "you go to a cemetery, which is something that Auschwitz also happens to be: to acknowledge the claims of the dead."[75] This is a compelling sense of how archives and artifacts, sometimes one blending seamlessly into the other, serve as a source of memory, further suggesting why so many homes are full of personal and family mementos, including photographs and documents. Mendelsohn also acknowledges what others have also observed, that there are limits to what can be experienced in museums and other repositories; they "can give us only the dimmest comprehension of what the event itself was like."[76] It is possible, perhaps, that homes can be transformed into more friendly and useful repositories and, like the archival repositories and museums now seemingly always under siege and distracted by public controversies of one sort or another, there is comfort to be found in personal archives where personal records can be lovingly interpreted and cherished.

Mendelsohn's book is a glimpse into why individuals seek to remember something about their own personal past, although in the case of families affected by the Holocaust, played out against the background of sweeping and horrific historical events. His efforts to confront the tragedy of his family's history become a story compelling to all of us. However, this interest in personal and family remembrance can be seen in the celebration of ordinary actions and events and as a means to see the world less through the digital panorama of the Internet, overwhelming in its scope and blurry with its colors, sounds, advertisements, and distractions.

We are sometimes disenchanted with digital writing and recordkeeping, and attracted to document forms that could hardly be represented by digital surrogates. The fascination with the doodles of famous and infamous historical figures reflects this to a certain extent. Paul Collins thinks we find Presidential doodles "so compelling" because "If they are significant, it is not because they are great art or the products of great men. It is because they are ordinary, and historians have fought to preserve open-access laws so that presidential doodles can be so ordinary. Anyone can view them – *they belong to us*. And when we view them, we see that they resemble our own words and our own idle lines. The drawing or scrawled comment on a yellow pad is like an ancient cave painting: a familiar image, but from an unimaginable distance of time and situation."[77] It suggests why so many of us regularly patrol flea markets and antique shops searching for the most intensely personal expressions of the past that we can find. Viewing the doodles makes us think twice about our own scratching done while sitting through a meeting or talking on the telephone.

If we value such documents, then we can extend the logic to want to preserve our own family papers. David Greenberg believes that these doodles "provide us with a glimpse of the unscripted president. They're the antithesis of the packaged persona. Made with neither help from speechwriters nor vetting by a focus group, a doodle is the ultimate private act; it's meaning may remain opaque even to the doodler himself. As a result, it renders the president human in ways that a staged family outing cannot. And if we can't make conclusive judgments about what a president's drawings reveal about his innermost fears or fantasies, his doodles can still be suggestive and provocative... Collectively they help in a benign and inviting way to demystify the office – to build a bridge between citizen and leader."[78] This is an apt description, especially in how it captures the kind of documents most archivists and the researchers in archives hope to hold in their hands; but it also captures some of the sentiment for why an increasing number of individuals seem to be hanging onto personal and family papers. Our own archives provide us the most intimate means to understand the past, seen through the eyes of distant family members or captured in our own innocent reflections when we were much younger and more earnest and hopeful about the world and our future. Just as the executive office grew is size and scope, and its own recording became more bureaucratic and formal, the informal doodles of our presidents became more valuable for personal perspectives.[79] Doodling is not an off-hand, superfluous exercise – not any more lighthearted than what happens with the creation of graffiti. It is a documentary form we ought to want to keep and a form we should be always on the lookout for. It is also the expression of an impulse for personal recordkeeping we can see in other ways.

We also can measure a society's concerns with the creation and maintenance of such basic documents as letters and receipts by the number and nature of manuals instructing individuals about how to produce and maintain such records. Such manuals have been with us for a long time and considerably predate the advent of the computer for personal use. If you frequent flea markets, antique shops, and secondhand bookshops, you have a good chance to find interesting books, photographs, ephemera, and artifacts relating to the production and maintenance of documentary materials. From time to time, you come across stuff reminding you of your own youth, another reminder of how old you are becoming.

One trip to a used bookshop rewarded me with a copy of Frank N. Freeman, *The Teaching of Handwriting*, published in 1914, a volume reminding me of my grade school days when I received a grade for my handwriting (not only was this the easiest grade to earn, but the day they stopped giving grades for this my handwriting lapsed into the chicken scratch it is today). Freeman's little book, in nice condition and picked up for $10, was designed to be an aid to teachers instructing students in handwriting. The book covers the physical aspects of writing, lays out a practice regimen, and provides what was then thought to be the aims and standards for handwriting instruction. I bought the book because I recognized it as a good teaching prop, one I could use in the classroom to help students growing up in the world of the personal computer and the Internet to understand something about the world where people mostly wrote in longhand.

The Teaching of Handwriting links the old handwriting to the new computer and other self-help manuals of today. Freeman starts his book with this statement: "Learning to write consists primarily in the requirement of a new form of expression." He describes how a student might be able "to form the letters fluently and legibly" but still be handicapped by how they approach writing. What Freeman describes is not that different from what one might discover in a software manual today, where the emphasis is on learning a new application so that it becomes second nature: "Writing has not been thoroughly learned until the child can give his attention chiefly to the train of thought he is engaged in expressing while the mechanics of the production of the letters are relegated to the realm of habit."[80] One can see how, after years of banging on a computer keyboard, a manual such as this appears somehow comforting or more user friendly, even considering Freeman's ruminations about the physiology and hygiene of writing, including the problem with writer's cramp, a "disease of the nervous system which affects writing by producing either the abnormal contraction or the paralysis of some of the muscles used in writing."[81] It suggests another reason for our interest in the old handwritten documents of our own families and those we stumble across in flea markets and antique shops. Samara O'Shea, who a few years ago created LetterLover.net, a source for helping people write letters, produced a letter-writing guide, suggesting something of the power of old documents: "One of my favorite things about letters is they can be experienced and re-experienced. The thoughts of one moment are preserved and you can encounter them again as an older, hopefully wiser version of yourself."[82] This sentiment is but one of many reasons people hang onto family papers and other mementos, and it is counter to the iPod era, the "symbol of media's future," suggests Steven Levy, "where the gates of access are thrown open, the reach of artists goes deeper, and consumers don't just consume – they choose songs, videos, and even news their way. Digital technology gathers, shreds, and empowers, all at once."[83] Immersing oneself into personal and family archives is a means for coping with such remarkable change.

If we fast forward just seventy years, to 1983 and the time just when word processing on a clunky computer (with the benefit of hindsight) was stepping forward to replace handwriting and typewriting, we can understand what began to be the basis for the creation of more recent family archives, as well as the foundation for the age of forgetfulness. If someone wants to gain the notion of how much creating documents has changed in just a few decades or more, picking up an old guide to writing with a word processor provides a remarkably graphic picture of this (not unlike looking at the mobile telecommunications technologies in a movie or television show of just a decade ago). William Zinsser's *Writing with a Word Processor* is a candid and valuable historical document for demonstrating how adjusting to such recording technologies has been transformed (and it only cost $3 in a secondhand bookstore).

Zinsser's brief book is no longer of any use for assisting someone to learn to do word processing. Describing an elaborate ordeal of shopping for a computer at the IBM store, waiting two weeks for a delivery of the equipment, working with technicians at home to get his equipment properly set-up, and working with a memory of about a 1000 words, this is a description of a long ago universe. What Zinsser's book now communicates to us is a world where one made a quantum leap from paper to digital (remember this is before the World Wide Web) and where one worked with a "constant fear of loss."[84]

Writing with a Word Processor is useful because Zinsser is an observant witness of one used to being comfortable with typewriters and paper. At the beginning of the book, Zinsser comments, "I belong to a generation of writers and editors who think of paper and pencil as holy objects." Zinsser continues, "The feel of paper is important to me. I have always thought that a writer should have physical control with the materials of his craft..."[85] All through this book, Zinsser struggles with his new world: "The hardest thing for me to think about was the idea of getting along without paper."[86] Zinsser attributes such attitudes to how writers work, although such attitudes extend far beyond just professional writers. However, Zinsser's perspective as a writer is quite revealing: "I found it hard to believe that I had brought into my life a set of writing devices that I would always have to activate. I couldn't just sit down and write; I would have to think about pushing certain keys and inserting diskettes. Now, just to push the ON switch seemed like a major decision."[87] No wonder so many would find themselves turning to the creation of handwritten diaries and handcrafted scrapbooks, desiring to feel the creation of documents.

What *Writing with a Word Processor* opens to us is the world of writing and recordkeeping we used to live in, where there was a lot of paranoia caused by the technology. "When everything is written down on paper it can be found and reviewed and put to use on some other piece of paper," Zinsser reflects. "But when words are mere shadows of light in an electronic box they offer no such security."[88] This is a world most of my students have no memory of, even if they have experienced the occasional loss of work. Most people born after 1980, or certainly after 1985, have no sense of a world where there wasn't the Web and where everything they created wasn't in a digital form. Zinsser's book reminds us have fast our world has changed.

Conclusion.

We have been seeing for years a sea change in attitude about the importance of personal archives. It is like those regular occurrences on the *Antiques Roadshow* where someone brings in personal papers or documents connected to their ancestors, discovering that they possess substantial monetary value. The usual reaction to this is surprise, followed by a comment suggesting that because they are intimately connected with their family they could never sell or part with them. Often our reaction is one of incredulity, but, as I argue in this book, this may be a true testimony and chart the future direction of what we will see with such documents being maintained, digitally and in paper, by individuals and families rather than by archives, historical societies, historic sites, and museums where these records use to go (except as a last resort to ensure the preservation of the more important papers). What this may mean, for the archival community and our society, is considered in the conclusion of this book. The splendor of personal archives is not diminishing, nor is the self-conscious documenting of people like Jonathan Edwards, even though the processes may be very different, and it is in these differences that the joy of new challenges and the possibilities of enhanced successes reside.

While many assume that personal papers and documents are more likely objects to be tossed aside, the very interest we have in these items when they are discovered suggests an intrinsic interest we possess in maintaining some degree of personal archives. Davy Rothbart, the creator of the popular *Found* magazine, writes, "Since grade school I've been collecting notes, letters, photographs, and other stuff I found on the ground," and he proceeds to describe examples of diaries, cartoons and drawings, wills, grocery lists, greeting cards, notices, school papers, and postcards. Rothbart continues, "It always amazed me how powerfully I could connect with a person I'd never met just by reading a half-page love letter left behind on a park bench or the city bus."[89] Isn't this what it is like to read a document in an archives, enabling us to connect with real people long gone in the past? And, isn't this another reason why so many hang onto their personal and family papers, engaged in an archival endeavor to preserve them?

The evidence offered by Rothbart suggests a lot about how people relate to archival materials: "Found notes and letters open up the entire range of human experience; they offer a shortcut directly into people's minds and hearts. We often feel most alive when we're glimpsing someone at their most honest and raw."[90] Of course, if we react in this manner to such tossed materials, why have people discarded them to begin with? And, does this suggest that society might see archives as only the formerly discarded, or, at least, might this explain why sometimes it is so difficult to be successful in explaining archives within an organization? Who knows, but I sense that such interest is also leading to more people themselves keeping archival records than ever before. Archivists need to help them.

Chapter Two

The Romance of the Document

Introduction.

You can find these people everywhere. They scour through boxes of stuff at flea markets, scroll through the latest offerings on EBay, search through the exhibitions at museums, and inquire at second hand book and antique stores. These are the people looking for the interesting document, one aged in just the right way, associated with a particular event or era, possessing an interesting or famous signature, or just possessing the desired appearance to be framed and hung in a study or den. Autograph and manuscript collecting has been a popular past-time in this country for nearly two hundred years, an avocation supported by a network of dealers, auction houses, and now online vendors. Americans, long accused of not being interested in history, defy such an assessment as they prowl and purchase such artifacts, seeking these items because they provide an intimate connection with the past or create a personal stake in the memory of the nation.

Archivists and records managers, the professionals responsible for maintaining the documentary heritage, sometimes become so involved in the clinical aspects of administering records that they lose sight of the general fascination, by the public, scholars, and other professionals alike, with the romantic appeal of the document. A few years ago, in an effort to counter society's focus on how much information can be stored and used with new technologies, a group of artists and writers explored the "productive potential of memory's failure – its technical dropouts, omissions, burials, eclipses, and denials."[1] Many of the contributors to this volume appealed to some of the emotional and other similar qualities of the record. Julia Creet, exploring the work of Danilo Kis, a Hungarian writer, provided such a perspective: "The truth of the historical record is provided by the richness of the literary imagination. The facticity of the document is not as important as the idea of the fact of the document itself and the emotional, intellectual, symbolic value with which we invest it."[2] Generations of commentators, especially artists,[3] have echoed such sentiments about the document, and while records professionals may have been attracted to their work initially because of such notions, the daily grind of preserving, cataloguing, and making these records available can dull such interests. Archivists have, for example, expounded often and loudly about the technical features of a record, necessary in this era of digital information systems, but this has not often included the sentimental or emotional elements of documents that have led so many individuals lovingly maintaining personal and family archives.

It may be difficult for many records professionals to reflect on the values people and organizations invest in the document when they are so busy striving to contend with huge volumes of paper records and growing quantities of digital information, complicated by the increasing demands of the organizations they work for and the constituencies they serve. The concerns of archivists and records managers run more toward legal and administrative needs, intellectual controls so that the records can be accessed when needed, and issues such as the reliability and authenticity of digital documents – all matters that may be minor for many others outside of the records professions but that remain central to the work of archivists and records managers. Someone acquiring a document because of personal interest or discovering an old document associated with their family may not be interested in issues such as that record's provenance (context), one of the concerns guiding the professional's activities. And they certainly are not going to linger over it and analyze first whether it meets the definition of a record or work through some elaborate checklist of appraisal values (and not the financial kind).

What archivists and personal collectors are interested in may not be that far apart. It is not difficult to see the more emotional and symbolic values of the ordinary record in the writings of autograph collectors, artists, and scholars such as historians. This chapter reviews a small array of recent publications that comment on many issues concerning the nature of documentation but that all have something to say about the romance of the document, reminding archivists and records managers of the need to be sensitive to this aspect of the records under their care. Records professionals have long struggled to build public understanding of and support for their work, and the message needed to accomplish this may reside somewhere in the popular fascination with the ordinary documents produced by them and their ancestors, such as with the journal. The archivist or records manager may be more interested in certain technical concerns, but they need to be sensitive to how outsiders view their work in order to promote their important mission, and they certainly need to understand the popular appeal of old documents in order to work with people interested in and committed to maintaining family archives.

The Most Personal of Documents: The Journal.

We are witnessing an upsurge in diary writing, journaling, and calligraphy – perhaps part of a reaction to the bits and bytes of the digital world. Publications appear regularly to assist individuals in taking up these pastimes. Gwen Diehn's guide for creating "decorated" journals is an example of such volumes. Diehn discusses, in well-illustrated detail, the use of materials, approaches to design and binding, and varying approaches to how journals reflect the world.[4] Writer and teacher Jennifer New's discussion of the journal as art provides ample illustrations from journals maintained mostly by artists, but also an engineer, a cognitive scientist, a composer, a landscape architect, a quilter, and a photographer. New writes that her book "celebrates these seemingly humble tools, beautiful objects in and of themselves like old Shaker chairs grown smooth from so many bodies, or a handmade quilt faded from decades of laundering and human contact, journals are utilitarian objects transformed by repeated and fond use. They hold life in them, which is why we cannot let them go."[5] And why there is so much reflection about them. New provides a broad definition of the journal, terming them a "place where we record personal reflections, observations of our world, playful meanderings, and plans."[6] In an interesting insight about journals, New argues that they "serve as file folders for future works."[7] Diehn and New's volumes can be useful for the records professional seeking some clues about the kinds of journals they may be seeing in the near future, and certainly they inform us a lot about the reasons so many are maintaining personal and family archives. While neither author provides the kind of analysis an archivist might draw on to make a final appraisal decision about such journals, they are valuable for understanding the forces shaping the creation of such documents.

These self-help books provide interesting insights into the nature and value of documents, such as Nick Bantock's attractive book on re-using old records for art projects, intended to function as a "handbook for those who wish to learn how to embellish and tamper with old documents, envelopes, and other ephemeral scraps."[8] Bantock, author of the popular Griffin and Sabine series built around the clever

portrayal of documents and their representation,[9] in this book utilizes
many different document forms (as well as other collectibles and
ephemera) -- maps, engravings, money, photographs, stamps, books and
magazines, commercial ephemera, postcards, rubber stamps,
photocopies, drawings, handwriting and type, and games – and plays
with creating new art forms, an approach that might concern archivists
and other records professionals about the potential needless destruction
of valuable sources. Yet, there is little to fear in anything Bantock says,
especially in what appears at times to be a discourse on the deliberate
destruction of historical documents, but there is much insight about the
popular notion of the document to be gained from following his
commentary.

    Bantock tries to assuage any fears that might develop from his
approach, noting that the "bits and pieces came from junk stores,
garage sales, online auctions, storerooms, and sometimes garbage piles.
There is no guilt or worry over the destruction of museum-quality
material because nothing here cost more than ten dollars. This figure
indicates not miserliness but merely a boundary that allows me to know
that whatever I do I am not defacing something of real historical
value."[10] Records professionals might continue to worry about whether
others, inspired by Bantock, might not be so careful and destroy
valuable materials. At the same time, records professionals ought to be
aware that the kind of writing Bantock has done offers considerable
insight into the value of archival and documentary sources, especially in
gaining a feel for how people interact, more emotionally and intimately,
with documents such as journals, letters, and receipts.

    There are some particular values for records professionals in
volumes such as Bantock's. Bantock stresses that he is not trying to
encourage anyone to create forgeries or fakes, but he is advocating an
activity that will assist people to understand better what artifacts suggest
to us about the past: "So what am I encouraging you to make? Not
forgeries or fakes. There is no pretense to hide the concept of fantasy
and no attempt to suggest something is other than what it appears.
What I want to show is that a little wit and guile can move us backward
and forward within an artifact's history, giving us an enhanced
sensitivity toward the archaic and the ever malleable. In so doing, we
allow ourselves to develop a creativity rooted in something stronger
than the transience of fashion."[11]   As many have observed, the re-
emergence of an interest in handwriting partly emanates from what it
reveals, versus that of typing or word processing: "At one time,

handwriting was commonplace and the literate were adept at reading it. Eyes were attuned to comprehend individualistic styles and letter formations; the handwritten word was a reflection of an individual's personality. You could establish whether your correspondent was tight and careful or open and gregarious by the letters shaped by his or her pen."[12] Most of all, however, Bantock likes to poke a bit of fun with old documents, such as when he notes, "Invoices, business forms, passports, visas, marriage and death certificates: there's almost no end to institutional and commercial paperwork... By their nature, official documents take themselves rather seriously, which makes them perfect for a little teasing."[13]

Archivists and records managers might welcome a little humor in their sometimes tedious efforts to handle the avalanche of records that characterizes the modern office and that seems to be synonymous with the negative meanings of bureaucracy and bureaucratic behavior. If nothing else, they can connect with a common interest in the records people normally work with, react to, and file away (except for those visually arresting or intrinsically interesting documents that tend to get taped or tacked to walls and doors). And they can begin to see why so many hang onto seemingly worthless old documents, such as a parent's or grandparent's old handwritten checks and receipts, as a means of connecting with their own immediate past and because such documents are curiosities (at least to them).

Such books may suggest all kinds of challenges in documenting the creation of such journals. Are any institutions making an effort to collect the variety of decorated journals these authors describe? What kinds of preservation challenges do they represent, even as their authors advocate the use of acid-free and archival materials? How do these paper journals relate to the online versions increasing daily? If nothing else, these writings suggest some immense practical preservation challenges for archivists and other records professionals because of the complicated layers of documents and mixed media that comprise these journals, suggesting that it is not merely the digital world that records professionals need to focus on. But this is the challenge facing archivists and records managers in maintaining the new world of personal archives. Archivists must ask the question whether they and their institutions will remain the primary preservers of such records, or whether private citizens will assume a greater role in this. Records managers, focused more on institutional records and information systems, will face increasingly more difficult tasks in distinguishing between institutional and personal records, especially as so many work as much from home and on the road as in the office. Journals are not the only documentary form undergoing change; the epistolary form has also drawn more attention by scholars and social commentators alike.

A Window into the Past: The Letter.

When was the last time you indulged in the polite art of social correspondence? If you are under the age of thirty, you may not even know what I mean by such a question. Selecting the right weight and feel of paper, searching for the pen which will best express your feelings, and practicing to gain the appropriate calligraphic style are activities very few of us indulge in today. Receiving a personal handwritten letter is now so rare most of us probably cannot recall the last time we have experienced this. For me, it occurred nearly a decade ago, when a beautifully penned personal letter of thanks from a professional colleague arrived. Not long after this happened, when I was speaking with this individual at a conference, I asked why she had taken the time to script the letter. Her reply was interesting, explaining that one's personal gratitude was best expressed by the extra effort expended in crafting such an epistle. And she was right. While unfortunately I did not hold onto the manuscript, and now I wish I had, I still fondly recall this experience and occasionally hope it will occur again.

If personal handwritten or typed (or word-processed) letters with annotations are declining in frequency, one must wonder about the impact of this on our personal archives and on the future of scholarship if we are someone who might be studied someday. We know, for example, that biographers long for the lengthy and candid personal letter, that these kinds of documents are often the subject of contentious litigation involving efforts to protect privacy or to control intellectual property, and that history reveals to us many instances where surviving spouses or children purposely destroyed personal and literary papers in order to protect reputations.[14] What is going into the archives in the place of the old handwritten or typed but heavily annotated epistles? What is being lost by their absence? One can speculate about this without too much difficulty. If, in past times, the novelist kept every draft of his or her book, the copy-editor's comments, and the author's subsequent corrections from manuscript through final page proof, today all of this is automated and prone mostly to be discarded or, with the same result, allowed to deteriorate in its digital form. Formerly, each of these stages would have correspondence with extensive commentaries; this does not mean there may not be electronic mail, but that mail will be easier to discard, along with the other digital documents, as well, endangering the existence of the kinds of evidence that we normally associate with the letter. The loss may be substantial. We lose the ability to re-trace our own work. Someone else wanting to understand the origins and process of bringing a book to press will find if difficult, if not impossible to do so. We will have to rely on memory or, worse, speculation, about what was involved. Multiply this by tens of thousands of times among our writers and millions of times among ordinary individuals and families, and we can begin to perceive the decline in our documentary heritage (and to begin to see why we need to re-evaluate how and why we value personal archives).

Most of us have experienced a manuscript letter from afar. When we visit a historical museum, we often encounter in an exhibition case an important letter announcing a discovery, revealing an intriguing personal tidbit about a famous historical personage, or providing some special insight into a well known past event. We gape with curiosity on the paper with the scrawling handwriting, and now, perhaps wonder about the nature of the mechanical movements required to produce the document, sometimes under adverse or extreme conditions. It is not a process many of us can relate to in our modern cyber-society. The physical nature of the manuscript letter is increasingly foreign to us. Stains on the paper, tears and smudges, crossed out sections, or words misspelled perhaps in haste all speak to us as much as the words in the letter about the past events and lives frozen for us. And reading the words may prove to be a challenge as well. As we become less and less connected to the process of creating letters using a pen, paper, and the simple, sweeping movements of a hand, we also lose the ability to read the cursive. It is more than likely that the museum has transcribed or enlarged the words in an accompanying label so as to assist us to read what now seems to be an ancient process of communicating. We may be more fascinated by the quaint artifact than the evidence or information it conveys.

Visiting an art museum brings many reminders of the technology of preparing a handwritten letter. Portrait painters used props, associated with their subject's livelihood or their life, to provide context, often using flattery, to the person they were depicting. The merchant would sit near a desk with account ledgers stacked on it. The cleric would have a Bible open on a table near them. The antiquarian scholar would be surrounded by the sculptures, coins, miniatures, and other objects in his collection. Many subjects, from the house mistress to the military officer, would be captured in the act of reading or writing a letter. The letter, with identifying marks of date and the recipient's name, would be held in an active way. The letter was a connector to the outside world, and a reminder of the networks of information and information that would demarcate the prestige and influence of the portrait's subject. For those contemporary with the portrait and the person depicted in it, no one needed to explain the significance of the letter. Gazing upon it from our vantage would raise many questions for us, because it is such a rare act to experience the need to read a personal letter or to have to respond to it in kind. Composing a personal letter seems artificial, almost an artistic expression whereby we pose over the paper and carefully scrawl the letters of one word after another (there are some who take classes in calligraphy in order to be prepared to write such epistles, almost defiantly protesting a complete reliance on the computer or, increasingly, text-messaging with a cell phone).

Writing the personal letter is a deliberative act, and today we reply to an electronic mail message quickly and effortlessly (and often not very carefully or deliberately). We tend not to weight a particular word or phrase over another, but we try to churn through as many messages as possible, often not concerned with diction or grammar, employing abbreviations and shortcuts to convey our thoughts and concerns. It is difficult for us to relate to the seventeenth century figure looming before us for whom writing the letter was a responsibility and a joy, the centerpiece activity of their day, and an act that they knew would bring in return another letter.

The writer Anne Fadiman provides some insights into how matters have been transformed in regards to the writing and receiving of letters, or nearly any mail. Fadiman commences her essay, "Mail," by describing her memories of her father looking forward each day to the delivery of mail, both junk and the more interesting professional and personal mail. She then contrasts seeing how her father received his mail with that of how people used to receive mail in the seventeenth and eighteenth centuries. Here she reminds us of something that might seem surprising; an individual living in a major urban area such as London would receive mail all day long, since it was the main form of communication for scheduling lunches, arranging meetings, and connecting to clients. For the mail lovers among us, this would be a truly hospitable environment. Email has, of course, transformed our experience with mail. Fadiman describes her adoption of email, and how quickly she made the adjustment to it. She confesses how quickly after starting to use it, that she was "batting out fifteen or twenty e-mails in the time it had once taken me to avoid answering a single letter."[15]

Most of us have made similar adjustments. Nevertheless, many of us worry about the legacy of documents we leave behind, as just one result of shifting from the personal letter to the electronic message. Fadiman lets us know what we might be missing when she describes her father's own papers:

> I also own my father's old copper wastebasket, which now holds my empty Jiffy bags. Several times a day I use his heavy brass stamp dispenser; it is tarnished and dinged, but still capable of unspooling its contents with a singular smoothness. And my file cabinets hold hundreds of his letters, the earliest written in his sixties in small, crabbed handwriting, the last in his nineties, after he lost much of his sight, penned with a Magic Marker in huge capital letters. I hope my children will find them someday, as Hart Crane found his grandmother's love letters in the attic.[16]

How many of us maintain similar archives of our parents or grandparents?

Attics, basements, and garages, even in the heralded era of cyberspace, often still contain boxes and bags of old family papers. Sooner of later, when we are moving or just in the need for a spring cleaning, we come across these papers, and they usually slow down the cleaning effort. As time passes, the kinds of documents we discover in these spaces seem more and more foreign to us. Old letters certainly may seem the strangest to us these days. We read a lengthy letter from a great aunt to one of our parents describing in detail a vacation trip, and we recall how little we may have documented about our own vacations. We might have fired off a quick e-mail message to a relative or a friend about one of our trips, but we probably made no effort to save it and we certainly never invested in a process whereby one of our children or grandchildren would be coming across our account. When we read one of these old letters, captured on quaint papers with sketches and doodles or folded about a snippet of a baby's hair or a pressed wildflower (providing physical evidence of the topics being addressed in the letter), we may begin to realize just what we are missing or losing in the so-called age of information.

Hermione Lee, in her musings about the art of biography, captures, at least partly, why we are so fascinated by the act of peering down into the past through the spectacles of those who left letters and other documents behind; she reflects that "when we are reading other forms of life-writing – autobiography, memoir, journal, letter, autobiographical fiction, or poem – of when we are trying ourselves to tell the story of a life, whether in an obituary, or in a conversation, or in a confession, or in a book, we are always drawn to moments of intimacy, revelation, or particular inwardness."[17] So, the question we have to ask is whether what we seem to be replacing letters with, those digital messages, are going to provide the same kind of moments? Clearly, if they are not saved, there will be no opportunity for this to happen, and the point is moot.

Letters have long been the staple of historians, and there are countless millions in archives around the world (more when we add in all the letters sitting in records centers waiting their final disposition and electronic mail not yet evaluated or preserved). Letters provide a glimpse into the lives of the ordinary citizen, and they are an important source for every form of historical research. Historian Deborah Montgomerie discusses, in one recent investigation into letter-writing, how the correspondence of New Zealanders serving in the military during the Second World War has been generally ignored and often not preserved. As she relates, some of this is due to the exigencies of war:

> During the Second World War New Zealand civilians sent thousands of letters to servicemen abroad, yet few have ended up in archives or public collections. Hardly any writers kept copies of their outgoing correspondence and the conditions of soldiers' lives made it difficult for them to hold onto the letters they received. Letters might be stored in kits, or back at base, but soldiers who made it through the war had hard choices to make when deciding what to bring home with them. A few especially precious letters might be kept; most were discarded. Souvenirs and presents often had more claim to limited baggage space than old letters. Families, too, seem to have been much more likely to preserve soldier-authored correspondence and later donate it to public institutions; civilian-authored correspondence was not regarded as worthy of preservation.[18]

In one sense, a few changes and leaping forward in time, and we could argue that this is what has occurred in our postmodern, digital era. As we have become more dependent on email, it is likely that we have become less sensitive to preserving much of what transpires via this but more aware of important personal letters, significant because they arrive as snail-mail and in handwritten form.

The callousness of our own time concerning such personal correspondence suggests the need for raising public consciousness about what may be lost – to individuals, to families, and to historians. Montgomerie hopes that her book will draw attention to the importance of preserving such documents: "It is to be hoped that as more of the war-time generation passes on, the friends and families clearing out cupboards and boxes of papers will choose to save papers relating to the war, either in private collections or by donating them to public institutions."[19] It is a worthy aim, and it attests to how much documentation of great potential value is yet to be accorded the attention it deserves. Yet, we are also aware that we will not have the same opportunity in the future to clean out the equivalent of cupboards, boxes, and closets – our computer hard drives – to save the emails that have replaced the letters or the word-processed versions of our epistles capturing how we drafted and revised these documents before printing them out and attaching our old-fashioned signature. Just as archivists working in institutional settings have long known that they need to intercede early in the life of a document in order to ensure its survival, they need to recognize that they need to do the same with individuals generating personal papers in a digital form.

Love in the Time of War builds around three sets of letters, with Montgomerie describing the nature of the documents, placing them in historical context and embellishing them with contemporary photographs, and reconstructing the very personal stories revealed by the letters. Montgomerie wonders, "Although letters are an important part of many war stories, historians have discussed them infrequently."[20] The letters, even with the oversight of wartime censors, "make sense of extraordinary events beyond their control."[21] Montgomerie notes how self-conscious the soldiers were about writing about letters and their utility in their lives and experiences: "Correspondents wrote about their conversations and conversed about their letters. Diarists noted the arrival of mail and the emotions evoked by writing."[22] These letters are particularly revealing sources as windows into the past: "The effort Wilson [one of the soldiers described by the historian] put into writing home, even when he felt he had nothing to say, his ongoing and insistent interest in home affairs, his idealization of home and family, his longing for a home-centered future, were shared by many soldiers. At best the letters provide only edited highlights of his army service, but they allow us to put flesh on the bones of friendship, family and place; faces on the official portrait of independence, single men."[23] Such letter-writing appeals to our perception of the very basic human impulse at play in such activity, and it suggests something of the human needs that are reflected in the creation of many forms of documents. Today, we are self-conscious about the act of formal letter-writing because it is such a rarity. Sitting down to write a letter in long-hand and in a personal fashion is as symbolic an act as the official bill-signing ceremonies staged by the White House and featuring the President of the United States.

A significant portion of this book evaluates the role of these letters as important artifacts worthy of preservation and care. Letters are "important symbols, tokens of remembrance and hope."[24] Montgomerie is careful to reveal how these documents take on values far beyond ordinary ones:

> Letters written and received in times of great stress, particularly those penned by soldiers killed during the war, became poignant artifacts. Like the photographs of departed soldiers enshrined on mantelpieces and living room walls, the treasured letters came to represent the heartfelt 'before' preceding a heartbreaking 'after.' Even when a soldier survived, his letters could remain a painful reminder of life deferred, and of friends and acquaintances who did not survive. Wartime letters carry with them a burden of sorrow and senseless loss as well as treasured remembrance.[25]

It is similar to the reverence accorded to the artifacts and documents associated with Holocaust victims and those killed in the World Trade Center on September 11, 2001 – and countless wars, rebellions, genocides, and other acts of violence. These letters also played a particular role, not just in sustaining morale for the solders, but they also "offered civilians the possibility of continued intimacy and hope for the future."[26]

It is important for records professionals to remember the emotions that might be associated with even the most mundane looking document. And this is especially the case when we consider personal papers. Sometimes it is easy for archivists to lament the times that they have been forced to watch and listen as someone carefully pulls out documents one at a time and tells a story about each one. Likewise, records managers have sometimes experienced something very similar when they are assisting an employee cleaning out an office upon retirement; the employee might linger over a routine document,

destined to be destroyed based on authorized retention schedules,
because it is associated with a meaningful or distressing event in that
individual's life. Archivists and records professionals will need to be
more patient and empathetic in these circumstances. These
professionals also need to be more understanding, perhaps learning
something that suggests some different approaches to their appraisal of
records and some modifications to their mission to assist individuals and
families to preserve documents of more meaning to them than
possessing historical significance requiring their placement in an
archives.

Letters, then, in the time of trauma such as war, also provide
compelling stories that connect us to the past. Montgomerie wonders,
"But what should we make of individual war stories? Are they just
sidelights on bigger battlefield dramas? I believe not. They are, in the
first place, good stories, worth telling. The more war histories we have,
and the greater their variety, the more ammunition we possess to resist
simplistic generalizations about what the war did to New Zealand
society and what it meant to those who lived through it."[27] These are
truly significant documents, as Montgomerie reflects about their
broader value for understanding history: "Thinking about these
people's letters and the place of war in their lives encourages us to
examine the process by which individual stories are transformed into
history, and history into nationalist myths. For all their apparent
simplicity they are complex documents."[28] And, given how routine so
many letters can be in our lives and institutions, they are also,
nevertheless, very important sources of information. Perhaps the point
here is that there is no such thing as a routine document, that even a
document passed by historians and other scholars or archivists in their
documentary work or records managers in their careful preening of
records with no continuing utility to the organization can have
substantial emotional and symbolic value to an individual. It is why
many archivists shy away from the knotty challenges of appraisal work
and others acknowledge, even as they turn down records or consign
others to the garbage heap, that all records are valuable for someone at
sometime.

And, it is because of such highly personalized sensibilities about
such documents that we have had a long tradition of individual
collecting. The recent publication of a collector about his autograph
collection, one built around letters, affirms the significance and romance
of the letter as a documentary form. Do Lago attests that "every letter,

even the most insignificant, is a touching relic of the person who wrote
it – a tangible link that defies the passage of time. Holding it in your
hands is unquestionably the closest contact you can possibly have if the
person is no longer with us."[29] And this is why so many people hold
onto their father's letters from the Second World War, their
grandmother's old handwritten recipe book, and the family Bible with
annotations about births, baptisms, marriages, and deaths – even if so
often these documents are jammed into shoeboxes on the upper shelves
of a hallway closet. This collector's account, beautifully illustrated,
describes 350 examples from his collection, provides advice about
collecting, comments on the history of autograph collecting, and even
plays with the psychology of collecting. Do Lago, the President of the
National Library of Brazil, also enumerates the kinds of documents that
attract collectors.

True to the Letter provides interesting insights of how autograph
collectors work, attesting to the romance of the document. There is the
tactile quality of the physical document, the "meeting" between the
document and the person holding it: "The paper has frozen from this
moment of time in the life of the writer. The pleasure of possessing it
contains a certain sweet fetishism, tinged perhaps with an element of
indiscretion; we are reading words that were intended for someone else,
but the collector will somehow feel that he or she is really the ultimate,
secret addressee."[30] The author plays with the limited range of
documents available to the collector, revealing how the collector views
the competition from established repositories; Do Lago notes that as
rarer or more valuable texts become more difficult to find, the
"collector is forced to turn to seemingly ordinary texts, which will
perhaps reveal something unexpected or even humorous, but which his
or her predecessors may have regarded as unimportant."[31] It may be
that this kind of enthusiasm for the document, especially as more and
more texts have moved into the digital realm, has ebbed in archival
programs and the community of records professionals. Records are
objects to be managed, not loved; documents are valuable for
everything but as an expression of our most human characteristics. The
kind of emotion Do Lago is describing is more likely to be found at
home as someone rummages through the old chest tucked in the back of
the attic or basement.

One senses that this collector laments the disappearance of valuable
documents into established archives, research libraries, and museums.
In a description of his Marcel Proust documents concerning the famous

writer and the architect of the modern novel, Do Lago writes, "Most of
the manuscripts passed down to the Proust family were sold to the
Bibliothèque Nationale de France. Nevertheless, during the last thirty
years a larger number of important Proust autographs have been found
than perhaps of any other major 20th-century writer, even though the
truly essential items have since been acquired by institutions and will
not be seen again on the open market."[32] Such sentiments reflect the
immense appeal of manuscript documents, even in this era of cyber-
hype. While one can read transcripts of such documents on the World
Wide Web or their digital counterparts by contemporary writers, the
experience between this kind of reading and possessing a document is
not quite the same. In the past, while there has always been tension
between private and public, institutional collectors, it has been the
institutional collectors –archives, libraries, museums, and historic sites –
that have won out. In the future, there may be less certainty about this,
especially as so many personal papers are digitally born and pose
challenges to the public archives. The good news is, however, many
private citizens care as passionately about the documents as do the
institutional repositories.

Do Lago also, somewhat dutifully given his interest in the
acquisition of original documents, makes a case for how manuscripts
will continue to be valued even in this era of high-tech developments.
This collector muses, "It has often been said that new information
technology will kill off the autograph. Perhaps it will, although during
the last hundred years the telephone and typewriter have already cut
the number of handwritten messages significantly. Faxes will certainly
not be seen as autographs, nor will emails – even if they are the
authentic words of the sender." And here is the main point of his
observations: "There is no doubt that methods of writing have changed
dramatically and are still changing. However, this will only add to the
value of autographs: manuscript messages from famous celebrities will
become rarities and, as such, all the more precious to collectors."[33]
People may be increasingly reluctant to turn over their original
documents to archives, libraries, and other institutions because of
sentimental and emotional meanings not being afforded by the new and
emerging digital documents. Before the computer, of course, people
worried about the increasing number of technologies encouraging oral
rather than written transmission, and their impact on written records.
However, there may be less to learn looking backwards because of the
remarkable advances in and increasing affordability of information

technologies. And, it may be that this collector is wrong about the new digital surrogates for letters, diaries, and other documents; individuals and families probably will rally to preserve the documents that are of importance to charting their own past.

Hearing the Past: The Oral Message.

Oral history has been alive and well for many decades, but it has floated tentatively about in the archival profession for almost as long, never ever going quite mainstream, often because of other priorities, the financial costs associated with the intensive form of gathering documentation, and lingering concerns about the veracity of evidence generated by this approach. Records managers have generally not bothered with any of this, except to worry about the legal implications of hearsay evidence in court proceedings, and how this may or may not affect their employers and records programs. More recent ruminations about oral history have suggested that in certain cultures oral testimony and evidence need to be given more serious attention, one of the main themes in a collection of essays about oral history in New Zealand edited by Anna Green and Megan Hutching.[34] Oral history and tradition can also add to the romantic view of the document, suggesting that there is considerable personal and family memory encapsulating any document that is personally maintained. Documents can take on extraordinary meaning when they are associated with personal and family memory.

The Green and Hutching book is a combination of basic primer and a set of case studies on oral history work. In the preface, the two editors note that they "hope … [the book] will be an interesting introduction to the field of oral history that will also suggest new ways of thinking about the original stories and how they are turned into written form."[35] It is the kind of new thinking archivists and records managers need to indulge in as well. As such, the book is a collection of general essays about various rudimentary aspects of oral history and some specific examples of research utilizing oral history. There are essays on how oral history relates to the broader framework of historical research, ethical issues in interviewing, and the matters generated by transcribing oral testimony. Most of the essays relate to various oral history projects, all based in New Zealand and some relating to the culture of indigenous peoples. However, anyone familiar with oral history and archival documentation in any cultural setting will find themes, issues, and processes that transcend the Kiwi nation and that will resonate with them.

The volume provides a good orientation to the normal range of concerns about the role and utility of oral history. Anna Green, in one of her essays, suggests why oral history has re-emerged as a topic engaging some historians and other scholars. Noting how historians turned away from oral sources as archives developed in the nineteenth century, Green asserts that what worked against the use of oral history has became an asset: the "subjectivity of individual memory became a positive resource for the study of history, not a liability. Through oral testimonies it was possible to explore the many ways in which individuals construct frameworks of meaning. The incorporation of myth, ideology, imagination or moral rhetoric into oral narratives about the past provided valuable insights into the making of meaning."[36] Considering how important oral testimony is to corporate culture, it is a wonder that records managers and archivists laboring in organizations have not been more aggressive in using and considering the importance of oral tradition or how to capture such testimony in order to supplement textual records. Moreover, the notion of constructing meaning is particularly relevant for individuals and families maintaining their own archives. Family photographs displayed, scrapbooks regularly re-examined, and old letters read and re-read all relate to rituals involved in such memory construction. It is how many identify and maintain their place in our complicated world.

Some of the oral tradition and testimony relates directly to the issues of evidence. Conducting oral history projects among the Maori provide a very different sense of how such sources can function as evidence. Danny Keenan describes how among this people the "past substantially converges into the present. Time, context and cognition easily connect within the memory of kaumātua who, standing on the paepae, recall the past and weave it into important tribal and hapu histories." For the Maori, oral testimony has always been accepted. "As a consequence, all important components of a tribal past, such as waka traditions, are readily acknowledged by Maori as perfectly valid history that is constantly maintained within vigorous oral forms like taupararpara (chants), whaikōreo (speeches), and waiata (songs)."[37] One wonders just how differing organizational cultures might reflect divergent notions of evidence, not too dissimilar from what we see in the various cultures across nations and indigenous groups.

One also can speculate about how the increasing presence of the World Wide Web might not also be collapsing time, space, and memory into one seamless process or product that challenges our traditional notions of what the document represents. If some wonder if we are entering into a new oral or visual culture, it might be prudent to look more carefully at cultures that have operated differently than us in our reliance on linear texts, hierarchical organizations, and regimented communications networks. Similarly, we should focus more on studying individual and family cultures to determine how personal records are generated, why personal archives are formed, and how such personal archives are maintained. We also need to determine whether how personal archives today differ from those of earlier generations and how more changes may be occurring.

These efforts in New Zealand demonstrate the importance of oral history in not merely adding to the documentary record, but in its ability to generate documentation for groups and individuals that are under-documented. Green, in another of her essays, articulates how this works: "So oral history gives us access to the world of the majority who do not leave written accounts of their lives. It can also increase the range of subjects we are able to explore, providing insights into aspects of social and cultural history that are difficult to research through written documentation. The often unrecorded private dimensions of family, working and community relationships become more accessible in oral accounts."[38] There may be, however, more personal and family documentation than she assumes, and new attention to oral history and tradition may include some suggestions about this.

A number of the essays, focusing on such topics as documenting a group of lesbians or considering how the Maori see the past, certainly suggest the very useful role of oral history in creating new archival documentation. Juanita Ketchel's interviews with individuals who endured domestic violence provide an opportunity to see how these individuals "are propelled forward by a desire and capacity to make some kind of sense of their cruel experience, to benefit rather than burden their lives." As Ketchel suggests, such a project can "convey the strength individuals can show in the face of adversity, and tell us that mental health promotion must focus not on people's disadvantages but on their strengths."[39] Individuals working in organizations or professions facing immense change, from new technologies to challenges from out-sourcing, might also be endeavoring to make sense of their world through the creation of their records and how they manage them. It is most likely the case with those providing more serious care to their own and family papers.

Oral interviews reflect document characteristics, and, likewise, they share features with personal recordkeeping. Kay Edwards, describing a project interviewing actors, makes, for example, an interesting observation about the difference between a transcript of an oral interview and the audio version:

> The tape of the interview remains the primary source of material, though the historian uses a transcript, a written translation, of the words spoken. The transcript may be an accurate account, in that it is a word for word copy, but it is impossible to translate the associated body language and the subtle nuances of speech – the deliberate pause, the ironic inflection, the raised eyebrow that accompanies a statement." [40]

Edwards was prompted to reflect on such matters because of the "irony" of creating oral history transcripts for individuals, actors, who make their living by the use of voice and body movements.

Oral history is also likened to capturing stories, and with this we can relate to other documents as well:

> Remembering is a complex process. Our brains do not store literal snapshots of the past that we can call up upon demand. Memories are partial and fragmented, and in the process of reassembling them for others we decide what to include or exclude. We also seek to make meaningful connections between the present and the past. Popular forms of storytelling provide the narrative structures that frame the story. To make sense of our past, we draw upon the vocabulary and metaphors of our time and culture, generating complex codes of meaning that can be opaque to later generations or cultural outsiders. Finally, oral history is recorded in a social context that rewards the skills of story telling and rhetorical persuasion. Because we need to take all these documents into account, oral histories have to be 'unpacked' to reveal the richness and variety of their contents. [41]

In the same fashion, other documents can be seen as social constructs. And, perhaps, archival records are also documents that must be unpacked from their storage locations in the repositories. At the least, the story telling aspect is one important ingredient of what attracts so many to reading documents, old and new and in paper and digital form, and, most likely, it is an important reason why so many individuals preserve family and personal archives.

Oral history is a deliberate means archivists and historians use to acquire evidence of the past that is not available in other documentary sources. Of course, archivists also have been striving to preserve one of the most prevalent documentary forms of the twentieth century, the audio record. Sound recordings, from oral history and tradition to music, are a ubiquitous basic documentary form and have been so for more than a century. Just as I am arguing, in part, in this book, that there is an increasing move by many individuals to care for their personal and family archives, a considerable part of the future administration of documentary sources such as sound recordings may rest with individuals other than professionals, from hobbyists to individuals maintaining family archives. Records professionals must be cautious and conservative, not necessarily taking a particular stance in debates about the value of one technology over another, but seeking ways to preserve all the document types that emanate from a constantly changing array of technologies. However, individuals, caring for their own recordings, besides looking for advice to professionals might have room for greater experimentation due to the necessity of taking some practical or preventive action.

It is in the storytelling aspect of the recorded oral testimony that we not only see the romantic aspects of this form of documentary record, but that we are also reminded of why so many people value old documents, artifacts and mementos, and stories passed down to us by our forebears. Archival repositories are, of course, full of stories. If you enter an archives, and you are real quiet, you can hear them, whispered among the researchers uncovering them or catching a glimpse of them in the finding aids, exhibition labels, and Web pages. Professional scholars, such as historians, often comment on how an ordinary document, buried innocuously in a repository or found in someone's attic, can provide astounding insights about the past. Well-known historian Adam Hochschild describes how in his book, *Bury the Chains*, he sought to depict a key meeting in 1787 at a Quaker publisher and bookstore in London. Hochschild reflects how the "only surviving direct record of the meeting is a one-page handwritten summary" recording the "date, list of attendees, and resolutions they had unanimously adopted that the slave trade was unjust and should be stopped, that they would open a bank account, and that a certain number of people would constitute a quorum for future meetings."[42]

Anyone who has ever been responsible for drafting the minutes of a meeting can immediately comprehend what this brief document looks like and the original purpose it served. Hochschild pondered about how he could bring this "important moment" back to life, and he turned to other documents, including newspapers and memoirs, secondary sources such as biographies, and "personal experience": "I found extensive biographical information about two of the men who attended the meeting. I can describe what another man looked like from a portrait. I learned that a fourth person in the group, the printer-bookseller, had stopped every morning on his way to work at a coffee shop just around the corner. These little details made a difference."[43] Hochschild draws on newspaper advertisements, his own walking of this section of London, archaeological reports, depictions of similar London bookshops, and an examination of period printing presses. And he also comments on how to write all this up so that "whenever you vividly reconstruct a scene you weren't present for, you want to be sure that readers know you're not making anything up."[44]

Individuals caring for personal and family archives most likely have an even better chance to provide meaningful interpretation of these records connected to their personal pasts. One can imagine visiting a friend or neighbor and being made to sit through the telling of stories about a family history, being shown old papers much like one might be shown travel photographs. If the collector can connect to the past by the beautiful handwriting of an old letter, understanding how it relates to a significant person or event, then oral testimony, especially when we can hear the voice from the past, can provide a particularly human portrait on old events and the people who have come before. Today, of course, we have the World Wide Web where text, voice, image, and moving image can be combined to form powerful windows into the past. Even though there remain many questions about how to preserve Web sites, ironically the ease of use of the Web may be a stimulant for the continued development of personal archives. Yet, before the Web, we had a great variety of recording technologies, such as sound and moving images, that were also bringing the past to life in innovative ways.

The Past Online: The Challenge of the Web Page.

If not too long ago, one might suggest that a couple of historians would compose a basic primer on using the World Wide Web for historical research and reporting, they would be met with extreme skepticism. Yet, this is precisely what happened with the publication of Daniel Cohen and Roy Rosenzweig's *Digital History*.[45] Cohen, Director

of Research Projects at the Center for History and New Media and
Assistant Professor of History at George Mason University, and
Rosenzweig, the late founder and Director of CHNM and Mark and
the Barbara Fried Professor of History and New Media at George
Mason University, are well-qualified to tackle this approach to historical
research and presentation. The two historians deftly provide
commentary on exploring history on the web, how to get started,
preparing historical materials for the web, designing web sites, building
an audience, collecting history online, copyright and intellectual
property issues, and digital preservation concerns. Their chapters start
off with intended learning functions, but this is no basic manual in the
sense that librarians, archivists, and preservationists have come to
accept such publications (it would have to include a bibliography, for
example, but it does not). Cohen and Rosenzweig have written a useful
book that addresses some very fundamental issues relating to the
digitization of historical and other documentary sources, one worth a
reading by both historians and the custodians of the documentary
heritage and, yes, even the average person curious about how the Web
supports historical research and digital preservation. At the center of
their book is the matter of the document and how it can and should be
used in new forms of historical research.

These historians stress that our world has changed with regards to
access to digital information, noting that their aim is to try to take a
balanced view between the "techno-skeptics" and the "cyber-
enthusiasts," and, in general, they succeed. They emphasize that they
desire to "critically and soberly assess where computers, networks, and
digital media are and aren't useful for historians – a category that we
define broadly to include amateur enthusiasts, research scholars,
museum curators, documentary filmmakers, historical society
administrators, classroom teachers, and history students at all levels."[46]
Their expanded view of both the historian and the user of historical
sources is a significant feature of their volume, reflecting a dramatic
enthusiasm and optimism they possess for the use of the Web that
sometimes has them writing a little more closely in the style of the
cyber-enthusiast role that they caution the readers about early in the
volume. For example, Cohen and Rosenzweig are strong advocates for
wanting historians to get involved in digitization work, mostly for
enhancing accessibility to documentary sources. After discussing a
variety of challenges confronting the maintenance and use of
documentary sources – "quality, durability, readability, passivity, and

inaccessibility" – they argue that such "questions and concerns should not lead us to throw up our hands in despair. Rather – and this is the key message of this book – they should prod us to sit down in front of our computers and get to work." They also are adamant that "historians need to confront these issues," "rather than leave them to the technologists, legislators, and media companies, or even just to our colleagues in libraries and archives."[47] What they stress about the role of historians is an interesting one, and it leads to some problems in their arguments in their book, but in a way that compels us to rethink how we approach the evidence found in records in whatever form they take and how individuals and families will organize and maintain their own records.

The strength of *Digital History* is the authors' knowledge of historical research and their commonsense approach of applying it to the Web world. They understand that historians and other scholars studying historical subjects create personal archives by virtue of compiling and analyzing documentary sources, and the Web provides an opportunity to share not just historical interpretations but the raw materials of historical research. They also understand the limitations that most historians bring to doing any kind of work on the Web. Amateur historians and individuals interested in their own personal and family archives may have been far more innovative and risk taking than historians (or records professionals) in the use of the Web. Cohen and Rosenzweig believe that historians should take to the Web and its potential in a very natural fashion, because "Historians are great documenters and in turn are great lovers of documentation."[48] The authors believe that historians will connect to newer approaches in using the Web, as when they write that a "significant feature of the web is that anyone who writes a web page also exposes to the world the code used to create it. Historians should find this nicely matches our discipline's emphasis on the open dissemination of knowledge. Whatever the future brings, the web will likely remain a place built on freely viewable text code, and if some historians feel uncomfortable with the technology, they should feel an affinity toward its underlying principles."[49] This is an illuminating perspective, even if it is not likely to convert many from their skepticism about digital projects.

Cohen and Rosenzweig are eager for their colleagues to explore new means of connecting with a greater portion of the public. They are excited that amateurs not only have ready access to the Web, but that they are actively engaged in using the Web to create sites. Part of this

relates to their recognition, shared by many, that "Now that the web
has displaced the library and perhaps the phone book as the first place
most people go to find information, it has become necessary for every
historical organization to stake out a home on the web so that people
can find them and learn about their activities."[50] Their belief in the
power and influence of history also relates to their sense about the
intrinsic interest in the historical document. And here we can hear the
echoes of sentiments that date back at least as far back as the nineteenth
century romantic historians like William Hickling Prescott and Francis
Parkman (both who mined archival stores to craft engaging stories of
the past). And it is why many private citizens are posting family
archives, crafting blogs, and sharing genealogical and other personal
information with the world. As people more fully exploit the potential of
the Web for their own use, their expectations for what others, including
institutions, such as archives and libraries, might do also increase.

Despite their enthusiasm for the potential of the Web in reaching a
broader public, Cohen and Rosenzweig are cautious about just what
should be done on the Web. They do not believe all historical projects
need a Web site. They recognize that building and maintaining Web
sites are laborious and expensive, and they devote considerable
discussion to the challenges posed by the use of the Web, while still
concluding that "digitization offers stunning advantages."[51] This kind of
assessment may explain why the general public has rushed to embrace
digitization (think of digital cameras); in other words, they may not ask
the harder questions about the maintenance of the electronic materials
and be less skeptical by vendors' claims. Cohen and Rosenzweig also
caution against advising everyone attempting to do a Web-based
project, arguing instead that potential Web historians must weigh the
needs and end results. For example, Cohen and Rosenzweig note how
"Local historians would ecstatically greet a fully digitized and
searchable version of their small-town newspaper, but it would not
justify hundreds of thousands of dollars in digitizing costs. Nor would it
make much sense to digitize a collection of personal papers that attracts
one or two researchers per year."[52] With such practical advice, these
historians join in with archivists and librarians who also have preached
caution and careful planning in their use of digitization and Web sites.
Obviously, there is a great need for records professionals to
communicate effectively with the public about such issues, but,
hopefully, they should offer advice that is positive and practical about

alternative approaches to personal archives (when alternative approaches are available).

Digital History focuses on the concept of professional historians connecting with a broader public. For example, Cohen and Rosenzweig believe good Web design pushes historians to rethink how they connect with the public:

> We believe historians can learn important lessons from both the usability camp and the creativity of the aesthetes, and that we can successfully navigate a middle way between these poles. Surely historians cannot blindly follow a design regime that relegates thinking to a secondary status; neither should we obscure historical materials and our ideas about the past in deference to pure artistic license. Clio is our muse, and she is the muse of history, not art (although some particularly creative individuals strive to crossbreed history and art).[53]

These two commentators perceive building user-friendly Web sites as being an ethical responsibility, seeking to "make their sites accessible to the greatest number of people, regardless of ability. Done in a modest, sensible fashion, following accessibility guidelines on your website not only will serve a larger and more diverse audience, but it will also improve the experience of your site for everyone else."[54] Their mission, in digital history projects, is not just compiling hits at their sites but in connecting to and supporting a community. What we may be seeing, however, is that the public, in its increasing use of the Internet, is reaching out to professionals such as historians and archivists. It is their zealousness to be so connected with the public that spells some problems for the approach of Cohen and Rosenzweig, and here we may have some cautionary tales for archivists and other records professionals seeking to connect with the public about the preservation and use of the documentary heritage by capitalizing on the growing use of digital technologies.

These two historians are eager to build sites that enable every person to write their own history, present their own interpretations, and participate in a broader discussion of the past. It is the same kind of expression being made by individuals concerned with personal archives. They see numerous benefits to this. For one, Cohen and Rosenzweig are excited about collecting history via the online world. Commenting on collecting the reactions to the events of September 11, 2001, they write: "Collecting history online may not always be this urgent, but these examples show the critical need for historians to find the most effective ways of using this new technology to supplement the historical record on paper, as we did in the twentieth century with tape recorders and video cameras."[55] This opens up the thorny question of just how reliable such sources might be, as well as how well-planned or constructed these documentary materials might be. They attempt to make the case about the advantages of online collecting, noting that it is economical -- "because subjects write their own narratives, we avoid one of the most daunting costs of oral history, transcription."[56] Yet, what about the problems of issues like authenticity or reliability that the two historians bring up early in the book?

Our intrepid historians believe that good basic human honesty and solid historical skills will protect us from any excesses in the digital history realm. They write, with sincere conviction, that

> We think the nonprofit mission of online historical archives generally produces even higher rates of honesty. Most people who take the time to submit something to your project will share your goals and your interest in creating an accurate historical record. Rogues and hackers have more interesting things to do on the Internet than corrupt historical archives. But our best defenses against fraud are our traditional historical skills. Historians have always had to assess the reliability of their sources from internal and external clues. Not only have there been famous forgeries on paper, but written memoirs and traditional oral histories are filled with exaggerations and distortions. In the past as in the present, historians have had to look for evidence of internal consistency and weigh them against other sources. In any media, sound research is the basis of sound scholarship.[57]

Only time, experiment, and experience will either confirm or contradict this viewpoint, but I remain skeptical about this approach.

One might question why such aggressive or open-ended acquisition must be in place. They have a rationale for it:

> Sites that require logins – usernames and passwords that you must register for in advance of your contribution – will almost always receive fewer submissions than those that allow all comers to proceed. This phenomenon is part of a larger tension between sound (and some would argue sane) archival practice and using the web to collect historical materials and narratives: the more you ask contributors to reveal about themselves, the less likely they will be to contribute.[58]

Librarians and archivists, they know, want metadata. Our historians are willing to jettison the archival principle of provenance, crucial to understanding and evaluating the evidence of a source, partly out of the conviction that historians, with their critical skills, will be able to sift through. What they don't address is, of course, what the amateur historians, lay public, and students – all possessing far less knowledge about such perspectives, might be able to do with such sources. And, just as some have argued when considering privacy issues, we should have doubts that people aren't willing to give up private information when they see other positive gains; for example, how else can we explain the explosion of interest in blogging?

These two scholars have faith that even a few nuggets, shining through the chaff of the digital documentary debris that might result from such efforts, will make it all worthwhile. They liken it to the traditional mode of research in archival repositories:

> A less obvious but perhaps more important measure of the 'quality' of a historical collection created online becomes apparent when the collection is assessed as a whole rather than on the level of individual submissions. Like any collection, online or offline, a minority of striking contributions will stand out in a sea of dull or seemingly irrelevant entries. Historians who have browsed box after box in a paper archive trying to find key pieces of evidence for their research will know this principle well, and it should not come as a surprise that these grim percentages follow us into the digital realm. Yet as we also know, even a few well-written perspectives or telling archival images may form the basis of a new interpretation, or help to buttress an existing but partial understanding of a certain historical moment. At the same time, the greater size and diversity of online collections allow you more opportunities to look for common patterns. Why do certain types of stories reoccur? What does that tell you about both popular experience and the ways in which that experience gets transformed into memory?[59]

This may well be the case, especially since the advent of the Web and new digital resources can allow historians to "search electronic documents in revealing and novel ways,"[60] but there may be other weaknesses inherent in the digital environment that generate larger problems than anyone has really anticipated. It may be that they are striving to challenge the traditional, and romantic, notions of the individual scholar painstakingly clawing through the old record, instead now seeing the promise of collaborative and speedier access to documentary sources. It may be that individuals are saving their own and family's records, or, collecting autographs and manuscripts, as a means of dealing, emotionally and psychologically, with what they see as the artificiality of the digital environment.

Work in the new virtual world brings with it, of course, challenges that are anything but romantic. The historians certainly pay attention to some of the most serious problems facing anyone working in the digital realm. They provide an interesting discussion of intellectual property issues, acknowledging that "working with the sources of the past, especially the twentieth-century past, puts you up against some of the thorniest copyright questions – and the most difficult issues to research." They are optimistic that such problems can be worked out, suggesting that the "good news is that vast swaths of documentary evidence of the past are in the public domain (the realm free of copyright restrictions), and you are free to post that evidence on your website with no questions asked."[61] This is certainly true, but it also suggests that digital history moves scholars and others into new realms that they may be unaccustomed to working in or where they do not yet possess good working practices.

One of the purposes of *Digital History* is to call academic historians into a more proactive world where they are more engaged with archivists and librarians who have traditionally held the responsibilities for such work. Cohen and Rosenzweig come up short in arguing that historians take a more aggressive role in preserving the digital documentary heritage:

> Although historians should be aware of these various efforts to save digital materials for the long run and should be part of this crucial discussion about what will happen to the records of today and yesterday in a digital future, a large portion of this discussion and almost all of its implementation lies beyond our purview. Computer scientists, librarians, and archivists are the prime movers in this realm, and properly so, though they could certainly use our input as some of the most important end users of their products and as professional stewards of the future of the past.[62]

Arguing that historians should open a dialogue with archivists and other custodians of documentary sources may seem like a step forward, and in many respects it is. However, participating in such an exchange requires that historians be more aware of archival practices, procedures, and perspectives than is evident in this book. In fact, their comments on how historians more broadly engage the public may be far more thoughtful than their recommendations about engaging colleagues in other disciplines. The road they are on may suggest the way to how a broader array of private citizens may assume responsibility for a portion of preserving the documentary heritage that archivists had never assumed before.

There is a pronounced weakness in the knowledge about archival work as expressed in this book, and in this is a lesson for archivists to heed. Early in the book, for example, Cohen and Rosenzweig grapple with the problem of whether the increasing use and reliance on digital resources is changing the way we think of preserving or documenting the past. Sensibly, they conclude the following: "One vision of the digital future involves the preservation of everything – the dream of the complete historical record. The current reality, however, is closer to the reverse of that – we are rapidly losing the digital present that is being created because no one has worked out a means of preserving it."[63] However, it is clear from later statements that the authors are uneasy about some of this, and that they do not possess accurate information about developments in the archival community. For example, in considering the question of what is worth preserving, they focus on the U.S. National Archives appraisal approaches, an institution that certainly has not reflected the most interesting or cutting edge discussions about this function (at least in recent decades). They also say that the "low cost of storage (getting radically less expensive every year, unlike paper) means that it very well may be possible or even desirable to save everything ever written in our digital age," eliminating the need for the kind of "selection criteria" archivists have used.[64]

So, which is it? Whatever professional perspective we might assume about shaping the documentary heritage through planned appraisal approaches, the truth of the matter is that private individuals will continue to save their own personal and family archives and, different than what has occurred in the past, we might see these documents not hidden away but visibly posted on the Web. The success of this depends on archivists working hard to explain and advise about the basic tasks necessary to maintain archival documentation. If historians, presumably with a lot more knowledge about historical documents, sometime struggle to comprehend the nuances of archival work, then how difficult will it be for individuals who come to the sources of the past with clear amateur status?

Conclusion.

The pull of the document can be an all absorbing one. We pause at the shared office printer to read someone else's document, ostensibly to check to make sure it is not ours but more likely out of curiosity about what this other document has to say and because it opens a window into someone else's world. Archivists and records managers also feel the pull to linger and read a bit more than might be practical into the records they store in boxes or in computers. Rather than feeling guilty about such emotions, records professionals need to realize that the romance of the document is a powerful means for understanding why our records are important in society. Each book described here, with a different approach or purpose, convey something about this.

It can be difficult to feel romantic when we also feel overwhelmed by the sheer mass of records being produced by individuals and institutions and the magnitude of the potential loss of records and information posed by this production. Alex Wright reminds us of just how much information we are processing today, noting that we now write "more than five exabytes worth of recorded information per year: documents, e-mail messages, television shows, radio broadcasts, Web pages, medical records, spreadsheets, presentations, and books like this one. That is more than 50, 000 times the number of words stored in the Library of Congress, or more than the total number of words ever spoken by human beings."[65] In the face of such volume, the archival community must look small and under-resourced. New approaches are needed, and one of these might be the creation of a corps of citizen archivists and new partnerships with them. If anything, such partnerships might help us regain some new sense of the romance of the document.

Chapter Three

Information Documents: How People and Organizations Acquire Information

Introduction: Speaking, Writing, Reading – and Recordkeeping?

Recordkeeping is part of a historical and cultural process, rich in its complexity and intertwined with humanity's efforts to communicate, document, and remember. Speaking came first, or at least so we imagine and logically infer, and reading developed at the same time with that of writing. Linguist Steven Roger Fischer's three-volume history of language, writing, and reading, published in 1999-2003, provides a rich historical context for understanding records in our lives, and a good orientation for us in considering the role of documents in our personal lives.[1] If personal recordkeeping is an inherent aspect of every human's life, then so is reading, writing, and speaking – and the former cannot be comprehended without a sense of what the latter activities represent.

When one looks at a document, at least the textual variety, one is faced with its language. The document, whatever form (letter, memo, or receipt), is covered with symbols representing words and numbers. It is intended to be received, to be read, and to be understood. As many have suggested, records speak to us, although much differently than the language we experience in face-to-face interactions. Resting behind such seemingly simple ideas and processes are very lengthy and complex histories of human language, although it would be the rare scholar or peculiar person who will spend much time or effort contemplating such matters as they open a letter, read it, determine if it requires a response, prepare the response, and file the documents (or simply toss the letter if it is unimportant). Most of us don't devote much energy to wondering how long a saved or stored document will be readable based on its language; instead we simply assume that the language is stable enough for our purposes and go about our business, even though we recognize that language is constantly changing and that more languages have died out than are presently actively spoken. Some of this has been transformed now as more people are becoming sensitized to the fragility of documentary sources, especially digital ones.

Individuals and institutions have faced awkward situations when they have discovered that those quick, convenient emails have disappeared or, just as critically, have reappeared after they thought them eradicated. Somewhere hovering behind all of these issues and concerns is the nature of language.

Language enables "information exchange,'" and this can involve everything from facial expressions to writing to computer programming.[2] Language, enabling complex communication, is critical to the major stages in developing human community. Linguists theorize that complex communications started about 150,000 years ago. By around 14,000 years ago, *Homo sapiens* had "already differentiated thousands of languages grouped into hundreds of language families,"[3] and the discovery of such languages has become the focus of linguists. Linguists are searching for language origins in the same way individuals may be searching for meaning when they preserve personal and family papers, revisiting them to hear ancient voices or to remember their own words from the not so distant past. If speaking is a basic human function, than so are our efforts to preserve what we have uttered over the generations.

Considering the basic notion of written language, Fischer comments on how some anthropologists formulated the idea that society evolved from barbarism to civilization because of the ability to read written language, while arguing that it is now better thought that writing should be seen as "society's principal lubricant: writing did not enable social development, but it did greatly facilitate social change,"[4] later adding that there is ample evidence of sophisticated societies developing before the advent of writing.[5] This is a particularly useful point to bear in mind as we so often hear about one's ability to use (effectively) a computer as an indicator of social status. Much of this emanates from the advertising hype about computers rather than any substantial data. A computer in the classroom is the hallmark of a sophisticated educational experience; a computer in the home indicates what side of the digital divide one is residing and whether one is connected and part of the modern era. Neither is true, of course. And, as well, language is far more flexible and adaptive than anything that computers represent. One of "language's greatest strengths" is a language's ability to borrow. "Human languages are not stones, they are sponges. This quality bestows on them their wonderful creativity as well as their adaptability and viability."[6] A sponge is not a bad way to reflect on the personal archives. We can continually soak up evidence of our actions, and those of our families, in way that provides an anchor or guide in times that seem more troublesome to us.

Writing is an essential aspect of humanity, and it is also impossible to discuss language without reference to writing, where "writing preserves spoken language, it levels, standardizes, prescribes, enriches and generates many other language-oriented processes with far-reaching social implications. Human society as we know it today cannot exist without writing."[7] It is imperative that we remember that it took thousands of years with language *before* writing emerged and that writing has been here as well for thousands of years. It is also important to reflect on such developments given the immense promises and values attributed to the World Wide Web that has existed for little more than a decade. If literacy is so essential an attribute of what characterizes a society or community, it is the manifestation of considerable changes, experiments, successes and failures over eons. Computer literacy, by contrast, might be important, but it is certainly a recent aspect of our culture. Looking at a technology with little more than a half-century of history pales when compared to languages with thousands of years involved in their creation and honing. It is possible to see the multitudes of individuals striving to preserve their personal and family papers as an expression of concerns about the fragility of organizational and public memory, an effort not to let the decisions about what and how to save old writing, whether a hundred years old or several seconds from its creation, depend on public institutions and professional experts.

The world is changing, at least in how it views expertise. Peter Nicholson, for example, believes that many people are not willing to defer to professional experts, what he calls a shift in "intellectual authority." Nicholson sees a change, detecting that the "agents we have relied upon traditionally to filter and manage information, and to broker formal knowledge – agents like research universities and their libraries, the serious media, and highly trained experts of all kinds – are less trusted as intermediaries than they once were." And much of what is happening challenges the very notion of an archives, of a documentary heritage, at least for Nicholson:

> The 'half-life' of *active* information has been getting shorter and shorter due primarily to the sheer rate of information generation. There is more and more to process, but not more hours in the day, and not more raw individual brain power to apply. So we graze, or we gulp, and then we move on. The half-life is also shrinking due to the very nature of electronic technology which makes 'overwrite' so easy

and natural. We are all becoming addicted to the 'refresh' button. Documents of every kind – certainly in my experience in business and government – are being revised continuously until the moment they become virtually obsolete. And as the shelf-life of any particular information product gets shorter – whether it's an e-mail or a position paper – fewer resources of time and money can be put into its creation.[8]

It may seem ironic, but the many preservation challenges posed by digital technologies also suggest more empowerment to individuals to administer their own personal papers. Individuals who are not archives and records management professionals may be more interested in developing their own expertise to administer their part of the larger documentary heritage (even though anyone will realize that solving the challenges cannot occur without such expertise or the larger quantities of resources, public policies, and laws and regulations needed to be thrown at the problems).

In our own era we devote considerable attention to the technical accomplishments of our information age, often turning a blind eye to the fact that information technology is usually under siege for being outmoded almost from the moment it is acquired and implemented. When we spend a couple of thousands of dollars on a new computer, we are immediately faced with the prospect that what we have will need to be discarded in two or three years in order to achieve greater memory, more functions, and faster speeds. The technological achievement of alphabetic writing, in contrast, a technology certainly featured in our computers and on the Web, seems all the more remarkable. Fischer describes how, some five thousand years ago, the "ingenious Greek scribes possessed a small, workable alphabet of letters for both individual consonants and vowels. All they had to do to write their language was to combine the consonants and vowels together in spoken sequence to form entire words, the same method we use today."[9] Other types of writing systems – the glyphs of Chinese and the logographic Mesoamerican writing – also stand as substantial, if different, technical achievements that functioned well for hundreds or thousands of years. That new digital technologies seem to threaten our documentary maintenance may be a very important factor for why so many are experimenting with keeping their own archives, both digitally and by printing out to paper. The human impulse to remember is as important as the one to craft tools.

Comparing systems that are so different in their functionality tends to lead to cynicism about the promises of our modern information era. Fischer is not as pessimistic as myself about the advent of the computer and its relationship to language. This is, perhaps, because he recognizes that "all writing systems, no matter how revered or innovative, are imperfect and conventional."[10] He connects writing and speech in a

> synergistic relationship, each now linked inextricably to the other, in much the same way that primitive thought was linked to the vocalizations of early hominids and thus continues to change and advance humankind with multidimensional magic. At the beginning of the twenty-first century, the hand no longer merely 'matches the mouth' but, through computer programming languages, is creating whole new worlds and giving voice to humanity's electronic future.[11]

We know that the electronic future will include records, but there is much diverse speculation about what these records might look like and how they might function. Or who, we might add, will be taking care of them.

Languages change in a variety of ways, with some changes taking centuries and others much less time. What is fascinating, for someone interested in records, about such changes is that the lineages of various languages are only possible to study in those languages with long written traditions. In other words, records are necessary. Time is always a critical element for scholars, and it has always been a source of concern for many worried about how we characterize the present era as *the* information age. Whether or not we accept whether things are changing more quickly now than before, it still has only been sixty years since the advent of modern computers – a mere whisker of time. Such analysis reveals how seemingly powerful languages (Celtic, for example) can wither and nearly disappear or how one language (Latin) can generate an entire family of Romance languages. Change is the order of the day with languages. We can discern individual words that are relics of older forms of languages, but the present tongues are continuously borrowing, adapting, and refining themselves as they edge up and bump into each other.

However one considers the earlier achievements of language, it is obvious that the ways languages function now are very different from anything that existed before, moving from being associated with "geographical territory" to being connected with "technology and wealth, a new borderless world with the only directions up and down, separating the haves from the have-nots."[12] Thinking of languages in such ways suggests how powerful they can be, much more so then anything we associate with the information technologies of the past half-century. If nothing else is considered, we need to remember that language is the foundation of what goes into records and that we have records going back thousands of years. Yet, we still worry that the documents generated by our computers will be readable even five or ten years from their creation. And such fears extend beyond governments, corporations, and other organizations into our own homes.

Writing is not as simple to define as one might assume (maybe because it is something we all do on a daily basis), and Fischer resorts to ascertaining criteria that make up "complete writing," such as "artificial graphic marks on a durable or electronic surface" and "use marks that relate conventionally to articulate speech (the systematic arrangement of significant vocal sounds) or electronic programming in such a way that communication is achieved."[13] The impetus for complete writing systems was nothing magical but simply social expediency, the need for "accountancy,"[14] attested to by the immense portion of Mesopotamian archives being financial and administrative records.[15] Alongside the more elaborate hieroglyphic writing of the ancient Egyptians there developed, for example, a cursive form ("hieratic"), "ancient Egypt's everyday script, used for business, administration, correspondence and general literary production."[16] While today, many records professionals lament that they often work with mostly routine records (making it difficult to impress their employers with their importance to the organization), it is useful to remember that the predecessors of these innocuous documents are tied to the creation and nurturing of the earliest writing systems, a hallmark of civilization. And, many people may hold onto older cursive documents simply because the handwriting seems so quaint, real, and even beautiful in comparison to the often sterile word-processed documents of our own era.

Fischer also strikes at another popularly conceived attribute of writing -- that it evolved along with humankind, especially in reflecting speech as it developed.[17] Fischer stresses the conscious design that is behind *all* writing systems. Indeed, when discussing some of the earliest writing systems, such as knotted ropes and notched sticks, Fischer identifies the level of sophistication that these primitive writing forms could attain. Looking at the notches, Fischer argues, "What is important here is that, tens of thousands of years ago, graphic marks, however primitive, were probably recording some sort of human perception, for whatever reason. This was information storage."[18] Such assessments are a reminder that all writing systems involve technology and, generally, that the technologies are innovative for their time. It may also suggest why some essayists, novelists, and other writers attest to their using pencils, pens, and paper for writing; for them, not only is this mode of writing more than satisfactory but it provides a tactile sense for their craft. And, as well, a better personal archives, documenting their writing progress, results.

Along with the advent and spread of writing appeared new experts with new roles, such as the scribes in ancient Egypt who could "attain great wealth, prestige and position," and who required specialized education.[19] This suggests the kind of influence that computer or information scientists might have achieved in the late twentieth century, at least if we think of the often esoteric knowledge that these individuals possess concerning the use of computers. As many have discussed the digital divide, more defined by the economic ability to have steady access to computers, there is also another kind of divide between those who can and cannot program and work with the more complicated aspects of the computers sitting on their desks at home and at work. But if the digital divide is to disappear then there is a lesson to be learned from the historical development of writing: computers will become so essential that they will become available to all and in ways that are seamless and painless, just as formal scripts were supplanted by the less formal cursives for everyday recording and communicating (think of the William Zinsser treatise on writing with personal computers mentioned in chapter one).[20] In a like manner, despite all the power of the modern personal computer or laptop, now capable of supporting all sorts of graphics and audiovisual applications, the vast majority of uses of these computers are for simple word processing (which has to be the closest to the cursives in application and sense) or reading/surfing the World Wide Web (additional applications requiring little in the way of sophisticated power). This is certainly how most people use the computer for their personal recordkeeping – sending emails, writing letters, paying bills online – but, in most instances, they also print out the digital versions for their own archives, sometimes freely annotating the documents as they organize and store them.

The idea that information technology is somehow a cause and effect relationship to literacy or democracy, as is oft discussed now, is something Fischer says cannot be supported by examining the history of writing. Fischer argues that "Society *as we know it* cannot exist without

writing, granted. However, writing is an effect of society, not a cause."
It is only considering such matters in the long-term that we can
understand the true relationship between such information systems and
society. Fischer argues that the "Greeks' vowelized alphabet did not
change the way people thought." This alphabet "fostered greater
literacy, more discussion and thus more complex domains of thought.
However, Greek writing did not spawn democracy, theoretical science
or formal logic. It helped to preserve the thoughts of those who
considered such things, and to train others to build upon these and
similar ideas."[21] It is worth noting that for all the similar claims made
about digital writing and the World Wide Web that the prospects for
preservation seem all the more dim. Yet, such a perspective also helps
us to understand that the reason people cling to old family papers or try
to administer their own records may have little to do with some noble
societal cause, but everything to do with personal interests, curiosity,
and self-identity.

Regardless of motivation, the individual seeking to maintain
personal and family papers will be concerned with technological issues,
from reflecting on older technologies used to create records to
determining what technologies to use in maintaining these papers for
the long-term. Fischer does not dismiss the impact or implications of
information technologies on writing. Technology and writing go hand-
in-hand, a fact that anyone seeking to preserve personal and family
papers can discuss in detail.

Fischer is very attuned to technological breakthroughs in writing.
He comments on St. Augustine's surprise in discovering his teacher St.
Ambrose reading silently, an event that "symbolically signals a new
notion of writing's role in society as an autonomous form of information
conveyance."[22] Fischer continues, "the notion that written language
now stood on a par with spoken language became principle, and it was
fundamental to all medieval thought. It was as revolutionary to Western
Europe as the later threshold that ushered in the modern world:
printing or graphic communication by means of multiplied
impressions."[23] This is an example that *technical* breakthroughs do not
require the kind of epic, computer-oriented transformations we seem
now to expect or require. Another example is the shift from the papyrus
scroll to the vellum codex, since "with vellum or parchment, one could
write on both sides of a sheet, thus doubling writing capacity."[24] While
on one hand it seems that the elegance of the scribal hands deteriorated
in order to allow for the speedier cursive writing required for

government, business, and social intercourse, on the other hand it is also the case that by the fourteenth or fifteenth centuries these scripts became the basis for the first printers' typefaces. Fischer also appreciates the importance of paper, noting "parchment and vellum could never have supported mass literacy, worldwide printing, modern offices, newspapers, government records, general education, and so on. These are the consequences of paper and the printing press," and these technologies are only now being challenged by the modern computer. Still, Fischer believes that "this hardly signals paper's decline, at least at present. E-mail communication and Internet access have greatly increased the frequency of personal messages and personally printed information. Everyone with e-mail, access to the Net and a computer printer usually makes several print-outs a day. The new technology has created a demand for paper not witnessed since the educational reforms of the mid-1800s."[25] Is it no wonder then that even as every home acquires a personal computer the shelves in the home are also being filled with leather-bound, acid-free journals for diaries and commonplace books? The only differences between these earlier revolutions and the present computer era is the amount of time involved; centuries have shrunk to decades, decades to years, years to months (and it is often the compression of time in new technical developments that are identified as the main attributes of the present information age).

Writing systems possess vitality and endurance, constantly borrowing from other systems and testifying, in this process, to the durability of writing. "Writing systems and scripts actually perish with far less frequency than the languages they transmit," Fischer reports. "Cuneiform writing continued millennia after the Sumerian language's demise. Latin has long been extinct as a living language, yet its script, a descendant of Egyptian, is today's most common one."[26] Whereas in the past we could observe writing ebbing and flowing over centuries, now we worry about electronic documents that are no more than five or ten years old. Those who cry out for maintaining paper as the best archival medium may seem out of touch to us today, except we know that multitudes of people are doing this in their own homes.

As alphabetic writing gained ascendancy over all writing systems, we also see egalitarianism in its victory. Where writing had once been controlled by those in power – government officials, scribes, and priests – now writing diffused through all levels of society.[27] We also see that the manner in which written language succeeded or failed was dependent on a wide array of social, economic, political, technological, and other factors. Fischer believes that "writing is the emblem of the social franchise."[28] In general, "it is seldom the efficiency of a writing system or script that determines its longevity and influence, but rather the economic power and prestige of those using it."[29] In this sense, the study of the evolution of writing reveals what we can expect to see in the continuing development of digital information technologies. It is certainly the case that there is a certain prestige, if not power, associated with an individual wending his or her way through the airport armed with laptop, PDA, and cell phone. The same individual may be quietly preserving old, handwritten family papers, out of affection, curiosity, or because it is a way of symbolically connecting with a past before such digital devices dominated one's life.

We tend to measure ourselves against the achievements, real and imagined, of the past. Literacy was more widespread in the ancient world than what we have normally thought. Fischer describes the excavations at a Roman military outpost (85-130 AD) in northern England where more than "two thousand letters and documents on wooden tablets" have been found, "attesting to writing's pervasiveness in ancient Roman society, even in this farthest reach of the Empire" and baring the "thoughts of ordinary men and women," suggesting the "great amount of correspondence that must have been taking place among Romans throughout the Empire."[30] It is interesting to reflect on such letter writing in our own era when so many lament what they perceive as the demise of personal letter writing due to the subsequent developments in telecommunications, ranging from the telephone a century ago to the more recent advent of electronic mail. It is also a bit unsettling, perhaps, to think that personal correspondence proceeded at a rate more like what we ascribe to our own times. Our laments over the personal letter are often due to a romanticized sense of a process whereby we would sit, quietly, in the evening writing long epistles that someday might be read by the historians of later times. Actually, for most of us, the personal letter is often a pedestrian document, more like the accounting records marking the emergence of writing. However, each of our households might be more like that Roman outpost, enclaves of personal and family letters and other documents waiting to be discovered at a later time.

Everything needs to be scrutinized as we speculate about the nature of such basic human functions as writing. It seems that personal correspondence, even in our digital era, may not be declining at all, if one measures its role via the number of personal etiquette manuals and letter guidebooks continuing to be published. But should we really be surprised about this? Fischer, in examining the writing of the ancient Romans, comments that they "appreciated that the medium was also a particular part of the message. Styles of lettering possessed particular cultural and social associations, each befitting a given class or circumstance."[31] It is unlikely that this has been different in any era populated by writing. This may have as much to do with the legacy of writing systems as anything, as Fischer indicates that the "Latin alphabet is Earth's most important writing system" and whereas "typewriting and computer print-outs have all but destroyed penmanship," the Latin alphabet is still the basis for subsequent technological breakthroughs such as printing and the computer. "The personal computer founded the electronic society on an alphabetic plinth."[32] The declining nature of penmanship may be just one reason why individuals want to save those old family documents, or why so many people seek out and buy at flea markets and antique shops, attractive examples of cursive documents. The neat handwriting is so different from what we are used to seeing or that we can ourselves produce (except with the most dedicated effort to produce calligraphic effects).

Reading is a universal activity, much like speaking, writing, and, for that matter, recordkeeping. It is something we do everyday, but most of us would be hard-pressed to define it in any precise fashion, other than "'the ability to make sense of written or printed symbols.'" Reading has changed over time, and it continues to change, including, the "extracting of encoded information from an electronic screen. And reading's definition will doubtless continue to expand in future for, as with any faculty, it is also a treasury of humanity's own advancement."[33] In ancient Mesopotamia, for example, reading was understood to mean reading aloud or reciting.[34] When we read the surviving letters and other documents from the ancient world, it is impossible not to notice that many of their features reflect their oral nature (that is, their intention to be read aloud). Fischer reminds us that some of what seem to be the strange characteristics of ancient texts results because these documents are the writings of a "speech-based, not a text-based, society."[35] Read them out loud and the documents come to life. Thousands of years later, passive reading and listening diminished, so the reader was now an active participant and interpreter of text, anticipating the rise of print. It is not too difficult to imagine someone today, sitting in their living room or den, reading aloud their old family papers to other family members, connecting one generation to earlier ones.

Reading is one of society's most noticeable activities, because reading consumes a large portion of everyday at work and on the computer checking email and browsing the Web.[36] Reading is also very different from writing or the nurturing of language, as Fischer suggests when he points out that

> Though reading and writing go hand in hand, reading is actually writing's antithesis – indeed, even activating separate regions of the brain. Writing is a skill, reading a faculty. Writing was originally elaborated and thereafter deliberately adapted; reading has evolved in tandem with humanity's deeper understanding of the written word's latent capabilities. Writing's history has followed series of borrowings and refinements, reading's history has involved successive stages of social maturation. Writing is expression, reading impression. Writing is public, reading is personal. Writing is limited, reading open-ended. Writing freezes the moment. Reading is forever.[37]

And what elevates the importance of records is that both writing and reading are critical to the essential aspects of what makes something a record.

Like writing, reading took a long time to develop and, in fact, writing was often a skill long preceding the notion of reading. In ancient Mesopotamia, the "goddess of scribes, Nisaba, had as her symbol the stylus, as it was the act of recording that embodied the scribe's primary role, not the act of reading-reciting. This tells us that a scribe was foremost the notary public of his and her era, the notarial stenographer of most of society's important activities, the executive secretary, the governmental bureaucrat."[38] While scribes were often employed to read aloud, "much of the material remained oral, neither written down nor read. Indeed, the vast majority of Babylon's social knowledge was transmitted orally and was never committed to clay."[39] In our modern culture, we intimately link reading and writing, unable to perceive of one without the other. In the ancient world, where sometimes the literate of a city could be measured only in the hundreds, the two activities were not so closely connected. Perhaps the sense we have of recordkeeping where records are created, stored, but seldom re-examined, is not so different from the ancient sense of what occurred with records. And, instinctively we know that individuals have been pulling out their personal and family archives for millennia and reading them for entertainment and edification (and for a variety of other purposes).

Many other scholars, considering reading and writing in the ancient world, have confirmed the importance of scribes as well. Karel Van Der Toorn recounts the development of the Hebrew Bible as part of the efforts of the scribal workshop of the Second Temple between 500 and 200 B.C.E. In order to understand this scribal workshop, he examines writing and the work of scribes in the Ancient Near East (Egypt and Mesopotamia). Van Der Toorn provides considerable information about the scribes and their culture. They wrote books mainly for other scribes; they were cosmopolitan, borrowing from scribes in other societies; they were formally educated (in Egypt, this training lasted twelve years); they were employed at the temples and in the royal courts; and the scribal positions often stayed within families, passing from generation to generation. Some of these characteristics challenge a direct comparison between modern archivists and the ancient scribes; for example, the "scribes were not merely penman and copyists but intellectuals." The scribes were the "academics if their time."[40] Moreover, in Israel, scribes were part of an exclusive group: "The skills of the scribes – of reading, understanding, and interpreting – commanded general respect. The scribes held the key to the symbolic capital of the nation."[41]

As Van Der Toorn suggests, there has been discussion from time to time in our modern era of the prestige or power of the individuals who held positions as scribes, that is, who possessed the power to read and write (of course, the prestige of scribes varied considerably between cultures, ranging from those holding offices to those who were slaves). In the ancient world and for many centuries later, many societies had a very small portion of people who were literate. Yet, historic illiteracy was a bit different than the way we view this today. Today, an illiterate is cut-off from much of society. In the past, there was dependence, and an expected one, on scribes to provide access to documents, to record transactions, and to navigate through the maze of texts that was no less daunting in the past than it might be seen at present. Rather than dwelling on issues related to computer literacy, in this volume I am focusing on personal archiving, and the image of the ancient scribe as a helping agent for hire may be the picture modern archivists ought to keep in mind. Today, we have those fancy diplomas hanging in our offices, documents that are fully ceremonial, to the degree (no pun intended) that they possess no legal standing whatsoever. And it is why individuals save these as part of personal archives, or seek them out in antique marts. Today many documents are so ceremonial that the paper is even made to look like parchment, no matter what the technologies may be to create them.

The kind of contrast that we see in the positions held by scribes leads to some interesting ironies, ones that should give us pause when we take for granted how and where texts are created. Fischer points out, for example, that "it is one of history's greatest ironies that this glorious society [ancient Egypt's], which is so identified with writing (that is, with hieroglyphs), whose temples, tombs, monuments and statues veritably brimmed over with writing, enjoyed the fewest actual readers." Fischer points out that the texts were written for the ages not their own era and the texts of ancient Egypt "were probably only seldom, if ever, read in the lifetime of their addressor. They were almost exclusively ostentatious propaganda for the divine as well as the living, and funerary messages to the gods of the afterlife and to the deceased, calling out the magical words to awake the spirit." Now this has a very interesting twist for those interested in records and their administration and use over time. As Fischer sees it, "What was actually read was mountains of administrative papyri, and these have almost entirely vanished."[42] And, in fact, many of the earliest documents that have survived tend to be more routine, more administrative.[43] The power of records persists even when they are often among the most routine of artifacts. And it may be in the future that archivists, researchers, and others will find millions of routine documents stored in closets and attics and billions logged into the hard-drives of personal computers.

Archivists often have been concerned with problems about access to records and their security, especially in this era of heightened concerns about global terrorism, government secrecy, and rights to information. It is with the emergence of the copying of books and scrolls that we see the first glimmers of censorship, an act that suggests the power of the word and reading.[44] Could it be that the narrowing of access to records and information influences individuals to preserve their own papers? What is amazing is, of course, that the targeting of the texts continues to this day. Libraries are targeted during warfare and civil strife as the depository of the memory of a people. The same is true with archives and museums. The power of reading, and of having access to the thoughts of previous generations, is evident if we examine such examples of destruction. It is why people through the millennia have collected books and other documents. Fischer suggests, "Among the most cherished possessions of a learned Greek or Roman were books, which comprehended an ardor otherwise reserved only for family, spouse or lover." And, he muses, "For many, books were even closer and dearer."[45] Today, we recognize that many of these books were documents, and, as well, that at present we might be inclined to dote as much attention on our personal and family papers, seeing them as endangered as anything.

Reading's development is closely connected to the technology of writing. In ancient Rome reading was more a public act rather than a private venture, and writers publicly read from their works rather than to cultivate readerships. Fischer indicates that in this culture, the "'reader' was a transmitter, not a receiver."[46] Partly this was due to the low percentage of people who were literate, but it also had to do with the often-difficult means of using scrolls for books and other documents. Despite the substantial technical achievements associated with papyrus scrolls, they were not easy to use. They need to be rolled out and back, causing searching for specific passages to be a tedious assignment. They were also easily damaged by the rolling and unrolling and, even if stored, they were susceptible to damage by rodents, dogs, children, accidents, and other mishaps. The scrolls were also quite expensive and only the wealthiest could afford the best specimens that were better made and more durable. Some of these matters reflect concerns that have carried down to our own era, including especially the nature990d of the production of books or documents and their preservation. Fischer cites Seneca in the first century AD who criticized how and why books were collected, in language suggesting that modern concerns about such collecting are not new at all. Seneca lamented that "Many people without a school education use books not as tools for study but as decorations for the dining room." Seneca also was appalled about the collector "who gets his pleasure from bindings and labels," where "you can see the complete works of orators and historians on shelves up to the ceiling, because, like bathrooms, a library has become an essential ornament of a rich house."[47]

With the exception of the reference to the bathroom, many have continued to criticize ostentatious collecting where books become furniture (as Nicholson Baker, of more recent fame, has written).[48] The emergence of the codex, fully in bloom by the third or fourth century AD, made ownership and collecting possible because of its revolutionary design features enabling easier storage, access, compilations of works in a single source, and, the relative lowering of costs for acquiring texts or producing other documents. In our own modern era we can watch the development of personal residences designed and constructed to display and store personal memorabilia, such as personal papers, photographs, scrapbooks, and diaries. Information technology is as much a cultural as a technical matter. Now, as more and more people buy into the use of digital technologies for all their documentary needs, the questions about the viability of such recording technologies are being dispersed from large governments and corporations down to the level of the household.

The creation, maintenance, and use of records require both a community and social structure. Archivists and records managers tend to think that these functions depend on their own professional communities and expertise. However, all processes associated with records and their administration also assume language, writing, and reading as activities. Steven Rogers Fischer's volumes provide little in the way of practical applications for archives and records management or for the private citizen seeking to maintain their personal and family archives, but they do provide an understanding about the origins and nature of documents. Records are a kind of universal language, even in the present era of digital stuff. We have to learn how to read these documents just as we have had to learn to read the languages that are in them. Fischer's scholarship even reminds archivists and records managers, and others, that the importance of records is all the more remarkable given the original and still often mundane purposes of records. His histories of language, writing, and reading suggest that, in a larger global historical sense, we can claim not just to be an information age but a records age.

Rethinking Our Frame Of Reference.

How do individuals relate to a variety of information sources ("documents"), both the most traditional (such as records, books, and newspapers) and nontraditional ones, ranging from television and movies to all the stuff found on the World Wide Web? By considering how people utilize the vast array of information available to them, it is possible to gain some understanding of how they view information found in the records they create, both as they work for organizations and the private records they generate because of their interactions with government, retail enterprises, and institutions of all types and serving all functions. Thinking about how people and organizations use information documents may seem like an academic exercise, but it leads to practical applications for the individual seeking to manage his or her own papers and family archives. We reflect on the vast range of records we generate, and this ought to enable us to appreciate better the role they play in our lives and society. The many complaints by records professionals (archivists and records managers alike) that they are misunderstood or unappreciated are often the result of not fully grasping the manner in which everyone interacts with the documentary enterprise. Each person is a virtual dynamo generating countless records, perhaps enabling us to understand why identity theft has become such a major societal problem. If archeologists can understand a past society by excavating an old trash dump, pulling up the shards and refuse of past activities, then anyone could appreciate our own Western culture by digging through our trash and discovering countless receipts, letters, bills, and other documents.

As they entered the modern Information Age and dealt with new concerns like information resources and knowledge management, records professionals seemed unprepared to understand that individuals and institutions seek information from many sources other than records. Instead, they focused primarily on records, often just substituting information or knowledge concepts for related notions of evidential and informational values. Looking for precision, in this day of computer exactitude, has been a useful exercise, providing the kind of details necessary for technical, legal, fiscal, and administrative purposes. Still, there have been problems with these definitions and perceptions.

Records managers and archivists believe that their institutions, bosses, and coworkers naturally understand that organizations create lots of information as transactional records and that, as a result, they would play a vital role in the ongoing life of the organization. One sign that this was not the case was the slippery slope of defining both information and records. A more recent indicator has been the broadening of the concept of information "documents" far beyond the more traditional notions of printed books, journals, magazines, and records. Archivists and records managers need to understand that this is more than merely a terminological matter. They especially need to understand that the average citizen, surrounded by personal and family documentation, has a broader perception of what documents mean than the ways in which modern professionals, for a variety of legitimate reasons, narrow their technical parameters for a record.

If we can move beyond all the hype or angst about the impact of information technologies on society and its institutions and inhabitants, then it is easy to discern that the increased attention on information has made us more aware of the complexities of information. Philip Agre, an expert in communications, argues that information is a rather messy notion, and that the "problem with information professionalism" is that "it treats information as a homogenous substance." Agre prefers to understand information through how individual "communities" treat it—or as he says, "conduct their collective cognition."[49]

The homogenous view of information is readily discernible in advertising by hardware, software, and other vendors marketing information services from the financial industries to other corporate entities. Advertisements slinging such mottos as "Because having too much information is just as bad as not having enough" do not provide clearer views of what information is, but they make you nervous that you could be in a lot of trouble *if you* do not purchase a particular product or service. Many such advertisements are being directed to individuals promising them solutions to managing personal and family archives.

The Agre concept, considering *how* particular communities use information rather than trying to define information, could be a useful approach for records professionals. Records professionals could (and should) define the nature of information derived from transactional records. A critical part of this definition comes from the perception of how people use records, archival and non-archival. Drawing on other existing definitions of information could, however, be extremely confusing as we find concepts, theories, descriptions, histories, cultural definitions, and mathematical formulas providing very dissimilar notions. Or, as two observers on the modern Information Society summarize: "Though information fascinates many social, biological, and physical scientists, no interdisciplinary agreement on basic concepts seems likely, and no unified theory appears imminent."[50] However, if records professionals assume that they need no overarching concept of just how records relate to information (or knowledge), they will become rudderless in how they plan and manage their programs or, as more relevant to the focus of this book, how they relate to and work with the public.

What records professionals need to do is to understand, at least, the context of information use in their institutional and societal environments. Just as archivists and records managers can break apart records into a set of components including context (structure and content being the other elements, at least according to one working definition of records), records professionals need to extend the notion of context to include other information or evidence sources that might rival or complement the information or evidence provided by records. As historians might argue that the concept of information must be understood in the terms of each era,[51] another method might be to seek such understanding by considering how individuals and institutions actually use (or seem to use) information. To do this, however, we must have some means to categorize different kinds of information-purveying entities, and, fortunately, there are some recently described approaches available that records professionals can draw on in commonsensical fashion.

Information scientists and technologists seem to have discovered that information is handled via "documents," not to be confused with how archivists and records managers restricted the notion to records emanating from transactions and the daily business of organizations and individuals. Documents become the primary venue for understanding information. David Levy guides us into the nature of documents: "So what are documents? My answer is that they are bits of the material world—clay, stone, animal skin, plant fiber, sand—that we've imbued with the ability to speak... What's useful about this perspective is the way it takes the focus off the technology per se. Any technologies or media that ensure repeatability will do."[52] In other words, documents are things everyone can relate to and comprehend.

These things are not inert, but active, as Levy argues. "Documents speak out, and by fixing their talk or otherwise making it repeatable, they make it possible for many people to hear what they have to say... But documents not only support the social order, they themselves are part of it. They themselves need to be tended and taken care of, just like everything else in the world."[53] This may be a rediscovery of a fundamental truth, as "documentalists" in the early twentieth century used "document as a generic term to denote any physical information resource rather than to limit it to text-bearing objects in specific physical media such as paper, papyrus, vellum, or microform."[54] No matter how theoretical one wishes to be when considering an entity such as a document, it may be that such constructions merely reflect what most already know. If one interviewed an individual reading through the diary of an ancestor or gazing upon old family photographs, the sense that these documents are speaking to them would be well articulated (even without references to or knowledge of academic theories about information sources).

What seems remarkably useful about such a concept is that archivists and records managers can fit *their* records into such parameters, and by following the implications of the idea of documents, they can see that individuals and organizations use a variety of documents to gain needed information. It provides a means by which archivists and records managers can begin to comprehend why their programs or responsibilities may seem to be underappreciated or, at the least, viewed in the manner they are at present. Rather than archivists and records managers rushing to embrace the latest information technology or by striving to change their titles, missions, and unit names to excise records in favor of information or knowledge, they can use the documents concept to ascertain how and why people and organizations use information.

This may be a liberating exercise. While there are those who express concern about how some information professionals—librarians are a notable example[55]—seem to have been left out of the perspectives hyping the Information Age and the pervasive value and power of information, a more useful way of thinking is to get various professionals to reflect on how information is being used and how it impacts their work and responsibilities. John Seely Brown and Paul Duguid's volume on the life of information extends this possibility. Brown and Duguid, an information scientist and a research scientist respectively, offer a focus as well on information documents, and they provide a more elaborate view of how information documents function. The key to the book comes quickly with its initial sentence: "Living in the Information Age can occasionally feel like being driven by someone with tunnel vision." The reason for this? The tunnel vision derives from the strident focus on information technologies: "This central focus inevitably pushes aside all the fuzzy stuff that lies around the edges—context, background, history, common knowledge, social resources." Brown and Duguid contend that this "fuzzy stuff" is not as irrelevant as it may seem, offering a "breadth of vision," suggesting choices, clarifying purpose and meaning. "Indeed, ultimately it is only with the help of what lies beyond it that any sense can be made of the information that absorbs so much attention."[56]

Records professionals, archivists and records managers alike, also have had a sort of tunnel vision in recent decades. Unfortunately, they often have ignored each other even when situated within the same institutional structure. The bigger problem, however, has been a stress on their own narrow range of records responsibilities while not striving to understand how organizations (or people) think of their own records or how they acquire and use information. Some years ago, I argued that archivists needed to identify, read, and respond to the management texts, trendy or not, that their institution's leaders and managers were reading, using, and emulating. By doing this, the archivists could better understand how to market their own programs to support organizational priorities and needs.[57] This present chapter examines another important aspect of understanding one's organizational environment, by considering the potential information sources or documents any person likely draws on.

While it may be tempting to simply express amazement at the bewildering array of information sources, this reaction to the rapidly transforming characteristics of the Information Age does not get us very far, especially those professionals like archivists and records managers who not only have responsibility for an expanding panorama of records technologies but who have to justify their work within organizations captivated by the latest technologies. Forest Woody Horton, Jr., for example, wrote an amusing and sarcastic commentary on the advent of the "wisdom administrator," lamenting the widening schisms of specializations and suggesting that "getting them to agree on even theorems and hypotheses and experimenting with and testing the `new' concept becomes extremely complex."[58] Rather than adopting such a perspective, it would be far more useful for records managers and archivists to broaden the scope of their attention so that they understand the manner in which their organizations and the people who staff them deal with information. The traditional information sources include records, books, and newspapers. Other information sources range from television and movies to the more recent developments of the World Wide Web. By considering how people utilize the vast array of information that is available to them, it is possible to gain some understanding of how they view information that might be found in the records they create and that the organization maintains.

There is no question that the speed by which some information is provided, such as through the Web, has changed expectations about how people want or expect to be able to retrieve information from their transactional records—or even whether they think they need to have access to such records. As the world of information source possibilities continually changes, the context by which records are created, maintained, and accessed also is transformed. Moreover, examining the context suggests how and why records might provide some unique values to information that may not be present in the other information sources. At the least, being observant within an organization (or even when at home) about how people seem to acquire their information will help records professionals to understand both the reasons why these same people use or do not use records for information and how records professionals might repackage their explanations about why records are important. Speaking, writing, reading, and recordkeeping all remain fundamental human activities in both the pre- and post-Web world, and these activities are becoming more transparent in our digital era and in the apparent new sense of personal and family archives.

Traditional Information Documents.

For decades, most information professionals and others with an interest in information thought of three primary ways in which people obtain information: books, newspapers or news magazines (and radio and television news programs), and records. It is not hard to imagine how people used such information sources. Daily they created records, both personally and institutionally. At home, they wrote letters, paid bills by writing checks, organized financial records for income tax purposes, and read and responded to their mail. At work, the same individuals filled out forms, wrote letters, authored memos, filed documents, and went to their files to gather information about or for their clients.

A simple glance at any individual's wallet or purse reveals a connection to vast record-keeping regimes, such as financial and government institutions, suggesting any individual's immersion into a records culture (whether or not they are cognizant of what this culture represents or how it operates). This individual also read newspapers and news magazines, both for personal and business reasons, focusing on local events, cultural activities, and sporting events, and for business matters. This same individual might also read other information sources, ranging from trade journals to news magazines. At some point, it is likely that this person would relax by reading a book such as a novel or a mystery. Printed information and written records represent a considerable part of an individual's daily existence.

Some might believe that what I have just described concerns the typical day of someone half a century ago. In some ways, this is true, as now this individual is likely to do much of his or her reading over the Web, and the news gathering might occur as part of an inundation in television and radio news programs, some of which is accomplished more as background noise. Yet it would be a mistake to think that before the advent of the computer or other media such as television that what and how this individual was reading had not been changing, although perhaps at a less noticeable pace. The late communications expert and social commentator Neil Postman wrote extensively about how newspapers have been influenced by television and radio to focus on the speed of reporting the news rather than on its accuracy or quality,[59] something we witnessed in recent presidential elections with exit polling.

In the midst of the expansion of the world through commerce and exploration, elaborate approaches to gathering and managing data were developed. Lisa Jardine, in rethinking the nature of the Renaissance, describes Vespucci and the Casa de la Contratacion de las Indias in Seville: "The responsibilities of the institution included the entering of new information on a master map (the *Padron General,* or official record of discoveries); the supervision of charts and instruments carried by seamen; and the examination of pilots,"[60] all leading to a brisk trade in both manuscript and later printed sea charts – as well as providing a stimulus for individuals, for both commercial and personal reasons, to collect such maps and charts. Two hundred years ago, as well, an individual could draw on routine document forms such as the day-book and almanac, and from receipts, expenditures, family and personal news into an archives that was a reasonably effective means of coping with a hard world to live in.[61]

Books and Newspapers.

Print has been around for half a millennium, but the manner in which it has been used has changed considerably. Five hundred years ago, only the wealthiest could afford a newly printed book, although the cost of such a volume was only a fraction of the cost of a book hand-produced by scribes. As the modern printed book emerged three centuries ago—modern in its size, use of a title page, and general structure and design—more people could meet the price of a book. Many of the earliest American colonists brought with them small libraries, something that could not have happened just a hundred years before. Then, in the mid-nineteenth century, the paperback book appeared, mostly to cater to the needs of those traveling on trains. Within a century of this development the modern inexpensive paperback book appeared, and it was common to see people at the beach, on trains and planes, at the lunch counter, and in other places of normal travel, work, and play reading from these books. The book industry eventually accommodated this reading public by producing a wider range of titles, from the purely popular to the scholarly, in cheaper paperback form. We have become so accustomed to having the book with us that those who predict the end of the printed book and its replacement by the electronic book ignore, as John Updike and others say, the value of books as furniture, sensual pleasure, souvenir, and societal ballast.[62]

At the same time that the inexpensive paperback book was emerging, the penny press—the inexpensive and much more accessible newspaper—was also being established. Newspapers date back to the seventeenth century, but even a hundred years later tended to be convey-ors of brief and often old news (although new to the reader), as communication systems were much slower and ineffective. Prior to the penny press, newspapers were mostly used by the wealthy and literate elite, but the cheap daily newspaper—supported by advances in printing technology that could print tens of thousands of copies of a newspaper in a few hours and the establishment of groups like the Associated Press gathering news from around the world more expeditiously—made its way into the hands of a larger portion of society than ever before. By the late nineteenth century, the newspaper was the primary means of information dissemination in this and many other countries. A century later, with such innovations as CNN and its "World in Thirty Minutes" segments, newspapers were supplanted by television, with many predicting that television itself was being taken over by the news venues offered over the Web.

Because of the intense pressure to have newsworthy material available every day, governments seem to have become primarily publicity agents, with implications about how news can be conveyed and read. While news retains its veneer of purpose and structure, its veracity has been questioned. Carlin Romano argues that "what the press covers matters less in the end than how the public reads. Effective reading of the news requires not just a key—a Rosetta stone by which to decipher current clichés—but an activity, a regimen. It requires a tough-minded, pragmatic nose for both information and nuance that alerts the reader to when a new key is needed. Instead, the very uniformity of American journalism tends to lull its readers into complacency."[63] While we know that newspapers and television news are at the heart of what many "informed" people rely on (although the numbers are declining)[64], we also recognize that newspapers and the media in general possess many limitations.

News, delivered every minute of every day, is a daunting information source to manage. Michael Schudson, in his exploration of the influence of news programming in democratic societies, counters many of the claims of bias leveled against the news industry while also explaining the difficulties it faces in reporting news in a fair and accurate manner. Schudson suggests that even if journalists could report on what they wanted with no restraints, there would still be problems with informing citizens: "A public with information available to it is not an informed public. Even a public with information in its head is not necessarily a public with the motivation or frame of reference or capacity to act in a democracy."[65] He also suggests that the critical ingredient is equipping individuals to know how to use the information they have, not to focus on giving them more information.[66] For our purposes here, this goal requires records professionals to comprehend both the variety of information that individuals and organizations have access to and how they use these sources.

Although reading has changed over the centuries, the love affair with print (and reading) has not died out. There are differences between reading out loud, as was the custom centuries ago, and reading in solitude. With the advent of the Web, the notion of reading text also has been transformed into some kind of communal experience.[67] Print remains a major information source, not just because it continues to be a practical way of examining information, but also because many individuals like print. Florian Brody writes, "In this age of textual ubiquity, a bibliophilic culture has flourished. Collectors are happy to buy books without reading them, valuing them as commodities independent of their position within the intellectual culture. Other bibliomaniacs cannot resist the temptation of a bookstore for different reasons. Their obsessions bind them to printed matter not as a commodity, nor simply because of the information it contains, but because the book has the quality of captured memory. Between the covers lies a promise: the possession of a book will mystically extend the mind of the owner."[68] Perhaps many will not consider records such as checks and income tax forms or newspapers in quite this manner (although many save these for generations as part of a personal or family archives), but it is clear that there are common characteristics of all information sources requiring us to consider how information is used and the method in which it is disseminated.

A book, for example, has a particular set of characteristics melding into a fairly common structure. As historian Robert Darnton suggests, "books are many things—objects of manufacture, works of art, articles of commercial exchange, and vehicles of ideas."[69] They are, in fact, technological products, and as they have reflected changes in printing technologies their content and form has shifted to provide a wider range of print sources featuring drawings, lithographs, maps, color reproductions, charts and figures, and other means of conveying information in powerful and effective means.

As printed materials worked in tandem with other emerging technologies, the use of information was continuously transformed. Historian Ronald J. Zboray connects print with the railroad: "The railroad and the printed word laid the foundation for an entirely different sense of identity, one writ on a national scale and within what would become an increasingly integrated and nationalized economic system. The self and the local community would not only have to make peace with this larger structure but, indeed, redefine themselves in relation to it."[70] Such an analysis suggests, of course, that the recent phenomenon of the Web is not new at all, except in its speed and potential capability to connect a larger group of people. This historian notes, for instance, that "with family and friends separated by wide distance, engaged in often different economic pursuits, and surrounded by different communities, reading the same books and periodicals could be one of the few experiences correspondents shared."[71] It may also suggest why families preserved documents and keepsakes associated with their parents and more distant ancestors. The diversity of Web sources and their immense capacity to be transformed regularly suggests that the Web might not be a means for community building, representing a substantial departure from the traditional information documents described here.

Considering print, whether in the form of a newspaper or a book, suggests that we need to think about how and what we read—and why. Do we read for information, pleasure, self-education, reflection, or all of these? Is the kind of reading we do in a book or newspaper the same as we do in front of a computer screen? How does reading fit into the modern information professions? I often hear archivists and records managers complain that they lack time to keep up with their own professional literature. These individuals are most likely absorbing information related to their responsibilities from other sources, even if it is not in the form of a dedicated reading program. While I read a lot, I also gain information from faculty meetings, interactions with students, gossip, and informal chitchat. While browsing might not be reading or indulging in gossip might not be as rigorous as careful analysis of a printed text, both are quite common and sometimes an effective means of obtaining useful information. Systematic reading of a monograph requires a different kind of exertion than reading billboards on a highway, but those highway markers are also often very useful information forms.

In my study at home, I have a Thomas McKnight print of a person sitting in an easy chair reading before a roaring fireplace and a large window revealing a snowy landscape. Would this scene be quite as pleasant with a laptop computer glowing in a corner or a television intruding on the scene? While many high-tech companies feature just such advertisements—an individual surrounded by computers and other electronic apparatus, as well as the family, a pet, and comfortable furniture—there is something a little menacing about such a picture. Self-reflective reading is a different exercise than worrying about being disconnected, but the reality of the twenty-first-century individual may be that the means by which they gain information requires such connectivity.

Manguel describes reading as a "bewildering, labyrinthine, common and yet personal process of reconstruction."[72] There is a place for this kind of acquiring information, just as there is a time and place for surfing the Net or chatting with coworkers around the office coffeepot. A thousand years ago people did not so much read as meditate. As Karen Armstrong suggests, people use religious texts in a different way than other texts, opening "their holy books not to acquire information but to have an experience."[73] She points out that Adam and Eve were not after information but wisdom: "What Adam and Eve sought from the tree of knowledge was not the philosophic or scientific knowledge desired by the Greeks but the practical wisdom that would give them blessing and fulfillment."[74] While many commentators have assigned near-religious qualities to the Web, it has not been because of seeking wisdom or a blessing. Still, such differences in seeking information are a necessary part of being realistic about how people and organizations gain and use information. And, as well, it may be a similar religious desire that has one holding onto, either systematically or informally, the papers of their families, seeking to have some sense of their place in the larger universe. French historian Roger Chartier asserts that "The fear of obliteration obsessed the societies of early modern Europe. To quell their anxiety, they preserved in writing traces of the past, remembrances of the dead, the glory of the living, and texts of all kinds that were not supposed to disappear." Chartier continues, "This was no easy task in a world where writing could be erased, manuscripts misplaced, and books existed under perpetual threat of destruction."[75] However, this might not be unique to any era, and in our own, it may be even more pronounced.

Maps and Photographs.

Some traditional records forms transcend their format and medium. Noteworthy in this vein are maps and photographs, both document forms that have had long lives as transactional records, collectibles, artifacts, and digital representations. Maps represent reality and serve functions such as taxation, ownership, and military exercises. Maps are also the products of changing technological, cultural, economic, and political approaches and sensibilities. From the ancient world, when geographers would strive to represent not just topography but cosmology (the nature of the universe), to our modern day when satellites and computers create eerily accurate depictions of landforms and natural features, maps have played a crucial role in society.

Road maps, atlases, news maps, maps depicting hiking trails, and antique maps framed and hung in our studies all attest to the continuing utility of the kind of information provided by a map. Maps, despite their commonality, must still be read, because, as Denis Wood suggests, they "claim to represent objectively a world they can only subjectively present, a claim made to win acceptance for a view of the world whose utility lies precisely in its partiality." Wood continues,

> Given that the usefulness of maps derives from their bias and subjectivity, these are qualities to be highlighted and celebrated. Maps need to be explicit about the choices they represent among potential sets of data and the ways of presenting them. Titles should make clear the nature of the limitations and distortion—the advantages and emphases—inherent in the map. And viewers should be better educated about what maps can and cannot do. The future of cartography lies in transcending the dichotomy between the utility of the subjective and the authority of the objective. Beyond lie maps that will be ever more useful because they will be more open about their real relation to the world.[76]

As an interesting aside, it is amazing how often we find maps both as part of personal and family archives, maintained as talismans for past adventures, and used in decorating homes and offices.

We need to be careful not to take for granted what maps actually convey. Mark Monmonier contends that a map is a "tale of power and compromise arising from the mapmaker's pursuit of an orderly process for naming and renaming that avoids confusion, preserves history, and serves diverse political aims."[77] Monmonier considers erasures, renaming, the processes of placing names on maps, and the regulatory role of government in naming on maps. Some of his comments provide insights about the potential roles of map custodians as well as those who compile maps. He describes that the mapmaker's responsibility is to record names, not censor them, noting that the fault for censorship and controversy often develops because of "local people who coined or perpetuated what the topographer merely recorded. Even so, by uncritically encapsulating local usage in a public document, mapmakers and the federal officials who oversaw their work made their successors responsible for defending or cleansing a cultural landscape tainted with ethnic and racial bias."[78] One only wonders when some controversy about old maps, with unpleasant names, might roil the normally quiet day of an archivist, librarian, or curator. The odds seem good that this will occur, when we consider how the role of these custodians is to preserve the older maps, no matter how unpleasant they may be. Monmonier hints at this when he writes, "Like other aspects of cultural preservation, archiving obsolete toponyms in an electronic repository has advantages and disadvantages."[79] Providing such an electronic archive might assist historians and other researchers, but this process also builds a foundation for later controversy. I have seen both tourist and military maps as part of the collections of former World War Two soldiers; they were clearly kept as mementos of the travails and pleasures experienced in that war.

If maps really require specific methods and skills for reading them, photographs are not only more ubiquitous but more challenging. Photographs are more commonplace than maps, liable to be found as part of our wallets, billboards, houses, offices, public buildings, and restaurants, as well as gracing our books and, now, especially, the websites we browse. In a photograph of a street scene, we can find information about transportation, architecture, costume, social issues, and a host of other societal aspects, in addition to the purposes of the photographer or the photographer's sponsoring agency. A historian reminds us that the term *photography* itself suggests that photographs are meant to be read: "The selection of the term `photography' placed the new process among the familiar practices of making legible inscriptions, the parallel crafts of writing and drawing. Lexically, photography means a kind of pictographic writing, communication through images."[80] As such, they have always possessed great appeal for us, whether we are operating as researchers or collectors or just looking for keepsakes to document our past and that of our families.

In order to appreciate fully the information provided by a photograph, we need to understand the motivations of the photographer, the nature of the photographic technology being used, the aims of the person or organization using the photograph, and our own perceptions—all in addition to the raw image being provided. John Tagg, a historian of photography, suggests that photography itself has "no identity": "Its status as a technology varies with the power relations which invest it. Its nature as a practice depends on the institutions and agents which define it and set it to work."[81] The same photograph displayed in an art museum, housed in an archives, held by an individual collector, or hanging as decoration in a public space can reveal very different purposes and information.

While the information provided by a photograph is affected by the kind of technology involved (the silvery daguerreotype provides a much different image than the cardboard-backed *carte-de-visite)*, discerning photographic information is a very complex task, as Trachtenberg and Tagg and many others have suggested. Our society is very visually oriented. The recent birth of the Web, with its ability to display text, still and moving images, audio, and other information documents, attests to the desire to incorporate visual materials as an information source, in much the same fashion as did social reformers and photographers (as Jacob *Riis's How the Other Half Lives* [1890] and James Agee and Walker Evans's *Let Us Now Praise Famous Men* [1940] did on behalf of the New York City tenement dwellers and Dust Bowl inhabitants). That we have new challenges posed by digital images—the ease by which they can be altered without detection, either to display new kinds of information or for deliberative purposes like advertising or false representation—suggests that our reliance on visual information requires a more critical eye and sensibility.[82]

Reading photographs in any era is a challenge, especially when we understand that these and other images followed certain conventions and that these conventions shifted over time. Katherine Martinez, for example, analyzed one well-known Victorian home to see how the family displayed visual images such as photographs and paintings, commenting that,

> Beginning in the 1850s, tastemakers encouraged homeowners to create highly personal, eclectic arrangements of household furnishings, decorative artifacts, and visual images as a manifestation of refinement and personal taste. Such eclectic arrangements would give owners the freedom to effectively personalize art, by assembling it in such a way that it would evoke particularly meaningful family lore or memories of an inspiring trip abroad. This Victorian aesthetic also emphasized the value of owners' distinct connection to individual works, suggesting that the narrative of owners' relation to the work was more important than its particular aesthetic qualities.[83]

No one today, except a curator in a house museum, will adhere to such an aesthetic, but it is useful for sensing how and why certain images would be created, displayed, and perhaps saved for later use as part of family archives.

When we look at information documents such as newspapers, books, and transactional records, it is not difficult to find common characteristics. Besides conveying information, they all possess a purpose, structure or form, symbolic value, history and tradition, social warrant for existence, social and organizational contexts, technological dimension, and identity with a particular community. All of these also build around language and writing systems, which, of course, operate according to systems reflecting cultural and organizational purposes. Most scholars, for example, connect the origins of writing back to the need for accounting and commercial systems, as stated earlier in this chapter, a mundane but very practical human need for communication. Though there are many schools of thought about how language evolved into writing systems, there is little disagreement that the motivations for such developments were based on business and religious purposes. Henri Martin's idea that "writing is nothing by itself" or that "the use of writing cannot develop spontaneously until small groups fuse and organize into a society"[84] is, in fact, part of the general characteristics underlying all of these information documents—a close affinity for the nature of social interaction and organizational culture. It is also an intriguing idea for explaining why and how families often strive to maintain their own archives.

Common But Often Neglected Information Sources.

Newspapers, books, and transactional records are common information documents that are well within the purview of records professionals' responsibilities. Archivists and records managers are aware of these sources and, just as often, they have some sort of administrative responsibility for them. Individuals also acquire information from other documents that are less often thought of as being within their scope of work. Movies, artifacts, landscape, maps, and photographs (and other visual materials) are critical for providing information to most individuals. While maps and photographs often are part of recordkeeping regimes, the manner in which individuals utilize maps and photographs extends far beyond the variety of these information documents that fill up the stacks of archival repositories and records centers. Movies, artifacts, and landscape are among the most ubiquitous information providers, and they are frequently not even considered as significant information sources. Yet it is possible that opinions and perspectives brought to the organization are just as likely to be molded by what people are seeing in the cinema or merely by looking around at material objects and landscape. And this may suggest another reason why archivists, in particular, need to re-think how they approach personal archives.

Many people's notions of society may be framed by their experiences in going to the cinema. Steven Spielberg's *Saving Private Ryan* not only brought to the screen the reality of the carnage and chaos of modern warfare, but it probably serves for many as the visual representation of this particular era in world history (just as the more benign *The Longest Day* did for my generation). Filmmakers can exert tremendous influence on how we see the past, contemplate the present, and view the future—sometimes influencing us in ways that we might not even be aware of. Oliver Stone's historical movies have been controversial primarily because this director "insisted that he had made an important contribution to historical understanding."[85] Stone's *JFK* is extremely powerful in telling a story about this American president's assassination, so influencing public opinion as to lead to a new government commission to review and open the records of the investigation into his death.

Movies that work often do so because they focus on telling a story rather than depicting an event or time in an accurate way. Robert Rosenstone, considering historical films, argues, "Because films lack footnotes, bibliography, and other scholarly apparatus, they have difficulty justifying the accuracy of their vision of the past to the audience. The usual strategy is to overwhelm you with drama, color, sound."[86] Elsewhere, Rosenstone contends that a historical film must be evaluated as we would other historical work, judging it `"not on the level of detail but at the level of argument, metaphor, symbol. It must be judged against what we know that can be verified, documented, or reasonably argued. In other words, we must judge it against the existing body of historical texts, and their data and arguments."[87] Rosenstone makes his comments, obviously, as part of an ongoing debate about the veracity of historically-themed film, but we can turn it to suggest that we might consider the film individuals and families acquire and maintain – both commercially bought home video and DVD's and home movies of family affairs – as important sources for understanding how individuals view the world.

The notion of *how* we view motion pictures (and similar sources) is an important issue in our present age. James Gleick describes how the chief attribute of our modern era has become the speed by which we can do things or learn about something.[88] Examined in this way, we can see that people go to the movies not just to be entertained or to do something different from their normal everyday activities but to gain quick insights into a particular topic or event. And the evidence for this is readily apparent. Claims about the influences of cinema have gone far beyond what we would normally expect for such an information source. One historian suggests, "With the exception of *Uncle Tom's Cabin* ..., *JFK* probably had a greater direct impact on public opinion than any other work of art in American history."[89] *Uncle Tom's Cabin* was, of course, a book that had to be read. *JFK is* a three-hour movie that you go to and watch. This explains perhaps more than anything else the shift from acquiring information by reading in a linear fashion to doing so in a form of participatory, multimedia experience. It also may explain why in personal archives of today we will find video or DVD copies of the *JFK* movie, just as we would expect to discover copies of the nineteenth century bestselling book in older family or personal papers.

Early in the development of moving pictures, crowds could be attracted just to watch, in amazement, film of people walking, parades, horses running, and other mundane events, suggesting that the technology was the focus rather than the subject being depicted on film. This focus began to change with Edward S. Porter's 11-minute film telling a story of *The Great Train Robbery* in 1903 and culminated in the

1915 release of D. W. Griffith's *The Birth of a Nation*, leading to nickelodeons in the United States and Europe and motion pictures as a vehicle for the dissemination of news and as entertainment. The connection between information provided by film and entertainment has never been disconnected, and today we see the two related in television news, the Web, and in how people view Hollywood, independent, and foreign films. How many people could distinguish between the fictional individuals and those in the Clinton presidential administration in the film version of *Primary Colors?* How many people really cared to make any distinctions? Films also seem to reflect popular views toward information technologies, from the out-of-control computer HAL in *2001* to the dangers of a networked society in *The Net* and *Virtuosity.*

While we go to movies or watch them on television, material culture or artifacts surround each of us, ranging from buildings to the normal household objects we use daily. They draw us to them. When someone mentions artifacts, most people tend to think of the objects collected and exhibited in history, art, or other museums. Yet only a small portion of the universe of objects wind up being acquired as a representation of style, culture, or historic events. While the field of material culture studies has emerged, focused on studying the remains of society and bringing together folklore, history, anthropology, ethnography, archaeology, and other disciplines, we have learned that ordinary people daily "read" structures and household objects as information texts.

Buildings are historical documents reflecting values, beliefs, ideas, customs, and technologies. While they are not literally texts to be read in that they are mostly symbolic or functional, buildings and the built environment are so strongly evocative of events and cultures that they speak to us as long as we learn how to hear and understand them. When we stand in front of a building, we can ask questions about who lived there, how the building has been used, how it has changed, who constructed it, how its neighborhood has been transformed, why it has survived, and whether it has been declared a landmark or historic site. We also can examine the influence of economics, politics, individuals, and other aspects on the structure. And since people often want to know about the history of the building and the people who lived or worked there before, these structures often become part or extension of the personal archives.

The survival of or acquisition of certain objects, from buildings to tools and cooking utensils, suggests that the means by which these objects can be read do change. Museum experts often argue that an object has no meaning until it is read and assigned value by virtue of being acquired by a museum, catalogued, and as part of an exhibition or study collection.[90] No one needs to rely on museum curators to inform them when an object should be read or how it should be read, only that what they add to the reading is substantially different than what most people do with it.

An object is examined as a product possessing design, manufacturing characteristics, distribution issues, and different utilitarian values that change over time as the object becomes useless or changes its values from a common household item to one with aesthetic or other higher value precluding its being used for what it was designed for originally.[91] While we can "read" objects, one pioneer material culture specialist suggests that seeing and reacting to real objects pro-vides a kind of information that cannot be readily described in words, which tend to generalize in subjective ways an object's nature.[92] While one might question just how much information can be gained from reading the things surrounding us, there are some objects that include text. Many of our household appliances, electronic devices, and other everyday objects incorporate text providing directions as to use, although some have commented that many of these instructions are poorly designed and confound easy application.[93] However, we can move away from household appliances to find better examples of texts intended to inform us, and that better illustrate how we are immersed in a world of information and have been long before anyone ever dreamed of a World Wide Web.

Some objects are more obvious as texts to be read. Monuments or memorials are the most obvious expression of man-made objects intended to communicate and inform. As Marita Sturken suggests, "The memorial is perhaps the most traditional kind of memory object or technology."[94] War memorials, the most prevalent type of memorial, are "designated common spaces for shared memories, sites that create the illusion that the residents of a town, region, or nation have a common past, present, and future. Creating a `common' memory of war is important in forming a national identity, creating an overarching frame-work into which particular and diverse local interests can be inserted."[95] Looked at in this fashion, it is obvious that these monuments, even if their inscriptions are missing (and often with older ones this is the case), are texts building community and sustaining collective memory, a matter I will examine in a later chapter in this book.

Texts are an integral aspect of memorials, even ones that have been controversial or difficult to design and construct, such as memorials of the Vietnam War or the Holocaust. Maya Lin, the designer of the Vietnam War memorial in Washington, D.C., has described her challenge in designing a memorial incorporating the names of all 57,000 casualties as required by the memorial's supervising committee, leading to a monument that is literally all text with symbolic features suggesting "taking a knife and cutting into the earth, opening it up, an initial violence and pain that in time would heal."[96] At first a design that was bitterly opposed, the "Wall" ultimately became a powerful memorial, one imitated by others: "The names act as surrogates for the bodies of the Vietnam War dead," writes Maritja Sturken. "It is now a ritual at the memorial for visitors to make rubbings of the names to take away with them, to hold with them the name marked in history."[97] The "Wall" is a good example of how simple text and very straightforward information can become powerful and moving, testifying to the success of Lin's efforts to make the personal names read "like an epic Greek poem."[98] Anyone who goes to the memorial will doubtless never look at a simple list of names in quite the same way again, or, they may think of the family records they have surrounded themselves with in order to maintain a sense of place in the world.

Monuments are also testaments to the fact that they reflect readings of a particular time and that they can become controversial readings as time passes. Historian Kirk Savage suggests, "To be erected, monuments usually had to mesh with the beliefs and aspirations of the majority, even when those were so deep-seated that they were unspoken. And once monuments were erected, they reshaped those beliefs and aspirations simply by giving them a concrete form in public space."[99] Savage examines the racism inherent in Civil War monuments, a racism that has become more evident in the past half-century with changing race relations in this country, as Law professor Sanford Levinson has discovered in his examination of how the meaning of monuments changes over time. Levinson describes the problems with the racist texts on many memorials dedicated to the Civil War dead, erected as evidence of a return to White control in Southern politics and society in the Jim Crow era. While Levinson struggles with what we should do with these monuments (remove them to museums, rewrite their texts, or destroy them), his description provides ample evidence of the prevalence of text in all areas of our society and culture.[100] Geographer George Foote recounts how places where violence occurred are often marked in different ways in order to provide readings to later generations. Some places are marked with memorials in order to be sanctified, while others are obliterated because they are the locations of particularly hideous or painful events. The fact that such places will be remembered and read suggests how individuals and society scoop up information at every turn.[101] Such shifts may suggest how individuals sense the value of their own and family archives changing, but more importantly their immersion into the documentation of their own personal past is likely more of a hedge against the vicissitudes of identity and meaning in the world. They are monuments for the individuals and families.

If one looks beyond the monument, into the surrounding landscape or cityscape, much more is discovered that can be read. Dolores Hayden sees urban landscapes as "storehouses" of social memories, because natural features such as hills or harbors, as well as streets, build-ings, and patterns of settlement, frame the lives of many people and often out-last many lifetimes."[102] While Hayden is examining how individuals see and understand such cityscapes today, others have looked more deeply into the past to consider the same issues. Historian David Henkin, revisiting antebellum New York, finds that people were reading things at every conceivable place and point. In antebellum New York, "writing and print appeared on buildings, sidewalks, sandwich-board advertisements, the pages of personal diaries, classroom walls, Staffordshire pottery, needlepoint samples, election tickets, and two-dollar bills, to name just a few locations and contexts."[103] Henkin believes that this "flood of written and printed ephemera created a now-familiar language of publicity linking political action, civic pageantry, and commercial promotion, and reinforced the use of the streets for impersonal address."[104] If we peered into houses, we would also see them covered with photographs, maps, and other iconic family images and texts tying them into the visages outside their door. This has only intensified through the decades since then, as televisions and computer monitors have enriched, if not always necessarily deepened, the information in the house.

If this much text can be found in the New York of 150 years ago, how do we even begin to describe what is there now? Consider the modern shopping mall, for example:

The Stanford Shopping Center in Palo Alto represents such a parodic and nostalgic *bricolage* of cultural and architectural history: Crabtree and Evelyn with its images of eighteenth-century life, Laura Ashley with its images of romantic and early Victorian life, Victoria's Secret (the late Victorian bordello with overtones of French fashion), Banana Republic (the late Victorian colonial outfitter), the Disney Store with its images of 1940s art, and nearby the Nature Company, closest to the sixteenth century and the rise of science, since it is full of simple instruments and simple observations of nature.... One walks through history, then, or, to be more precise, through the images of history, just as one did in the formal garden, but now it can be appropriated by the act of consuming. One buys images, but learns "history."[105]

Again, we have the sense of being immersed in information as we put on our consumer hats and go shopping. Perhaps the ultimate success of e-commerce may occur because we have been prepared by our routine experiences, such as going to the mall.

Shopping malls do not sit, of course, in isolation. A crucial part of any landscape or cityscape is the buildings that make up the vista, give it character, reflect its changes, and document its uses. Architecture has long been known as something that we read and that informs us. Buildings often bear the signature of their architect or, if they are a form of vernacular architecture with no particular architect, they reveal cultural and other influences.[106] Particular architectural styles are often associated with certain types of building functions. Gothic architecture is often used for university buildings and churches, whereas neoclassical or Greek Revival styles have been used in government structures. The Greek Revival architecture made strong associations with classical tradition and democratic forms of government, and it is a style that sometimes still reemerges when traditional symbolism is seen as important. Even photographing buildings requires careful approaches (depth of field, perspective, etc.) so that all the details and features of a structure can be read clearly. Architectural critic Witold Rybczynski reminds us that the "importance of buildings ... was not what they said about the vision of individual architects, but how they reflected the values of the society of which they were a part."[107]

We can see this in our own homes. Alain de Botton argues that any "house [where we have resided for a time or in some way have come to know] has grown into a knowledgeable witness."[108] In his view, we often interact with buildings as not just artistic statements or functional structures but as critical documents of human activity. Thinking of buildings as documents is important, especially as such a process also will help archivists or scholars better understand the limitations of textual and visual records in documenting any aspect of society leaving behind such notable physical artifacts as buildings. A house is another memory device, especially as we "construct and decorate buildings to help us recall the important but fugitive parts of ourselves."[109] While we may select a particular architectural style, or even mix various styles, the manner in which decorate our homes often involves the use of personal and family documents; our homes, as de Botton suggests, can function as a "repository of our ideals,"[110] but they also just function as actual archival repositories.

Given the extensive discussion about an imaginary place as a real landscape (cyberspace), it makes sense to look at digital information sources as something requiring special attention. Books, newspapers, records, photographs, maps, and the other sources already discussed in this report are all regular features of the Web. On the Web, however, they seem different.

Conclusion: The Digital Information Source As Culmination.

The advent of more pervasive, faster, and powerful information technologies has led many archivists and records managers to want to reinvent themselves as information or knowledge professionals. Some even want to cast off what they think of as antiquated sources, such as records, in favor of an expanded knowledge role (at least they do not want to discuss records and be thought of as clerks). There are, of course, good and bad reasons for such concerns. The poorer reasons involve an interest in professional or personal security or, at worst, a desire to tie into trendier and more lucrative approaches to information management and use. And, as this book is suggesting, there may be other roles, more directly working with a broader sense of the public, that make a lot more sense.

The better reasons involve a real awareness of and interest in the manner in which information has become a much more dynamic focus of how organizations and society function. Given that many archivists and records managers have always displayed a broader mission in providing information to a variety of constituents, it is easy to see an expansion beyond transactional records to a variety of information sources, including those generally maintained by private individuals, as their mission. Also, since many records professionals may be the closest already on staff to a knowledge or information function, it is easy to see why archivists and records professionals might wish or even be asked to expand their mandate.

If records professionals want to expand their roles they must comprehend how their employing organizations and constituents use information. The shift to wanting to encompass electronic information sources within the realm of records programs ignores the fact that individuals and organizations have been utilizing a vast array of information sources beyond the traditional transactional records—such as maps, photographs, landscape, artifacts, and others described here—for generations. This avoids the nature of the Web/Internet, in that it brings together some of the chief characteristics of how the typical person or organization uses information—as especially reflected in the Web's serendipitous qualities. Recent studies like to point out the increase of information possibilities between an individual today and someone from a half-century or century ago;[111] while quite useful in describing the potential of modern information sources, these studies ignore how people have *always* used information.

Turning to Web resources, especially listservs, provides clues as to how individuals have used information. One of the most common information sources has always been verbal communication, attesting to the fact that humans are social creatures. Most people absorb information or create the context for how they gather and use information by informal chatting with family, friends, and coworkers or, in a more structured way, by attending guest lectures, workshops, or meetings. Listservs are really just extensions of this kind of verbal communication, evident by the often informal nature and tone of their discussions as well as how easily a formal announcement—such as for a job or a special event—might spark discussion and debate far from the topic or issue prompting the new discussion thread. Individuals probably even today rely as much, at least on a daily basis for most practical concerns, on informal networks of family members, friends, and co-workers as they do more formal searching in databases or on the Web (although Web search engines are often designed to mimic the informal query mode one might find in a living room or the neighborhood pub).

The Web and the listservs are not that different from the traditional vehicles of gossip columnists hatched by Walter Winchell in the 1920s and alive and well today in the cable television talk or, perhaps, the reality shows.[112] In fact, an entirely new focus on manners and etiquette may be another bit of evidence about how the nature of networked communication mirrors oral communication. Historian Mark Caldwell suggests that "Gossip, media buzz, and anecdote are the richest archives for a study of modern civility...,"[113] noting that the emphasis on speed has recreated a concern for manners or etiquette, with Americans always seeing new communications technologies as a challenge to civility—from the telegraph to telephone to computer. He sees total quality management and corporate reengineering, two of the most discussed management concepts, as really being "Social Person management. ... In both systems the aim is to codify and control workplace behavior, regularizing relations among bosses, workers, and customers."[114]

That there is a direct connection between new information technologies and very common and traditional ways of gaining information can be seen in the way e-mail has caught on. In a recent *Economist* survey on e-management, there is a discussion about how e-mail is a solution for companies with "more fragmented" and "geographically dispersed" work forces. "In a stable, slow-growing and well-established company, a common culture may be easy to maintain. You take each year's new recruits off to boot camp for a fortnight and teach them the company history. But few companies today can afford to be stable or slow-growing. Instability and speed make culture-creation harder." In these circumstances, e-mail "allows companies to ensure that every employee has access to the corporate news, views and vision." E-mail and Web-based "company portals" (whereby workers access company information and resources through a common entryway) are essentially substitutes for the old chatter around the office coffee pot.[115] Whether they will become part of personal or family archives remains to be seen. Such concerns as these point to a way of rethinking how archivists in particular approach the twenty-first century personal and family archives.

Chapter Four

A "Therapeutic Function": Personal Recordkeeping

Introduction: Personal Records Go Public.

Many institutional archivists, records managers, and information managers become so absorbed in their daily demands and responsibilities that they forget the connection between personal and organizational recordkeeping or the usefulness of being able to explain the importance of records by appealing to each person's own need for creating and maintaining records. Most archivists and records managers acknowledge the difficulties they face in explaining why records and information systems need to be managed, but they forget that everyone knows something about this responsibility because of how they need to maintain personal records. Some of this disparity between personal experience and knowledge of the public requirements for records and information management has begun to break down in the grand and testy debates between civil libertarians and government or national security advocates.

We can document this tension relatively easy. In early 2005, the government announced a plan to "embed U.S. passports with radio frequency chips," making "passports work more like employee ID cards that can be passed over an electronic reader to gain access to a building." According to one account, "State Department officials said the new technology, commonly known as radio frequency identification (RFID), would allow customs agents to quickly process passengers at airports and borders." The reaction to the plan was swift and negative. "Groups representing travel-related businesses and privacy advocates say the high-tech chips would do more harm than good. Each chip has a built-in miniature antenna that uses radio waves to transmit information to a machine reader. Critics contend that terrorists or thieves could use hand-held chip readers to identify U.S. citizens, even on a crowded street, anywhere they travel."[1] No one questioned the basic need for passports, affirmed as crucial long ago for international travel and government identification. Another way of understanding this recent controversy is to see that this was a major intrusion into how we are accustomed to perceive the nature of personal recordkeeping.

Here is another example of a recent controversy that captures a
sense of our concern about personal records and the information
contained in them. The theft of a laptop from an office at a University
of California Berkeley office contained 98,000 names with Social
Security numbers and sent people running to fix the threats to their
privacy and financial information. "Victims spend an average of 175
hours and $800 to resolve identity theft problems, according to the
California Office of Privacy Protection,"[2] the media reported.
Unfortunately, Social Security numbers can be easily obtained, with
many Web sites offering means for obtaining them. It is not illegal to sell
these numbers, but privacy and other experts worry about the
implications for personal privacy that wide access to these numbers
provides. Another news story quoted one of these experts. "'For identity
thieves, it's their magic key ... that gets into every door,' said Daniel J.
Solove, a George Washington University law school professor who
specializes in privacy law." The news story went on to report that
"getting a number can make it possible for criminals to access to bank
or credit-card accounts, establish credit to make purchases, or find
someone they wish to harm."[3]

Such stories appear in our newspapers, news magazines, and other
news sources on a daily basis. As one freelance writer opined in 2002,
identity theft is "considered one of the fastest-growing crimes in the
United States." This writer notes that the U.S. Federal Trade
Commission tabbed "identity theft... [as] the number-one source of
consumer complaints in 2001, totaling 42 percent of all the complaints
it received."[4] The rising problem with identity theft led to the passage of
the Identity Theft and Assumption Deterrence Act of 1998, establishing
such theft as a federal crime with penalties of up to 15 years
imprisonment and a maximum fine of $250,000, and the increasing
attention about such identity theft can be linked to the concerns that
government agencies and corporate entities have with protecting their
own records and information assets.

The examples linking personal recordkeeping with that of
government, corporate, and other institutions continue to pile up. A
decade ago, the Health Insurance Portability and Accountability Act
(HIPAA) was passed, with a mandate that the health care industry
develop procedures for safeguarding medical information of patients,
probably the most personal of all records systems and one that many
probably ignore or don't think about. In the two months (February
2005) since the requirements became active, "there have been nearly

11,000 complaints filed to the federal government by patients and others." There is, at this point, less than stellar public confidence that the medical establishment can safeguard such information found in electronic systems. "A survey conducted earlier this year [2005] by Privacy and American Business and Harris Interactive showed that 70% of Americans are concerned that their personal health information could be disclosed because of weak data security, and 69% think electronic health records could result in the sharing of their health information without their knowledge. Sixty-five percent think patients will withhold information from doctors because of those concerns."[5] The problem just may be the glut of recordkeeping being administered by the health care system. Columnist Paul Krugman, writing about the bloated costs of health care in the United States, attributes the high costs to a number of problems, including recordkeeping: "Above all, a large part of America's health care spending goes into paperwork. A 2003 study in *The New England Journal of Medicine* estimated that administrative costs took 31 cents out of every dollar the United States spent on health care, compared with only 17 cents in Canada."[6] It is no wonder that there are fears about unauthorized or inappropriate access to personal health records.

Government use of personal information is not unprecedented. Even seemingly innocuous government records, like censuses, can have sinister purposes when they focus on gathering personal data. Discussing the Nazis use of the census process, a group of historians conclude:

> Precisely in the light of historical experience, censuses, with their seemingly objective data and usefulness for policymaking, constitute an assault on the social imagination. Humanity is in danger of being run over by a steamroller of data. What is at stake, however, is not only information about consumption, but also information about desires. A basic need that we have encountered throughout our research is the need for equality among all people. The continuous counting and singling out of the weakest and those who are isolated by sociopolitical constellations only serves to deepen inequality and break up social existence, rendering it into splinters and particles.[7]

Census data is, of course, one of the most basic documents capturing personal information, and the census has held this place for centuries. As these historians continue, "The murders of millions of Jews has been researched more extensively than any other historically relevant topic, but many of the bureaucratic and scientific techniques used by the

Nazis have not been taken into account. This is probably because they are, in many respects, considered normal techniques of the modern state – used, to be sure, in extreme cases, but by no means considered shady."[8] In other words, we can become accustomed to the mechanics of record making and keeping, unless we are ever vigilant in asking why certain records are created and how they are or might be used.

Privacy in America is a mess. James Rule, examining the implications of technology, the role of government, and the activities of private institutions, depicts how privacy has expanded beyond any sense of limits – except whatever we (society) might care to establish. Comparing what is going on in the United States with other nations (Canada, France, the United Kingdom, and Australia), Rule suggests that the way America manages privacy is poorer than just about any democratic state. Rule asserts, "Today in America, virtually any publicly recorded personal data are subject to sale, for almost any commercial purpose – as are many data intended to be anything but public."[9]

Not surprisingly, technology plays a role in all this. Rule argues that before new information technologies, there was little need to distinguish between public and private information: "Before the rise of special technologies for preserving the unfolding daily 'record' of human affairs, personal information generated in public normally had a short half-life, passing unnoticed in the first place, or quickly forgotten. Rather, special steps from diaries, to social scientists' field notes, to the archives of the daily press, were necessary to preserve it."[10] Concerns about personal privacy have increased because of the growth in the "sheer amount of personal documentation accumulated on Americans. They have also grown through the linkage [most often enabled because of the new information technologies] of crucial intakes of personal information with situations and relationships that most people cannot afford to do without."[11]

In America, then, we should not get too smug, especially in the post September 11 era of national security and the war on terror. Long before such events, however, various levels of government engaged in dubious activities of gathering personal information. The case of the Mississippi State Sovereignty Commission is one graphic example. One reason for doing the study about the Commission, remarked the scholar engaged in this work, is that "no southern state has preserved such a nearly complete set of official records of a similar type of pro-segregation state agency as Mississippi has done at its Department of

Archives and History in Jackson."[12] The road to recognizing the difficult decision to preserve these records was an arduous one. In 1977 the state legislature passed a bill abolishing the commission and authorizing the destruction of its files – but it opted instead to seal the files for 50 years (until 2027). In 1989 a federal judge ruled that the public should have access to the records, with the proviso that those represented in the files could add information to them. A method was devised in 1994 to open the records and protect privacy, and in 1998 the records were opened, yet another example of the crossing over between public and private recordkeeping. This, and other of our examples, should serve to remind us of the importance not just of personal privacy and recordkeeping, but why the notion of personal archives remains so important in modern society. Indeed, it is sometimes difficult to imagine the implications of some government activities and policies about records until we remember what it is that we tend to capture and maintain in our own personal files, a world of stories waiting to be told about us.

Another example of this is the result of continuing discussions about reparations to the descendants of slaves. Brown University has been in the news in recent years for its efforts to deal with its legacy of involvement in the slave trade. A new report, *Response of Brown University to the Report of the Steering Committee on Slavery and Justice*, has just been released this month. This is a response to a report issued in October 2006 about this institution's historic ties to the slave trade and stressing a commitment to memorials and social justice activities rather than monetary reparations or public apologies.[13]

In 2003, Brown University formed a committee of 17 to assist the university to "come to an understanding of the complicated question of the extent to which Brown University benefited from the Rhode Island slave trade."[14] This university committee also had a specific archival mission: "We hoped that the Committee would demonstrate how we might explore and make ongoing use of important historical documents in our collections as well as identify outside experts to help us interpret this complex history and our place in relationship to it." And it also demonstrates the connection of historical documentation to matters of accountability, as the intention was to facilitate the university community to be able to "debate the legal questions, moral issues, and ethical choices involved in issues of retrospective justice."[15] This is an example of an organization drawing on the existence of both institutional and personal archives, suggesting just how deep issues of accountability may go. The recommendations suggesting that the university sponsor exhibitions "to make relevant archival materials available to the public" and that "fellowships will be established not only to assure that these exhibitions can be appropriately curated, but also to ensure that knowledgeable individuals will be trained to staff museums, libraries, and historic sites with holdings relevant to slavery and memory.[16] Sometimes it is difficult to draw a line between personal archives and organizational records, and such issues might become even more problematic in the future. Such a case might be an example of a new trend in American society; as Cass Sunstein concludes, "The last decades have seen an extraordinary growth in the use of a simple regulatory tool: the requirement that people disclose what they are doing."[17] This even extends backward, into the past, and encompasses organizational, governmental, and personal records.

Traveling in the Archives.

Travel somewhere, anywhere different than where you live, in this world, and you may find that you never left home. It is becoming more difficult to find unique places to see, because we are striving to make the world into a Holiday Inn. Holiday Inn was the hotel chain, of course, that wanted to meet the traveler's expectation that they could stay in exactly the same room no matter where they might be. There would be no surprises, no unpleasant experiences. Today, the Holiday Inn's official mantra is that its origins in 1952 are the "result of one man's refusal to compromise his standards," an "entrepreneur" who started the chain "after he had repeatedly encountered uncomfortable, inconsistent and overpriced accommodation on his leisure holiday."[18]

This kind of homogenized world, even with an emphasis on quality standards, is antithetical to what happens when one travels into the archives or the records center and through the different countries that each box of records, each document, might be willing to reveal to the explorer. Every document is different. Each has a different voice, a different perspective. There are many adventures awaiting anyone who might venture into the archives, or any records repository. We find the voices of an eighteenth century priest, a nineteenth century cobbler, and a twentieth century novelist. There are women, children, the aged, men plotting revolution, and men planning how to resist the upheaval. With some, we have their stories told directly, in their own scrawls and misspelled words and awkward phrases. With others, their stories are revealed to us through court reporters, relatives, friends, and enemies. We find diaries revealing secrets, and letters trying to heal wounds between old friends. We read elegantly composed thoughts about the events of the day, and incoherent mutterings about these same events. The documents yell to us different interpretations, rising in a cacophony of noise that threatens to turn the visiting scholar into a member of a lost expedition.

If one is a devoted follower of Holiday Inns, of finding a Starbucks anywhere in the world, or who believes that shopping in a strange city is successful only if one finds a Gap just like the one around the corner from your home, then an archives is a place to avoid. If one believes that the value of life is the little surprises, the serendipities of discoveries, the shock of something new, run as fast as you can to the nearest archives or records center. There is no standard look to an archives or a records center or feel for the services they offer or even for the possibilities of discoveries that might be made in them. The closest to the experience gained in visiting the archives is that of delving into one's own personal or family records. A Southern columnist describes how his parents kept records:

> They kept lifetimes of records, and they did it, generally, in houses far smaller than ours. They hadn't yet learned that each person needs 1,000 square feet of personal space to live in. So they filed the records in accordion files and put them behind a door or in a corner.
>
> And it was good. They had done what they could. The world, which they knew was a dangerous place, had sent them important papers, and they had mastered them.
>
> Today, of course, we have no paper records to speak of, just a few tax files, maybe an insurance policy or two and some stuff about the kids. All other records are digital - back up your hard drives, please - and we don't worry much about those. We assume the record is out there in a database somewhere if we really need it.[19]

What ought to scare us is that such personal records might be out there in some institution's computer, and that these agencies and corporations might not have learned at all about how to protect or to use such information responsibly.

The joy of reading through the documents involves all the unexpected events, insights, and actions that you might find. In our age of pseudo-scientific everything, where all knowledge is intended to be presented as if the results of careful clinical trials, it is humorous to try to describe to a colleague how research in archives and other documents is unlikely to be anything like that. The visiting researcher might start off with a distinct roadmap, a AAA "triptik" prepared in their graduate seminar or outlined in a book contract, but it is more than a little likely that the archival traveler will end their journey in a very different destination. Great books and great articles can be accidents.

We can find ample testimony about the continuing significance of personal archives. Anne Lamott, in her fabulous book about writing, tells about her heart-breaking story of anguish over a book manuscript that just didn't want to come together. Drinking heavily, hearing rejection from her editor, and running out of money, Lamott describes how she stuck with the book through countless revisions. She recounts how her editor forced her to sit down and write a chapter-by-chapter treatment, even as the pages and rewrites had already piled up around her. Lamott does this, painfully and slowly, with plenty of self-doubt about where any of this was going, until ultimately one of her best novels emerges from the debris. Lamott uses this story in her writing classes. She describes what happens when she gets to the end, and the happy results: "Whenever I tell this story to my students, they want to see the actual manuscript of the plot treatment. When I bring it in, they pore over it like it is some kind of Rosetta stone. It is typed on paper that has become crisp with age. There are annotations, smudges, and rings left by coffee and by red wine. It strikes me as being a brave document, rather like the little engine who could on the morning after."[20] Is there anything that conveys as well as this the essence of a document? Or, for that matter, the reasons why individuals take on the role of records manager and create personal archives?

Archives and records centers are full of documents like Lamott's manuscript. Each is trying to tell a story. And one does not need to go too far away to experience this. Many individuals are surrounded by personal archives, generations of records documenting their family, their house, and their community. Some commentators suggest that much of our life is undocumented or under-documented. Howard Mansfield argues, for example, that most of the houses we live in possess "private, untold lives." He believes that the "history of the private house is one of hearsay and conjecture. We know very little about our own home. We may know the year it was built or thereabouts; we may see an old photo or two of the place with different trees and flowers, or heard a story about our house from a neighbor." Mansfield thinks "houses are taciturn," that "its history is unwritten."[21] However, I am here to tell a different story, suggesting that we are surrounded by records, including those documenting the houses we live in and including the houses themselves as a record of sorts of our past and continuing activities. Filling a hallway with personal and family photographs transforms the house into a personal archive.

The power of personal recordkeeping does not just emanate from being organized or being able to retrieve information from them efficiently. These records are part of our place in the world, marking how we and our ancestors before us have gone through life. And we don't have to think too deeply to understand the importance of records to us personally. April 15th always generates news stories about personal recordkeeping, as millions of federal tax returns are filed and billions of personal records (receipts, vouchers, letters, notebooks and calendars, and other documents) are maintained as backup verification for what has been filed, providing a sense of the broader reasons why personal documents should be kept. One commentator writing near the tax deadline wrote about how the federal tax system, in terms of records generated, pales in comparison to many other federal paperwork activities, musing that the "goal of simplified paperwork collides with the need to prevent fraud and the intricacies of government regulation."[22] Roxie Rodgers Dinstel provided another practical view:

> Why keep records? It's the sensible thing to do. Think of your household as a mini-business, performing the tasks of planning, buying, saving and investing--only on a smaller scale. Some records are required to assist in tax preparation. Others are needed in case of a crisis, such as death, fire or theft. Others are necessary to show proof of payments and ownership of property. Records provide a useful summary of financial situation, medical, employment and lifestyle history. It is critical that family records be maintained to ensure easy access to necessary information when needed.[23]

Adopting such a thoroughly utilitarian view is important for some aspects of our personal archiving, but it is also only one aspect of such recordkeeping. As our personal records pile up around us every day of our lives, we are mindful of the many witnesses to our life and our activities, no matter how mundane our own existence may seem to us.

A Cloud of Witnesses.

We are surrounded by documents marking the activities of our lives, the history of our families, and the unrelenting passage of time. Bills to be paid pile up on our desks at home. Papers from our workplaces can usually be found nearby, or, if we are efficient and organized, in our briefcases, packed and ready to be consulted and worked on. We save certain documents, an interesting letter from a family member or an annotated greeting card from a friend, as mementos of important events in our lives. We assiduously maintain our financial records, carefully organized by accounts and functions, and usually reflecting our sense of how we will tackle the unpleasant annual chore of filing our income tax statements. Photographs, diplomas, and certificates of awards are framed and decorate parts of our houses and offices. We regularly search on the Internet, and whether we are aware of it or not, we are often examining documents there as well – government reports, news accounts, and personal blogs are all documents, many traditional documents that have tracked our world for centuries.

The importance of texts can be seen in other eras as well. Not surprisingly, historians continue to provide ample commentary on the nature of records and the creation of archival documentation, but not always in a manner one might expect. Peter Fritzsche provides an analysis of how individuals came to consider the past from the period of the French Revolution to the mid-nineteenth century, carefully charting how the past became "an object both of mourning and desire," as people struggled with a deepening sense of loss and fear of the future.[24] The historian, focusing on individuals rather than institutions, describes a revolution in the importance and use of personal letter writing, where letters became "privileged forms" for private individuals to speculate about the past and the future, including a new interest in maintaining such letters as part of family heritage.[25] Fritzsche also considers the interest in collecting artifacts, souvenirs, family portraits and photographs and the production of scrapbooks, commonplace books, and souvenir albums. It may be that the present era shares much with the earlier one, in that we strive to document our every activity, perhaps as a hedge against the rapidity of change and the uncertainty of economic, political, and global attributes that are so much a part of our culture and threaten to eradicate our identity and individuality.

It is a different form of collecting, this accumulating of our own papers and the maintaining of the archives of our parents and families. Under normal circumstances, individuals who collect passionately and who work in cultural and other organizations with recordkeeping responsibilities would need to be aware of how such activities might connect to their professional lives. Individuals who work in cultural institutions or serve on their governing boards with active collecting agendas must be aware of their institutional and professional codes of ethics. The American Association of Museums code, dating back to the late 1970s, promotes individual museums adopting policies and procedures that prohibit employees from engaging in personal collecting. Some leaders in the field have argued for policies that resist any kind of collecting, while others argued for more lenient interpretation because of the "historical and practical reasons for the different rules about personal collecting in art museums, compared with those for science, history, or culturally specific museums."[26] It is a code of ethics typical of many such professions, but it is not one anyone need seriously worry about if their focus is acquiring and administering their own personal archives – unless, of course, there are records involving national security or trade secrets.

What drives a lot of people to reflect on their personal recordkeeping is their residence in what is constantly called the Information Age. The immense hype about the newly emerging digital world also provides a clue about the documentary universe that is as much a part of humanity as birth, love, and death. MIT professor William J. Mitchell, in the last volume of his trilogy about the digital society, mused, "I am part of the networks, and the networks are part of me. I show up in the directories. I am visible to Google. I link, therefore, I am."[27] We can say the same about the documents that have been with us over the millennia. Unlike many commentators about the new cyberworld, Mitchell is not disconnecting our modern era from earlier ones. Instead, he merely notes there are different means for creating and using documents, arguing that we have evolved from text you went to (like clay tablets) to text that circulates (like that on papyrus, parchment, and paper) to text that comes to you via the Internet.[28] In the same way that Mitchell describes an immersion of ourselves in cyberspace, we can describe our connection to a documentary universe.

Wherever we go we leave behind a trail of evidence in the form of documents, just one reason why the authors of the Bill of Rights affirmed the "right of the people to be secure in their persons, houses, papers, and effects, against unreasonable searches and seizures, shall not be violated, and no Warrants shall issue, but upon probable cause, supported by Oath or affirmation, and particularly describing the place to be searched, and the persons or things to be seized" and the earlier writers of the Declaration of Independence listed as one of their complaints against the King of England that "He has called together legislative bodies at places unusual, uncomfortable, and distant from the depository of their public Records, for the sole purpose of fatiguing them into compliance with his measures." Jefferson, Adams, and the other Founding Fathers recognized the importance of records to each person every day, especially as they assiduously preserved their personal papers in order to secure their legacies.

It is interesting to note such public historical documents, especially since their preservation and display often provide an impetus to individuals to deal with their own records and, as well, also represent a kind of national therapeutic function. Historian David Armitage, considering the international influence of the Declaration, enumerates more than a hundred variations of declarations in the post-1776 world. Making the point that the Declaration primarily introduced a new state and "inaugurated the very genre of a declaration of independence,"[29] Armitage plays with the idea of how the manuscript and printed versions highlighted the words UNITED STATES OF AMERICA, GENERAL CONGRESS, and FREE AND INDEPENDENT STATES. In the manuscript, he notes, these words are in a "distinctive italic script" and continues: "So faded is this manuscript of the Declaration now on display at the National Archives in Washington, D.C., that these are almost the only clearly legible parts of the text. That is only appropriate, for these words made up the central message of the Declaration as an assertion of sovereignty as independence."[30] Based on Armitage's work, it seems that no other declarations include explicit references to the issue of access to government records in quite the same fashion, suggesting that Americans may have a unique national source for inspiring them to keep documents.

Family papers can be remarkably powerful testaments to the past and one's place in the world. At the June 2003 Association of Canadian Archivists annual meeting in Toronto I had the privilege of hearing the well-known Canadian actor R. H. Thomson talk about and perform excerpts from his play *The Lost Boys*. Thomson's play about his five great uncles who went to war during the First World War and led to the death of four of them, based on his reading of the 700 letters written by them during their military service, is a moving recreation from archival sources of the power of documents to speak to us long after their creators are gone. Thomson's presentation, marked by his interruptions when he was caught up in the emotions of his own family's loss, was a stirring discourse on why documents are saved and continue to be used by subsequent generations.[31] We might not write plays about our own lives or families, but many of us possess personal documents with the power, sentiment, and drama that could be transformed into a play, a novel, or a short story. And, as we visit with these papers, we hear the voices of the past, and we connect to the time that has gone before us.

Personal loss and tragedy are common ingredients in the impulse to save and re-examine personal archives. Ken Dornstein, in his assessment of his brother David's life, snuffed out in the explosion of Pan Am Flight 103 over Lockerbie, Scotland in late 1988, has ample occasion to comment on David's personal archives. David Dornstein was not a typical compiler of personal archives; desiring to become a writer, he compiled notebooks, wrote diaries, and sent lengthy letters, at various times in his brief life indicating that he wanted to write down everything he saw, experienced, and thought about. His brother digs into these voluminous documents first in order to write a book about David and then to reflect on his struggles to write such a book and to make any sense of this short life. Throughout Ken Dornstein's memoir, we gain a sense of his brother's creation of his own archives. "David had filled a great cardboard box with his notebooks and manuscripts," his brother recounts. "He labeled it in thick Magic Marker: THE DAVE ARCHIVES."[32] We see how Ken visualized his "literary estate," "believing that a tragic early death would ensure his literary greatness. He wrote notes on in the margins of his notebooks 'for the biographer'; he instructed his correspondents to 'save this letter or you'll be sorry.' He imagined scholars trying to figure out the riddle of his life in light of his untimely death. He suggested topics for graduate student theses... He pictured his friends poring over his pages to see what he had been working on all of those years, to look for their own names if nothing else."[33] At one point David began to "keep a meticulous record of his artistic coming-to-be, a portrait of the artist as a young man, all the more interesting, he thought, for being written by the young man himself as his youth was actually unfolding."[34] Perhaps these are indicators that writers, even failed ones, are not only self-conscious of their craft but are very aware of the need to produce their own literary estate in their manuscripts, correspondence, notes, and ephemera.

Dornstein reveals other characteristics of his brother's personal papers, aspects that many archivists can relate to from their own work. For example, "In his letters, David had a habit of enclosing artifacts from his life, found objects, things lying around at the time he sealed the envelope: a box of cigarettes to show what he was smoking, clippings from the local newspapers to show what he was reading, condom wrappers, manufacturers' inserts from spermicidal jellies."[35] Archivists often have found such items and even more bizarre objects; I once found parts of a shattered collarbone in a letter describing a sailor's wounds in the naval battle on Lake Erie during the War of 1812. It may also suggest a more expansive notion of personal and family archives, as well as why we hang onto such materials as a means of connecting to the past. The author describes his struggles to make sense of his late brother's papers, resolving a number of times to finish working through them, write his story, and "then put this stuff away for good."[36] As Ken Dornstein candidly reveals, this book is as much about him as it is about his brother. He concludes the book with a letter to his brother, writing that "In some ways this whole project has been a struggle to get back to the present from wherever it was that I blasted off to after you died – a fall to earth just like yours, but with hope and possibility opening up as I near the ground, not closing off for good. I feel like I've been scratching and clawing my way back for years and I'm almost there."[37] David's archives provide the means for Ken to finish up with the death of his brother, and in his descriptions of reading the papers and musing over their eccentricities, we also discover something about why individuals and families hold onto old documents. They are markers, clues, signposts to the past, and they are the best we have as windows into our own past and a road to understanding that past.

Thomson and Dornstein's experiences are by no means unique. We can get emotional or sentimental about our family when we read old letters or view photographs of our ancestors. A letter describing a death of a relative might bring back a flood of memories of our youth and a person whom we loved. Even a cancelled check, documenting the purchase of a household appliance or the deposit for a momentous trip, might prompt remembrances of activities we had long forgotten, perhaps for reasons suggesting the pain we now recall. Testimonies of Holocaust victims describe how they secretly held onto a bar of soap or a photograph in order to remind them of the civilized society that then seemed such a remote world, giving them the simplest hope of their return. Personal and family documents can stimulate the same kind of feelings.

We might also have other feelings, such as guilt or shame or fear, when we reflect on the documentary trail following us. Documents provide evidence of our existence, and, depending on the nature of our activities, this can be good or bad for us as people. If we are engaged in criminal, unethical, or questionable practices, it is likely that the trail of records we leave behind will be an unwelcome outcome of what we are doing. Public officials sometimes seek to pass laws that will make it difficult for their activities to be discovered by the media and, consequently, the citizens. Often these efforts are wrapped in patriotic language suggesting the need to protect national security or reflect sentiments about the importance of individual rights and personal privacy, but, in time, usually the real motivations come to light. Likewise, business leaders sometimes have had their companies illegally shred records in efforts to thwart legal inquiries about their practices. And, as well, they have often pleaded ignorant of regulations governing their documents or, more probably, they have argued that their actions are the result of their efforts to protect proprietary information in highly competitive industries. The actions of government officials and business leaders mirror very well the human impulse to sometimes cover our tracks. Individuals try to destroy hotel receipts when they are engaged in illicit affairs, attempt to not use credit cards when they are involved in an extra-legal activity, or strive to get paid under the table with no documentary trace of the income so as to avoid reporting it to the Internal Revenue Service. But, as always, we leave behind a cloud of witnesses.

These witnesses have been with us for a very long time. The impulse to record extends back tens of thousands of years and is seen in the cave paintings, decorated objects, and other material culture remains left us by early humans. Writing systems are, of course, much more recent innovations, but they tell us remarkable things about ancient societies, including what they ate, how they traded with each other, who the rulers were, evil acts perpetrated on people, stories of miracles and great beneficences, natural disasters, wars, what they wore, and how they built residences and public buildings. Although we view our own age as the time when great quantities of information are created, maintained, used, and abused, the honest truth is that such recording is endemic to human nature – and that all eras are eligible to be termed "information" ages.

The Oldest Recording Impulse: Personal and Otherwise.

Writing and recordkeeping emerged from our needs to engage in commerce, keep track of property, and accumulate possessions – all part of our most basic need to survive and, if possible, prosper. Even if one could argue that the impulse to document our activities is not part of our human nature, it is hard to argue that the sources for driving writing and recording were not at least connected to the most basic of human functions. None of these personal recordkeeping activities are new, even though the technologies have substantially changed, especially in the last couple of decades with the globalization of the financial industry enabled by increasing powerful computers and computerized networks.

The most mundane of all recordkeeping, tracking financial transactions, is probably the oldest records system known to us. Some scholars of the history of writing have connected the origins of writing to the evolution of tokens used in commerce to the emergence of writing systems. When we look at the oldest records known to us, they read, in translation, like modern day grocery lists, probate inventories, or checking records. While not especially glamorous, these documents attest to the ubiquity of recordkeeping even in the ancient world as well as to the universal roles such records play in tying people to other people, governments, and merchants from around the globe. And, as it turns out, these kinds of documents are a gold mine for scholars trying to unravel the history of the ancient world, providing a lesson for us as we contemplate our own personal archives. Most people probably do not realize how much time they spend in creating financial records nor how valuable these checks, receipts, and bank statements can be for reflecting on our own past, providing markers that trigger our memories about ourselves and our families. They also do not realize how the large quantity of financial records mirror the government and corporate records and information management systems, as well as the innumerable archives and records center operations.

The most common financial record is our checking book. Although many banks have ceased sending cancelled checks back to the customer, there are billions of these checks floating about. Not too many years ago, 49. 1 billion checks were annually written, representing a decrease from 60 to 70 billion annually or 250 checks per person per year, with direct electronic payments growing to 30 billion a year.[38] An assessment a few years later revealed that paper checks were decreasing about 4.3

percent annually while electronic payments were increasing 13.2 percent annually.[39] Most of us have experienced, when we clean out the homes of deceased relatives, finding old shoeboxes and grocery bags stuffed with cancelled checks going back decades, and while this seems to be changing as digital payments replace paper ones, records of the digital versions are still being created and kept in the financial institutions. Perhaps all that may change is the kind of romantic process writer Thomas Mallon experienced in cleaning out his father's possessions, noting that "Like the grid of streets in the suburban development on Long Island, New York, where I was born, my father's neatly stacked checks map a whole postwar way of life." Mallon contends that checks are more faithful windows into a person's past because

> What was never meant to be saved, like what was never meant to be overheard, is usually what contains the truth. Letters and diaries (which my father never kept) are supposed to be the preserved written instruments by which the dead are revealed to posterity, but each of these is a formal communication, and any written communication, from even the least self-conscious soul, is a performance.[40]

The more sterile experience with computerized financial accounts may only prompt more people to hold onto some of the older paper versions long after they are needed or are useful for much of anything. It is such attitudes that might explain why archivists and records managers encounter individuals in their organizations who want to cling onto old checks, no matter how much evidence is introduced that these checks have been accounted for by other records systems or are not necessary to be kept for any administrative, legal, fiscal, or historical purposes.

For some, saving and revisiting checks can be a complicated business, perhaps the result of never wanting to toss any document once deemed to have an importance or possessing some sense of an authority because of its issuance by a large financial enterprise. For others, this is the result of viewing, at least partly correctly, these checks as a form of diary of one's life, as Thomas Mallon contends in looking at his father's routine checks. Spread out chronologically, checks can provide a view of a person's activities, marked by their spending habits. We can see a person's basic fiscal priorities, when they dip into a more luxurious mode, their generosity, or their niggardly habits. These most common of documents can provide lots of information about a life lived, but few keep them longer than they have to mainly because there are so many other records providing far better evidence of one's activities. Nevertheless, the familiarity of checks, even as they are increasingly becoming an online activity, may explain why it is we want to cling to them.

The Art of the Letter.

So it is with many records we take for granted today, secure with their familiarity in their place every day in our lives and comfortable even as we witness their transition from paper to digital form. Letter writing has been around since the ancient world, and it shows little signs of disappearing, with the United States Postal Service estimating that it handled 206,106,000 letters in 2004.[41] The practice of learning the polite art of social correspondence or what once was the manly craft of business letters seems to have disappeared except as a subject for scholars to study, but letter writing manuals and etiquette books continue to sell; there is a form and style for a letter for every occasion. Many have predicted the demise of social letters, and, indeed, it has always seemed to be that such correspondence was an endangered species. When someone died a hundred years ago, a carefully composed, handwritten letter was sent, filled with personal touches and commentary and memories of the deceased. Such letters seemed to have been displaced by greeting cards with their pre-manufactured sentiments. Also, a century ago, people regularly set aside time to read and answer personal letters, partly because there was little alternative to doing this if one wished to stay in contact with friends and relatives. The telephone threatened to undo the role of such documents, and more than one historian or biographer has wondered about the impact on the documentation of their subjects wrought by such electronic telecommunications, especially the switch to the much more transitory electronic mail.

We can recall, however, that the delivery of mail, especially letters, was an important social activity as well as a function changing almost from the start because of technology. Most Americans take for granted the daily arrival of mail at their doorsteps. Some may have reflected on the existence of the postal service only because their increasing use of electronic mail has affected how, when, and why they choose to write a letter, affix a stamp, and drop it into a corner mailbox. Historian David Henkin reminds us that the old style postal service remains important even in our digitally networked age and that its nineteenth century version laid the "cultural foundation ... for the experiences of interconnectedness that are the hallmarks of the brave new world of telecommunications."[42] As he demonstrates over and over again in his study, "Before telephones, before recorded sound, before the transcontinental railroad, and even before the spread of commercial telegraphy, postal exchanges began habituating large groups of Americans to new expectations of contact with distant places."[43] The postal service was initially established to serve business, but like the later experience with the telephone, it quickly became a critical system for supporting individuals in their personal and family lives. Henkin points to the experiences with the post during the American Civil War as particularly important:

> None of this intense and enduring interest in solders' letters is remarkable, and it is hardly surprising that Americans on both sides of the conflict preserved, circulated, and published Civil War correspondence – and have continued to so ever since. What is worth noting, however, is how a national investment in these letters as historically significant and personally poignant served, in the 1860s, the secondary cultural function of dramatizing the role of mail in everyday life. By 1865, the war experience had given most Americans additional reasons to think of the post as the repository and conduit for the sort of epistolary self-representation that united families across great distances and preserved family identity over time.[44]

What Henkin tracks is certainly a major transformation in American life. Over less than half a century, Americans move from being a people who experience the arrival of mail rarely to being accustomed to receiving it daily. Henkin indicates that

> despite the exaggerated aura of secrecy and privacy that surrounds personal correspondence (and despite the flimsy materials, ephemeral purposes, and unheeded wishes for self-destruction that attended so much epistolary contact), an extraordinary number of letters have survived, filling historical societies, manuscript collections, and private attics throughout the country. The sheer volume and diversity of this archive is daunting – and potentially confusing – but there is no better repository of information concerning the uses to which Americans put their increasingly accessible postal network and the expectations they brought to it.[45]

Henkin also draws on diaries of the period, mixing their discussion about the mail and reading letters in with newspaper accounts, literary journals, government reports, etiquette and letter-writing manuals, and

an array of other documentary materials. Using such sources, Henkin
reveals how the letter, and mail in general, became such a pervasive and
desired item that many social commentators of the day warned of its
more pernicious influences on the morals of youth, women, and others,
especially as strangers could now interact more freely and threaten one's
privacy, livelihood, and time (very much like some warn about the
impact of the cell phone and email). As Henkin concludes, in relating
our present era to the earlier one, the "persistence of mail as a slower,
seemingly more immanent form of communication in the age of
instantaneous electronic exchange is potentially misleading. Despite all
the changes that separate us from the postal culture of the mid-
nineteenth century, our pervasive expectations of complete contact, of
boundless accessibility, actually link us back to the cultural moment
when ordinary Americans first experienced the mail in similar terms.
The world we now inhabit belongs to the extended history of that
moment."[46]

Somehow, however, the letter continues to hang in there. People
certainly use short-cuts in our faster-paced world, such as writing long
messages in pre-fabricated greeting cards or postcards or mass-
producing on word processors what appears to be personalized letters,
but the function and allure of the letter remains intact. Even as we work
with organizational records, it is always an interesting experience to
come across an old letter with its antiquated style and expressions that
capture the detail of a transaction or provide an insight into the
evolution of the institution. We can even see in letter writing manuals
extending across the centuries, advice that connects the art of the letter
from one age to the next. Linda Mitchell, considering one 1712 letter
writing manual, indicates that this manual suggests that the "ability to
write letters brought some degree of power to anyone who had to
conduct legal or commercial business."[47] Mitchell believes these
manuals "reflect social, economic, and educational changes that are
taking place" in the era of their publication. And, for this reason and
others, the rules enumerated in these earlier manuals "appear today in
business English books, software programs, and e-mail etiquette
guides." [48]

The major change in letter writing has come in the form of
electronic mail, where individuals write lengthy messages with
colleagues, friends, and relatives and the time involved in sending,
receiving, and responding to messages has shrunk astronomically.
Electronic mail is one of the primary features of our modern networked

society, where one can communicate nearly instantly with others where it used to take days or weeks before. One estimate was made that each person on earth was sending over 2000 electronic mail messages annually, a figure that must be quite higher for those with access to computers at home and their offices, but a figure that provides a sense of the scale being added to what is now called snail mail (letters and other documents in paper and dispatched through the postal system and via overnight delivery services).[49] Etiquette guides have appeared assisting people to know how to use the venue, a sure sign that this communication form has both become a dominate means for staying in touch and that it has been influenced by other, older document forms. One recent guide, for example, not only details problems with how we use e-mail, but it also suggests what its limitations are: "A handwritten note makes it personal; a typewritten letter on company stationery makes it official. Each in its own way comes with a weight that email will never have."[50]

Electronic mail has also developed an interesting self-contradiction about its societal role. The use of digital letter writing poses interesting, complex, and cumbersome problems regarding the maintenance of the documents traversing the Internet; most people resort to printing out to paper the letters they send, if they want a lasting record, but the general informality, the ease of use, the speed of transmission all work against the sense that one is utilizing a venue that can lead to a personal archive. However, the uneasiness about the archiving of the digital documents and the general sterility of typing on keyboard rather than writing with pen has led to a resurgence of interest in fine writing instruments, nice paper, calligraphic skills, and a host of other traditional writing approaches.

Despite whatever impact electronic mail may be having on the art of letter writing, it is certainly the case that the personal letter remains a critical part of our private archives. Just as scholars such as biographers find letters of their subjects essential or historians use letters describing the events they are investigating as key evidence to determine what was going, so we can read with profit, interest, and amusement the letters of our parents and grandparents. Scholars have given us substantial clues into why this is so. One historian's study of Abigail Adams, the wife of John Adams, describes her letter writing as having a "therapeutic function." "Abigail had the rare capacity to express her grief, anger, and fear in words on paper. In doing so, she also helped to raise her own spirits. By transferring her emotions to paper and then mailing the letter, she banished her unhappy temper." Abigail's letter writing was a means for her to "unconsciously transform the raw experience of her daily observations into a strongly formulated system of values. Writing to the folks at home about the strange scenes encountered in her travels confirmed their reality in her own mind as well."[51]

We can identify such aims in our own social correspondence, and we can also sense such purposes when we browse through the correspondence of our family. It is why personal and business letters are generally so essential for individuals studying the past, investigating decision-making, and seeking to unravel the mysteries of past events – letters often provide candid, detailed, and revealing perspectives on our activities; the particular nature of letters – their candor, intimacy, and richness of content – also explains why we protect those of our parents and grandparents. It is not too big a leap to see how we can explain the importance of archival and records management to organizational leaders by exhibiting to them an old letter with its window into the institution's past. There are only a few types of records, such as those documenting property, that are more important, revealing, and common in our personal and professional lives.

Property Records.

Most of us, at least those of us at a socio-economic level where we own a house, a car, and some other substantial property, also are cognizant of the need to maintain property records as a form of protection and a manifestation of the responsibility that comes with property. Today, when we buy a house, we may sign forty different documents, constituting several hundred or more pages.[52] Like financial records, property records extend back to antiquity. As commerce and government developed, the need for documenting the ownership of land and houses emerged, and the nature of marking physical features on the landscape soon proved unreliable as the ownership of property became more complicated (although the earliest records, predating scientific systems of surveying and mapping, often documented immense amounts of these features and that of oral tradition as well). As soon as groups stopped wandering and cities began to evolve, people needed to provide proof of what they owned.

Property records, because of their antiquity, provide numerous clues about the origins of writing, government, and earlier means of communicating and remembering. The well-researched transition to a textual society often first revolved about the development of charters and deeds demonstrating the ownership of an estate, and, indeed, many of the earliest property records mimicked owner evidences for property in their describing of natural landmarks and solidifying of oral traditions about ownership. The famous eleventh century Domesday Book, created when William conquered England, is an elaborate record of property, one used for centuries by people claiming both property and lineage. A marvelous achievement for its time, over the past millennia we have generated millions of records systems more elaborate than what it provided for the protection of property. In nearly every government agency and financial institution, there are major systems of recordkeeping documenting property; likewise, in every house, copies and other records accompany these evidence systems, and sometimes provide the focus for our day-to-day activities. We pay monthly mortgages, make sure property taxes are met, file away home insurance policies, and carefully document improvements and repairs to our houses. And, we do nearly the same with other major assets, such as our automobiles and appliances such as refrigerators and stoves.

Most of us know precisely where we keep records documenting ownership. We have safe deposit boxes at remote sites, in case a fire or flood or other natural calamity besets the place where we live, although we often leave behind as unclaimed materials valuable documents such as autographs and stock certificates and other possessions.[53] Some of us opt to store our property records in fireproof metal boxes in a remote corner of our house, not a bad plan as long as we have copies offsite, and, as it turns out, a particularly smart thing to do as banks don't insure the contents of the boxes and the boxes themselves can be susceptible to destruction.[54] All those old metal document boxes we find in antique stores and flea markets are testimony to the fact that people have been maintaining property and other vital records in safe places for a very long time; examples of the predecessors of such document boxes date back to ancient society, and the storage devices and the function they represent provide an easy to comprehend link between what organizations and governments do with their records and why we manage our personal papers. We keep records of the house, the car, valuable art, and antiques likely to grow in value as part of our personal assets, ones we intend to hand down to our children. Some of us keep carefully written descriptions of the more valuable possessions in notebooks, often accompanied by photographs, just in case we need to make an insurance claim, but as much as a kind of archival record compiled for the use of future generations.

Maintained for personal practical use, these records assume significance for many others and for reasons far beyond eventually reselling some property or for re-assessing its insurance value. Historians studying colonial-era probate records find a treasure trove of information in those accounts where room by room descriptions of the possessions were compiled as part of the probate process, and while historians studying us someday in the future may find less information of this kind across society, it is clear that these scholars will discover plenty of examples of individuals and families keeping meticulous records of their possessions. While our modern day wills generally tend to be far less detailed some still compile fairly detailed records of what they own, perhaps as a means of charting their place in the modern world. Even computerized financial systems provide the means of keeping at our fingertips a full financial assessment of our net worth, in rich detail that enables us to compare ourselves to national trends and norms. I always laugh when I compile my tax forms and discover where I figure in the grand scheme of income, information I really don't need or care to have but which I am given anyway, but all testifying that we remain a nation of personal recordkeepers (and often forced to do so by our government).

Closely connected with our care of maintaining property records is the meticulous fashion most collectors maintain information about their acquisitions. This should not be surprising, of course, since the accumulation of property can be profiled as a form of collecting. Much has been written about the psychological aspects of collecting, but whatever the reasons for individuals building collections of one sort or another such efforts are usually accompanied by fastidious records. Individuals maintain detailed notebooks or computer files documenting every purchase and every detail of the objects they acquire, often maintaining information about desiderata as well. The impulses of such recording are closely connected to the impulses associated with the earliest examples of writing. It is not that far a step to move from the lists found in the ancient archives to the archives constructed to document one's collecting efforts. Indeed, ideas of immortality and religious-like functions seem endemic to both scenarios. Collectors record their collections with the same zeal and detail that religious sects, government agencies, and other organizations indulge in their recordkeeping most often associated with popular notions of bureaucracies. Given that so many individuals identify personal meaning and worth with their collecting activities, it is no wonder that this part of their lives will be well represented in their personal archives. Recording a newly found and formerly missing part of one's collection brings almost as pleasure as the quest for and ultimate acquisition of the object. All of it is a way of documenting our selves and our place in society.

The evidence of such self-documenting through meticulous care of personal records can be found nearly everywhere. Dan Koeppel, in the memoir about his father being a birdwatcher, considers people, such as his father, seeking to record a sighting of every bird species: "My father is a brilliant man who has lived a life that, in so many respects, didn't turn out the way he wanted. He buried the sadness of his disappointments by watching birds, by tending his logbooks and checklists the way a gardener nurtures his blooms... The triumph of the list is the triumph of that hidden heart because it is proof not just of obsession, but also grace, and glory."[55] What Koeppel is describing here is the compulsive recordkeeping that many energetic collectors indulge in, creating the kind of archival trace that most archivists love to see, assuming they are able to sort out the peculiar aspects of their notation and documentation.

Koeppel also captures the obsessive recordkeeping that can accompany the efforts of birdwatchers. In describing the work of Phoebe Snetsinger, Koeppel writes,

> Snetsinger's preparation for a trip was as tightly woven as a military campaign. She prepared a special notebook for each excursion, complete with a handwritten paragraph on each target bird's key identifying features. She was a stickler for scientific accuracy, making sure that she knew both the English and Latin names for each species, as well as whatever it might be called in local languages. During the trip, Snetsinger recorded details of the birds she'd seen in the notebook, then transferred that information onto individual species cards when she returned home. She insisted on copying each sighting, word-for-word, sometimes twice, as a way or reinforcing and remembering what she'd seen.[56]

This is, of course, not unusual activity at all.

Such compulsive personal recordkeeping, as a means of coping with life, pops up everywhere. Jennie Erdal's memoir of her life as a ghostwriter includes this interesting reference to Leni Riefenstahl's personal archives in the basement of her home just south of Munich:

"Every part of her life had been recorded and labeled and catalogued, and it was all stored in box upon box, shelf upon shelf. The boxes were even color coded: yellow for press cuttings, green for de-nazification documents, red for American correspondence, grey for German, white for personal letters and black for court cases – more than fifty of them."[57] Whether this captures the archival impulse of an individual focused on rebuilding or reinventing her reputation or is simply another reflection of the compulsive documenting of someone associated with the Third Reich, it is an interesting portrait of a personal archives.

It probably should come as no surprise that individuals reflecting on their love affairs with various sports enterprises sooner or later also are discussing recordkeeping ventures. Robert Benson, discussing his love affair with baseball, provides a couple of interesting passages about his maintenance of personal documentation about the sport. Describing how he started to keep score at baseball games, Benson writes, "I was in a place in my life in those days when it was very important to get everything down on paper and not miss anything, good or bad, that was happening to me. I was going through a rebirth of sorts, in virtually every area of my life, and things were coming at me so hard and so fast that I was afraid something would get away if I did not take notes."[58] Benson was struggling with depression, a recent divorce, a new job, a new girlfriend, and a renewed commitment to writing. Reading passages such as this one suggests how complex the motivations for personal recordkeeping may be and how interesting an area for future research it might be.

Benson also reflects on his keeping old scorecards and related documents. "My old scorecards and scorebooks are on a shelf beside my old journals. Next to them is a box of old calendar pages going back some years now. I designed a way of keeping track of my days on those pages beyond making and keeping appointments. It is complete with little boxes and marks and abbreviations for weather and naps and stuff. For some reason it is important for me to be able to recall whom I wrote a letter to and whom I called and where I went and what I was reading on a given day."[59] At another point, Benson confesses that he does not know why he is interested in "keeping track of such things. If someone were to ask me to defend it, I would not have much to say, except that I must not want to miss anything. Or maybe that I want to be sure that I know what I did today or yesterday, so that I can point to it sometime and say this is what I did today. Here it is, the real stuff that I spent my day doing."[60] Again, such comments provide some insights into the motivations people develop for maintaining personal archives, in this case, as markers for their place in the world.

Others involved in sports have written memoirs with some interesting commentary about family archives and personal documentation. Roger Angell, in his memoir, provides this useful insight into watching his father write letters:

> Every night when I was a boy, I sat and read in our living room, listening to my father writing letters. He wrote on his lap in longhand, with the letter paper backed by one of his long yellow legal pads and the scratch and swirl of his black Waterman pen across the page sounded like the scrabblings of a creature in the underbrush. There were no pauses or crossings out, and in time I realized that I could even identify the swash of a below-the-line 'g' leaping diagonally upward into an 'h' and the crossing doublezag of an ensuing 't' and soon after the blip of a period. When he reached the bottom of the page, the sheet was turned over and smoothed down in a single, back-of-the-hand gesture, and the rush of writing and pages went on, while I waited for the declarative final 'E' or 'Ernest' – the loudest sound of all – that told me the letter was done.[61]

It is doubtful that we can hear such sounds in letter-writing anymore, although the collecting and use of fountain pens is a growth industry (I own several fountain pens and use them). I suppose we can replace such sounds with the sounds of our computers (although my Apple iBook G4 is so quiet, although perhaps no more quiet than what the writing of Angell's father). There is, obviously, a very different sensory experience with subsequent generations of record making. However, Angell's testimony about watching his father write letters is perhaps a telling example of the collective process of memory building that the creation and maintenance of personal and family archives represents.

Conclusion: Peering Into Closets.

A visit to most homes will not provide substantial evidence that anyone understands *how* personal and family records need to be maintained. The most common scenario is to discover papers jammed into a miscellany of boxes kept in out of the way places, usually with only a modicum of organization and often revealing little concern for long-term preservation. This is why we often hear of fabulous discoveries of important archives found accidentally after someone has died or fallen upon in a closet or attic after a house has been sold or an apartment vacated and occupied by a new tenant. Daily news emerges about a lost and unpublished novel by a well-known writer or a cache of old documents throwing new light on a famous or infamous event. While bibliomania, the quest for rare books and manuscripts, rages quite unchecked, there is also the sense that rare and historic treasures will bubble to the surface if one simply waits around long enough. While such events are intriguing, playing to our most romanticized notions of what archivists, librarians, and museum curators do for a living, there is little lesson in these stories except that, sometimes, historical records can survive even in the most adverse conditions. Most of us would not want to play the odds with our own papers or those of our family.

It is not unusual to find the worst storage materials, boxes and folders made of highly acidic materials, housing important records, not because of willful neglect but generally due to ignorance about what the appropriate supplies should be. Archivists regale each other with stories of historically valuable papers brought to them in old shopping bags or decaying suitcase or their treks, finding documents stashed in leaky basements and attics. Archivists almost always can top a colleague's recent worst experience with one of their own. The best care might be assigned to those documents framed and hanging, such as certificates and photographs, but even in these cases it is likely that one will find the records poorly framed with acidic materials and displayed in areas with too high a light intensity (even the Declaration of Independence suffered irreparable harm by being displayed across from a window for decades at the Department of State). I have seen swimming pools filled to the top with record boxes, documents covered with dead pigeons and their droppings, and records stored next to steam heating and water pipes.

And the paucity of care extends to include other challenges as well. Sometimes people with large accumulations of important personal archives die without wills, and the state steps in to auction off and disperse valuable materials. When Joe Nash, a pioneering African-American dancer and choreographer died in April 2005, this seemed to be the fate for his large collection relating to his career and those of other African-American artists and performers. And, it seems that his collection led to his demise as well. As the newspaper report states, "Joe Nash's vast archive on black dance in America made him a leading figure in the dance world. It also may have helped kill him." Apparently, Nash had "stumbled over a pile of materials in his packed apartment in a West Harlem housing project. As he fell, he clutched at a stack of books, which tumbled down on him, according to Rashidah Ismaili AbuBakr, a friend who took care of him. Mr. Nash, a lecturer and essayist whose flowing African robes made him a familiar figure at dance events in New York, lay on the floor for five days, until friends heard his cry for help, she said. 'Every single room was storage - his bathroom, his bedroom," Ms. AbuBakr said. "He just had enough space to lay down.'"[62] While one can imagine a novelist having a field day with this, commenting on the vagaries of old age and compulsive collecting or romanticizing the circumstances to demonstrate how Nash warded off his ultimate fate by surrounding himself with the reminders of his long life, it still does not represent what anyone would want to see happen with their personal archives.

Such poor care may be the result of people not understanding the importance of their personal archives. As we are inundated with advertisements persuading us that paperwork is merely an obstacle or burden to be overcome, it is easy for us to transfer such attitudes to the documents that we create and the records that are sent to us (although it may also explain why certain people hoard newspapers, magazines, printed ephemera, and their own documents, as a hedge against the artificiality of the virtual, digital world). We begin to see the paper and digital records as only problems, when this is far from the truth. Although journalists and much of the public equate paperwork with needless or senseless bureaucracy that ought to be eradicated, a considerable portion of such paperwork provides not only evidence of our lives but also protect us and establish our place in the universe. A little thought and a modicum of care can transform our documents from problem piles to assets assisting us on a daily basis. And, much of this is just commonsense.

The problems associated with improper care of personal papers have become far more complicated these days, as we live in our highly networked society. A little sloppiness in tossing out records or in browsing on the Internet can result in one of the pernicious aspects of our modern world, identity theft. With the use of a Social Security or credit card number, someone other than you can access considerable amounts of personal and financial data, leading to misappropriation of money and the borrowing of an identity to generate transactions building on one's credit history and good name. While spam in electronic mail may be annoying, identity theft can lead to far more disastrous results. In thinking through the administration of personal or family archives, one needs to build in safeguards against identity theft and other inappropriate behavior that challenge our concepts of privacy, work, and place in the world. And, if we contemplate on matters a bit more, we discover that in many ways our personal archives mirror how we view the management of the records in the places we work and how we feel about the administration of the records by our governing bodies. Personal recordkeeping is a topic worth exploring more.

Chapter Five

Human Impulses and Personal Archives

Introduction: Why Personal Records Exist.

The negative attributes often associated with records suggest that documents are one of the great burdens of our living today. Try to imagine living your life without the use of records, such as with the financial and property records and personal letters described earlier in this meditation on personal recordkeeping. You cannot do it. Records do not miraculously appear without reason, and in more cases than none the reasons are good. No person or business is creating records just for fun, but they are doing it because they are required to do so. Every record exists because of a particular reason, covering a variety of legal, administrative, and other purposes. Some archivists describe this as the *warrant* for recordkeeping, suggesting that every document emanates for a reason deeply embedded in the fabric of our society and its culture and organizations. Even when writing a personal note of condolence or congratulations, something not legally required, we are still responding to deeply embedded cultural impulses.

Some records are created because of legal and regulatory mandates, and this is easy to discern in our daily activities. When you conduct a banking or business transaction, you have reason to expect that there will be a variety of records generated as a result. Anyone who has purchased a house, for example, has probably been amazed at the number of documents they have had to sign, every one required by some legal, government, or industry regulation – with some of these documents resulting in quite unsettling thoughts (when we bought a house in Pittsburgh, we had to sign a document protecting us against the possibility of damage caused by an unknown or old coal mine). The legal and regulatory aspects of records suggests that there are activities for which it is absolutely necessary for records to be created, that, in fact, without the existence of a record the activity is an incomplete one (or, even, the transaction cannot be proved to have occurred). Individuals preparing their own annual federal, state, and local tax returns also can understand something of the importance of maintaining a carefully chosen set of documents, governed by tax and other government regulations. If it were not for such regulations, it is unlikely we would maintain as many financial records as we do and even possible that some of these records (receipts for charitable donations, for example) would not even be created in the first place. However poorly organized these financial records might be (ask most accountants about their experiences in helping individuals prepare their tax returns), the fact that we put any energy into keeping them at all is completely due to government laws and regulations. And, as we so often discover later, these records provide many insights into how we and our parents or grandparents have lived their lives.

Many records are also created because of professional best practices, rules that have evolved over time that govern the creation of certain documents and the manner in which they are administered. Accounting and auditing rules are perhaps the best well-known example of such best practices, and, until very recently, these rules were a pillar on which many organizations built their records management programs. A very large percentage of organizational records, whether government or corporate, not-for-profit or a citizen advisory and action group, have always focused around financial transactions (just as any study of the evolution of writing systems will attest to, that commerce is a great motivator for documenting human actions). The recent corporate scandals have both tarnished such reliance on auditors and accountants for determining when and how certain business and organizational records should be destroyed, but the scandals have also generated more discussion and created more regulations that draw attention to the importance of reliable and ethical professional best practices. Many Americans still rely on accountants to help them sort through their financial records in order to prepare their final tax returns. Likewise, the same citizens also rely heavily on lawyers and other specialized advisors to assist them to prepare wills and retirement portfolios that can adhere to laws and regulations and still provide for their personal interests.

Whether one likes or dislikes having to check in with the accountant or lawyer is besides the point here; the need to consult with such individuals is part of the reality of the importance of records in our daily lives. Social pundits, from all parts of the political spectrum, have commented on the power of government to force us to create and maintain records. Conservative scholar Dinesh D'Souza writes, "What distinguishes the government from the private sector is the power of coercion. In some ways the most insignificant government bureaucrat –

the parking meter attendant, the IRS examiner, the guy at the Department of Motor Vehicles, the immigration official – has more power over me than the CEO of General Motors or General Electric."[1] Whatever one's views about government power, there is still much that we can learn about the nature of records by examining how it has utilized records and information systems. The adoption of fingerprinting systems to be able to track habitual criminals is a case in point. One historian of fingerprinting states, "a person's fingerprint set is … a permanent and unmistakable record of his identity. It is like a biological seal which, one impressed, can never be denied."[2] In the same fashion, personal archives, in what they contain and how they are organized and displayed, also is a record of identity, although with a wider range of latitude about the governmental influences.

Financial and legal concerns are often cited by records managers as reasons for administering their organizations' records and information systems. Notions of copy, reports, and other documentary management approaches have emerged from the need for organizations to be compliant with government and legal requirements, and the case can be made for the extension of these ideas to the individual as well. These same professionals also often cite administrative values as a key reason for carefully overseeing such systems and the countless documents they generate. There is no hard and fast definition for what constitutes administrative value in records, except that it is intended to indicate how long the creators of records need to make reasonably active use of the records. Working guidelines vary from organization to organization and even among particular departmental and other administrative units within one organization. Administrative value is very subjective, but it is a useful concept for helping individuals to know how to approach their personal and family papers. If records are never consulted and never needed, it is a safe bet that they do not need to be maintained at all.

But we do have great need to consult regularly many of our personal archives. We re-examine property records when we are contemplating selling them or refinancing them. We take inventory of all our capital when we are working on a will or updating one. We check financial records when we believe we have been over-charged for a purchase. We pour over old family papers when we need a photograph of an ancestor or a remembrance of a past event to be used in the production of a greeting card, wedding invitation, or renewal of wedding vows. These are activities not that dissimilar from what happens in corporations, civic groups, churches, cultural organizations, and other institutions. In one of the most detailed histories of any corporation's recordkeeping, that of the Hudson Bay Company, we learn how the company slowly learned about the value of its archives for internal administration, public relations, and various forms of scholarship.[3] This is not all that dissimilar from what happens as we maintain personal and family archives.

Records are also produced because of societal customs and traditions. Document forms have been around for a long time, and the forms not only mirror the functions they are meant to perform but they also reflect social conventions and traditions. There are events dictating the creation of a document, if one is to be socially responsible. The death of a friend, for example, requires the writing of a letter of condolence, even if today we might scribble the letter into a pre-packaged greeting card or send it via electronic mail, short-hand approaches indicating that the societal customs and traditions are always evolving, even if slowly. Every document we examine, from a letter to a check or receipt to various legal forms, are the result of generations and even centuries of development. We instantly recognize the intent of a document by its form. The purpose of a receipt rests with its structure and content, providing the date of a transaction, information about the seller and buyer of goods or services, the price, and any conditions (such as time frame for the return of the item because of defects or other problems). Even if we cannot read the language of the document, we can usually guess its purpose (if not its specifics) by the form and structure of the information.

The most common forms of documents found in personal and family archives suggest reasons why care needs to be given to such documents, a topic I explored some in the first part of this book. Checks chronicle the daily expenses and these daily expenses suggest the nature of our lives and those of our forbears. Receipts, such as for book purchases and vacation travel, reflect our sense and use of leisure time. Personal letters document our network of friends and relatives and often capture the details of both our and their lives. Tax and property records show our financial worth and our social standing. Diaries are more purposeful personal interpretations of one's life, usually started for a specific reason, such as illnesses or a desire to chart progress in a particular area. Scrapbooks are purposeful compilations of the bits and pieces of documentary evidence that has survived, providing a glimpse into how someone interprets their life or the history of their family. All of these kinds of records emanate from purposes that are important, in many cases crucial, to how someone comprehends the meaning of their life and their position in the present time, place, and society. It shows why archivists and records managers can explain the importance of administering records in their organizations by appealing to a person's sense of their own documents and that of their family. It also begins to suggest why archivists need to shift some of their attention to working directly with the people who are creating such a large portion of our documentary universe.

One of the most powerful sources for understanding the cultural and traditional form of records rests with the array and long history of etiquette manuals that one can still find in great masses in nearly any bookstore. A walk into the self-help, writing, or reference section of the local or chain bookstore will lead to the discovery of many volumes dealing with the writing of letters for all business and social occasions, etiquette books with advice about when to compose and send certain kinds of letters and invitations, legal references guiding one about the making and filing of legal records such as wills and business papers, and those often wonderfully bizarre dummies or idiot's guides to nearly every aspect of life. Most people believe that these guides are a modern phenomenon, and while they have certainly proliferated in the modern era, these kinds of publications have been around for a long time. Letter writing manuals, replete with samples of letters for every occasion, date back to the Renaissance. Gentleman's guides also date back to this era, and most contained examples of letters and other documents for purposes of social etiquette. Early American colonists used farmer's almanacs and basic legal primers that were filled with document forms and instructions for their use. Handwriting manuals of this era also taught young boys how to write business letters and what business documents to use and taught young women how to write social correspondence. With centuries of such advice and assistance, it is natural that we instinctively comprehend so many different document forms, and that we can even find on our personal computers templates for preparing letters, memorandum, receipts, and other business and social recordkeeping.

While the warrant concept is a relatively recent formulation of basic archives and records work, it is only attesting to a long held notion about the natural creation of records. Based on archival and records management principles we know that every record possesses structure, content, and context. The structure of a record is its form. The content is the information and evidence contained in the texts and statistics of records. And context, building on the trusted principle of provenance. is the principle that reflects the source of origins of records, referring back to the individual or administrative entity and the legal, administrative, best practice, or other authority generating the document. Every record is also a transaction as well, indicating that there is both a creating and receiving source, such as writer and addressee of a letter or memorandum. All of these professional principles are not arcane facts or ideas to remember, since each precisely and practically captures aspects of why records are created and why they are important. They are principles with some relevance even for individuals maintaining their personal and family archives, and they will be referred to again, especially since avoiding them opens the possibility of playing havoc with these archives in ways that could harm their significance and use.

However, something may be forgotten in all this. These notions of records are the result of archivists struggling with how to manage electronic records and information systems. Alistair Tough and Michael Moss see recordkeeping as a "relatively new field of study. The boundaries of the field are poorly defined and porous. This is characteristic of emerging disciplines and need not be a cause of professional insecurity."[4] The editors and contributors in this volume are looking forward, missing that there is much to be learned by looking back to learn by studying historically records and recordkeeping systems. Seamus Ross's essay, "Approaching Digital Preservation Holistically" is a good example of what can be found in this volume. Ross believes that we have often tended to overstate the fragility of the digital materials, when the larger and more serious problem is the lack of collaboration among records professionals, IT workers, and managers. Ross seems to accept the custodial model for digital preservation – writing about the need to "ingest" these materials into a secure and stable repository, but I am not so certain about this as a strategy, at least an effective one. Ross comes down hard on the notion that we have not had much success in digital preservation, but his seven steps for fixing this – keeping skills current, better advocacy, ensuring organizations have the right approaches, avoiding proprietary standards, and so forth – doesn't really seem to add very much to the debates and discussions that we have not already read or heard. This worries me that this new book from Glasgow reflects more about how far we are from solving the digital challenges than in providing some better answers and better directions. It also largely ignores the needs for administering personal and family archives, as this volume, as so many others on electronic records, focuses on organizational and governmental cases.

Sentimentality and the Personal Archive.

While individuals certainly must be mindful of why records are important, especially for legal and regulatory obligations, these are not the first reasons that come to mind in thinking about personal and family archives. What initially come to mind are the emotional and sentimental reasons, what professional archivists often more formally term cultural values, attached to such documents. If books can be furniture, and used as decoration, as Nicholson Baker describes,[5] then so can the archival records of one's family and past. It is not uncommon to walk into a house and find family photographs, coats of arms (real and imagined), diplomas, award certificates, marriage certificates, and other documents framed and hanging on walls, resting on mantle places, and artfully arranged around on tables. No one must do this. There is no law or regulation requiring people to display such documents, such as when you travel internationally and must produce passports, visas, medical information, and other records. Rather, there is something in us, in each person, pushing us to want to do this, an impulse that leads to most individuals and families holding onto older records long after there is any requirement that they do so. Philosopher Nigel Warburton wonders if there is not something "hardwired into us" that makes us assign such value to such objects, ones that often seem to possess the most common characteristics and values. He wonders if it just the fact that someone, now long dead, once touched, used, or looked upon these other documents or objects: "The objects' particular histories do not usually leave their traces on the objects; yet we treat them as if they have done."[6] And such activities generate from the same basic impulses that led to the creation of the earliest writing and recordkeeping systems, the desire to extend humanity's memory. As Denise Schmandt-Besserat argues, the origins of the earliest writing systems occurred when writing extended beyond accounting to encompass art and the expression of narrative (or the telling of stories),[7] It is worth exploring why this happens, especially since storytelling is so critical to any understanding of personal and family archives.

Each document form, of those most commonly displayed, has reasons why they might be used in this fashion. Photographs are an easy place to start, bringing obvious practices to the fore. Ever since the advent of photography in 1839, individuals and families have posed for portraits, often marking special occasions such as weddings, births, and deaths. Photographs of interior scenes in the mid-nineteenth century reveal that photography was used to decorate domestic quarters, and, given the much cheaper process than painting, it is not unusual to find rooms nearly buried in images. The somewhat macabre photographing of deceased infants, family members, and even pets – all often neatly posed with their family or owners – may seem strange by our standards, but the practice indicates the power of this documentary process to allow people to remember and to chart their place in the world. The ease by which individuals now can transmit digital photographs of their daily life and most intimate moments via the Internet or by posting them on personal Web pages is not only merely another step in the evolution of our love affair with photography, but it does not suggest any diminution in the way in which we interpret and remember our past via the visual record. The new technology makes it just as easy to print out quickly and inexpensively high quality images that can be framed and displayed in our homes and workplaces. One change is that we can tamper more with the image in order to clean up the evidence, a matter that speaks more to the interesting challenges photography has always brought to the human record as both powerful and potentially deceiving and manipulated documents.

Digital photography may be challenging how individuals have thought of photography and how families built photographic archives of generations of their ancestors. It doesn't take much to realize how digital photography has thrown photography, and all its various manifestations and theories about the process, into another realm. Digital photography has a more tenuous relationship to reality than that of earlier photographic forms. Now a photograph is information and does not become an image until called up and tinkered with, exaggerating all of the earlier debates about just what a photograph's image is – art or reality, for example. Critics, historians, and other scholars long ago abandoned thinking of any photographic image as just a frozen moment in time and space, adopting far more complicated concepts of what the image is, but a digital photograph seems more complex by many orders of magnitude, mainly because it is so much more malleable.

James Elkins, in a recent collection of essays and reflections on photographic theory, provides a compendium of views and attitudes about the nature of photography, representing a wide range of theoretical perspectives. The core part of the book reproduces a dialogue among nine artists, photographers, and experts on photography about the nature of photography and various conceptual notions of what it represents. One emerges from this with a lot more to think about when looking at a photograph. Sharon Sliwinski writes, for example:

> In a sense, I suspect photography theory has begun to evaporate, for a whole range of reasons. Perhaps the main one is that photography itself in its analogue form has already been dispersed by scientists, media institutions, the police, artists, and travelers: its dispersion began as soon as it was invented, so that photography has served a myriad of institutional purposes. Now photography is mutating into a digital environment where the boundaries are even less clear."[8] If this is the case, how has the description by archivists of photographic sources changed or does it need to change? We know that we face greater challenges in such tasks, especially as Martin Lister reminds us, "The oldest of modern media, photography (and radio and the telephone) now exists in a media ecology that was probably unthinkable even fifteen years ago.[9]

No one is suggesting, certainly not me, that individuals interested in maintaining personal and family archives were also engaged in reflecting on the theoretical implications of new photographic imagery; indeed, the rise of personal photography in the nineteenth century occurred in the midst of great debates about the medium, as Anne McCauley writes,

> Established artists, aristocrats, and intellectuals attacked the new technology as mechanical, mindless, inferior, vulgar, and servile, while the new practitioners, equipment manufacturers, scientists, progressives, populists, and positivists had to defend it as contributing to knowledge, amazingly detailed, better than the handmade, efficient, true, real, and possibly even beautiful, artistic, and immortal.[10]

Nevertheless, what this does suggest is the resiliency of individuals maintaining their own documents even as the nature of the technology creating such documents changes and is debated as to meaning and utility.

Iconography is the study of images and their symbolic role in our lives, institutions, and society. And, as such, it also speaks to the use of documents in displays in our homes and offices meant to provide an interpretation of our life. Just like the recent phenomenon of roadside memorials for traffic accident victims or the public outpouring of remembrances in the deaths of public figures such as Princess Diana or the workers in the Twin Towers in New York City on September 11, 2001, many set aside spaces in their houses or offices to display photographs, certificates, and other documents about their lives and families. Often displayed with the care of a museum exhibit, these spaces tell us much about how and why people want to preserve at least a portion of their private archives. Of course, in many instances, the individuals assembling these displays may not distinguish much between the documents and what can only be called kitsch. Interspersed among real documents are other sources, such as mugs and ceramics with vacation spots emblazoned on them, which can also be read (although in different ways). However, these artifacts are also part of the personal or family archives, especially since traditional documents, such as letters or diaries, often have their meaning diminished without them. In one sense, the manner in which these documents are displayed is an important context of meaning for these documents.

The public display of documents is a means by which we connect with the past. The mere retention and management of our personal archives suggests this purpose as well, but such administration is often done behind the scenes, with records neatly stored in boxes and folders, on disks, and on personal computers. The public display employs a much more selective process of interpretation, whereby we assemble key documents – sometimes selected as much for their aesthetic value as for their evidence – to portray a certain image or to assume a particular identity. The National Archives, for example, handles millions of documents, in both paper and digital form, but it only displays permanently a handful of documents, usually referred to as the charters of freedom (the Declaration of Independence, the Constitution, and the Bill of Rights) as possessing such powerful meaning for the nation that they are singled out for display, extraordinary care, and reverence. Likewise, many corporations, even those with underdeveloped archives and records management programs, also choose to have small public displays, some might call them museums, where key documents, with more symbolic than legal or other importance, are displayed along with the shovel that broke ground on the first corporate headquarters, the corporate seal, some select photographs, and an architect's model of an early building. New employees are taken to these corporate shrines, where they are immersed into the memory, mission, and traditions of the company, a process that might not have immerse financial value or immediate monetary payoffs but one that will help these individuals to understand and buy into the corporate culture. In the same way, displaying photographs, certificates, and important documents in the home can assist parents to help their children to understand something of their family heritage. Such displays, whether those by government entities and corporations or done on a personal level, reflect an important function of archives, but they also must not be totally confused with what archives are about or the many other roles of evidence, security, accountability, and memory that they play. And if these documents are removed from this context (say, into an archival repository), is it not the case that they lose some of their important meaning?

Sometimes even well-established government agencies and archives fumble the ball when it comes to comprehending the symbolic value of archival and other documentary sources. Sometimes we learn about this in what might seem to be unlikely places. *Wired* magazine has been a window into cyberculture and our so-called information age since the start of its publication.[11] *Wired* also provides continuing commentary on the notion of documents and archives, such as occurred in the January 2007 issue. One article in this issue – Gareth Cook's "Untangling the Mystery of the Inca," – describes the work of Harvard anthropologist Gary Urton in deciphering Incan khipu, knotted string or rope. The article describes how about 750 khipu survive and how Urton and others are using computerized technologies to decipher the rules governing the language of these artifacts. As Cook writes, "Urton's great insight has been to treat the khipu not just as a textile or a simple abacus but as an advanced, alien technology."[12] As such work continues, we have the prospects of gaining a greater understanding of one of the oldest recordkeeping systems in the Americas; but even if successful translation never happens, the khipu present overwhelming evidence about how simple documents become symbolic tokens of a culture (in this case, even as their meaning diminished, the sentimentality attached to them grew.

Later in the same issue of *Wired* David Kushner recounts the story of one of the more embarrassing moments in American government recordkeeping, the losing of the videotape of the July 20, 1969 moon landing somewhere in the archives of NASA. In this essay Kushner describes the "4 million musty boxes at the Washington National Records Center"[13] and the discovery that the "government's data storage system is a shambles." He continues, "There's no barcoding or computerized tracking when a box is checked out, the only record of its removal is a sheet of paper placed loosely on the shelf in its place, The placeholders can sit there yellowing for decades – assuming they don't fall behind the stacks."[14] I doubt that the boxes at the federal records center are musty, and in this description we have just another example of the use of stereotypical notions of what archives represent to make a point – in this case, how one of the most famous and important iconic records of the twentieth century could be so easily misplaced. What this incident relates, perhaps, is that understanding the symbolic importance of documents is not enough to provide adequate care for them. And how many times have we, as individuals, discovered that documents with sentimental value can no longer be found?

We can understand more of this role of the personal archives if we understood about why we carry certain records with us. The photographs, receipts, credit cards, licenses, and membership cards we transport with us every day in our wallets, purses, and briefcases speak loudly about us as citizens of the world. Some of these cards, such as a driver's license, we carry with us because we are required to by government agencies. If you want to travel internationally, for example, you will need a passport and maybe even a visa and other documents; there is no discretion left to you about this – comply or don't travel. Some of the material we have with us we have to facilitate our work and shopping habits. We don't need to have a credit card or ATM card unless we expect to need it to entertain clients, shop for a wedding present, or just because we don't wish to carry larger amounts of cash. For most, there is little latitude about keeping these cards with them.

But this is not the case with other items that we carry, such as photographs and personal memorabilia. We keep these documents with us because they provide some identity for us, especially as we relate to others. And, with the aid of laptop computers, PDA's, and cell phones, we can now carry far more personal information, some of it quite symbolic of who we are and much of it as carefully arranged and catalogued as an exhibition at a museum. Even so, these new portable digital devices only increase the need for the bags we carry with us everyday. Desks, cabinets, shelves, wallets, purses, and other such devices can tell us a lot about the evolving nature of records and recordkeeping systems. Even as recent trends in women's fashion have increased interest in carrying handbags that are stylish and branded, these trends have not overcome the need for them to be functional.[15] The records we transport daily run the gamut of reasons from needing evidence and staying compliant to reasons that are laden with emotion and sentimentality.

Vital Records and Government Licenses.

Recordkeeping we associate with government responsibilities as public data managers, such as vital family records — like death, birth, marriage, and baptismal documents — have seemed to be with us nearly forever. Many people do associate such vital records with government responsibilities, and, indeed, such recordkeeping did become an essential and ubiquitous aspect of government bureaucracies as social, health, and legal services expanded. Spurred on for reasons related to public health, taxation, and planning of all sorts, government at all levels created systems to track demographic shifts and trends; and, even when governments were not deliberately seeking to do this, they tended to generate such records through legal proceedings and the assorted work of the courts; the bigger challenge for researchers, especially those working in early American history, has been the issue of what has survived. Richard Godbeer, studying the late seventeenth century witch trials, indicates that "reconstructing" these trials and what led to them can be very "challenging." He continues,

> In most cases we cannot be sure that we have all the official papers and in some instances only a few depositions or none at all have survived. Even relatively complete court transcripts rarely provide all the information that we would like to have about the context from which an accusation emerged." Here we see the limitations of records, even government and legal records that in the colonial period tend to be complete and richer in detail than personal papers. Godbeer notes that for "every useful piece of information that historians unearth, there remain many questions that cannot be answered.[16]

Some associate such government recordkeeping as being synonymous with bureaucracy, the filling out of endless forms that every citizen experiences every time they visit a government office. Nevertheless, our effort to complete such records or to provide the information essential for their completion leaves traces everywhere of us, adding to the accumulation of personal records we generate on our own volition. Most of us are engaged regularly in completing some government form on a weekly or monthly basis and, as well, we

unknowingly regularly complete other forms that generate information
to government programs.

Vital recordkeeping was not always a government responsibility.
Non-governmental organizations, most notably churches, recorded
births, deaths, marriages, and baptisms as part of their sacramental
responsibilities – and it is reasonable to assume that if government had
not become the official agent for this that private groups, such as
churches, would have continued to perform more fully this function.
Many of us have copies of these documents in our family scrapbooks or
framed and hanging on the wall, especially since many of these
documentary forms are in beautiful calligraphic hands and are
associated with landmarks in our lives and those of our families; in
many instances, we transform the data from these records into family
trees and other documentary expressions that can be framed and
displayed. Such records have also been inscribed into family Bibles or
other keepsake volumes, including volumes specifically designed for
documenting basic genealogical information. In fact, when many reflect
on the nature of their personal or family archives, it is often done in
conjunction with an interest in genealogical research. The rapid growth
of interest in genealogy through the twentieth century and into this new
century shows no signs of abating and, along with other hobbies such as
scrap booking and diary writing, suggests a continuing interest in
personal archives. The growing genealogical industry has certainly been
a positive factor in drawing attention to the importance of personal and
family archives, especially as many of the hundreds of basic genealogical
manuals offer at least a modicum of advice about the maintenance of
family papers, ranging from basic documents on births and deaths but
also often including advice on photographic archives as well.[17]

Our personal archives are also reminders of how we live in our
world and are affected by numerous forces and institutions governing
our activities. Even a casual glance into our stacks of personal records
will reveal the evidence of how pervasive government is in our lives. We
maintain copies of licenses for driving cars, fishing, hunting, and a host
of other activities that we normally engage in but that are regulated for
one reason or another. In the year 2000 the government issued
15,044,324 hunting licenses and 29, 585,728 fishing licenses.[18] The
government also issues a variety of professional licenses as well, such as
for operating taxi cabs or for certifying lawyers and physicians. Some
take on more importance than others, such as driver's licenses, as we
use them for a host of other purposes, mostly for identity checks when

engaging in a financial transaction or traveling. Indeed, the largest records-generating agency in state government is that of the motor vehicle agencies, pumping out millions of records annually, with many making their way into our wallets and personal archives. In the year 2003 there were 196,165,667 licensed drivers in the United States, a staggering figure suggesting an immense recordkeeping enterprise.[19] Whatever the range of government-issued records we might have, it is clear that such documents have become a more prevalent part of our personal archives than ever before, the result of what modern government has become, whether we like it or not. For example, legal scholar Lawrence Friedman uses the licensing of drivers as a means of understanding the concept of personal freedom in the American democratic system:

> Freedom is not an absolute; it is something relative, and it is also quite subjective. Consider, for example, that twentieth-century miracle, the automobile. Now that most people have cars, they have opportunities that were denied most people in the past. They can live, work, travel in ways that expand their horizons. In this sense, the automobile makes an enormous contribution to 'freedom'; it carries the priceless gift of mobility. It provides a kind of 'freedom' that the nineteenth century could hardly dream of. Yet the automobile also generates a tremendous volume of law – a mass or rules about roads, traffic, driver's licenses, all of which regulate and restrict and set limits.[20]

Some government records have become much more important in very recent years. Passports, in the wake of the terrorist attacks of September 11, 2001, have become very newsworthy, but they are not at all new creations. Martin Lloyd, a former employee of the U. K. Immigration Service, has provided a reasonably in-depth account concerning the use, misuse, forgery, and technical aspects of passports, especially how the development of usable photographic technologies and the growth of commerce and the rise of classes of people more interested in travel all affected the evolution of officially-issued passports. Such document forms are closely connected to the manner of government machinery and international diplomacy: "Documents such as passports and safe conducts could only perform their purpose in an atmosphere of international recognition and within the burgeoning structure of diplomacy."[21] Particularly interesting in the book is Lloyd's candid analysis of various attempts to provide international standardization of passport design and content, reminding us how relevant the passport is as a document in our post-9/11 world. Lloyd speculates that the passport "has survived centuries because of two factors: it is a concept that is adaptable and there have been persistent demands upon it to adapt."[22] With all the intensified interest in national security, government control, national identity cards, and the like – as well as the apparent forgeries of passports by some of the terrorists involved in the events of September 11, 2001 – the passport will continue to be one of the most intensely analyzed documents of our own era.

Government, in its incessant recording of ourselves, perhaps has done a service for us. We hold onto many older government records, old passports or licenses, for sentimental reasons, connecting the use of the records with trips, vacations, and various fond memories. It is fun to go back and look at old passport and driver licenses photographs, partly because they are often so unflattering in their efforts to capture clearly facial details and partly because they help us remember where we have been and what we were doing at particular times in the past. If government was not recording so many of our activities, even with all the reasons of privacy invasions and misuse of personal data that should concern us, would we simply ramp up our own self-recording? The relationship between governmental and organizational recordkeeping and the individual impulse to develop personal archives is a complex, but quite real and useful, one.

Recording Ourselves.

We might believe that the creation of our personal archive is an involuntary process, as we leave remnants of evidence about our activities wherever we go. Every transaction results in a document, and these documents often form the substance of what become credit reports and Internet profiles. However, many of us do not worry about such matters since we are heavily engaged in sculpting our own personal archives. Much of what we may choose to do in documenting our personal property is just that, a matter of personal choice. We accept ATM cards, acquire bonus cards, buy subscriptions, and make other choices fully aware that we are leaving footprints of our journeys that will result in unsolicited mailings and offers. Much of this is not a worry. I hope that my subscription to the *New York Review of Books* will generate my receiving additional book catalogs. I am not at all worried that my subscription to *Golf Digest* will bring solicitations from golf club manufacturers or additional catalogs from golf supplies firms and clothiers. Indeed, I want these other intrusions into my life, although I will probably not make a decision to maintain any of this stuff in any long-term fashion as part of my personal archive. Gary Wolf, writing about personal data in *Wired*, argues that it is "hard to find any logic in the idea that our personal data is private property." Instead Wolf contends that the "very existence of our reputation arises from the fact that information is shared. As we buy and sell, borrow and repay, our identities multiply, accumulating new qualities and scars. This is a good thing. Yes, the promiscuous accessibility of personal information has given rise to a spectacular crime wave, but it has also vastly expanded our networks of trust."[23] Examinations of the kinds of records we maintain about ourselves would certainly confirm such seeming contradictions in our behavior. Indeed, much of what will constitute our personal archives will be the byproducts of activity that creates a kind of virtual or shadow archive in the financial and institutions around the globe.

There is then, what we see of ourselves and what others see of us; perhaps, one motivation for maintaining our own personal archives is our effort to manage what we consider to be the more accurate portrait of ourselves. Perhaps it is this kind of motivation that explains what former National Security Advisor Sandy Berger was doing trying to smuggle documents out of the U.S. National Archives (NARA). His story is well-known, mostly depicted as an effort to impede the work of the 9/11 Commission. Berger removed classified notes, dumped classified records, and removed and subsequently returned some additional classified records. Ultimately Berger was given two years probation, ordered to perform a hundred hours of community service, fined $50,000, and lost his security clearance for three years. The report issued about this incident criticizes NARA's handling of the Berger situation, ranging from their supervision of Berger, "lax procedures" in handing classified records, allowing Berger to work in an area that was not authorized for viewing such records, and operating with outdated law enforcement procedures.[24] However, what emerges from the various reports and news stories about Berger is the odd way he seemed to be functioning when seeking to examine his own documents created when he was a government official. Perhaps his behavior was no more odd than that of others who have tried to control the document trail they have left behind. In Berger's case, of course, his actions reek of illegal activities.

Others have even created complete fictional archives of families and organizations in order to try to leave a smudge of their own on the documentary universe. Rohan Kriwaczek's *An Incomplete History of the Art of Funerary Violin*, published just in 2006, is a complete forgery. It is not a particularly well-written or organized book, with historical chapters followed by chapters of varying lengths on important personages in the funerary violin tradition, and including even claims by the author that he might be the object of death threats. The book is heavily illustrated, including some reproductions of portraits, book title pages, and documents, with many clearly looking like fakes. Throughout the book there are detailed and quite believable references to archives. The author notes at the beginning of the volume how he meets a fellow musician who talks to him about the Guild of Funerary Violinists. "After a couple of meetings, where we discussed the Funerary Aesthetic, and the terrible events that befell the Guild, I was almost ready to leave for good, but then mention was made of the Guild's archives," and he begged for access to them. And he describes what he finds: "Never in the history of record-keeping has there been a more chaotic, disorganized or neglected archive than this. The conditions were atrociously damp, pages were rotting, trunks were falling apart on top of each other, objects were stacked with all the coherence of a landslide, and I realized, at that moment, that it was my mission to preserve, collate and study whatever was not beyond saving."[25] And on and on this author describes the amazing and quirky archives of this society. There is no direct explanation of why the author created this fictional archives, but as in most forgeries it is a mixed bag of the thrill of fooling the experts and the creative act of compiling the archival record. It is only a thin line separating this kind of behavior and the more legitimate efforts of individuals and institutions to maintain their own real archives as a mechanism for personal and institutional memory.

The level of commitment we might want to invest in such personal documentation, even to the point of forging our own documentary past, can also be seen in other document forms, such as diaries. The writing of diaries has been a human activity for centuries, and nearly everyone can think of a famous one that has been published, such as that of Samuel Pepys in seventeenth century London, and hailed by some as being a great literary achievement. Diaries, with their daily or weekly accounts can be mesmerizing documents, providing elaborate and rich detail about a person's existence and the world of the past. In some instances, scholars have taken the most ordinary of diaries, such as one of a frontier Maine midwife, and turned it into an extraordinary document revealing unknown insights into early American life (even after many other historians and scholars had read and chosen to ignore the diary).[26] Diaries are deemed to be such a revealing and critical source of information about one's life that from time to time elaborate hoaxes have been attempted, such as in the forgery of Hitler's diary (a fraud that also revealed how tempted we are to want to accept such obvious fakes penned by famous and infamous historical figures), in order to influence our interpretation of the past or, more mundanely, to cash into the wild, unpredictable but often quite profitable market for such documents.[27] There must be a vicarious thrill in creating a diary of a historical figure, not all that unlike the pleasure a real person feels in generating one's own diary and building layers of evidence about one's place in the universe. The impulses driving one to forge a document such as a diary are not far from those prompting individuals to create genuine diaries or to search and collect historical records and artifacts.

Many explanations have been offered for why people write diaries, such as using the process to mark their place in the world or as creating a mnemonic device. Louis Menand provides one particularly interesting interpretation of the impulse to write a diary:

> 'Never discriminate, never omit' is one of the unstated rules of diary-keeping. The rule is perverse, because all writing is about control, and writing a diary is a way to control the day – to have, as it were, the last word. But diaries are composed under the fiction that the day is in control, that you are simply a passive recorder of circumstance, and so everything has to go in whether it mattered or not – as though deciding when it didn't were somehow not your business. In a diary, the trivial and inconsequential ... are not trivial and inconsequential at all; they are defining feature of the genre. If it doesn't contain a lot of dross, it's not a diary.[28]

There has been debate over whether people write diaries primarily for themselves or to be read by others, although I have always thought that the nature of diary writing is a fairly transparent process for trying to be remembered by others (and this is certainly supported as people shift to writing online, very public, blogs).

And, perhaps, the best window into the process can be seen in the words of diarists themselves, such as in the those of Rev. Francis Kilvert, a nineteenth century English curate, quoted by Bret Lott in his book on writing: "Why do I keep this voluminous journal? I can hardly tell. Partly because life appears to me such a curious and wonderful thing

that it almost seems a pity that even such a humble and uneventful life
as mine should pass altogether away without some record such as
this."[29] Needless to say, perhaps, but the process of diary writing is the
quintessential act of personal recordkeeping, where the daily – or some
regular occurrence – of scribbling in a bound book can become an
obsession of trying to record every activity, or, at least, an interpretation
of every activity. Even if the words written may prove to others to be
useless, the act of compiling a diary (like collecting) can be a significant
process for the diary writer. One commentator on the increasing
creation of personal diaries, including the sale of ten million blank books
a year, argues there has "been a shift in emphasis from documenting
facts to exploring feelings. For many of the millions of folks who keep
them now, journals are tools for self-discovery and personal growth."[30]

Diary writers are shaping their world, even if someone else might
deconstruct the form offered to them. One historian, Rhys Isaac,
provides an interesting view into the extraordinary diary of the
eighteenth century Virginia landowner, Landon Carter, suggesting that
Carter's diary was a kind of epistolary novel: "It was a kind of open
letter to Landon's family that unfolded the household's life as the
patriarch would tell it. Yes, if only they would all read its self-justifying
narratives, they would understand not only Landon's feeling but the
rightness of his conduct. Perhaps then they alter their own conduct
accordingly."[31] Many observers have wondered if diary writing is, like
that of the more formal memoir, a kind of fictional writing or, at the
least, a form of creative non-fiction. Certainly diaries, if kept, are
essential components of the personal archive; it is also possible to argue
that they could be the backbone of personal and family archives,
providing a kind of meta-narrative linking all other documents,
ephemera, and artifacts.

Whatever diaries might be, they have become popular again. It
seems that nearly everyone at least starts compiling a diary, although
most do not sustain the process (committing to a diary over an extensive
period of time has about the same success rate as dieting and New
Year's resolutions). There is a contemporary revolution in diary writing,
with a great portion of the populace at least having tried to keep up a
diary for some period of time (it is, obviously, not an activity for
everyone). Not too many years ago, anyone needing a good blank book
in which to start or continue a diary had to travel about looking for a
fine stationary store and also had to shell out top dollar for the privilege
of acquiring such a book. For a long time what passed for a book were

those gaudily designed books one used to see in use in elementary or middle school, handed about in those teen or coming of age movies, and often stamped with something like "My Secret Diary." Diaries were portrayed as the place to write down those salacious thoughts about illicit or immoral activities, a kind of protest against parental and other authorities (but, also, I would argue, ones really intended to be read as well). Now, of course, every bookstore chain devotes an entire section to "archival" quality notebooks, beautiful and sleek fountain pens, and books about how to compile a diary (along with family histories, photograph albums, and scrapbooks). There is a public invitation to creating personal archives everywhere one looks, and it is sometimes hard to ascertain whether the vendors are driving and creating a market or whether a market has emerged all on its own.

There is big business, it seems, in the solitary art of writing a diary, and nearly everyone feels, at some point or another, that they must try their hand in writing one. The popularity of diary writing can be seen in the growing presence, since 1995, of online diaries on the Web, with their writers searching for an audience, a connection with others. One scholar studying these new diaries notes, "Sharing one's inner life and one's life story with others is a way of inviting society to bear witness to the discovery of one's historicity, one's position in time, one's progression from earlier versions of oneself to the time of writing."[32] Blogging started in 1999 with the availability of the Blogger Weblog development software, with estimates of two to four million people blogging by the end of 2003.[33] In a sense, blogging eliminates the middle agent, removing the question of whether the diary is intended for personal use or for public consumption by going instantly to a public (one much larger than when occurs when diaries are placed in archives or even when they are published, something usually happening only for the more famous among us or occurring when a diary provides remarkable insight into a momentous historical event). Blogging also indicates that personal archives are becoming more public, as people also put scrapbooks with family photographs and scanned images of memorabilia online for their family and friends, also suggesting the changing notions of privacy in our modern culture. John Seabrook, writing about the growing popularity of genealogy, says, "As the family Web site gradually takes the place of the family Bible as the standard repository of family history, the controlling structure for the family seems to be evolving from a tree into something more like a root system, hairy with adoptive parents, two-mommy families, sperm-bank daddies, and other kinds of family appendages that don't fit onto trunks and branches."[34] All of this, warts and all, is openly displayed on the Web.

While the diary form is easily recognizable, with its dates, places of composition, and paragraph or note form, diaries are also remarkably idiosyncratic, each matching the purpose and personality of its creator. As one consciously thinks about their personal recordkeeping, it is not difficult to imagine a clear or precise role for the diary. In a sense, it is the backbone of a personal archive. It can provide the basic outline of a life and its varied activities, a frame of interpretation about which all other records hang. Interpretation is the key word, of course. Unlike most records, created in an immediate transaction, the diary is often written long after the fact and, even if it is not, the diary entry is a highly personal version of events through one individual's eyes. Most records, the great majority of them, are rarely interpretative at all; rather, they document a simple, straightforward transaction – a purchase, a donation, a transferal of ownership – and, unless deliberately forged or intended to deceive, there is nothing particularly interpretative about such records. Indeed, one could use a diary to comment regularly on the records that follow their life, from the selection from among junk mail that stimulates other activities and generates new records to the mundane but important receipts documenting daily expenditures, such as grocery registers and dinner receipts, reminding us of how we are connected to the previous millennia of recordkeepers.

Reflecting on this business of recording ourselves should cause us to consider the motivations for the creation of many record forms such as diaries discussed most immediately. Sara Paretsky's memoir of how she became a writer and her concerns with the role and prospects for writers in what she sees as an increasingly oppressive America reminds us of such matters. Here is how she describes the life of the writer; "Every writer's difficult journey is a movement from silence to speech. We must be intensely private and interior in order to find a voice and a vision – and we must bring our work to an outside world where the market, or public outrage, or even government censorship can destroy our voice."[35] Anyone who endeavors to write in a diary or to go online with a blog can relate to Paretsky's observation.

There are a number of ways in which the archival impulse manifests itself in Paretsky's memoir about how she learned to write. Paretsky's stressful relationship with her parents comes through in a number of spots in the book, including the recounting of the incident of their purposeful destruction of her youthful manuscripts:

When I was a teenager, both parents wanted me to use my words to make their points – my mother demanding poems describing her entrapment, my father stories proclaiming his unlauded glories. I dutifully created both. But beyond that my writing roused so little interest that my mother told me my father burned all my childhood papers in some housekeeping frenzy or other. I kept hoping she got it wrong. Before they died, I spent hours hunting through their attic for some story, some diary, a remnant to connect me with my past, something that might tell me what dreams I used to have. Nothing comes to light.[36]

Many of us, in far healthier environments, can recall similar events. My grandmother, battling her own demons, destroyed many of my family photographs in an effort to eradicate painful memories and to inflict hurt on others who might have wanted some connection with the family past. I think maybe I became an archivist out of some deep personal resentment about such deliberate affronts to the past and documentary record. It is clear that from such events in her own life that Paretsky becomes a writer and that her background shapes the kind of writing that she does.

At another point Paretsky compares the mass protests of the 1960s and 1970s with the relative apathy of today, attributing the change partly to the kind of digital haze and information glut we are enveloped in:

In the sixties and early seventies, when we encountered this kind of hatred [such as racism], we would take to the streets and organize for change. Today, I see few signs that anyone wants to organize for change. I don't know if people feel so overwhelmed by the war in Iraq, the threat of terrorism, the damage to the environment, the destruction of women's rights, the loss of jobs, the long decline in real wages, along with the gutting of federal anti-poverty programs, that we don't know where or how to start. I don't know if people are in narcissistic cocoons of cell phones and iPods that make us oblivious to the world outside.[37]

This is especially important for Paretsky, evident by the way she historically assesses the challenges for writers to be vocal in an age seeking to silence them: "Silence can come from the market, as it did for Melville. It can come from public hysteria, as it did for Kate Chopin. It can come from the government as outright censorship. Today in America we are finding pressure to silence coming from all three sources."[38] If an author such as Paretsky sees such challenges for a writer, how should archivists see barriers today in their own mission and work? Clearly, the same challenges are pernicious threats to archivists as well. After all, what is the point of trying to preserve any sense of a documentary heritage if it is sanitized before the public can see it and blocked by elaborate ruses of national security threats and intellectual property restrictions that only lawyers can seemingly unravel?

There is, however, always reason to hope. Paretsky, at the conclusion of her book, notes, "When I enter a library, when I enter the world of books, I feel the ghosts of the past on my shoulders, urging me to courage."[39] Many archivists, certainly I do, may feel the same when they enter an archives and see researchers using the materials reposing there. When we read in the manuscripts and other documents left behind by individuals their own courage in speaking out in their families, workplaces, and society, I hope archivists are likewise encouraged to become more effective advocates for a free and open society. An age of silence is not one that will strengthen the archival mission or endorse the work of archivists. It is an era that will lull archivists into believing that they can perform their tasks without worrying about the issues that allow or block access to the records they maintain. And all these issues may be factors partly driving individuals to keep diaries, post blogs, and maintain an enhanced sense of both personal and family papers.

Family Photographs.

Many people may associate family photography as the penultimate expression of building a family archive. More probably has been written on photography than any other aspect of a records generating technology, partly because of the dramatic quality of appearing to capture the reality of the past. We can see our ancestors as they looked a hundred or more years ago, and what is more sobering, we can see what we looked like in our youth or as we started out in marriage. Two scholars writing about the importance of photography in the nineteenth century argue that it "opened up new worlds to nineteenth century viewers, enabling them to visualize – with unprecedented accuracy and ease – themselves, their families, their immediate surroundings, their wider communities and the world beyond their doorstep. And, as never before, photographs made the past a palpable part of the present."[40] Photographs continue to do this. And they represent the most memorable, if not always most informative, aspect of the personal archive. Even photographs generated as part of corporate or government activities often tend to stimulate different reactions from their creators or caretakers than what are associated with other records.

Photographs tend to stir up more reactions than the typical document, doing more than merely holding information: "they also evoke memories, elicit stories, and stimulate ideas. And such associations are more likely to be triggered and shaped by a viewer's own experiences than by a photographer's intent."[41] Another scholar, analyzing the painful photographs of the Holocaust, notes, in a similar fashion, "The photographic representation of the Holocaust does not give a comprehensive account of the historical events which photographic narratives generally lead us to believe; that is not possible. Photographs are fragments. They illustrate stories, they do not tell them. It has been left to curators, film-makers, historians and propagandists to determine how they are interpreted."[42] In other words, photographs can be distorted or used in distorted ways, partly because they have a surreal kind of authority about them. At their best, however, photographs speak to us and tell stories in ways as compelling as any documentary form available to us. And it is the stories emerging from our personal archives that we are often most interested in retrieving (and somehow preserving).

Since the emergence of low-cost photography, heralded by the Kodak Brownie camera, in the late nineteenth-century, individuals and families have merrily clicked away, taking photographs on every topic, event, and activity imaginable. For the first part of photography's history, images were staged and posed. Family photographs were taken in studios with predictable poses and decorated backgrounds, with the family members staring out at the photographer. These photographs remind us about the technologies of photography, that individuals did have to remain motionless for long periods for the images to be captured or that many images were staged. And while we prize these images today as a means of connecting with our past, we also marvel at the limited range of poses and activities our ancestors seemed capable to perform. Traditions of photographing the dead, houses, and landscapes added to the scope of photography's legacy and enrich our sense of what our family history encompasses, but such images also remind us of the limitations of photography's earliest years. All these limitations are minimized by the uncanny ability that photographs provide for us to see almost precisely (almost since clearly photographers play a role in shaping the reality of the image) what our ancestors looked like, in ways far more dramatic than what portrait painters and sculptors were able to accomplish before the advent of photography.

The technology of photography advanced rapidly and with it, as well, did its subject matter. As photography became cheaper, more portable, and more adaptable to a wider range of activities, individuals and families took to photography as a means of documenting all facets of their lives. Photographs of their travels and tourism became a normal personal pastime for the use of the camera. Family events, such as picnics, baptisms, and reunions were all documented in less formal ways than before, although official photographs continued to be produced. Informal images, people reading or talking over dinner, all began to proliferate and fill scrapbooks and document boxes. A fuller sense of the personal archive became possible and evident because of the advent of photography, and it is safe to say that new technical developments, such as Polaroid instant photography and portable digital cameras, have only continued to add to the possibilities of a richer documentary foundation for our lives (although posing new problems in the preservation of such documents). Everyone is now taking photographs. In 2000, a survey of 1000 individuals over fifteen years old found that 9 of 10 use a camera of some sort, 7 of 10 use 35 mm cameras, 31 percent use video cameras, 23 percent use disposable cameras, and 16 percent use digital cameras,[43] with indications that digital cameras will be replacing other camera types within a few years.[44] For most, the personal archive builds about the photographic image, both staged and informal. As Jay Prosser speculates,

> For photographs may be the closest we get to another's autobiography. The photographic collections we leave when we die are approximations of the life story that remains typically unwritten. And because in our life we view them through our eye and our I, photographs that have significance for us are often autobiographical, although often they are those in which this is not conscious to us. Photography's approximation of autobiography remains true even with the appearance of home movies and video cameras.[45]

Personal archives also seem to be a kind of autobiographical assemblage as well.

These kinds of concerns might play out in personal archives as well, where photographs become house decorations to remind us of our past and are interpreted by their owners in ways that might seem to be out of bounds in terms of any accurate representations. As you walk into my house, you quickly encounter a wall of individual and family photographs, documenting four generations, a reminder for us that we have not just generated out of the vapor but that we carry forward both the DNA and hopes and aspirations of others who have come before. Photographs can be wisely used as a form of personal recordkeeping and identity, and most of us hang onto old licenses and passports because of the images reminding us how different we looked then than we do today. These displayed items convey stories and connect us to both place and time (and sometimes people have even displayed older images of individuals and families, purchased at flea markets and antique shops, representing them as ancestors). Archival records, real and imagined, can be powerful.

The possibilities of these image technologies have expanded rapidly in the last couple of generations, both with the advent of portable and affordable movie cameras and more recently with the emergence of digital cameras enabling us to produce both moving and still imagery easily housed in our computers and designed for use on our personal Web sites. There is a touching scene in the hilarious movie *National Lampoon's Christmas Vacation* where the main character, portrayed by Chevy Chase, is trapped in the attic and discovers old film footage of Christmases from the 1950s. It is a scene we all can identify with, as Chase sits enraptured by the retelling of his family's interest in the holiday and we learn that his family was just as dysfunctional then as it is now. Home movies, now digitally re-mastered, are a vital part of our personal archive, although the new technologies, as will be discussed in a later chapter, also remind us how vulnerable our archives can be to the passage of time and the shifts in recording technologies. Whether moving or still, these images are all part of a kind of personal scrapbook that is the personal archive.

Conclusion: Symbolic Archives.

Another essential part of any personal archives is the array of certificates that one gathers over the years. We accumulate diplomas, award citations, and certificates indicating the completion of a special course or program through the years, with the largest clumps coming in our earliest and latter years. Our parents dutifully keep those certificates we receive in grade, middle, and high school, and we generally start holding onto them when we enter our college years. Most of these documents are intended to be framed and displayed, much like what we do with personal and family photographs. These documents are markers of personal progress, expertise, and authority, and they are most often displayed in public spaces such as our offices. Many individuals, especially academics and professionals, build their identity around these records, displaying them to both reassure and impress their students and clients who are paying for access to their knowledge. They are as much a part of our public lives in government, corporate, and other institutional venues as they are a component of our personal archives.

These kinds of records are interesting parts of our personal archives since they exude symbolic value and provide a connection between modern records and their ancient antecedents. Documents such as modern diplomas have little, if any, legal value as they are issued merely for decorative purposes, mimicking older parchments and more ancient forms of records. They speak eloquently for the symbolic role of archives, a role whereby the documents take on more of a cultural rather evidential purpose. For example, one could argue that the original manuscripts of the Declaration of Independence, Constitution, and Bill of Rights have taken on more of a symbolic function, even though they are completely genuine records. However, the massive amounts of other documentation supporting the independence and creation of a federal government, along with the numerous copies of the texts of these documents, have more than made the original versions superfluous except as societal icons and curiosities. Likewise, the handsome high school or college diploma is only a shadow of the official school files documenting our education, but our versions of the diplomas possess symbolic and even sentimental value for us. They provide a source of identity, prestige, and status, especially as they are nicely framed and displayed around us, usually hung in the place where they will be best seen. These documents manifest much of the overall symbolic value of our personal archives, including those parts of the archives that we carry around with us.

The legal aspects of these documents are something worth pausing about, and it is something that many people probably make more assumptions about than actually reflect any real knowledge. Archivists and librarians have always been concerned about the laws affecting their work and that of their patrons. Some issues, such as intellectual property, have been plagued by conflicting and confusing advice or, even worse, advice that suggests that one will know that they have stepped over some boundary when they are sued or threatened with litigation. It's a crazy world out there. Bryan M. Carson, in his primer on legal issues in libraries and archives, reviews contracts, copyright and patent and trademark law, fair use and intellectual property, copyright issues in the classroom, search warrants and library records, Internet use policies, and how to read a legal citation. Drawing on trade secret laws, Carson believes that these laws can be used by librarians and archivists "to help protect the confidentiality of our patron interactions."[46] Carson writes, "I believe that trade secret law gives library [and archives] patrons an additional protection beyond that of professional ethics and state nondisclosure laws. My theory is that, under trade secret law, courts could enjoin libraries [and archives] from revealing patron information."[47] Carson believes that "librarians [and archivists] adopt the standard that psychologists, psychiatrists, clergy, and other professionals use. What a patient says to a counselor is confidential, but if the person is a danger to himself or others, the counselor has a duty to report this situation to the potential victim and to the appropriate authorities."[48] Nowhere in such discussions will anyone find anything related to the legal value of those old certificates and diplomas or, for that matter, the importance of the symbolic value of older documents.

Certificates and diplomas often wind up in scrapbooks, another essential aspect of our personal archives. Another modern industry relating to personal archives has been the scrapbooking fad, now a two billion dollar a year industry[49] and with reports of four million people creating scrapbooks in one recent year, partially enabled by software that enables digital scrapbooks to be created as well.[50] Scrapbooks are what many people think of if you ask them about their family archives, and, in many ways, they are another form of symbolic personal archives, with their artificial arrangements seeking to create order and meaning. Assembling a scrapbook is the amateur's approach to the classification and ordering of information done by professionals such as librarians and archivists, providing an ordering and meaning assigning to what their families have been up to through the decades. Individuals compiling these books, engage in both selecting documents and enhancing the informational value of these documents, as they often sort through boxes and file cabinets jammed with records, ephemera, and artifacts and give shape to their own and family's history by arranging the materials in volumes with narratives and interpretations. Menus, postcards, ticket stubs, letters, receipts, and other items serving as mementos of favorite or benchmark events make their way into scrapbooks. Individuals carefully construct a narrative of their past, designing scrapbooks as deliberatively as others write diaries.

Although archivists and conservators often lament the possibility of facing another scrapbook, with yellowing, brittle pages and acidic materials chewing up the original documents, programs, and souvenirs, the exercise of compiling these volumes is as natural a human impulse as eating and sleeping. One scholar suggests that individuals create personal scrapbooks to cope with the deluge of print, and "each clipping scrapbook maker ... created a private and idiosyncratic catalog, a reflection of personal identity made from mass-produced and distributed publication as much like Netscape Bookmarks or Microsoft Favorites as a library's vertical files."[51] And even the scrapbook has gone online as well. A company, TravelPost.com, "launched a free service designed to let people store and share personal travel experiences online, using tools for creating illustrated diaries and itinerary maps. Users are encouraged to rate cities, hotels and restaurants they have visited, information that becomes searchable by other users to help them plan vacations and business trips."[52] While it is debatable from an archival perspective that scrapbooking should be encouraged and continued, even with the more careful use of archival materials, it is evident that scrapbooks will always be an important part of the personal archive. If nothing else, we must recognize that they are as ubiquitous as government records.

It is in the often mundane, but sometimes highly charged, exercise of compiling scrapbooks and framing photographs and certificates for display that we see the quintessential symbolic process of building and maintaining personal archives. In the deliberate preserving, ordering, and displaying of documentary scraps we can begin to understand how people fundamentally understand something of the significance of records in their lives, workplaces, and society. And it is an understanding archivists and records managers should use to advocate for their mission, and something they should continue to strive to comprehend in a personal way.

Chapter Six

Traces of Ourselves: More Thoughts on Personal Recordkeeping and the Roles of Archivists

Introduction: Personal Archives and Our Place in the World.

Most of us have become sensitized to the significant symbolic roles archives, libraries, and museums play in modern society because of the devastation of so many of these kinds of cultural repositories as a result of civil war, international warfare, genocide, and natural destruction or neglect. The deliberate destruction of these repositories as a means of obliterating a people's heritage and memory especially speak to why records, even those seemingly far less important personal papers, can transmit such critical values across generations. A loss of documents translates into a loss of memory and identity, the equivalent of the onslaught of a kind of societal Alzheimer's. We can make the same assertion with our personal records. Letters, checks, receipts, deeds, birth certificates, diaries, scrapbooks, and other documents all help secure our place in the world. Without the evidence and information found in these records, we lose our moorings, self-assurance, and connection to society and other people.

We can see this role for records nearly anywhere we work, visit, or reside. Many management experts have been attracted to the concept of knowledge management as a means of tapping into the collective insights of an organization's staff. There are many conflicting ideas about the nature of such knowledge, but there seems to be essential agreement that its core is the information found in people's minds and based on their experiences rather than in an organization's records and information systems. This seems a bit short sighted, and it probably reflects more of the general stereotypes associated with redundant and inefficient bureaucracy, often symbolically represented by stacks of paper documents and forms in offices and organizational storage areas. One merely has to visualize the countless advertisements in magazines or scenes in movies playing on how most people react to stacks of paper and clutter.

In those stacks are lots of valuable and even essential evidence and information that any organization or individual needs to tap into from time to time. Even the way in which we stack and organize the documents tells us something useful. Personal archives can be viewed as crucial aspects of the knowledge of ourselves, our family, and our times that we need, as much as the licenses and memberships that enable us to function on a daily basis. There is some security in being surrounded by evidence of our lives and families. And there ought to be a feeling of insecurity when we lack such requisite knowledge, equivalent to being illiterate. When we lack the right records, and hence the necessary information and knowledge, we also lack the ability to read the world and to cope on a daily basis.

These records, even if inspiring negative images of bureaucracy and institutional inefficiency, still provide a kind of security, similar to the comfort we feel when surrounded by familiar books and other furnishings. Sven Birkerts suggests that the "decision to re-read a book is not usually an amnesiac's search for clues about what is lost. More likely it is prompted by some kind of flaring up of memory, by a longing to be immersed again in a feeling that we know as important, gratifying, or somehow defining. We return, often, out of curiosity, no question, but also in the hope that something will be given back to us, or reawakened."[1] This is a description that is apt for us when we revisit our personal or the family archives. These recurring visits are usually motivated by some need for evidence about our past or by the sense that we need to reconnect with our own heritage in order to make sense of our place in the universe.

Sometimes we can discern deeper meanings in the most mundane of our actions involving records. The act of stacking documents, often done as a means of organizing our work, also suggests other aspects of why we manage personal records. There is the tactile nature of the document, suggesting that records are something not only to be prized for their information and evidence but for their feel and texture. Some scholars have tried to expand the notion of what we mean by "archival" to include both the text and the artifact, engaging in debates over how records should be preserved. Historical bibliographer G. Thomas Tanselle, who has cogently argued for the importance of the material book in studying book and publishing history, argues that "treating archives merely as collections of words and numbers shows no awareness of the fact that every physical characteristic of every document is the trace left by a human action or a natural event in the past. The artifact has its own story to tell, one that can never be separated from what the words say or what the text as a whole signifies in social terms."[2] Tanselle's concern may be intensified because we now take so much for granted when we can easily copy documents quickly and inexpensively.

When we look at an older, original document of a century or two ago, we tend to become fascinated with how the document looks and why it feels the way it does, especially now since so many of the documents we generate digitally have no feel at all but only a look as we open them up on the computer screen (although clearly our sensibilities are changing as we become more accustomed to the virtual world). It may be a safe prediction that individuals will hang onto older personal and family documents, or turn to collecting other interesting records, as we become more of a digital society. Even as we contend with preserving personal archives that are increasingly in digital form, from photographs to our correspondence, we will continue to devote resources and efforts to preserving documents in traditional formats.

Admittedly, some of our fascination with old manuscripts, photographs, and other original documents derives from the more romanticized aspects of creating and interacting with such materials. In Ross King's fabulous novel about booksellers and antiquarians in seventeenth century London, the author provides an interesting description that suggests why we might be so intrigued by older records. King has Isaac Inchbold, the London bookseller and antiquarian who is the main protagonist in the novel, remembering his father, who was a scrivener (copyist) in this way: "I can still picture him hunched as if in supplication over his battered scritoire, his hair hanging over his face, a turkey quill pivoting back and forth in his slender hand." Inchbold continues to reminiscence: "my poor father must have been writing passages of the dullest possible sort. Letters patent, court rolls, parish registers…" "The scrivener led a life of rare drudgery," he reflects. "Only when I was older did I realize that my father's back was permanently bowed from hunching over his desk and his eyes dim because he was too poor, much of the time, to afford a candle. His labors in the tiny garret room that served as his study were relieved once a week when he visited the shops of ink-makers and parchment-sellers, or when he delivered the fruits of his efforts to the Inns of Chancery in whose pay he was so precariously kept."[3] While this is a literary fabrication, King captures something of the work of the professional scribe, and, as well, something about the magic and hard work that went into the production of original, handwritten documents that still continues to haunt and fascinate us.

King's mythical bookseller connecting to his father's craft also suggests something of another reason why some, today, want to maintain something of their family's archives, rather than dumping them into the trash, scattering them among other family members, or donating them to an institution. We often wish to reach back and touch the artifacts created by our ancestors as a way of reconnecting to the past and learning about where we have come from; it is similar to the same motivations driving us to read history, visit museums and historical sites, and collect documents and antiques. And it is one reason why we find so many powerful fictional accounts depicting individuals pawing their way through family documents.

An interesting novel concerning records is one by South African Shaun Johnson, building around a large box of records of the main character's father who committed suicide. Suggesting that the box is like an "archaeological anthropological site,"[4] the son, reading through the box, reflects:

By the time I was able to conjure the voices from the ward [where his father spent part of his last days] and the kitchen, I had already spent months on my project. I had read the letters from dozens of thick paper-clipped bundles, looked at hundreds of photographic slides neatly ordered in old-fashioned plastic circular canisters. I had pored over scrapbooks, yellowed newspaper cuttings, programs and souvenirs of theatre shows long forgotten, speeches, stories written in another age. I had put together scraps of diaries, read school reports, seen medical accounts, old bills; I had fingered the faded insignias of rank from wartime. I had listened to tape recordings, hours upon hours of them, from an Africa and Europe of earlier generations; heard the scratchy radio announcements of the times, the voices of politicians long dead. I had touched the locks of hair even, found amateur poems shyly written then hidden so long ago. I had immersed myself in this private cornucopia, an extraordinary archive of an ordinary family which happened to be my own; it had unlocked in me memories I did not know I had."[5]

Later in the novel, the protagonist discovers that there are documentary gaps in the box. "My mother had hoarded plenty of documents from the Witbank years, but there were unsatisfactory, tantalizing gaps along the way, suggesting to me that in my father's troubled state he must have begun not to write things down so diligently, so there was less for her to squirrel away. In Witbank the papers became more wayward: swathes of rich detail interspersed with silences, holes."[6] These gaps send the narrator back into the national archives looking for more evidence. While sometimes archivists scour through fiction looking for references to their profession, and often becoming irritated at the ways in which they are depicted, novels and mysteries often provide perceptive glimpses into the human tendencies to create and preserve documents.

Truth can be so much stranger than fiction, however. Simon Worrall, in his analysis of a literary forgery, describes the efforts of manuscripts dealer Todd Axelrod to broaden the autograph market by opening stores in up-scale malls: "Axelrod's target customer was a new, eighties breed of collector who did not want [to] keep their purchases tucked away in vaults or safety deposit boxes, as old-style collectors had. They wanted to see their money hanging on the wall."[7] While the financial aspect of this assessment reveals a certain cynicism, the desire to display openly the purchased documents nevertheless captures something about our interest in immersing in and connecting with the past rather than burying it into a repository. One might ask someone whether the photographs on the wall are all of their ancestors or merely a collection of older images, but it is doubtful that we would question why these items are displayed publicly. Indeed, we are not only immersed in a documentary universe, we are also surrounded by the artifacts used in producing and storing these documents. These records represent a world we can see, touch, and, with a little imagination, experience.

The Material Culture of Personal Archives.

The next time you are walking on a busy street or traveling through an airport, observe what people are carrying. Nearly everyone is laden with a briefcase, a large purse, or a backpack of some variety. Some of these devices indicate a businessman or woman or a student, but they have become so ubiquitous that it is difficult to assign such identities so easily. What kinds of things are in these various contraptions? Some are filled with their business documents and readings, especially since so many carry laptops now in these cases so that they can fire up and work anywhere (in the year 2003, laptops began outselling personal computers).[8] But they also carry many parts of personal archives. Photographs, credit cards, membership identifications, drivers' licenses, and other items either include or represent the trail of documentary evidence that follows us everywhere we go, work, and play. With the laptops and digital cameras, most of us seem quite able to take nearly our entire personal archives with us wherever we travel, provided we have taken the time to scan in the older personal and family papers and photographs. One will also find in these cases personal and travel diaries, usually attractively bound in leather and specifically designed for such specialized jottings and now easily found for sale in major bookstores and office supply centers.

Some of these carrying devices are ancient in tradition, but some, such as the briefcase, are products of our being part of the modern world, reflecting the business of the Industrial then the Information Ages. In our so-called Digital era, we are connected 24/7 to our work but also to our family, church, and recreation – all indicating that we must be able to transport considerable amounts of present and past information in order to function. Much of our community is cast in virtual terms. I sit in my hotel room while away on business and casually converse with my family and my colleagues spread across the world. The ease of communication is unparalleled in the early twenty-first century, providing we have the financial resources and educational background to join into the information ranks. While I attended a conference in Wellington, New Zealand, I stayed in touch with family, friends, and colleagues with no difficulty, and I returned from the expedition to the other side of the earth without missing a beat in my professional or personal activities.

A briefcase loaded with my laptop, passport, notepaper, and movie DVD's for relaxing is a typical piece of baggage that we carry with us, but it is also an extension of our personal archives. I can bring up family pictures and other personal documents from my laptop or navigate into password protected Web sites to examine private information. We can now transport more of our personal archives with us wherever we go and get into it whenever we want. As I sat on the airplane I observed other passengers watching movies they had transported with them, creating documents, writing emails they would send later, and listening to their music catalogues carried on their portable music players or downloaded into their laptops; on one of my recent international junkets, I also read about how the airline industry is working to develop the means for passengers to stay connected to the Web and their electronic mail. Of course, I was engaged in all the same activities, but in addition I was reading some archival records I had copied onto my laptop for a conference paper I was preparing for the next month.

Some observers of the increasing power and portability of the digital devices have pontificated about new kinds of power they bring with them. David Weinberger, for example, suggests that the traditional emphasis on order may be becoming irrelevant in our digital era. Reviewing our historical preoccupation with order, especially emphasizing how professionals such as natural history scientists and librarians have developed cataloguing and classification systems, Weinberger seeks to demonstrate that now we can achieve new means of using information and evidence from the artifacts around us. Weinberger wants to demonstrate the advantages of a new order that moves us from a preoccupation with the physical manifestations of knowledge to the digital aspects whereby we can shape it in unlimited ways to our advantage. He writes, "The gap between how we access information and how the computer accesses it is at the heart of the revolution in knowledge. Because computers store information in ways that have nothing to do with how we want it presented to us, we are freed from having to organize the original information the way we eventually want to get at it."[9] This new order replaces older systems such as library catalogs, and it transforms the notice of expertise in such ordering of information. Weinberger suggests that professionals, such as librarians and editors of reference works, may be sounding "hysterical" because the "change they're facing from the miscellaneous is deep and real. Authorities have long filtered and organized information for us, protecting us from what isn't worth our time and helping us find what we need to give our beliefs a sturdy foundation. But with the miscellaneous, it's all available to us, unfiltered."[10]

Such commentators imply that the new information technologies can transform average citizens into assuming roles only in the past reserved for specially trained professionals, a prospect that has some worrying about the loss of older expertise. Andrew Keen opposes the elevation of the amateur, fearing that the "voice of a high school kid has equal value to that of an Ivy League scholar or a trained professional,"[11] searching instead for a way that will protect the needed expertise while allowing us to utilize the full power of technology. One way to do this may be getting these established experts to redirect their attention to working with the public in ways that empower more directly the public. Archivists may not be assuming the role of taking archives from individuals and families, but in working with these people archivists can assist them to manage more effectively these documents.

Not all of the material effects of our personal recordkeeping can be moved about so easily. The briefcase is part of the material evidence of our personal archive, just as will be the laptop someday when it becomes obsolete. We can trace the development of personal archives (and all archives, public and organizational, for that matter) by the evolution of furniture, architecture, and other material remains of our universe, and obviously much of this won't be able to be moved as we want, at least in any convenient fashion. We can find in early domiciles chests used to store not only blankets, extra clothing, and utensils, but we can see the outlines of personal archives as these chests were often designed for the storage of important documents and books, such as Bibles with their family genealogies inscribed in them. By our standards today, these chests appear small, indicating that the quantity of personal documents was much less than what we have to contend with in our modern society; it may be that we can store immense amounts of information in smaller spaces in digital form, but there are many documents that we will choose not to scan and discard and we still possess more paper records than any other generation since paper was first introduced. In fact, we can buy a greater variety of paper now than ever before as traditional diary writing, calligraphy, and scrapbooking have grown in popularity.

Much of what was created in the past few hundred years regarding records and recordkeeping were aimed at easing our burden in both generating and maintaining paper documents. Desks evolved, for example, through the centuries to include more and more spaces for the storage of documents. The eighteenth century divine Jonathan Edwards, discussed earlier in this book, morphed a standard writing desk into one with special compartments for his notes, sermon and book manuscripts, and personal papers. In the late nineteenth century the Wooton company designed elaborate desks with multiple pigeonholes and other spaces for storing documents, hailed as a marvel of modern efficiency and now prized as antiques. Mission furniture, emphasizing simplicity of lines, often included desks with drawers, bookshelves, and ergonomically sophisticated designs that enabled office workers and those outfitting home libraries to utilize new technologies such as typewriters and to store the byproducts of their modern efficiency. Specialized forms of furniture emerged as well, including at the end of the nineteenth century the vertical file cabinet, a furniture form that has continued to be a central fixture of home and organizational offices for more than a century despite the ongoing promises of paperless offices.

Home designs evolved to feature libraries and offices as central points of the private life, often including built-in shelves and cabinets for the storage of documents and other personal artifacts. Today, we have specialized stores and mail order companies focused on the creation and maintenance of writing, archival, and library supplies and storage, making it easier than ever to support the notion of a personal archives and attesting to the viability of this feature of our daily lives. Nearly all of these companies are merely building on previous generations' attitudes about the production of documents.

Much of our personal space is occupied by older devices, from furniture to built-in shelving and filing cabinets, reflecting very traditional document systems. We reside in a world where we are bombarded by advertisements suggesting that most of this is obsolete or that it should be only of interest to us if we are engaged by the use of antiques and more comfortable with obsolete technologies (and I write this on a laptop on a hundred year old desk where sits a fountain pen and an old letter sorter). The maintenance of personal archives will be contested in this environment, raising many of the same issues archivists and records managers face in striving to administer both paper and digital systems in what seems to be a transitional era in terms of documentary formats. How we engage such challenges and incongruities with our personal and family records ought to make us better in how we explain, engage with, and resolve such situations in our employing organizations.

Forces Opposing Personal Archives.

There is evidence of personal archives extending all the way back to the ancient world, but it is in the past century or so that we have seen the proliferation of the interest in and existence of such archives. In Colonial America and into the nineteenth century, individuals and families with vast real estate holdings and financial empires generated and maintained sizeable family archives. In the 1990s, for example, I examined the archives of Helen Clay Frick's estate (Clayton) in Pittsburgh and discovered that the Fricks seemed to have kept nearly every document pertaining to the estate and its operation, their business dealings, their art collecting, and other social and political ventures over more than a century. This is not unusual for families of such wealth and social prestige, but individuals and families operating at much lower socio-economic levels have tended to accumulate fewer records (although they have not necessarily been less interested in caring for their personal archives). Propelling enthusiasm for maintaining such personal records has often been the threats, real and imagined, posed by a variety of social, economic, and technological forces.

We have no lack of pundits who claim that we are immersed in an unprecedented "information" age, pointing to the variety of information professions, computer networks, and access to immense amounts of information best typified by the existence of the World Wide Web. Indeed, we have been the beneficiaries of a succession of information systems over more than a century, including the telephone, wireless technologies, and the Internet. These and other technologies have both given us greater access to information and threatened our ability to manage evidence we want to archive (although many of the later devices also enable us to capture more evidence than ever before). While there is no precise information about the impact of the telephone on personal letter writing, it is logical to assume that a lot of people who previously wrote letters to friends and relatives started to call them instead. This is a reliable conclusion if only because the telephone, originally thought to be financially viable for business, became an immense commercial success because of the rapid adoption by individuals for social purposes. Individuals were spending time talking with each other on the telephone that they might otherwise had spent in writing letters, and the result was a reduction in the documents that could go into personal archives (although personalized telephone directories and logbooks began to be included in these archives). The addition of the cell phone, an instrument that people cannot seem to be away from even when they are with friends or in places where it is socially unacceptable to use them, such as movie theaters and church services, seems only to have accelerated the decline of interest in traditional social correspondence. One wistfully longs for the declining art of polite correspondence when observing group after group of people wandering through malls and parks and chattering, not to each other but to unseen friends and acquaintances. The privacy of letter writing seems to have been lost as everyone publicly airs out his or her most personal thoughts for the world to hear and wonder about.

Although many scholars and other researchers are assessing the implications of the various information technologies on society, there have been few efforts to consider just what they have done to the creation and maintenance of records. Rich Ling, in an interesting analysis of the impact of the cell phone on society, considers what this device has meant for social interactions, the creating of new networks, formal meetings, and the notion of safety and security. Ling describes how the cell phone has outstripped conventional rules and collapsed traditional notions of time, arguing that the "mobile phone's appearance in society has resulted in turbulence."[12] Still, there is no consideration of the impact of the cell phone on personal (or organizational) recordkeeping, even as certain features of the phone's use ("texting") combines speaking and writing.

It is also difficult, at this point, to know just what the impact of the Internet has been on the sense of the personal archive. As I have discussed in this book, the Internet has provided a new space for mounting or displaying personal archives, such as blogging and personal photograph galleries, but there has been enough debate about the preservation of digital records that no one should view the newly emerging digital personal archives with unbridled confidence. Electronic mail has proved to be a particularly testy challenge, as it generates great gobs of documents that test maintenance and control systems, pose new problems of security, and, like the telephone, has probably lessened the reliance on the traditional letter (see the next chapter). A child writing from college is now likely to ask for money by dispatching quickly an email, perhaps with digital images attached, a scan of a professor's positive comments on an essay, and other documents. Saving these kinds of records suggests both greater problems and more imagination. No longer can we casually jam stuff into a box in the closet, planning to look at and assess the records at a later time. Now we must more consciously plan out what our personal archives will look like and the functions it will serve, understanding that it will consist of paper records, printed ephemera, photographs, memorabilia, and digital materials.

Despite the increasing dependence on digital communication and the sense that we are both comfortable and take for granted such systems, we must acknowledge that we are still in a transitional era. There is little question that the nature of the records surrounding us is changing. In early 2005, an article described how the shift from paper to electronic airline tickets had run its full course, reporting that now "paper airline tickets are quaint but occasionally annoying reminders of a time when computers didn't control all aspects of travel. Airlines still issue paper tickets in some circumstances, but most travelers don't want them - though there are holdouts who prefer the security and comfort of paper."[13] At nearly the same time, another report surfaced suggesting that the next generation will be handling it's checking and most of its financial transactions "almost entirely by debit card, credit card and computer." As the report continues,

> Checks are still used more often than either credit or debit cards, so it is too soon to write their obituary. But the declines reported recently by big banks - as much as 10 percent from a year ago - are so steep that checks over the next two decades are likely to become as prevalent as electric typewriters.

> The trend toward electronic payments illustrates that consumers who were once skittish about managing their finances online are now more comfortable with the new technology. Retailers have been encouraging customers to use credit and debit cards because the fraud rates are lower and the store is paid faster.[14]

This is happening with every kind of record. It is surprising, although it still occasionally happens when you buy something in a shop, to witness the clerk write out a receipt in longhand, and give a copy to you. Sometimes, I have found myself holding onto an antiquated receipt form just because it is such a throwback to how documents were created a generation or two ago. And I realize that much of what used to make up the personal archive won't be available in the future, at least in the same way. Will the personal archive be a paperless repository?

It is likely that the increasing use of digital formats will enhance interest in the preservation of personal archives and that this will strengthen the public's awareness of the importance of archives, records, and information management. For example, as digital photography has captured the public's interest, now constituting a billion dollar a year industry, with its ease of making and reproducing images, other problems have emerged. One aspect that has been debated concerns the longevity of images printed on specialty photo paper marketed by retailers like Staples and Eastman Kodak. A testing laboratory hired by printer manufacturers concluded that photographs printed in this way fade quickly because of exposure to ozone pollution. As one reporter described the problem, "From a consumers' point of view, digital photo fading shouldn't be a big problem - provided the consumer kept a digital copy of the picture on a CD or online photo-storage site. But with software standards, Web sites and storage devices constantly changing, a print on paper may be the best way to assure that your great-grandchildren see what their ancestors looked like." The reporter indicated that archivists suggest "subzero refrigeration of prints," storage in albums or shoeboxes, anywhere where the images are protected from "light, pollution, smoke and moisture."[15] The point may be as those home photographs in digital form begin to disappear that the public will ask more questions and demand more answers about our documentary heritage than it has ever before. Archivists and records managers need to be prepared to supply the answers, and they need to be prepared to deal with how such questions may prompt new discussions about the administration of corporate and government records and information systems as well.

Will the personal archive eventually go paperless? Earlier in this book, I noted how certain kinds of personal documents were disappearing, at least in their longstanding paper form. Paper airline receipts that once helped to document our vacations and business trips are rapidly disappearing. The Christmas 2002 issue of *The Economist* included a revisionist essay on the promises of the paperless office, "In Praise of Clutter." The essay mostly draws on the Abigail Sellen and Richard Harper book, *The Myth of the Paperless Office*, published earlier that year by MIT Press. The essay provides an interesting commentary on the dynamics of paper in the office: "The more digital information sped around the world, the more people wanted to print it out."[16] Moreover, "People spread stuff over their desks not because they are too lazy to file it, but because the paper serves as a physical representation of what is going on in their heads..."[17] Increasing attention to the resurgence of paper documents, not as some bureaucratic obstacle but as a representation of legitimate work practices, should be of interest to archivists and records managers, as well as all individuals who are interested in the maintenance of their own personal archives. Many individuals will print out their digital files and store them as paper copies, partly because they like the sense of being surrounded by the markers of their life's activities. Walking about in one's own archives is like walking through a stately cemetery, observing the names, dates, epitaphs, flowers, and other objects left behind but also clearly speaking to the present. It marks our place in the universe.

However, there are other countervailing forces suggesting that if we are ever to be truly paperless, it is a long way off in the future. Fax machines, for example, continue to churn out paper documents. As one journalist reported in early 2005, "In an office world that has gone largely digital, hand-held and wireless, the fax machine is ancient technology that just won't go away." This relates to our home offices as well. The reporter continued, "Some 1.5 million fax machines were sold in the United States last year for use at both businesses and homes, according to the Consumer Electronics Association, based in Arlington, Va. Manufacturers estimate that they sold 500,000 more machines that combined a fax function with other functions, like copying and scanning." The fax provides certain advantages over digital documents, such as "reproducing signatures on documents like contracts, business proposals and medical prescriptions," providing additional personal security against the ever-present computer hacker.[18] And, so, it is likely that our personal archives will contain at least a few faxes; in fact, each of us should save some examples of received faxes just to document this technology and its role in our lives. It is in all of our personal archives that a true memory of society begins to form and take shape. We all share some archival responsibilities, as I suggest here.

Reality, Theory and the Power of Personal Archives.

Scholars, primarily from literary and historical studies, have devoted considerable attention to comprehending just what a document means, often probing into what we can easily term personal archives. One literary scholar, for example, candidly argued, in an analysis of Emily Dickinson's manuscripts, that "observers may see the same papers and sites as the Dickinson family, but we do not see them from the same place in time. Contemporary readers come from a point in literary history that is different and distant from the point at which these documents emerged."[19] This scholar continues,

> Being aware that reading a manuscript at the beginning of the twenty-first century may not be the same as reading it in the nineteenth century is an important means to descriptive accuracy as well as a moral and intellectual exercise: it reminds us of the difference – the interesting difference – of the historical (for surely one of the fascinations of older literature of any kind is precisely its difference from our own). Emily Dickinson's autograph lyrics continue to speak powerfully to the present, but they travel immense distances from a foreign country called the past, and we would do well to accept that some of their accents may be alien from our own.[20]

We learn that there is an immense difference in reading the manuscript versus the printed poems, with considerable meaning possibly lost in the print version as "line arrangements, the shapes of words and letters, and the particular angles of dashes are all potentially integral to any given poem's meaning, making a graphic contribution to its contents."[21] Dickinson's personal archive is left behind because it is her literary legacy, but the fact that she never left explicit instructions about how the poems were to be set in print form makes the manuscripts both exasperating and enchanting for all interested in her writing.

What such studies are reflecting is what is usually termed the "linguistic turn," whereupon different disciplines have rediscovered both the primacy of text and language, as well as how difficult it is for scholars to discern just what a particular document really says. Historian Joyce Appleby argues that,

> For postmodernists the most important social element is obviously language. It is through language that everything from our dreams to our career plans acquires meaning. Even the visual field in front of us relies on language for meaning. When we describe what lies in front of us, we marshal the full array of interpretive tools of our society. In this sense postmodernists have applied the word 'textuality' to everything that exists in our world. Everything is a text because everything has been socially interpreted.[22]

Appleby is, however, one historian who is concerned about what this emphasis on text has meant in terms of our sense of being able to understand what happened in the past. She perceives that

> Textuality for the postmodernists explains far more than written documents. It is a concept that highlights the social medium through which all experience comes to us. Gone is the raw encounter with reality celebrated by the Enlightenment and in comes the insidious instruction of society, interpreting the world before we discover it on our own, naming for us its elements while categorizing and codifying, sanctifying and profaning, organizing and energizing.[23]

Postmodernists play with the notion of text so much so as to give up its having any meaning or veracity whatsoever: "The claim is," argues Appleby, "because I cannot control all of the meanings that readers will find in my text, my acted-on intention to write this text is not a causal force."[24] Even though most historians have tended to ignore philosophical musings on history, keeping focused on sources and evidence, most "historians now admit that the remains of the past are fragmentary," suggests another historian, "that our knowledge of it is partial, that *all* written records (including documents) are conveyed in language."[25] While some discount the primacy of the traditional document, the elements that lead them to question these records also leads to new approaches to analyzing them and a greater appreciation of the complexity of the breadth and depth of the documentary heritage left behind.

While scholars muse over the ultimate meaning and veracity of any text, people everywhere gather, preserve, display, and use documents generated as part of their lives and of the lives of their family members before them. While certainly one must pause and meditate about the meaning of a document, there is little debate of the value of creating such personal archives. The ultimate postmodern spokesperson, Jacques Derrida, revealed something of both his musing over the meaning of text or words and the value of what they are contained in a recent collection of his essays. Derrida did not think that text is disappearing but that it was reaching for something new. We can see the end of the book as either its destruction or as its achievement; Derrida believes that "we know that the book isn't simply going to disappear," but "we should analyze the retention of the model of the book, the *liber* – of the unit and the distribution of discourse, even the body, the hands and eyes that it continues to orient, the rhythm it prescribes, its relationship to the title, its nodes of legitimation, even when the material support has disappeared..."[26] It is likely that few playing with their own family archives, except the rare scholar who might be involved in such an activity, are mulling over such literary or historical theories.

Derrida sees nothing necessarily of intrinsic value in the meaning of any storage or communication medium. For him, paper can be valuable or it can be trash. Derrida argues that there is a wide range of meaning of the value of paper:

> On the one hand there is the condition of a priceless archive, the body of an irreplaceable copy, a letter or painting, an absolutely unique event (whose rarity can give rise to surplus value and speculation). But there is also paper as support or backing for printing, for technical reprinting, and for reproducibility, replacement, prosthesis, and hence also for the industrial commodity, use, and exchange value – and finally for the throwaway object, the abjection of litter.[27]

Derrida contends that the culture of paper remains, evident when we notice that online journals are usually seeking print norms (constituting preservation, formatting, selection, and even printing out).[28] And we can also discern a paper culture in the existence of personal archives, the collecting of printed ephemera and books, and in a variety of other activities dispersed through our early twentieth-first century culture.

And we can look beyond paper. Derrida admitted that some like the computer as an artifact. When asked if we will love CD-ROMS or floppy disks like books, yes, Derrida argues: "Probably. Some particular draft that was prepared or printed on some particular software, or some particular disk that stores a stage of a work in progress – these are the kinds of things that will be fetishized in the future." Derrida continues, "Even the computer belonging to the 'great writer' or 'great thinker' will be fetishized..."[29] Some of us already know people who continue to own obsolete computers because of events and activities that they associate with them.

Creating and maintaining personal archives are activities undertaken to assist us to place ourselves in societal context, a process that gives us meaning. It is interesting that both technologists studying the impact of the computer on society and individuals and literary and other scholars investigating the meaning of texts have focused considerable attention on context. William J. Mitchell, in the fourth of a series of volumes on our digital culture, suggests that the "meaning of a message depends not only upon the information that it contains, but also upon the sort of local ignorance or uncertainty that it reduces – in other words, upon what the message's recipients require information *about* ... Information becomes useful and messages serve their purposes in particular places at particular times. Context matters."[30] Mitchell believes that the continuing emergence of networks result in a different kind of context, one that keeps shifting: "Digital networks now form a vast, growing, indispensable backdrop to our everyday lives." "As a result," Mitchell writes, "the physical settings that we inhabit are increasingly populated with spoken words, musical performances, texts, and images that have been spatially displaced from their points of origin, temporally displaced, or – as in the case of email and Web pages downloaded from servers – both spatially and temporally shifted."[31] The assemblage of both paper and digital documents into personal archives may be one way that individuals cope with such shifts. The personal archives are their context.

We can understand the role of personal archives in another way. William Mitchell, acknowledging that new digital storage and computer networks have enabled more decentralization, still comprehends the importance of real, physical space. Mitchell, at one point commenting on the phenomenon of wealthy residents in Cambridge, Massachusetts ordering groceries online, mentions that the same people are going to another store to sample expensive wine and cheese. Why? "A place that is pleasurable and unique is still a powerful attractor," Mitchell comments, "and busy people will devote some of their scare leisure time to visiting it."[32] Mitchell also romantically reminiscences about the old university computer lab, as a place for people to come together. "The computer center was not a very pleasant place – freezingly air-conditioned as the big hot machines required, noisy, and industrially lit – but it had its compensations. Like the village well," he remembers, "it generated a lively public space in the surrounding area. You could rely upon seeing other computer users there, and it was a place to *be* seen. As you waited for your job to process, you could socialize, and exchange news and gossip. Most importantly, it concentrated the specialized expertise of an intellectual community, and became a place of intense, round the clock, peer-to-peer learning."[33] While Mitchell recognizes that the ubiquity of wireless networks and laptops establishes the "potential of *every* sort of space to support intellectual activity, and in doing so, they encourage new, fluid, and potentially creative combinations of research and scholarly practices," he also recognizes that something may be lost.[34]

Commentators on the digitization of the universe often hedge their bets about the social and geographical implications of such changes, and both William Mitchell and Jacques Derrida are no exceptions. Mitchell hints that empty spaces, such as libraries and archives, might not be so positive, remembering that Stanley Kramer's "On the Beach" "does not rely upon special effects at all. To suggest a world turned uninhabitable by clouds of nuclear radiation, it simply shows us empty city streets."[35] Mitchell believes that both virtual and real worlds converge in the new world, such as a "city [his focus] [that] functions as collective memory and as a crucial site of shared cultural reference depends upon its power to provide virtual as well as physical settings for interchanges among its inhabitants."[36] From a very different perspective Derrida speculates that even if the library or archives were empty would the function disappear? He asks,

> Will we continue for long to use the word *library* for a place that essentially no longer collects together a store of books? Even if this place still houses all possible books, even if their number continued to hold up, as I think can be envisaged, even if for a long time books still represented the majority of texts produced, nonetheless the underlying tendency would be for such a place increasingly to be expected to

become a space for work, reading, and writing that was governed or dominated by texts no longer corresponding to the 'book' form: electronic texts with no paper support, texts not corpus or opus – not finite and separable oeuvres; groupings no longer forming texts, even, but open textual processes offered on boundless national and international networks, for the active or interactive intervention of readers turned coauthors, and so on."[37]

What we might be seeing, even in the realm of the personal archives, is a shifting towards a world of both digital and paper documents, with increasing levels of comfort and facility in working with new media forms. N. Katherine Hayles, in examining literature and its digital forms, notes that digitizing a document or text is a means similar to translation that is "also an act of interpretation."[38] People are increasingly converting older files to digital form and creating more and more digital files from scratch. The challenge is that many learn, quite readily, how to utilize the new technologies, but they do not understand the long-term consequences of the digital systems for their personal records. Derrida discourses on the fact that he knows how to use the computer as a word processor but he does not know, really, how the computer works: "This secret with no mystery frequently marks our dependence in relation to many instruments of modern technology. We know how to use them and what they are for, without knowing what goes on with them, in them, on their side; and this might give us plenty to think about with regard to our relationship with technology *today* – to the historical newness of this experience."[39] This is not an uncommon confession, whether one is a scholar or a dentist experimenting with new recording formats.

The challenges of maintaining personal archives mimic those facing every organization and government agency. Personal archives are not time capsules – "deliberately sealed deposits of cultural relics and recorded knowledge that are intended for retrieval at a given future target date" – but they are in active use as a means of assisting every individual and family to navigate in the world.[40] What goes into our personal archives are very different than what we have tended to surround ourselves with, at both home and work. Chris Hedges, considering popular religion in America, laments that,

> We are burdened by household gods, no longer made of clay, but all promising to fulfill us. Our computer, our television, our job, our wealth, our social status, along with the brands we wear and the cars we drive, promise us contentment and inform our identity. These

household gods seem to offer well-being, health and success. But all
these gods create cults. And all these cults circle back to use, to a
dangerous self-worship fed by forces who seek to ensnare us in
idolatry.[41]

Personal records and artifacts immerse us into the world in a way that
gives us meaning beyond the superficial material stuff we acquire. All
we have to do is to determine how best to care for the archival goods,
recognizing that the personal sensibilities associated with family archives
may be far more important than all the scholarship and theorizing
being devoted to studying such documents. All we may need to do is to
read the testimony of a writer like Ivan Doig rediscovering his mother
and his childhood after he receives a packet of his mother's letters years
after her death, suddenly "sensing the carrying power of ink as a way to
go on."[42]

We Are All Archivists.

Most people have little sense of what an archivist does, or even
know that such a profession exists (and this probably extends to the
notion of the records manager as well). Daily newspaper articles and
other media coverage confuse archivists with librarians or museum
curators, even though there has been increasing attention on issues such
as the importance of records as sources of accountability and evidence,
the continuing challenges to preserving the evidence of the past, and
steady coverage of popular hobbies, such as genealogy, that rely on the
availability of archives and historical manuscripts. As many individuals
try to cope with the maintenance of their own personal and family
archives, they often fail to realize that there are professionals and many
published and online guides that could assist them in this endeavor.

It has become difficult for the public to understand archival work
because of the shifting notions of archives in scholarly and popular
usage. A lot of scholarship about the nature of the "archive" has twisted
and expanded the concept beyond any sense of the traditional meaning
of the term as a repository where scholars use historical records to try to
decipher the past. Antoinette Burton, for example, studied three
twentieth century Indian women writers who "used domestic space as
an archival source from which to construct their own histories and
through which to record the contradictions of living as Indian women in
the context of colonial modernity."[43] Along the way, Burton defines and

redefines the archive, challenging what she sees as the "preoccupation of a modernizing, Western, bourgeois, Victorian professional class,"[44] whereby one moves beyond older textual forms such as the letter to other sources such as memory shaped by autobiographies, family history, and artifacts. Some of Burton's ideas are dangerous in that they minimize and threaten any authority of records for purposes such as evidence and accountability, yet in her views there is also a valuable concept as well: "At a time when the practice of professional history appears to have so little grip on the contemporary imagination -- when History of the academic variety is thought to be so persistently irrelevant to the average person's experiences, identities, desires -- it seems fitting that we are, effectively, all archivists now."[45] Individuals striving to manage their personal and family archives can certainly agree with this.

Fortunately, there are places to turn for assistance. Enough people struggle with administering their own personal papers that a number of self-help books have appeared offering advice and promising solutions. Liz Davenport starts her volume off with the general problem most of us face, namely growing volumes of information being hurtled at us, compounded by ineffective methods of organizing and dealing with the information. Davenport states, bluntly and coolly, "The average businessperson receives 190 pieces of information *each day*. The average businessperson wastes 150 hours *each year* looking for stuff."[46] I am not sure how she calculated the scope of the problem, but it is as good an assessment of what one finds in their workplace as anyone could find. The problem with personal information and personal records is probably occurring on a somewhat lower scale, but it is nevertheless the case that each of us is receiving far more information than we can easily manage. And her concern is echoed in numerous other volumes about managing personal and professional papers and information. Patricia J. Hutchings, in her book about managing information, writes, "It is easy to become frustrated when you walk into your work area and find piles of paper, mountains of messages, reams of reports, thirty-five e-mail messages waiting, stacks of reading, and your message light blinking. If your work area is cluttered and disorganized, it will lower your productivity, cause procrastination, and lead you to feeling overwhelmed and burned-out."[47] Well, sure, but we might also speculate that this may be precisely how many personal and family archives are like, minimizing their utility except for the comfort that the knowledge of their existence provides.

Self-help author Davenport promotes the idea that the disorganized personal archive generates from the creative instincts of people. She offers her advice, because she faces the same problems as all naturally talented and motivated people:

> What qualifies me to help those of you who are by nature disorganized? Because I am just like you. *I* am, by nature, disorganized. I have the same personality profile as most of my clients; that is, we are creative, we hate details, we are spontaneous, and we like to leave things open-ended. We are the creative geniuses of the world. Our energy is focused on the future – the next project, the next idea, the next grand scheme. Unfortunately, paper belongs to the past or, at best, the present. Our attention is on the future. Therefore, clutter is the natural side effect of being creative.[48]

Of course, one needs to resist being so creative that the problems in maintaining personal records increase.

Some of Davenport's advice is pure commonsense. She describes needing to clean off one's desk at the end of each day, creating a kind of vacuum. "A vacuum is the empty space in drawers, bookcases, filing cabinets, and closets in which to put all the new stuff that is coming in each day," Davenport suggests. "Each file drawer should have at least two inches of play in it so when you want to file something, you can easily open the file with two fingers and drop in whatever you need to file. When files are too jampacked to easily file in, most people quit filing!"[49] This author follows some of the commonsense dicta that have characterized records management textbooks for decades.

And then Davenport gets to the main point, when she argues that each person needs an archive. "Archival stuff includes things you don't use very often (less than once a month) but that need to be kept for future use. To archive your old stuff does not mean just tossing it willy-nilly in boxes and hiding it away. Your archives stuff needs to be organized so that you can find individual items again, if you need them."[50] This is, admittedly, a pretty superficial view of what an archive is about, and Davenport only compounds this when she offers advice on making clear labels, the rules of filing, designing the office space, and discarding most (95 percent) of one's papers, except for "tax papers, legal documents, and anything you are required by law to keep…"[51] Yet, the fact that she suggests the need for such personal archives is significant in its own right.

Davenport's motivations for writing her book is in helping a person to be more efficient, and efficiency and effectiveness are attributes that are part, but only part, of the responsibilities of an archives. She implores people to write down things needed to be done in a time sensitive manner, creating a system that "replaces the 500 floating pieces of paper: sticky notes, backs of envelopes, and odd scraps with pertinent data on them, reports, agendas, meeting notices, and copies of things you lost once already."[52] She suggests that people take stock of the miscellaneous documentation all around them: "You will be amazed at how many of the pieces of paper lying around can simply be thrown away once you have written down what they were there to remind you of. Much of that clutter was simply because you knew you could not trust your memory for something due days or weeks from now."[53] Davenport argues that one starts with gathering all of their papers:

> That means, go forth into your life, find every scrap of paper you have created. Yes, that means the ones behind the tissue box in the bathroom, the ones behind the toaster in the kitchen, the ones over your sun visor in the car, the ones at the bottom of your briefcase or knapsack or purse, the ones under magnets on the fronts of the fridge – everything, everywhere. It is time to put them into your one all-encompassing system, because each of those other stashes represents a system, whether you can verbalize what the system is or not. And the more systems you have, the greater the likelihood you will miss something![54]

And with this we begin to see the development of what can be termed a personal archives.

Even the vendors of the latest glitzy software products have gone after the market for managing personal records. Many different suggestions have been made for how individuals can keep track of their property, as well as their records, for example. Software packages – such as Personal Record Keeper, Quicken Deluxe, Managing Your Money, and Personal Home Inventory – all include ways of tracking personal property.[55] Specialized software is also on the market for tracking art works, jewelry, and other such valuable personal property.[56] As one essayist advises, "Whether you choose the high-tech route or prefer a handwritten list, you first need to grab a notepad and start walking. Go through each room and closet methodically, jotting down all items worth the $25. Think like an insurance agent or police officer. Note the makes, models, and serial numbers. Save sales receipts, especially for big-ticket items."[57] There are even vendors who will come into one's home and take a digital photograph of every major item, room, and closet, and then put the images on a CD with an inventory that can be shown to an insurance agent.[58] Individuals who have camcorders are encouraged to film everything in their house as a supplement for more traditional inventories.[59] And so the advice keeps rolling in.

Maintaining one's own personal or family papers is a crucial activity for preparing a family history, and while there are similarities between archiving and writing there are also differences. Americans have been blessed with an abundance of state, regional, and local historical agencies that provide many programs offering advice and instruction on family history work. And these organizations have been doing this for a long time. Many professional historians, and some public historians laboring in organizations other than the academy, have taught workshops and institutes on the topic, orienting interested individuals about the nature of historical sources, where these sources can be found, and connecting ancestors and the family to various historical periods and events. Much of the advice offered to individuals interested in their family histories will sound useful for those also concerned about maintaining their own family archives, such as follows:

> Careful research entails keeping neat and orderly notes indicating the reason for every search made; maintaining a list of sources searched to avoid needlessly examining the same source over and over; making notes simple enough so that anyone can understand them, but also complete enough to adequately reflect research; classifying family members according to jurisdiction or location to avoid clutter; establishing a cross-reference system; filing notes alphabetically by surname and under each surname chronologically by location; and taking precautions never to lose or dispose of research notes.[60]

Similar to the process of writing family histories is that of writing memoirs, a source identified by local historians as possessing particular value. As one historian describes it, these sources are fairly abundant in archives, libraries, and museums, and they assume all shapes and forms: "Preserved by families or deposited in libraries and in the archives of local historical societies, local memoirs vary in form and length – from complete books to a few handwritten paragraphs to any number of unbound typed pages" (now, we can add that they will appear as well in digital form on personal websites). "Usually," the historian continues, "they have an informal style of writing and somewhat disorganized

content that rambles from one topic to another as much as memory
itself works, inspired randomly by some phrase, word or chance
recollection." These memoirs can provide unique information and
perspectives on particular places and events, along with eyewitness
accounts and factual errors and faulty or incomplete information that
must be checked against other sources.[61]

The main differences between compiling family histories or writing
memoirs and that of creating and maintaining personal archives may be
the intended audiences and final purpose. Authoring family histories
and memoirs is intended to reach an audience of some sort, while
generating a personal archives may just be for the use of an individual
or immediate family. These activities probably share one common
attribute, an effort to understand our past. The prolific essayist, novelist,
and poet Wendell Berry recently wrote that "we know almost nothing of
our history as it was actually lived. We know little of the lives of our
parents. We have forgotten almost everything that has happened to
ourselves. The easy assumption that we have remembered the most
important people and events and have preserved the most valuable
evidence is immediately trumped by our inability to know what we have
forgotten."[62] Clearly, the efforts of writing memoirs, compiling
genealogies, and establishing personal archives are intended to eradicate
such ignorance.

Archivists and records managers can gain some valuable assistance
by understanding the nature of personal recordkeeping. For the
archivist, some of these personal archives may ultimately be offered to
their repositories, and it behooves the archivist to provide advice about
the care of such documentary sources to ensure that they arrive in good
order. Some professionals have awakened to this role, as reflected in the
recent book by Don Williams and Louisa Jaggar on *Saving Stuff*, offering
basic advice on the care of personal artifacts and documents.[63] Of
course, the vast majority of personal records will not be offered to
archives, as they are of much greater value to the individuals and
families they relate to. But for both archivist and records manager, the
key importance may be in tapping into the concept of personal archives
as a way of explaining the importance of administering records. Too
often we assume that others do not share any sense of this important
work, when, in fact, many are quite engaged in trying to preserve their
own family and personal papers, providing a good starting point for any
discussing of the needs for administering organizational and
government records.

Conclusion: The New Archival Mission.

I started this volume with a brief discussion of how the documentary holdings in archival repositories often started life as individual collections. Are we now seeing a reversal, where individuals and families might be shifting their attention to administer private archives and less inclined to transfer their records to an archives? Where personal archives reside in cyberspace, available to anyone who wants to consult them? Where the public controversies often surrounding archives, museums, and libraries may give pause to someone handing over the personal or family papers? Where venerable cultural institutions, strapped for cash and facing declining revenue and public interest, curtail or limit their once vigorous collecting programs?

Perhaps, the archival profession needs to concentrate on developing new mechanisms for educating the public about how to care for their personal and family archives. Perhaps, this has already started to happen, as we note that one of the expanding sections of the major chain bookstores is the self-help section. In this section there is a growing number of books about organizing personal papers, what to keep, how to avoid cluttering up one's life, preserving family archives, and so forth. One of these self-help guides provides as good a reason as any why there is a need for people to follow the advice being offered. Denise Dale and Alexandra Bradley write, "Years ago, all of a household's important papers could fit quite nicely in a single briefcase. This just does not seem to be the case today. Consider the mail. As one records organizer has observed, we receive more mail in a week than our parents did in a month. We receive, in a month, more mail than out grandparents did in a year."[64] Dale and Bradley then discuss what to keep, where to keep it, how to re-evaluate and purge from time to time, developing filing classification systems, and how to deal with electronic records. However, professional archivists can do better than most of the advice currently being offered in such self-help guides, but, in order to do so, these archivists need to shift their attention from mostly serving the needs of academic and experienced researchers engaged in mostly long-term research projects to working with amateurs committed to preserving their personal and family archives.

There is a negative way to interpret this potential new role for the archivist. As mentioned earlier, Andrew Keen attacks the idea of the rise of the amateur in the Internet era, seeing the failure of experts and the failure of newspapers, magazines, and every organization and professional with some stake in the maintenance of societal and cultural values. Keen argues, with our fixation on amateurs forming our news and all other information, that we are getting "superficial observations of the world around us rather than deep analysis, shrill opinion rather than considered judgment."[65] To make his point, Keen considers the difference between the professional journalist and all those amateurs building news site on the Web:

> When an article runs under the banner of a respected newspaper, we know that it has been weighed by a team of seasoned editors with years of training, assigned to a qualified reporter, researched, fact-checked, edited, proofread, and backed by a trusted news organization vouching for its truthfulness and accuracy. Take those filters away, and we, the general public, are faced with the impossible task of sifting through and evaluating an endless sea of the muddled musings of amateurs.[66]

Keen tries to shift the attention from playing with new technologies to preserving the systems of expertise that we have built over the generations, worried that it will be difficult to rebuild such knowledge structures. Keen believes we need to "use technology in a way that encourages innovation, open communication, and progress, while simultaneously preserving professional standards of truth, decency, and creativity."[67] I am not advocating that archivists turn their work over to amateurs, but given the changing nature of the documentary universe it is clear that they need to form new and improved working relationships with them if their objective is to help preserve and maintain valuable documentary materials. Of course, if archivists are only interested in acquiring and preserving sources in order to enhance their own institutional reputation and to assist relatively small clusters of researchers than business as usual is fine.

Archivists need to be careful in how they might criticize the role, old or new, of individual preservers of documentary materials. A historical perspective clearly indicates that the source of many holdings in now established archival repositories is that of the work of individual collectors or the efforts of some family member to preserve the family archival legacy. While archivists often see or portray themselves as the documenters or collectors of our society, if the truth be told many of their holdings were already somewhat formed by individual collectors who built aggregations of documents or who worked to preserve their own family archives; their disposition into an established archival repository with a more public mission was simply the last stage of a process. However, what I am getting at is that we may be seeing a very different role for family archivists because of the digital platform on which they work. Whether this new archival desire emanates from simply a utilitarian interest in maintaining personal and family papers or whether it reflects a new kind of competition with archival repositories, it is too early to tell. However, we know that even with the most basic form of collecting there is some inherent competition with institutions like museums and libraries. As Bill Brown reflects about the impulses driving collecting, he notes,

> Indeed, if there is an overriding principle of private collecting, it is that the collector, establishing a different order of things, enjoys the fact or the fantasy of wresting authority away from institutions and even from that thing we call "culture," establishing a different system of value and meaning. The collection becomes the source of specialized knowledge-about Venetian glass, or baseball cards, or swords, or Barbie dolls, or stamps. And the collector can claim some mastery, some exhilarating expertise. Collectors collect more than objects; they collect the knowledge (however pedestrian or profound) that empowers them to take pleasure in those objects and to take advantage of someone else's ignorance. More than any mere consumer, the collector lives for the thrill of the bargain because the bargain is the theatrical mark of a knowledge both superior and secret.[68]

Brown's focus is more on the tangible objects that collectors pursue, whereas the new form of private archivist may be more focused on the digital surrogates of personal documents. As Keen suggests, this may be another manifestation of the elevation of the amateur against the professional, here testified more as the individual collection against the institutional collection.

What should the archivist be rethinking about when they function in the light of new possibilities for personal and family archiving? The traditional paradigms, over the course of the twentieth century, have shifted from building repositories and letting the records accumulate to more planned and strategic acquisition programs, but in most of the various changes proposed the emphasis always remained on the archives and archivists as custodians of documentary sources. The transformation of archival perspectives has usually occurred because of rapidly growing volumes of documents and increasingly complex hybrid documentary technologies. Over the past two decades especially, new networked digital technologies have pushed archivists, at least some, to rethink the custodial model and to consider new kinds of distributed or post-custodial strategies. This seems to be where we now are with personal and family archives, and the prospects for continuing archival work are both daunting and exciting.

Continuing archival work is challenging because the digital recordkeeping and information technologies continue to perplex archivists, especially those working in smaller institutions with limited resources, in their abilities to apply traditional notions of record reliability and trustworthiness to the new environments; the result has been almost an avoidance of dealing with these documentary forms, an approach bound to cause problems with the future prospects of the archival profession. Dire predictions of the demise of the archival community have not come true, although it is also the case as much because there are still vast reservoirs of paper records to be analyzed and administered. It is unlikely that sanguine predictions will continue if archivists working through society simply do not deal with digital formats; this avoidance will result in other disciplines or new disciplines stepping in to fill the void.[69] Many of us have heard working archivists at conferences testify that they are avoiding working with digital formats, even when the documentary sources (such as photography) have made major shifts into the digital realm. If the archival community expects not only to take care of its own materials but also to assist others in caring for their documents, it must be more engaged in working with and solving challenges to digital recordkeeping systems and their products.

The exciting aspect of rethinking how archivists will work in preserving personal and family archives is that it may re-open a much greater possibility for reaching the public with a clearer sense of the archival mission, an objective archivists and their professional associations have struggled to do for several decades with very mixed results. Archives and archivists have done fairly well, usually on the local level, in installing exhibitions, running special events, celebrating anniversaries, and marking institutional and societal benchmarks – all with some positive results in improving the profile of the archival field and its work. In more recent years, there have been some ambitious efforts to celebrate national archives week, and this is encouraging. However, most archivists, when candidly asked, would indicate that theirs is still a largely unknown and under-appreciated profession. While there are been isolated happy experiments with meeting the public where it is and making it more aware of the importance of archives and of what archivists do, most would agree that there is much work to do. However, we are on the cusp of getting some grand new opportunities for working with the public and assisting them to understand and preserve its digital documentary sources.

It is, however, clearly the case that the public itself is actually sowing the ground for archivists to seed. As individuals and families continually invest in new technologies that are portable and use them to store ever-growing amounts of records and information, they will encounter increasing challenges for maintaining these sources. Even as people grow more aware of the potential loss of these materials because of technical glitches and design weaknesses in the long-term maintenance, they will be loath to give up on them because of their convenience and ease of use (similar to people being hesitant to stop using credit cards and retail discount cards even as they become more aware of the increased threats to personal privacy). Even in Lee Siegel's angry polemic about the influence of the Internet – challenging concepts of privacy, leisure, work, and culture – Siegel nevertheless states that the "Internet is now a permanent part of our civilization. We can either passively allow it to obstruct our lives or guide it toward the fulfillment of its human promise. The choice is ours. Things really don't have to be the way they are."[70] Archivists, in examining the evolving nature of digital personal and family archives also must embrace the challenge in an open and positive fashion.

In addition to archivists adopting a broader campaign to assist the public, they must redirect part of their attention and resources from acquisition of archival materials and to assisting onsite researchers to developing workshops, self-help publications, and other tools for the purpose of equipping more and more citizens to care for their own archives. This requires, as well, a new attitude by archivists, one that has them offering (even giving away) rather than protecting their expertise. There are a number of sources and approaches archivists can connect into in order to help them make this transition.

There is an emerging scholarly discipline, personal information management, archivists need to begin both to dig into and to influence. Personal information management is defined as follows:

> Personal information management (PIM) is the practice and study of the activities people perform to acquire, organize, maintain, and retrieve information for everyday use. PIM is a growing area of

interest as we all strive for better use of our limited personal resources
of time, money, and energy, as well as greater workplace efficiency
and productivity. Good research on the topic is being done in several
disciplines, including human-computer interaction, database
management, information retrieval, and artificial intelligence. This
two-day workshop will continue momentum towards building a
community of researchers doing PIM-related research.[71]

This definition derives from the conferences now being offered on this
topic about every year and a half, conferences offering a lot of
interesting insights in how individuals are seeking to management
information but also revealing a lack of knowledge about the practical
work of archivists and records managers or the emerging historical and
other scholarship on personal records.

The historical and other scholarly research on personal and family
archives, much of it occurring outside the archival community, is
building a strong foundation for understanding why we create and
maintain documents. I have cited a good deal of it throughout this
volume, but it is worth mentioning an example or two in this
concluding segment. Samuel D. Kassow's study of the secret Warsaw
Ghetto archive in the early years of the Second World War provides
important insights into the nature of why people, especially in times of
great duress, create and maintain historical documents – and it is a
good example of what such historical study can bring to our
understanding of the origins and development of personal and family
archives. As Kasson notes, "During the Holocaust hundreds of
individuals wrote. They wrote diaries, laments for murdered children,
essays, poetry, and fiction."[72] The Oyneg Shabes Archive in the
Warsaw Ghetto is one of the most critical clues about just how and why
this occurred. Kassow approaches the archive in this way: "Countless
individuals worked on their own to record what they saw. In hundreds
of ghettos, hiding places, jails, and death camps, lonely and terrified
Jews left diaries, letters, and testimony of what they endured. For every
scrap of documentation that surfaced after the war, probably many
more manuscripts vanished forever."[73] The Oyneg Shabes Archive is a
rarity because so much of it survived.

Kassow's work centers on the efforts of historian, and Warsaw
Ghetto resident, Emanuel Ringelblum, who tried to create a record of
the atrocities inflicted on Polish Jews by the Germans in order to
provide testimony to the world that would follow. His efforts were a
kind of resistance, and Ringelblum, as Kassow documents, wrestled

continuously with the kind of objectivity he could bring to his task while promoting the study of the past as a means to resist what was happening in Europe during the Second World War. And his effort was sweeping in its scope, as his archive "collected both texts and artifacts: the underground press, documents, drawings, candy wrappers, tram tickets, ration cards, theater posters, invitations to concerts and lectures."[74] What we learn, among many things, is that the experience of working on the archive functioned as a mean of building and sustaining community, something archivists have always sensed and promoted in their advocacy about their work and mission. Kassow, examining this real historical example of archive building, argues that the participants "drew their strength from the collective energy of dedicated workers who would pool their talents and establish a hierarchy of priorities and objectives."[75] And with this we see something of the power of records in society, extending to what individuals may want to do with their personal and family archives.

While archivists have been contributing modest work on the history of archives, records, and recordkeeping, they have not as yet begun to produce a scholarship that has been noted by other disciplines or determined how to relate such scholarship to their more ongoing practical concerns as working archivists. I am sure this will occur. One of the most encouraging recent signs has been the holding of three International Conferences on the History of Records and Archives in Toronto (2003), Amsterdam (2005), and Boston (2007). The most recent conference focused on personal archives, including papers on "forms of personal records," "motivations for making and keeping personal records," "collecting of personal records by individuals and archival repositories," "cross-disciplinary perspectives on personal records," and "needs for research in the area of personal records."[76] In general, these conferences have been noteworthy for the excellence of the research represented, but my personal impressions of the third conference was that these papers were the weaker of the three meetings and reflected less of the rich emerging scholarship on the topic. However, perhaps this conference, especially after a portion of the better papers are published in *Libraries and the Cultural Record*, will be a catalyst for more analysis about the meaning of personal and family archives.

Partnerships with other disciplines to develop solutions for personal archives management and a greater dedication to research about the reasons why personal and family archives are formed and maintained are good commitments for the archival community to make. Archivists, either on their own or in collaboration with others, also need to write and publish guides about the management of personal and family archives directed at the lay audience. Maybe we are becoming poised to do this as we begin to see new attempts to provide such publications. The Council of State Archivists, for example, published in late 2007 a guide on saving family records in disasters.[77] This publication provides basic advice on safeguarding family records, determining what records are the most important, and checklists and questions for one to work through how to maintain such documents in the event of a disaster. Written in the wake of the disastrous Hurricane Katrina, this guide points the way to new efforts for archivists to work with the public. Now, we need publications, workshops, training videos, and other such efforts to assist ordinary citizens to maintain family and personal archives. It may be that some of these records will ultimately come to reside in archival repositories, and when they do they ought to be in far better shape than what archivists normally find.

Advisory publications such as this are a by-product of what might be a new role for professional archivists. In this role archivists will function more as advisors rather than acquirers, educators giving their knowledge away rather than protecting the secrets of a guild, and advocates rather than reactors in seeking to preserve the portion of the documentary universe that possesses archival value. Some of this should seem familiar because it relates to some notions promulgated by those working with electronic records a decade or more ago, although some of these views have been greeted with criticism or silence.

Before I am misinterpreted here, I want to state clearly that I am not arguing that established, institutional archives will not acquire and preserve personal and family archives in the future. What I am suggesting is that the vast and rapidly growing digital documentary universe of such archives requires that archivists first try to advise the creators and amateur caretakers of these materials and only intercede when valuable or unique personal and family archives are endangered. This will require new and more intense archival appraisal approaches, ones that have not been devised yet, as well as new standards for the maintenance and use of personal and family digital archives. These are interesting and engaging problems that should be the increasing focus of what educators teach, what doctoral students conduct research about, and what working archivists experiment with and develop into reliable systems. The attitude we need is the kind Terry Cook ascribes to Verne Harris in Harris' quest for the relationship between archives and justice:

Archives, Verne insists, are about dynamic recordmaking, and remaking, re-remaking, over and over again, without end, rather than the traditional record-*keeping*, looking after and keeping safe some fixed records product as a sacred artifact. The correct stance for archivists, then, is ever questioning, never complacent, always seeking for the grail of memory, while allowing forgetting, always celebrating the ever-changing contingent, which continually reinvents (remakes) the archive.[78]

Cook additionally indicates that for Harris archives and archiving are "profoundly spiritual … [a] transcendent faith that tomorrow will care about the records we preserve today."[79] These are topics and issues I will address in the concluding chapter, after considering in some additional detail digital technologies and their impact on personal and family archives and the modest archival response to such concerns.

Chapter Seven

Electronic Mail and Personal Recordkeeping

Introduction.

Electronic mail is one of the most ubiquitous, commonly accepted, and easiest to use of the modern records and information technologies. Every professional worker, government official, student, and grandparents and parents rely on e-mail for daily communication. More e-mail messages are being sent than handwritten letters or postcards, and few think it is unusual to be daily or hourly checking communications or even, in a bit of sleeplessness, to be sending messages to friends, relatives, and co-workers in the middle of the night. In my own case, a considerable part of my professional and personal activities revolve about e-mail communication. I rely on e-mail to carry out administrative responsibilities, collaborate with colleagues around the world, work with editors on my publications, communicate with students, set lunch dates, and stay in touch with friends. Not too many years ago these same activities would have been dependent on the postal service, the telephone, and face-to-face meetings, but this is certainly not the case anymore. And I suspect my experience is much the same as others.

There seems to be a common consensus about the fact that e-mail plays not only an important, but crucial, role in the activities of organizations and the lives of individuals. Where at one time, e-mail was seen as little more than the equivalent of informal conversation – something to be quickly discarded after its immediate use and because of its seemingly short-term value, now it is recognized as a required tool for communication, decision-making, planning, and other business and personal functions. On the personal side, individuals rely on e-mail for everything from social correspondence to running households and working remotely in order to keep up with their professional responsibilities. On the professional side, e-mail is being used to convey every kind of official record and to support every organizational or business activity. There are few examining institutional or individual records who do not recognize that e-mail has replaced or superceded other documentary forms as a window into understanding what organizations and individuals do.

There is additional consensus that e-mail has presented new challenges to administering records and information. Records managers have tended to see e-mail as a specific threat both to their own ability to control records and information systems and, perhaps more important, a liability risk and invasive threat to proprietary information of their employing organizations. Archivists, on the other hand, have viewed e-mail as a threat to one of the most important documentary sources they administer, personal and organizational letters, and, as a result, symbolic of the challenges of the digital era to our documentary heritage. We need a middle path between these viewpoints that enables the critical e-mail for documentary and research purposes to be maintained in an effective fashion that is appropriate to the records generating organization (and, as well, by individuals creating e-mail in lieu of more traditional means of writing letters). In this chapter, I spend considerable time discussing the administration of e-mail in organizations because I believe how organizations approach this medium suggests a lot about how individuals approach the use of e-mail (there is little separating personal use and the workplace and, as well, the workplace often equips individuals for relying on such a messaging system). In this chapter, I also examine how archivists and records managers have viewed e-mail in very different ways, since this suggests issues about how well such records professionals are prepared to communicate with individuals about the management of personal e-mail (and before the suspense kills anyone, these professionals are not particularly well-prepared for providing real assistance at this time).

E-Mail and Society.

Electronic mail is a communications system that many Americans can't imagine living without in any capacity. A few years ago, a study by the Pew Internet and American Life Project suggests that the "average wired American worker spends only about 30 minutes a day dealing with e-mail." It was also discovered that more than 60 percent have Internet access at work and nearly all use it at work, more than double (57 million) with Internet access just two years before. Electronic mail is valued greatly, no matter how it is actually used: "E-mail use on the job has become so pervasive in American offices that half of the Pew study participants said they consider it essential to their work."[1]

Such assessments bombard us on a regular basis, and it is difficult to find anyone who does not have access at least to the use of e-mail (even though we all have experienced personal frustrations with colleagues, friends, and relatives who seem less capable than ourselves in using e-mail – or at least responding to our messages in a timely fashion!). One observer indicates that "email represents a staggering 75% of all corporate intelligence," partially explaining why U.S. businesses expended nearly $6 billion in 2005 in discovery efforts related to litigation.[2] Just after the Enron debacle and the passage of the Sarbanes-Oxley Act (SOX) and the Health Insurance Portability and Accountability Act (HIPAA), a study was released by the Radicati Group entitled, *E-mail Archiving Market, 2004-2008*, predicting revenue growth of more than $2.5 billion in a few years for automated systems with provisions for routinely deleting e-mail after a specified time.[3]

This was testimony to how ingrained e-mail had become to most organizations. And it represents a major shift in a very brief time span. A survey firm in 1992 estimated that 2 percent of the US population had access to e-mail, a percentage that grew to 15 percent by 1998.[4] By late 2006, it was estimated that e-mail volume was growing by 30 percent a year, including everything from spam, business, and personal e-mails.[5] Another study suggested that 171 billion e-mails are sent daily, with about 70 percent of these messages being spam.[6] While it is difficult to ascertain precisely the accuracy of such estimates about the volume and frequency of e-mail, everyone willingly acknowledges that the pace of e-mail messages piling up in our electronic mailboxes is staggering, if for no other reason than the personal testimony each of us can make about what we find in them every morning when we log on. We are accustomed to relying on e-mail at both work and in play, at home and when we travel.

While e-mail grows every day in its use and importance for individuals and institutions alike, the challenges posed by e-mail also grows. When a few years ago Google announced the introduction of Gmail, a free Web-based service offering 1 gigabyte of storage to each subscriber, privacy groups spoke out. For taking advantage of the free storage, Google intended to "scan users' incoming e-mail and then deliver targeted ads based on key words in the messages." When Google defended its program by arguing that no humans would look at the mail (only computers would be involved), many were not reassured. Still, some skeptics cited advantages of the program, with its faster loading and ability to search email, and enabling users to flag messages with labels and to apply different labels and file in different ways.[7] Roughly at about the same time, President Bush's (George W.) plans to create an Internet-wide network operations and monitoring center to defend against cyber attacks were criticized widely and ultimately scaled back. The Bush administration sought to get Internet Service Providers to work together to share information, but the ISPs were concerned about privacy risks.[8] These are classic cases of how technology had outraced some of the safeguards against intrusive prying into one's personal activities. And they also represent the potential consequences for the passionate embrace by both individuals and institutions of the utility of e-mail.

Most individuals working in industry or government have grown accustomed to having their e-mail regulated in some fashion, perhaps a practical trade-off for the ease of being able to use it at their place of employment. A survey released by the American Management Association in April 2000, indicated that 54 percent of mid-size and large companies monitor employees' Internet use, a dramatic increase in just a few years, with others wrestling with issues with privacy, the potential of surveillance software, and how to disseminate to and instruct employees about the monitoring policies and procedures.[9] A survey carried out by the American Management Association, *U.S. News & World Report*, and the ePolicy Institute in 2001 found a majority of employees having their email monitored by employers. The Electronic Communications Privacy Act provides employers the right to do this in order to protect them, and many organizations are adopting email policies and training employees about how to use (properly) e-mail on company computers and time.[10] There are obvious reasons why employers may be concerned about the most mundane of uses of e-mail by their employees, with evidence that employees using e-mail at work waste time or cause them to fall behind in their work (often because they are tending to personal business and because they have lost any sense of a divide between work and personal activity).[11] Most of us have observed these traits in other, less formal, ways. A few professional listservs I monitor show the distinctive signs of being used by most people during the normal working hours, and it is dubious how many of these postings could be said to be directly related to work responsibilities.

We have become so accustomed to living with e-mail that we also are used to contending with some of its most common problems, such as the constant receipt of spam messages. Internet service providers, such as AOL and Yahoo!, have debated charging senders of mass e-mail a fee, with the goal of reducing spam mail (the assumption being that only legitimate senders of mass e-mail would be likely to pay the fee). However, all sectors of society, not just the cranks and pranksters, have grown dependent on e-mail, leading to criticism of such a proposal because it would have a negative impact on charities, small business, legitimate lobby groups, and others.[12] Most of us use the various filters provided to restrict the flow of such messages. Many, myself included, just matter-of-factly delete the next message from Nigeria about a money-laundering scheme and report it as an unwanted message. We so value the e-mail we receive that we are willing to live with such inconveniences, no matter how annoying they may be.

In all organizations, the amount of e-mail being created and stored is on a rapid ascent. A few years ago, e-mail, Web, and IM provider Orchestra stated that 1/3 to 1/2 of all electronic communications kept in company storage did not need to be there and was being re-routed to more expensive storage. Many are personal e-mails and spam with no value to the organization. Orchestra argues that putting in a software system to analyze incoming and outgoing messages and archiving them according to their business relevance could resolve this problem.[13] Nikki Swartz, in an essay describing compliance and records management issues, presented some astounding statistics related to such basic administrative concerns from a group of recent reports. E-mail creates 500 times more data each year than that generated by the addition of new web pages. The total amount of e-mail created annually by businesses exceeds more than one exabyte, equivalent to all the information found in the Library of Congress 24,000 times over. Thirty billion e-mails are being sent each day. And, and no wonder, e-mail is the most requested business record in court cases.[14] Of course, one might also argue that this makes e-mail one of the most critically important components of the modern documentary universe, a characteristic that ought to merit the work of records professionals to not only determine how to contain it but also how to extract its most significant content according to some agreed upon selection criteria. We already have seen many claims about the importance of any organization's records being the "best source of legacy information"[15] or organizational knowledge.[16] Given the importance and scope of e-mail in any organization, such arguments must encompass e-mail as an essential documentary form needing careful management, and given that a large percentage of this organizational e-mail is going to or coming from individuals, it is also a challenge in the management of personal and family archives.

There are few research benchmark studies in the archives or records management fields to provide any kind of foundation for understanding how far we have moved in addressing the challenges posed by e-mail. A 9-month study conducted at the Graduate School of Library and Information Science at the University of Texas at Austin a decade ago and examining how a variety of organizations manage e-mail concluded that organizations have embraced e-mail as a way of doing business, but that they are not administering e-mail as a records system. Organizations are not following appropriate federal rules of evidence or classifying e-mail in a manner that can be tracked. It was obvious that a decade ago that email, in its loose administrative and technical framework, was creating an enormous legal burden for many organizations.[17] The Texas study also discovered that there are very few real e-mail management programs taking into account the evidence found in e-mail. Requirements seem well enough articulated, but there are few real case studies to explore.[18] Organizations had no software solutions available, but they were working on employee education and developing policies. It was also hard to find models or advice from any professional associations. The study concluded that there were four approaches to managing e-mail, but none were proving to be very useful.[19] None of these, we know now, have been very useful in helping us administer e-mail possessing archival value or can be scaled down to assist individuals to manage their personal e-mail.

Matters have only slightly improved since then. Even with standards for integrating electronic records management systems with electronic document management systems,[20] there is still a long way to go in administering e-mail. A 2005 survey concluded that only 51 percent of organizations have formal e-mail retention plans, although this was a vast improvement (with a 24 percent growth) from just two years before.[21] At home, most of us probably contend with e-mail by printing out copies of selected critical messages, not observing just what might be lost or gained by such approaches.

Both archivists and records managers have expressed concerns about communications technologies such as represented by e-mail. While some experts have cautioned organizations to be careful in focusing on e-mail independently from other records and information concerns,[22] a real problem for sure, the fact is that e-mail has loomed for some time as a major compliance and documentary challenge, with one expert suggesting that although "everyone loves the convenience of e-mail, ... e-mail is striking fear into the hearts of many in the world of records management."[23] Enron and other corporate scandals have brought these concerns to the fore. At the present, there seems to be no way to administer e-mail – it goes into individual mailboxes, overwhelming the organization with its volume and presenting a range of divergent responses (delete everything, save all the mail, or just leave it up to the individual user of e-mail). Technologies such as e-mail should force organizations to see records management in a completely different way, as a real responsibility, and not just something to be left up to individual departments and units. At home, individuals should be striving to understand how their use of e-mail is transforming the activities that once upon a time generated expressive correspondence often saved for their penmanship and personal connections to earlier generations.

Some vendors are beginning to offer slightly different variations on the solution to the problem, moving beyond records, information, or strategic information management to concepts such as enterprise records management, the latter providing a "common infrastructure supporting the wide diversity of enterprisewide records types—from formal electronic records to informal memos, emails and discussion threads, to traditional paper and microfilm."[24] One easily recognizes in enterprise records management the basic components of what has been traditional records management – such as a focus on records retention, an organizational policy governing records and documents, and classification and metadata approaches – with a twist, it builds a structure that backs off from a concern with centralized control to one empowering individuals to operate with more confidence to administer their records and other information.[25] The issue, considered from a more holistic records perspective, is just what these rules ought to contain and the purpose they ought to support. This is a more complicated issue than it seems.

Records Managers, E-mail, and Lessons Learned.

Risk is an essential word in how records managers consider e-mail. The typical essay about e-mail commences with a litany of risks the modern organization faces. E-mail and the breaking news of the latest scandal go hand-in-hand, one contributing to the other or one unable to occur without the other. John Phillips describes e-mail as both an "indispensable communications tool" and a "nightmare for company executives attempting to reduce business risk."[26] Maurene Caplan Grey writes, "Protecting the organization by ensuring regulatory compliance is paramount in today's business environment."[27] And such risk is real. A survey on e-mail and instant messaging by the American Management Association and The ePolicy Institute in 2004 discovered that one in five companies have had employee e-mail subpoenaed. The survey finds that 43 percent of employees do not adhere to requirements governing e-mail retention or are not sure if they are compliant, as well as that over three quarters of companies have written e-mail policies (although only 20 percent have policies on IM).[28] E-mail is the antithesis of the control records managers have traditionally sought to exercise over records and information systems, perhaps more a legacy of the old industrial era office when the foundational records management principles were developed. Since the advent of the personal computer and its array of related technologies, ever more portable and powerful, control has been a chimera for the records manager. We need to understand, of course, that control ought to be of interest to individuals administering their personal and family records and information systems; the stakes might seem less of an issue, but the problems are no less complex or challenging as those organizations face.

It is not hard to determine why e-mail, one of the hardest of document creation systems to control, has viewed in the context of security and compliance issues. Recent studies suggest that almost ninety percent of U.S. corporations are involved in some type of litigation, and that the typical company has about 37 lawsuits in process (larger companies, operating at the $1 billion level, typically have at least 147 lawsuits).[29] Extending standard records management approaches to the growing quantity of records makes the challenges of e-mail and other digital records appear that much more difficult.[30] Many organizations simply made a decision to save everything, but then discovered they were overwhelmed with huge quantities of e-mail. Organizations going to the opposite end of the spectrum, establishing a system by which they dumped e-mail quickly and efficiently, only learned that workers found ways around such requirements.[31] We seem to have records managers tilting at the proverbial windmill here, concerned for centralized control in an environment where control seems to rest with each individual employee. This is additional evidence that the designers of various information systems seldom have any concern for the kinds of issues records managers have had, and the efforts by records managers to re-invent themselves as strategic information managers or knowledge managers have not necessarily alleviated such problems. Individuals seeking to administer their own personal documents also discover that they face security and compliance issues, although they have less resources to harness and often contradictory advice to follow about how to manage their personal and family records.

Such concerns were not always the case. Early on, hardly anyone really noticed problems with the use of e-mail, as there was little in the way of messages from outside of the organization or anything like the junk or spam mail that now invades our mailboxes. Now we hear regularly of the challenges posed by e-mail and other messaging systems, although most of these concerns are posed from larger organizations and businesses. While archivists worry about what might be lost with communication and decision-making via e-mail, records managers worry that it might be far more permanent than what is desired. John J. DiGilio, considering e-mail, notes that a "nightmare of electronic incrimination may lay in ambush for the unsuspecting, unprepared records and information management professional."³² What attracts people to use e-mail, DiGilio reasons, is "its simple and seemingly transitory nature. People will often write things in e-mail that they would never consider putting into other forms of writing."³³ E-mail is like conversation, except that it is more permanent than telephone or memos, because it is difficult to delete effectively. Although both lawyers and records managers initially ignored electronic documents such as e-mail, declaring it to be nothing more than the digital equivalent of a telephone conversation or an informal chat around the office coffee pot, we now know that e-mail meets the federal rules of evidence guidelines that records are made in the course of regular business, as part of the business practice, made by someone with knowledge of the business, are created near or close to event, and can be identified as having a chain of custody. Individuals need to be aware that e-mail can pose problems for them as well as they generate larger volumes of more personal and complex messages.

Such perspectives are not without considerable evidence, of course. The government's case against Microsoft set the precedent that e-mail can be used in litigation, and ever since there have been questions and debates about when organizations should keep or discard such records, especially since those ubiquitous backup tapes can be screened to recover even deleted messages.[34] In the post Sarbanes-Oxley era, corporate compliance estimates, in terms of their financial costs, are high, ranging for larger corporations from $1.6 to 4.4 million a year.[35] While the financial costs can be great, although in terms of the overall financial aspects of the corporate entities these costs might not be as burdensome as it seems, there are other benefits, as Grey suggests: "Many argue that although the cost of becoming compliant is high, the upside is well-structured accountability, improved organizational creditability, and customer protection."[36] One must wonder, however, if this is the only way to consider e-mail or, for that matter, any record or information source. And, we might reason, archivists and other records professionals will have to develop new means of expressing concern, probably other than compliance or accountability, for individuals who need to manage their personal documents.

News about companies paying huge fines or losing court cases because of mismanaged e-mail regularly reverberates through the records management profession. A U.S. Federal judge ruled that e-mails written by a J.P. Morgan Chase & Co. staff member could be used as evidence in a civil trial. The company was trying to reclaim more than a billion dollars from insurers concerning deals between J. P. Morgan and Enron Corp., indicating that the company assisted Enron in concealing its debt issues. This case suggests that corporate e-mail accounts need to be used wisely, that you know what not to write down, that you know what needs to be recorded, and that organizations must stop using e-mail as a personal knowledge management tool.[37] Such advice reflects the crossing between work and personal lives, but, generally, it is also useful advice for individuals as well. An individual can be held legally responsible for what they send in e-mail messages, just as companies and other organizations can be.

Other such cases regularly make the news. Philip Morris was fined because it destroyed e-mails sought by the Justice Department in its suit against the company. U.S. District Judge Gladys Kessler described the company's "reckless disregard and gross indifference" to the order that it preserve the mail. The company continued its monthly deletion of e-mails, protesting that it had already given millions of pages of documents and acted in good faith.[38] Merrill Lynch and Co., Inc. also was fined in 2006 $2.5 million by the U.S. Securities and Exchange Commission for not turning over 17 months of e-mails in a timely fashion. The company agreed to review its own e-mail and to develop policies for managing it, especially to comply with securities laws stipulating that companies must preserve e-mail for 3 months. In 2004 the Bank of America paid $10 million for similar problems, and Morgan Stanley is paying the SEC $15 million for the same reasons.[39] These settlements almost always require new efforts by the companies. In the case of Morgan Stanley, after destroying and failing to retain e-mails, totaling tens of thousands from December 11, 2000 through July 2005, as well as making "numerous misstatements" regarding the availability of and procedures concerning e-mail and other documents, the company agreed to "implement policies, procedures, and training focused on the preservation and production of e-mail communications."[40] Where would such a company look for model policies for administering its e-mail? How do we scale any of this down to individuals and their personal e-mail?

One case in particular, *Zubulake v. UBS Warburg*, has led to some particularly disturbing decisions for corporations, where the judge issued five opinions and orders focusing on electronic discovery and costs associated with such discovery. By all accounts, the case, concerning alleged gender discrimination, was fairly routine, but the judge's various rulings about electronic discovery were noteworthy, declaring what email and other documents a company should maintain when it knows or suspects that the documents are relevant to an action, including those that might be on backup tapes. What is important is that the court made a series of decisions about the preservation of evidence, finding that at UBS Warburg the lawyers had not instructed employees about how to preserve evidence, request appropriate evidence, or to consider how employees were maintaining evidence, with some of these problems relating to the maintenance of e-mail. In considering lessons from this case, legal expert John Montaña argues, as others have, that we need to incorporate these into records management procedures, learning from such past decisions.[41]

Other court cases have produced other disturbing aspects of the implications of using e-mail. In March 2003 the Federal Energy Regulatory Commission (FERC) released more than 1.6 million emails and documents by Enron employees on the Internet in a searchable database. These messages had been gathered as part of investigation into Enron's energy market manipulation case, and the FERC believed that posting these messages would help the public understand the case. Enron employees complained, and some of the more sensitive messages were removed. Enron also was given a 10 day shutdown to petition for the emails it wanted removed, resulting in about 100 Enron volunteers sorting through the messages (with the FERC ultimately removing about 8 percent of the messages [141,379 to be specific]). Nikki Swartz discerns the moral of the story: "Be careful how you use your business e-mail. You never know where your electronic messages may end up or who may be reading them, especially if the company you work for is sued or comes under investigation."[42] The same principle may apply to personal e-mail as well.

E-mail is one of those recording and information producing systems that generate records managers' concerns about new federal regulations, and, judging by the professional literature, this may be the foremost concern of records managers. On December 1, 2006, amendments to the U.S. Federal Rules of Civil Procedure went into effect, with the purpose of trying to make guidelines clearer for companies handling discovery requests for electronic information. These amendments declare all electronically stored information subject to discovery, even stating that an organization must be able to produce partial or fragmented data if there is a reason for it,[43] adding additional reasons for companies and other organizations to prepare written policies, take actions to provide greater control of electronic data, determine what data will be accessible, and have a systematic records retention schedule governing these electronic records. Records managers not only believe that they must be ever vigilant about such matters, but they seem to think that this is how they promote themselves to their employers. Whereas a generation or two ago they focused on the matter of the efficient and effective administration of records, now records managers are tied up with keeping their attention on matters of compliance, legal issues, and professional best practices that serve as new forms of regulations. Records professionals need to provide similar advice for individuals seeking both to manage their personal records and to preserve their family archives.

Records managers operate within a rapidly evolving set of guidelines and regulations regarding the nature of electronic records, such as represented by e-mail, and how they are to be managed. In a 1999 decision in the United States Circuit Court regarding the nature of maintaining federal government e-mail, the court "ruled that retention of a paper printout of an e-mail, as opposed to retention of the electronic record itself, constituted compliance with the Federal Records Act."[44] The outcome of this case derived from some ambiguous issues in the primary federal records law, most notably that "The Federal Records Act contains little substantive guidance on how to implement its strictures." In this case, the "court took the position that this absence of guidance permitted the archivist [the Archivist of the United States] to construe and apply the act in a discretionary manner, so long as the results were not inconsistent with demands of the act."[45] Such a decision suggests how not just records professionals but the courts themselves have been struggling to contend with how communication systems such as e-mail are being used by organizations and how these messages can be captured, maintained, and interpreted.

It is not just federal laws that are the source of concern for records professionals when considering how they should view e-mail. Increasingly, federal, state, and local governments are being forced to preserve e-mail and make them available to the public. A Wisconsin state law requires county offices to have approaches to save e-mails about county business and make them available for public viewing. In this state, one county had many of the county officials conducting official business from their home personal computers, a procedure that violated many laws, such as when email is used to continue a public discussion and violates that state's open meetings law.[46] It is another example of the blur between personal and professional use of e-mail. New professional standards are being developed in order to assist courts to be able to ascertain the reliability of electronic evidence, such as in the recently developed Canadian standard *Electronic Records as Documentary Evidence* (C**CGSB-72.34). The need for this standard emerged when the Personal Information Protection and Electronic Documents Act passed in 2000, legislation deriving from the fact that electronic records were increasingly being admitted in court cases, and that there needed to be a mechanism for courts to consider the reliability of electronic evidence. The standard's focus is on setting procedures for organizations to ensure the use of their records in court. The standard builds on principles of an organization having a records management program and having the proper procedures to support the program. The standard also lays out the guidelines for legal requirements, establishing the essentials of an electronic records management program, the nature of a quality assurance program, and the nature of creating and maintaining an audit trail.[47]

It is in the government arena that some of the earliest landmark cases emerged. David Wallace has documented the implications of two interrelated cases – Armstrong v. Executive Office of the President and

Public Citizen v. Carlin, both concerning e-mail, how it is viewed as a records systems, and how it should be administered. Referred to popularly as the PROFS case, after the system being used to create and manage e-mail, this legal case reinforced e-mail as a legitimate record necessitating the application of a substantial records management program encompassing e-mail with other records. The PROFS software was introduced into the National Security Council in 1985, bringing considerable functionality for using and managing e-mail.[48] This mail system was featured in the Iran-Contra Affair investigation in 1986-1987, because it was used by Oliver North and National Security Advisor John Poindexter. North and Poindexter tried to delete 6000 e-mail messages before the official investigation was underway, but backup tapes provided the copies of what Poindexter and North believed they had permanently deleted. In 1987 the NSC policy was that e-mail was a surrogate for the telephone, meaning that individual users were to identify a message as a record and then taking the necessary actions to ensure that any official records were to be printed out and the electronic versions would be dumped. When Reagan left office in 1989, it was expected that all e-mail would be deleted, but this plan was challenged by the National Security Archive, a non-governmental research institute and library using the Freedom of Information Act to gather government concerning "national security, foreign, intelligence, and economic policies of the United States."[49] The National Security Archive took this action after it was learned that NARA approved such deletion because it believed that it had the official records all printed and filed.

The basis of the suit brought by the National Security Archive was quite simple, or at least it appears to be with the advantage of two decades of hindsight. The National Security Archive (NSA) did not agree with e-mail being assigned as having a non-record status, especially since valuable and essential metadata would be lost if printed out. The NSA also disagreed with the then prevalent view among many records professional that a printed version of an e-mail message made the digital version a non-record. The case took four years, seemingly ending in 1993 with a ruling in favor of the plaintiffs about their argument that the deletion of the electronic versions of the e-mail would present nothing other than an opportunity to destroy federal records. The federal court ended up directing the U.S. Archivist to preserve electronic record versions and to develop new guidelines for e-mail management. It seemed that a new day had arrived for how records managers and archivists would perceive e-mail, except for the outcome of another lawsuit.

The second lawsuit related to the earlier one because the government in 1995 issued new general e-mail rules along with the General Record Schedule 20, supporting the notion that the official record of e-mail could not be supported electronically and that once printed out and properly filed that the electronic versions could be destroyed (in other words, circumventing the previous judicial ruling about federal e-mail and its administration as a government record). The plaintiffs filed another suit because they thought valuable administrative, legal, research, and other values in records would be lost. The court again ruled for the plaintiffs. The government appealed and in August 1999 the Appeals Court ruled for the government and reversed the lower ruling, basically deferring to the Archivist's judgment, especially in how it interpreted the notion of a formal recordkeeping system. Ultimately, the Supreme Court decided not to review the case. As David Wallace states, "As records management applications for maintaining electronic records in electronic form were just being commercialized in the late 1990s, the government was able to convince the Appeals Court hearing the GRS 20 case that the technology and practice infrastructures for managing electronic records electronically just did not exist across the federal government."[50] Undoubtedly, many records managers and archivists probably concurred with the decision, given the technical and administrative solutions that were available at the time. And, meanwhile, even as individuals increasingly grew dependent on e-mail, they mostly knew nothing about such cases and what they might be suggesting about their own electronic documents.

An article appearing just about the time the final appeal was being heard suggested that the existence of electronic document management systems, electronic imaging systems, and records management software all fell short of providing the kind of systems needed to maintain records such as e-mail in their digital form.[51] Paper printouts also won the day. Wallace surmises that although the government argued about how e-mail systems were not records, most experience with e-mail systems suggested that they were being used in this way. The litigation made the government back away from this perspective of e-mail messages not being official records, forcing it to begin to rethink how to manage these records. It also forced the rethinking of printouts versus electronic versions and to at least redirect attention to the recordkeeping dimensions and proper filing. From this point forward, few would argue that e-mail messages were anything other than records to be administered, and there is no reason to believe that such a development did not also reach out to individuals and their use of e-mail in the private sector; e-mail was now a document form that could compromise, as well as support, activity across society.

While government agencies squabbled over the definition of e-mail messages as records, information, or just convenient communications, businesses, universities, and organizations of every variety struggled to control how their employees used and managed their e-mail. The increasing reliance on e-mail and other digital documents for all organizational business also revealed how porous organizations have become in terms of managing their proprietary and confidential information. We see more and more cases of proprietary information compromised by stolen laptops, lost hard drives, and hacked company computers. Three Coca-Cola employees tried to sell trade secrets to PepsiCo for $1.5 million, and although PepsiCo worked with its rival and FBI agents to nab the three and charge them with stealing trade secrets, the case has disturbing implications. According to the U.S. Department of Justice, insider theft is growing at a rate of 15 percent annually, costing U.S. businesses and other organizations $60-120 billion annually. Protecting corporate information of any proprietary value is becoming more difficult because of portable electronic devices, with estimates that such devices will contain up to 40 percent of all corporate data going out each day with company workers. Nikki Swartz, reviewing various cases, comments that companies need to take steps to screen all employees at all levels, train employees about the value of information, protect confidential documents and records, control access to sensitive data, and not let employees leaving employment to take information with them.[52] Private individuals also need to be educated about the potential problems with their own digital archives.

Electronic mail, seen as such a threat, also has been a factor in shifting the attention of records managers in their work. Records managers need to equip themselves to understand how to contend with privacy concerns and legislation, as well as how to advise the corporations in how to avoid legal actions that stem from employees using e-mail for sending offensive sexual materials, discussing corporate proprietary and trade secrets, and revealing organizational practices. Given the nature of e-mail and its ease of use, however, this is a considerable challenge. It may be why so many records managers have examined publications written by vendors marketing e-mail technological solutions, some of dubious value.[53]

Many observers have commented on how they see records management work being transformed. As Randolph Kahn argues,

> Cases of records mismanagement, improper destruction, and falsification have cost billions of dollars, ended careers, decimated reputations, and caused some companies to wither away. Clearly, something is seriously broken. Although many records management programs probably never functioned as they should have to begin with, for most corporations it was not until the last few years that anyone took notice. Now everyone ostensibly cares about records.[54]

And here we can see a powerful lesson for the potential of archivists and other records professionals working with the public, concentrating on issues also relating to personal and family archives that will provide new opportunities for educating them about records issues. Such organizational issues have emerged because of the immense volume of e-mail being used to transact business, often with a sense for the administration being reliant on voluntary employee action. Companies and other organizations need stronger commitment to compliance to government and legal requirements and regulations, including policies and procedures, top executive support, employee training, auditing, the means for enforcement, and a commitment to improvement in how these records are handled. All of these matters can be scaled to personal recordkeeping.

Others have seen e-mail as a litmus test for the health of records management programs. Phillips believes that if we can figure out a way to administer e-mail, then it is indicative of progress being made in electronic records management efforts. Indeed, the problems with e-mail are a reflection of greater problems with administering records.[55] E-mail becomes a problem in the absence of records management standards and best practices. In fact, Phillips thinks, "E-mail, more than any other software application, is a default repository of both risky and valuable business records."[56] If e-mail can be administered with some degree of effectiveness, it is an indicator that an organization's records management program is working well in other areas. In the same fashion, if archivists can ascertain how to work with the public on such issues, this will reflect their own success in finding solutions posed by technologies such as e-mail.

The very nature of e-mail is contrary to what has been the purpose of records management operations. E-mail emerged as a tremendous challenge to records managers and their interest in order and control of records and information systems. Many have pointed to how e-mail's primary challenge is its casual nature, one that lulls workers into using it for a variety of purposes that can cause problems for the organization.[57] Randolph Kahn describes records retention, and records management in general, as a "broken" process because the increased use of electronic records systems has made "every employee with a computer a *de facto* records manager." As a result, employees tend not to pay attention to records schedules or other records management directives.[58] It is because of the decided lack of control that many organizations have adopted an extremist position on the management of e-mail. Since employees can't spend time analyzing every record or complicated schedules, records managers and legal counsel have suggested a variety of options, including getting rid of everything or saving everything.[59] These same kinds of issues also concern archivists who desire to identify and capture e-mail messages critical to documenting an organization or an individual; the only difference with their perspective is their focus on the maintenance side rather than the destruction of these messages. However, as I have argued in this book, perhaps archivists and records managers need to adopt the idea of equipping everyone to function as private records administrators.

Perhaps all that e-mail represents is the early wave of new communications technologies promising to re-invent the fundamental mission and nature of records management work. Many records managers, still struggling to deal with e-mail, now are facing even greater problems with the growing use of instant messaging (IM), a communications systems which can be synchronous, asynchronous, group, and parallel all at the same time. Even with these differences, we see two similarities between IM and e-mail. The "messages tend to be casual and often cryptic," leading to greater sloppiness and less control, and IM is a "free-flowing" process, not lending itself to be captured and controlled in standard document management systems. And, just as in the earlier days with e-mail, many records managers have opted to treat IM like telephone calls and voice mail, placing their organizations at risk.[60] From a legal perspective, are these records? Must they be formally administered for legal purposes? Legal expert John Montaña contends that e-mail and other messaging have no "ideal solution," arguing that the "spontaneous and informal nature of messaging is an attribute that contributes greatly to its value as a communication tool. The more we attempt to control and manage it, the more we interfere with that spontaneous and informal nature, and, thereby, with its value to us. Ultimately, a balance must be struck between control and utility, recognizing that these two needs are at odds with each other."[61] In the same manner, individuals face decisions everyday where they weigh convenience or ease with other issues like privacy and documentation.

The informality and pervasiveness of e-mail have prompted most records managers to develop, or adapt other, policies that describe a code of conduct, how the organization handles spam, procedures for the retention of messages, all in an effort to both regulate and educate their employees.[62] Rae Cogar contends "establishing a company e-mail policy protects not only the employer but also the employee and creates a better working environment."[63] It is because of a conviction that strong policy and accompanying procedures may be the most effective approach to controlling e-mail that we have witnessed so much emphasis by professional associations on e-mail policy,[64] but this is not an approach that will enable archivists and records managers to assist individuals (except to point to such policies as guides about the challenges of e-mail use).

Despite all the policy and technical attention to electronic communications such as e-mail, it is painfully obvious that progress in administering them has been far from adequate. In survey after survey, there is bad news about such matters. The 2006 AIIM study, *Compliance: It's Real, It's Relevant, and It's More Than Just Records*, surveying records and information management professionals (with 52 percent identifying themselves as records managers) in 128 state and local agencies, discovered that only about a third have any confidence about electronic records management. The "majority of respondents said their efforts to preserve and secure information on computer hard drives, e-mail, and portable devices is very weak." Another 41.5 percent "described their processes for managing information stored on portable electronic devices (e.g., cell phones, PDAs) as 'complete chaos.'"[65] This is a survey occurring a reasonably long time after ARMA had issued its well-known e-mail policy, suggesting that such a policy framework fell far short of organizational realities. What the public might ask, when it gets around to doing so, is what are they supposed to do with the information and evidence they generate on such devices if the experts can't figure what to do? We have time before such questions are asked, but not much.

The fatal flaw, at least for archivists, is that poor records management policies and practices seem to consign e-mail to oblivion, perhaps making the corporate lawyer happy, but befuddling anyone interested in the long-term memory and documentation of an organization. John Phillips contends "e-mail's transitory nature illustrates the difficulties associated with storing records for long periods on electronic systems. Very few users have e-mail older than two or three years because e-mail systems, software, and data migrations typically destroy or distort these records periodically."[66] And recommended policies seem not to make provision to correct this problem, even if organizations and individuals want to maintain such records longer. The earlier ARMA e-mail policy mentions appraisal, for example, but not in a manner that will fill archivists with confidence, actually suggesting that if an organization lacks an archival program, then there is no need to worry about such issues. [67] The lack of a holistic records program and policy may be one key to understanding why new information technologies such as e-mail seem to be breaking down standard notions of records management operations.

What Does the Future Hold?

While many records managers have one eye on their current status within their organizations and the other on where the future may be directing them in terms of the changing technologies of recordkeeping, few have made specific predictions about the future (most have provided more hyped up versions of the importance of records and information management professionals). One exception is Deborah Juhnke who peers half a dozen years into the future and sees where instant messaging has become preferred over e-mail, when there are no e-mail archives to search, and the old paper document paradigm is over. "The quill pen has given way to the digital pen," she speculates, "creating a responsibility to respect and protect this more fragile form of evidence."[68] The new emphasis on digital data goes beyond the notion of the document where there is a "beginning, an end, and a logical structure."[69] She sees that "storage has become personal. Corporate servers are no longer the exclusive keepers of corporate data. Thumb drives, flash cards, and micro-drives are now capable of holding gigabytes of data that can be downloaded simply and secretly. Employees can more easily take their work (or anything else) home or to a competitor."[70] This is a prediction about the shift to personal recordkeeping, or, at least, where organizational and personal archiving has become interchangeable. It is a time when declining storage costs means that companies and organizations are keeping more and making them more liable.[71]

Predicting what the future holds is always a risky business. What may be significant is grasping that records managers now understand the importance of e-mail, so now the issue is how best to manage it. As Johannes Scholtes suggests, we must sort through the matter of whether e-mail is a technology issue, a concern related to sales and marketing (or customer services), or a legal and liability problem. Scholtes argues that we need balanced approaches that take into account all these aspects.[72] And such a balanced perspective is impossible unless we embrace the foundational principle of the records life cycle and consider how archivists, who must be present in the equation, view e-mail and its management.

Enter the Archivists.

Even if it is not difficult to understand that electronic mail is an essential means of communicating, transacting business, and living out one's daily existence, apparently it is a challenge to figure out how these messages ought to be administered as part of the documentary universe. Records managers have generally viewed e-mail as a threat to controlling records and information, a liability risk for their organizations, and a potential sieve for leaking out crucial proprietary information. While records managers certainly understand how and why e-mail has virtually replaced correspondence as a documentary form, a fact that archivists are particularly sensitive to in their work, they have generally adopted practices whereby they routinely destroy e-mail (accept for those messages connected to actual or potential litigation), an extremely different perspective than that held by archivists.

Archivists have tended to see the emergence of e-mail as a threat to one of the most cherished of documentary sources, the letter. Historians and biographers, as well as researchers engaged in some form of historical enquiry from nearly every discipline, have both praised the value of correspondence as a window into the past and lamented the potential loss of this rich documentary source caused by the growing use of e-mail and the technical, administrative, and legal issues generated by this communications technology. Archivists have adopted similar strategies to those of their records management colleagues in developing policies, educating e-mail users in their organizations, and seeking technical solutions through vendors and their own research and development issues. There is, of course, a major difference in the objectives of archivists and records managers in their efforts to administer e-mail. While archivists generally want to identify and preserve e-mail with continuing historical and other research values, records managers aim to remove as much e-mail as quickly as possible, fearing potential legal and other problems. The varying views of archivists and records managers on e-mail is testimony to the deep cultural, historical, and professional divisions between these records professionals that seem counter to the unifying concept of the records life cycle.

While records managers view e-mail through a lens clouded with concerns about risk, litigation, compliance, and control, archivists have tended to consider the same messages as another challenge to identify and preserve the important segments of the documentary heritage, within corporations, governments, other institutions, and created by individuals. While both segments of the records community adheres to the notion of a records life cycle – tracking records from creation through use and storage to an ultimate disposition either to be destroyed or to be placed in an archival repository (real or virtual) – it is hard to accept that this is much more than rhetoric given the practical activities carried out by archivists and records managers when they face information systems such as e-mail. Mostly, they express opinions on the far ends of the spectrum of what should be done with records and information systems, and it is difficult to know what an individual working as a records professional with both records management and archival responsibilities ought to do with e-mail messages. However, the nature of the archivists' concern with e-mail as an important historical source, one often created by individuals, ought to position them for working directly with individuals and families concerned about their own archives.

E-mail and the Threat to the Documentary Heritage.

More and more of us, whatever our occupation, are relying on e-mail. The consequences for documenting organizations, individuals, families, and society are potentially devastating. Robert P. Crease, historian at the Brookhaven National Laboratory, provides a glimpse into the challenge with his assessment about the impact of the Internet on the history of science. Providing a number of examples about where historians have discovered critical insights into scientific research through the discovery and analysis of letters, Crease notes that "now that e-mail has replaced letter writing as the principal means of informal communication, one has to feel sorry for future science historians, who will be unable to use letters and telegrams to establish facts and gauge reactions to events." He argues, "letters are also useful to historians because the character of scientists can often be revealed more clearly in informal communications than in official documents." Historians rely on letters as well to "reconstruct thought processes." However, this will be more difficult in the future given how scientists are using the Internet and computers for their work: "E-mail is, of course, cheaper and encourages quicker thought, and it introduces a peculiar blend of the personal and professional. The AIP historians have also detected a decline in the use of lab notebooks, finding that data are often stored directly into computer files. Finally, they have noted the influence of PowerPoint, which can stultify scientific discussion and make it less free-wheeling; information also tends to be dumbed down when scientists submit PowerPoint presentations in place of formal reports." Crease indicates that this is not about the ease of use for scientists or the "romantic" thrill of examining old letters; "Far more worrying is the question of whether e-mail and other electronic data will be preserved at all."[73] Such concerns can be extended out into nearly every aspect of our society, including the family and personal archives.

This is not a new story, of course. A decade ago, Susan Lukesh wrote about the potential loss to historical documentation that might be caused by the growing use of e-mail. Starting off with the usual refrain of how important letters have been to historians and biographers, in both formal and informal communication, Lukesh argues for the importance of preserving e-mail as a critically significant part of our modern documentation and she draws on the views of archivists, librarians, records managers, historians, and corporate and legal experts to build her case. She argues, among other things, that "scholars should be urged to keep paper records of all e-mail correspondence," even though "doing this clearly eliminates the full record and as more e-mail products provide direct hotlinks this loss will increase;" "archivists should develop standards and recommendations for preservation of this form of informal communication, and librarians and archivists together should actively seek to alert scholars to the dangers that future research (and even their own) will face should these documents no longer be available"; and "vendors ... should be urged to develop products for use on a personal level which scholars could purchase and implement." Lukesh also believes we need more "funding for research in the preservation of electronic records, including e-mail correspondence," and that "all current efforts investigating the preservation of electronic records should make explicit the inclusion of personal e-mail preservation in their efforts, separate from web sites and listservs."[74] Just how much progress has been made in such recommendations since Lukesh made her observations is debatable. And the growth of dependence on e-mail, made more complicated by the proliferation of hand-held and other portable devices making e-mail available at all times, is something archivists and other records professionals need to recognize and embrace as an area requiring their immediate attention.

It is possible, of course, to hang onto the notion that e-mail will never completely replace word-processed and handwritten snail mail. Edward Tenner provides a sense of the tensions between the new possibilities of digital information technologies and older methods, such as print, in generating societal and individual documentation. We can feel "empowered" because "we can send what are basically free telegrams to people around the globe, create and distribute photographs and video at little or no cost, broadcast our ruminations through blogs, and browse many of the world's greatest art museums and library collections — all from our own desks. Public libraries and Internet cafes around the world assure free or cheap access to those still without home computers. If that isn't progress, if this isn't empowerment, what is?" Tenner stresses some of the economic, logistical, and marketing challenges faced by publishers of print sources, while explaining why even with the digital technologies some old-fashioned means of communicating, such as printed greeting cards, have not been replaced by digital surrogates. Tenner thinks that e-mail has not replaced the influence of older means such as snail mail: "And although executives may spend hours sending e-mail communications and instant messages, their most important sentiments are likely to be expressed as handwritten notes — one of the reasons for the luxury fountain-pen industry's niche in the digital age. Legislators and their staffs are also said to take handwritten letters more seriously than e-mail notes, although it remains true that an original and thoughtful electronic message will be more influential than canned talking points in any format."[75] Although Tenner, along with others, sees some possibilities that new digital sources will complement and even enhance some traditional print sources, there is no way to be sure about this. From my vantage, there will remain an interest in collecting older documentary forms, and the continuation of some forms such as handwritten diaries, but it seems doubtful that older technologies will remain prevalent while newer ones become convenient and less expensive.

While it may be heartening to think that some letters are still being sent in the old-fashioned way, there is no doubt that e-mail has made major inroads into this. There is probably little question that archivists value correspondence as one of the most significant forms of historical documentation. There is nothing better than rich detailed letters by various protagonists to add both insight and color to any historical event. There are few greater pleasures than discovering a personal letter in which an individual explains the reasons why he took a particular action or his explanation about why a certain event occurred. But I suspect, along with others, that this kind of detailed explanation is being expressed in e-mail, and, what is more, that e-mail captures even more by text than what was occurring before its advent. Now, individuals send e-mail messages rather than letters because e-mail is easier, faster, and more efficient. E-mail has also replaced telephone calls and a considerable amount of even face-to-face conversation. Archivists hunger to capture this depth of documentation, while records managers worry about legal and other implications of it. Someday, it may be that historians and other researchers will have much better documentation from which to do their research.

The implications for how e-mail might affect the fabric of our documentary heritage are only a relatively recent recognition. David Bearman, in 1994, predicted that e-mail would become a major organizational and professional issue,[76] seeing a combination of policy, design, implementation, and standards as the way to resolve an organization's needs to administer e-mail in a seamless process by which individuals could identify what e-mail messages needed to be archived. More than a dozen years later, archivists and others are still wrestling with the implications of e-mail and how to administer it, approaching the challenge in nearly the same fashion as Bearman did.[77] Some archivists and other records professionals are rolling up their sleeves and working with the e-mail systems, recognizing that this is no longer an issue that they can ignore and still maintain some degree of presence in the quest to administer any organization's documentary universe. They also need to look for solutions outside of organizations, assisting people with their personal and family archives.

It is difficult for most archivists to try and pretend that electronic records, such as e-mail, do not exist when their lead program, the U.S. National Archives, already acknowledges that the "majority of government records are electronic."[78] The National Archives is carrying out research in four areas – archives and records management; requirements analysis; computer science and operational concepts; and operational prototypes, with some of these projects being tackled on an immense scale apropos to the scale of government recordkeeping. It is working with the San Diego Supercomputer Center to develop new means of access to electronic records, while also working to establish a records management profile in the Federal Enterprise Architecture.[79] On smaller scales, archivists are also seeking practical solutions to administering e-mail (although it is questionable whether archivists are thinking about how to scale down to the level of the individual, private citizen. While some may long for the old-fashioned handwritten letter, archivists generally comprehend that e-mail is now the surrogate for that letter.

How Have Archivists Considered E-mail?

How have archivists approached the issue of e-mail? Has it been similar to what records managers have done? More archival work was done initially on harnessing e-mail as part of a reference service (rather than in managing it as a documentary source) that can be run all day every day with advantages such as developing a litany of common questions.[80] Considered this way, e-mail is simply part of the challenge archivists are facing in the changing expectations of users (some new because of the advantages of connecting electronically) who are becoming more and more savvy with compact, ubiquitous information technologies.[81] Yet, if researchers are adopting e-mail as a means of seeking connections to archives and to transact research projects, archivists must recognize that every one else is using e-mail to carry out their own business, both generating important records and replacing other forms of documentation.

Archivists, like records managers, have tried to manage e-mail through policy promulgation, mostly as a means of creating a broad approach to identifying and capturing, in a usable fashion, e-mail messages of continuing value to organizations (what individuals create would not, of course, be captured through such policies). Many examples of archival policies on e-mail are available, and we can see e-mail policies extending from more than a decade ago. A resource guide on automated records and techniques in archives, issued by the Society of American Archivists in 1990, reveals little evidence of interest in e-mail issues (most of the archival focus was then on matters like databases, scheduling and appraising records, and an assortment of technical issues).[82] There were some early studies of e-mail, such as one conducted by Carol Nowicke, where she confirmed that in a federal government agency that "electronic mail is the nearest written equivalent to the correspondence of pre-World War II era" and that this e-mail also captures information previously lost in telephone conversations, the perspective initially conveyed in an effort to contend with the impact of e-mail on organizational activities.[83] In fact, a decade after Nowicke's small study, archivists were still both hopeful and concerned about the use of e-mail, in that it seemed to capture information lost in telephone conversation and was a return to a form of correspondence, assuming that appraisal and technical matters could be worked out.

By then, some archivists were more worried about the implications of e-mail for the shaping of personal archives, as one archivist notes:

> The proliferation of electronic mail has substantially increased personal documentation, partially supplanting telephone communication. Although it would be false to assume that the content and method of e-mail communication mirrors speaking on the telephone, its convenience and relatively low cost allow people to supplement and often substitute it for telephone communiqué. The impact of the telephone replacing the letter as the primary method of distanced communication has long been a source of lamentation for archivists who have been forced to acknowledge that much reflective information about an individual's personal life now takes place over an unpreserved medium. The relative ease with which one can save e-mail messages provides an opportunity to regain documentation of perhaps intimate exchanges, if archivists can find a way to preserve them.[84]

A focus like this on personal documentation is, without question, a far cry from what records managers have been interested in. Records managers would be interested in individuals and their records only if these were somehow connected with organizational business or were threatening to reveal, inadvertently or in some planned way, proprietary and other confidential information of the organization. It also suggests that archivists have understood how communications technologies such as e-mail affect personal recordkeeping, the kind that many archives have been eager to acquire.[85]

Archivists are not, then, new to the business of recognizing e-mail as important records systems or in trying to administer effectively e-mail. The Australian national archives promulgated standards a decade ago for this purpose, stressing that electronic messages are records, need to be captured as part of recordkeeping systems, and that they need to be maintained with their content, structure, and context. The Australians were pioneers in arguing that archival programs were not just about cultural agendas but that records were to be administered for accountability and evidence as well.[86] This particular national archives required that e-mail rules be set in every agency, whereby critically important records were to be printed out and filed in appropriate places. While certain technical requirements were spelled out, as much attention was devoted to matters of e-mail etiquette.[87] Armed with this broader notion of societal values in administering records, it is not difficult to see that e-mail would be incorporated into such management as more than a legal or intellectual property liability but as part of a larger objective to preserve the documentary heritage.

Other government archives in Australia were developing similar approaches, such as exemplified by the Archives Authority of New South Wales, built around policy, legislation, standards, best practice, guidelines and manuals, and training and support. All of this mimics to some extent what we see in the records management literature, except that here archivists are given a more explicit role.[88] Such emphases appear in many government archives and records policies around the world in this era, such as with the issuance in 1995 by the New York State Archives and Records Administration of a policy on e-mail, affirming it as official records "when they are created or received in the transaction of public business and retrieved as evidence of official policies, actions, decisions, or transactions."[89] We understand, however, just when this policy was issued, as it states that there is an awareness that "technological constraints and practical considerations may preclude some agencies from retaining e-mail records in electronic filing systems at this time."[90] There is affirmation that e-mail can possess archival value, as the policy indicates that e-mail is subject to retention schedules, with state archives staff available to help "identify records with long-term or archival values."[91]

Other various government archives have supplemented policies with technical and other administrative actions. The Texas State Archives has experimented in using the Open Archival Information System (OAIS) Reference Model to design a repository for managing email records. The attraction to the OAIS model exists "because it provides the elements that research indicates are necessary: a closely audited, well documented, and constantly maintained and updated system," elements suggesting its utility especially in a government agency. The Texas Email Repository Model (TERM) provides for a classification of email messages "by using standard email metadata to determine the record creator and then linking this identification to job function or job activity and an associated records schedule set." This is obviously a system enabling the holistic administration of e-mail messages, encompassing archival, records, and preservation management perspectives. This is built around a virtual repository, or what they call a "trusted" repository, ensuring that "records of a truly transitory nature are destroyed efficiently and legally rather than left to accumulate in ever increasing numbers in an unwieldy manner in networked computing systems. The repository preserves the official business records of state government and can expand access services to a customer base that includes the agencies within state government and the public it serves."[92]

Generally such approaches as these have substantial fault lines in their foundations for implementation. Despite this interesting proposal in the Lone Star state, the present policy (at least when this chapter was written) for e-mail messages in the Texas state government makes little provision for retaining e-mail with archival value. While the policy declares that "all e-mail sent or received by an agency is considered a state record" and that "all e-mail messages must be retained or disposed of according to the agency's retention schedule," there is little indicating that this means any e-mail will be retained because of an archival significance. It is indicated that e-mail will be part of administrative correspondence, "subject to Archival review"; general correspondence, needing only to be retained for a year; or "transitory information," meaning that it can be disposed of after the "purpose of the record has been fulfilled."[93] Whatever such weaknesses may be, these and other efforts at least recognize the documentary resource that is inherent in e-mail messages for government and its citizens. How much of a step would it be for such an archives to move from working with government agencies to working with state citizens?

A more ambitious proposal for administering e-mail has come from the Digital Curation Center in the United Kingdom.[94] The Center believes e-mail includes critically important records for organizations not just to administer from existence (via strenuous deletion) but also to manage because they provide important evidence for organizations to archive and to maintain for organizational purposes such as corporate memory and knowledge management. This proposal provides a very different perspective about the archival issues posed by these messages that raises a whole set of new issues, and it is a perspective worth quoting at length:

> Correspondence of notable figures is traditionally collected and used by institutions, private individuals, and researchers as a historical record of events or social/private discourse. There is often no legal reason why the correspondence is created or should be preserved. The value and preservation of the materials arises instead from its cultural heritage and historical context.
>
> E-mail is the modern-day equivalent of paper-based correspondence. Many types of institutions, particularly in the library and museum sectors, will therefore collect and curate e-mails that have no legal context or value, and with no explicit legal obligation to do so. Such organizations may simply have an implicit or explicit mandate to preserve. For example, a library may accession a collection of e-mails from a significant author that it wishes to curate and make accessible for future generations. Record-keeping is not the driver for managing and curating objects in such institutions; the driver instead is the preservation and accessibility of the objects themselves. In the absence of legal requirements, the institution's mandate to provide continuing storage and access to items is itself a powerful impetus for ensuring proper e-mail curation practices.[95]

Such perspectives must seem to be nonsense to records managers concerned only or preeminently about the legal and other liabilities created by e-mail, since here we observe historical and cultural reasons to preserve a portion of e-mail.

This report additionally observes that vendor systems have little to offer for the archival maintenance of e-mail: "Although such systems may help ensure that inappropriate e-mails are deleted, provide good search facilities and fairly instant access to stored messages, and relieve the general burden on e-mail servers, there is little published information about their ability to ensure the management of e-mail messages for the long-term of fifty, a hundred, and two hundred years or more."[96] The lack of such information ought to be a reason for considerable alarm among all records professionals, although the recommendations for organizations establishing digital repositories for the storage of e-mail messages make a lot of sense.[97] In the remainder of the report, there are practical steps for creating a policy enabling the creators of e-mail to assume some responsibility for e-mail curation, as well as describing the reasons for capturing e-mail messages with long-term value (although no one will discover here concrete or established procedures for a successful capture of e-mail with archival value). As the report notes, "The proper and active curation of e-mail messages, as with websites, is still in a period of immaturity."[98]

There is, then, much work to be done, even if we recognize that when archivists began to formulate agendas for research about electronic records management, there was little reference to e-mail.[99] Mostly now, however, we find analyses of the use and administration of e-mail in various organizations, with recommendations for policies reflecting how to administer such records. One such study reveals, as most have, that it is left up to individual workers to administer their e-mail. This is why so many organizations keep hoping that policies will help (or that vendors will offer up viable technical solutions that take away the serendipitous reliance on individual approaches). This study also suggests that individuals rely on memory and association to manage their email, and that "this storage and retrieval strategy allows the least transferability of the information because it relies on the individual manager's heuristic devices and memory for successful retrieval."[100] Maybe somewhere in such notions, there is advice that will help archivists recommend approaches for the effective preservation of e-mail found in personal and family archives.

Are We Witnessing A Shift in E-Mail Management?

Perhaps the various federal and state laws, so often cited by records managers and the many vendors serving these professionals as almost a kind of scare tactic, may be bringing a shift in thinking and working that might be closer to how archivists have approached e-mail. Lawyer Douglas Seaver, trying to get the attention of the administrators in higher education, where more archivists are employed than any other sector of society, warns them that universities are now expected by the courts to be able to produce their electronic data.[101] Seaver emphasizes the need to be more diligent in *preserving* the digital information and evidence than in destroying it.

Is this kind of advice part of a shift from the interest of many records professionals, legal and fiscal officers, and administrators to destroy e-mail as quickly as possible? Seaver, surveying the legal landscape, provides very practical advice to the leaders of universities and colleges, namely, "establish a litigation team to handle e-discovery issues"; "preserve all relevant evidence"; "be inclusive in identifying information that should be captured"; "outsource information-gathering, if necessary"; "train other staff members about e-discovery"; "adopt a clear e-discovery computer-use policy"; "preserve attorney-client privileges"; and, "establish an e-discovery plan." Seaver argues that lawyers and judges are both becoming savvier about the digital recordkeeping and information systems, leading him to caution that everyone working on the campus "should understand that their electronic documents may become evidence in litigation, and that, as a result, they should be judicious in the information that they create, receive, retain, or send. They must also be ready to preserve and protect electronically stored information once they learn that litigation against the institution is likely or has begun."[102] While it is tempting merely to acknowledge that what is being described sounds very similar to what records managers have been saying or reading for years, there is one difference; there is also an added incentive of being careful to identify and preserve the critically important records. It is easy to see how archivists, if they can do this in an effective fashion, could harness such principles and use them to support an archival mission that relies on a much broader based argument than merely saving old stuff that may possess limited research value.

E-mail and the Documentation of Individuals and Families.

The computer is ubiquitous at all levels of society, and, as a result, e-mail has increasingly replaced the personal letter as a major means of communication. Archivists who identify and collect individual and family papers for their archives now are not only examining basements and closets but computer hard drives. Canadian archivist Lucie Paquet provides a glimpse into this, writing, "When I visit my donors, I bring an external disk drive with me in order to copy electronic records of historical value so that I can take them back to the National Archives of Canada. On entering their homes, I find that, as is the case in my own home, the computer is an integral part of the rest of the furnishings. Installed in the living room or a study room, its role is to process and transmit information and to create many different kinds of records. My donors look upon the computer as a space for their work and leisure."[103] Paquet describes how she "have had to adopt different archival approaches: one is a proactive approach for recently-created records, characterized by their diversity, by the increase in the quantity of software and electronic formats, and by the integration or interconnection of equipment."[104]

Paquet's comments about the implications of e-mail represents a very different perspective than what we have seen with records managers: "Donors are happy to show me how their computers and accessories work. They tell me that they communicate daily with friends, colleagues, former colleagues, and especially their children, and have been doing go for almost ten years. They are writing far more today with electronic mail than they ever did via traditional letters," although they are not saving as much. "Some messages have been printed out but, unfortunately, most of the mail sent and received has been erased..." Paquet continues, "Electronic mail generates a phenomenal amount of messages that can, over time, become difficult to manage. Their solution in the short term is to destroy the messages or print some of them out on paper." E-mail is generating a gap in the documentary record, since "we are losing a considerable amount of personal information, a step backward in terms of personal archives. This major loss also diminishes the quality and value of their records since the electronic correspondence contained information that might have shed light on their activities and the evolution of their thinking during a particular period."[105] In other words, archivists need to become much more proactive in their efforts to save such materials.

Archivists tend to see not only the potential damage to the documentary universe caused by the use of e-mail, but they also see its potential for wonderful new insights into the activities of individuals and families:

> Electronic mail, as well as the records generated by chat groups on the Internet, are important records to save for private archival holdings. Exchanges by electronic mail are a form of communication that, by its dynamism and its occurrence on a daily basis, allows for direct contact between people and leads to dynamic, spontaneous, informal and personal interaction. The historical value of this personal information can be extremely important. In some sectors of society, this form of

communication acts as the medium for new ideas, new hypotheses and new research projects. Compared with the traditional communications, this new system of communication is simple, fast, efficient, secure and inexpensive. Preserving this type of record would enable researchers and historians to easily access, research and manipulate the information.[106]

Paquet reveals that individuals and families often have some of the same concerns about e-mail that corporations and governments do, namely that

> Unfortunately, donors are not very receptive to the idea of retaining their electronic mail messages, mainly because of the volume of personal and sensitive information it may contain about their lives, their families and their friends. Some donors want to save their correspondence. But the simplest and fastest solution in their eyes is to make a paper copy of the most important messages. It is necessary to explain to them that a paper copy is not the solution because the messages lose their important archival value. Unique information relating to form and technique can be lost when a paper copy is made, including, among others, the information relating to the structure of the messages.[107]

What all this suggests is that unless archivists seek to educate these individuals about the nature of digital records such as e-mail, much of it will be lost before we even have a chance to evaluate it.

Finding the Middle Ground.

If archivists see e-mail as a potentially important historical resource needing to be preserved in some form and records managers perceive the same e-mail to be an administrative liability needing to be destroyed or managed in a way that reduces potential harm to the organization, can we discern a middle ground between these two perspectives?

Assisting archivists and records managers in finding a middle ground, we have some existing tools that could be adopted and adapted. Mark Moerdler notes that even with considerable variation among e-mail archiving systems, every system contains certain essential features such as storage management, e-mail capture, e-mail discovery (for compliance purposes), mailbox management (for user management), and lifecycle rules (internal regulations directing users to take certain actions, such as when a certain storage capacity is reached or setting certain time limits for when e-mail should be moved into an archive).[108]

Johannes C. Scholtes describes the basic e-mail capabilities that can be supported in an XML application, including capturing, storing, analyzing content, searching, de-duplication (removing near duplicates), reviewing e-mail quickly, redacting (in order to remove confidential or private information), and disclosing (where documents can be made available to other parties when needed).[109] So, yes, we may be moving, even if too slowly, towards some technical solutions for managing e-mail. However, it may be that the real important role for archivists is to seek to assist the public in preserving personal and family archives, a task records managers certainly have expressed little interest in fulfilling.

For many years archivists expressed dismay at the use of the word "archive" by software and records management software vendors who used the word in every way except in the manner that archivists intended. Now we see vendors and other experts using the notion of archiving to distinguish from simple backup tapes for electronic documents such as e-mail. While back-up tapes can be effectively used in the case of major disasters and system failures, it is not a good way to be able to search and locate specific documents since both content and context of the documents are necessary. Nevertheless, archivists might be troubled by certain limitations of e-mail archiving systems such as described by Nick Mehta, where "archiving takes copies of older primary data that are typically no longer accessed on a daily or short-term basis and moves that data to another location, ideally less expensive storage, where it is indexed and searchable by the organization in a long-term archive. Given the amount of duplicate data that exists within enterprises, especially within email systems, reducing primary storage through active email archiving can substantially improve backup and restore performance."[110] Joe Romanowski describes an email archiving system as one that will "automatically apply corporate policies to offload messages from email servers based on any combination of parameters such as age, size, status, sender, location, etc."[111] We need to ascertain how to scale down such systems to the level of personal and family archives as well, or risk losing a massive portion of our documentary heritage.

We also can detect the differences in attitudes between archivists and records managers when we read a report sent from ARMA about new technologies allowing voicemail messages to be automatically converted to written messages that can be read as e-mail or written transcripts. The written versions provide essential metadata such as the sender's telephone number, message date, and the time of the message.

It is not difficult to imagine that archivists could see some extraordinary potential in such technologies to generate new documentary sources relating to critical organizational functions and activities. However, here is how the ARMA news release reported the potential of these technologies:

> Stored voicemails represent a new, potentially negative consequence during legal discovery. Most large companies do not save or archive voicemail. But converted to e-mail, these messages *are* likely to be stored and be subject to discovery. Unfortunately, because it is regarded as transitory, voice communication is often used for subjects that should not be discussed in e-mail. Voice messages that are stored as e-mail on employees' mobile devices, forwarded to their work and others' e-mail accounts, or made available from a third-party service will give litigators a new treasure trove of easily accessible, electronically stored information that delivers dramatic evidence in text – and possibly even in the defendant's own voice.[112]

How do we reconcile such perspectives with the need to advise the public about how to care for their personal and family archives? Certainly, we need to advise them about the dangers associated with maintaining personal information, but we also cannot advise them to resort to wholesale destruction of their documents.

Without question, one of the most important steps needing to be taken with e-mail is to place the archiving process for e-mail within the information technology structure, such as maintaining metadata, keeping together e-mails and their attachments, and moving e-mails and attachments into formats enabling them to be kept over time. Technical approaches, while important, are not the most critical step, however. There must be a commitment to a broader archival-records management agenda with both a view on administrative and archival matters; while archivists and records managers in their organizations need to work to ensure that personal e-mails and other records are not in their systems, these records professionals also need to determine ways to advise the public how to deal with their personal and family archives. In enabling organizations to manage their record and information resources, we should not be ignoring or destroying another important component of the documentary universe.

It is especially important that archivists and records managers work together in order for them to place conditions on vendor products, nearly all of which do not deliver on the functionalities for e-mail management that are needed. Most of the off-the-shelf solutions have problems with securing data on the context of e-mail messages, classification, administration of attachments, capturing of the complete record, and too great a reliance on the creators and transmitters of e-mail messages.[113] Stating this, I do not mean to imply that the solution to e-mail management is a technical issue; indeed, I think the problem is that records managers and archivists need to develop an approach whereby the organization is protected against unnecessary litigation or the loss of proprietary information without resorting to wholesale destruction of e-mail messages. Archivists and records managers need to collaborate so that they can identify key organizational functions and activities that must be documented in the long-term and that require identifying all records, information, and data – including e-mail – that is crucial to achieving this. Archivists need to take the lead in working to preserve personal and family archives in digital and other forms, including e-mail messages.

Some individuals have at least pointed us in the right direction. David Bearman's early essay on e-mail management presages the needed middle ground for archivists and records managers. Writing with a sensitivity to the archival perspective, Bearman also stresses organizational accountability and institutional administrative, legal, and compliance needs.[114] Bearman also suggests how e-mail strained then present archives and records management approaches:

> As a new documentary form, electronic mail is not governed by many conventions. In its management we are forced therefore to educate the users about how these systems and our in-house files work, design systems that recognize records of specific business functions and treat them accordingly, implement systems which segregate the creation and storage locations so that records must cross over software switches that can assess how they should be managed, and deploy standards that contribute to better documentation of the content of electronic mail, particularly metadata documentation standards.[115]

How far we have come since Bearman wrote this is debatable.

In all these various elements that we can associate with a middle ground, the most important one might be the idea, more deftly articulated by archivists, of records as resources. In one of the SAA teaching case studies from the mid-1990s, Barbara Reed and Frank Upward describe the case of a hypothetical banking establishment where email has become the "preferred method of communication throughout the organization," but where there are "no instructions on

how to manage electronic mail ... beyond a guide providing a few
protocols for communication and advice on how to use the system."[116]
In the accompanying teaching guide to their case study, Reed and
Upward describe how archival science concerns understanding records
as resources – "It deals with recordkeeping, including document
creation, records systems, the establishment of the archive as corporate
memory, and the wider role of providing access to records beyond an
organizational context, embodied in corporate memory."[117] This is the
main meeting ground for archivists and records managers to seek to try
to develop mutually beneficial solutions for the administration of e-mail.
It is especially important since e-mail has become the "preferred
method of communication" for large segments of society.

What ought to be the middle ground for archivists and records
managers for determining how to manage e-mail? First, it is a
recognition that the aim is not to destroy all e-mail messages as
ruthlessly as possible but, instead, to develop criteria and procedures for
identifying e-mail that are critically important to an organization's
administration and memory. Second, that the value of records (and
information) for organizational and cultural memory is as least as
important as the value of records for institutional management and
performance. Third, that the organization has a responsibility to
manage its records in a way that reflects its responsibility for a public
good. Fourth, that the concept of a life cycle of records, so foundational
to all archives and records management work, mandates that records be
considered in both their active and inactive stages, encompassing all
potential values, including the archival value. And, fifth, that archivists
and records managers work together within an organization via a
macro-appraisal approach, such as an emphasis on identifying and
documenting critical organizational functions. All of these elements are
well documented within professional literature, but it is also obvious
that when considering something such as e-mail that archivists and
records managers seem to row in different directions. We can also add
to all this, the need for archivists to adopt energetically methods of
advising the public on how to administer their personal and family
archives, especially those in digital form such as e-mail.

However, the question really may be whether there is any hope now
for finding such a middle ground.

Is There a Middle Ground?

When I started writing the original version of this essay, I envisioned a much more coherent statement about what archivists and records managers need to do in order to manage effectively and appropriately e-mail. Then, before I finished two things happened. The Society of American Archivists (SAA) embroiled itself in controversy with an initial decision to destroy the online archives of the Archives and Archivists listserv, and Carol Chosky's book on records management was published.

The SAA decision, announced in mid-March 2007, to remove the online archives of the primary archives listserv brought with it an intense discussion. The SAA Executive Director, Nancy Beaumont, announced the decision to the listserv by citing a range of reasons for the decision, including an appraisal report indicating the list to possess little continuing value, financial and technical issues working against its retention, intellectual property matters, and questions about SAA's responsibility for maintaining the listserv as documentation of the archival community. Very few expressed opinions on the open forum for any support for this decision, with many comments questioning SAA's appraisal decision, it's apparent disconnect from this virtual community of archivists, dismay about the lack of understanding about the insights and practical uses this archives has for the profession, and the remarkable absence of savvy revealed by the SAA leadership in terms of public relations. Some speculated that the SAA leadership seemed to be waffling about how to deal with the long-term maintenance of a digital resource made up of e-mail messages. Given that archivists have long recognized the potential value of e-mail as a documentary resource, this seems unlikely to be the main explanation, but the subsequently released appraisal report, thoroughly redacted, suggests that the kinds of interests normally expressed by records managers (litigation problems, intellectual property, and administrative control) now seemed to be voiced by archivists.[118]

There may be a severe price to pay for such a shift if that is what we are seeing in archivists' attitudes toward e-mail. The Chosky book, in my estimation, is an invitation to open warfare between archivists and records managers, a needless warfare and one that may be potentially destructive of both professions.[119] Chosky's purpose is to show how records management differs from what archivists and librarians do, and in seeking to do this she builds an argument about why records managers have too complacently followed archivists and librarians in conceptualizing their mission and practice. Throughout the book, Chosky argues about how records managers are concerned only with meeting the business needs or requirements of the organization, even to the point of narrowly defining records according to such requirements and rejecting notions about authenticity, reliability, provenance, and other such matters that have so animated discussions, debates, and research among archivists over the past decade or more. Records, in her view, are largely determined by the courts and government regulations, and they are administered only to the extent needed to satisfy such concerns. Because she holds to the existence of some basic records management principles, such as the records life cycle, one might think that she would see a stronger connection between the work of archivists and records managers because they are necessary to support the life cycle. Such is not the case. In her chapter on the records life cycle, Chosky dismisses the importance of preservation because the "vast majority of documents that we [records managers] manage are kept for a total of six years or less."[120] Indeed, Chosky is so preoccupied with records managers breaking their shackles from archivists and librarians, that challenging issues such as the management of e-mail for administrative, legal, and corporate and societal memory purposes are completely lost. It almost seems that e-mail, posing many challenges to standard records management practice, is simply to be shuffled aside as documents needing to be destroyed as quickly as possible or simply ignored when possible. This is worrisome, and it seems more likely to weaken the mission and work of archivists and records managers. It also particularly weakens them being able to see new ways to work with the public.

Conclusion.

There is little doubt that new digital records and information technologies such as e-mail have brought major changes to how archivists and records managers work or conceive of themselves. Just a few years ago, ARMA tried to shift dramatically the focus of the work of records managers. In one commentary about this change, Patricia Franks starts off by discussing how records management work "emerged in a time of the Industrial Age office with its emphasis on paper record forms, assembly line office procedures, and hierarchically structured decision making."[121] The implication is that new technologies have changed this. She suggests, because of the shifts in information technologies, that records managers really now need to function more like knowledge managers: "The original goal of records management, to either dispose of records for economical purposes or identify records for archival purposes, has given way to identifying records with continuing value for the organization's knowledge repository."[122] Of course, this is not what we see in the Chosky manifesto described earlier. And records managers, often in search for a new rationale, may have found it in the work by Carol Chosky. For a while, there was a new purpose, what ARMA leadership briefly called strategic information management, giving new life to records management. Email, it would seem, is a significant part of this new emphasis by records professionals of all varieties.

Moreover, records professionals, whether archivists or records managers, when they seek to deal effectively with e-mail also serve notice about the importance of electronic records management and records management in general. When we consider something like e-mail, here is what I fear the most. Ben Macintrye, in an op-ed piece in the London *Times*, sounded yet another alarm about the digital age: "The digital age brought with it the false promise that everything written, filmed, photographed or recorded might now be preserved, for ever. The 'save' key would eliminate the need for filing and storage. Since 1945 we have gathered 100 times more information than in the whole of human history up until that point. Entire libraries could be preserved on disks that fitted into a pocket. Paper was dead." Yet, this seems to be a false promise. As Macintrye reflects,

> Who, save the most fastidious self-chronicler, takes the trouble to embalm their own e-mails electronically? Historians of the future may look back on the 1980s and 1990s as a black hole in the collective memory, a time when the historical record thinned alarmingly owing to the pace of technological change. Future biographers may be reduced to trying to extract personality from whatever electronic fragments survive, cheque stubs and those few ritual moments (birth, death and overdraft) when a subject still puts pen to paper."

For some, like Chosky and her followers, there may be a complete sigh of who cares, because this does not meet the present demands of the organization. However, some, like myself and many other archivists and records managers, fear the loss of a core element of our humanity if we approach matters so coldly. Macintrye believes "we may be denying

future generations the chance to witness the warp and weft of our lives."
And he asks the inevitable question -- "What will we bequeath to our
grandchildren? At best a bunch of antiquated disks that they may well
be unable to open and read."[123] Archivists, and hopefully records
managers as well, need to embrace the public and deal with its concerns
about the long-term maintenance of personal and family archives in
digital form.

And, there is more at stake than the loss of a portion of our
documentary heritage. If archivists and records managers do not figure
out how to develop a middle approach to administering e-mail, it is
clear that other disciplines will step to the plate and assume the role.
While records managers, considering the challenges of managing e-
mail, might downplay the need to consider such messages as records
needing to be managed over the long-term, opting instead, to seek ways
to destroy such messages as efficiently as possible, others are seeing that
we need a new kind of cyberinfrastructure, such as in the realm of
science and engineering research. A recent report from the National
Science Foundation states in the executive summary: "Responding to
the challenges and opportunities of a data-intensive world, NSF will
pursue a vision in which science and engineering digital data are
routinely deposited in well-documented form, are regularly and easily
consulted and analyzed by specialist and non-specialist alike, are openly
accessible while suitably protected, and are reliably preserved."[124] This
report sees new disciplines, like data curators, emerging or, at the least,
new mixes of existing professionals:

> Ongoing attention must be paid to the education of the professionals
> who will support, deploy, develop, and design current and emerging
> cyberinfrastructure. For example, the increased emphasis on 'data
> rich' scientific inquiry has revealed serious needs for 'digital data
> management' or data curation professionals. Such careers may
> involve the development of new, hybrid degree programs that marry
> the study of library science with a scientific discipline. Similarly, the
> power that visualization and other presentation technologies bring to
> the interpretation of data may call for specialized career opportunities
> that pair the graphic arts with a science or engineering discipline.[125]

Perhaps there will be a new profession of archival mentors working with
the public to advise them about their personal and family archives,
much like the ancient scribes who prepared documents who lacked the
necessary literacy skills. With this in mind, it seems like there is an
interesting and exciting future ahead.

Chapter Eight

The Web of Records: The World Wide Web, the Records Professions, and Personal Archiving

Introduction: The Web as the Incredible Disappearing Library or Archives.

At one point in time, information was associated with physical or material expressions – such as in printed, bound books and handwritten manuscripts. As H. Curtis Wright, just thirty years ago and before the personal computer revolution, reflected, "information exists only in minds. It comes through the physical media of human expression, but does not originate or reside within them."[1] Now, of course, if you ask nearly any person on the street with an average amount of resources and education about information, what it is and where you find it, they will think immediately of computers and the World Wide Web. While we can touch computers, much as we used to touch typewriters, what we see on the computer screen is something very different from the paper we used to see in the typewriter. Given that the Web did not exist before 1991, this is a remarkable seismic shift in how we perceive information, something as seemingly so practical and necessary for living and working. While there has always been philosophical and other academic discourse about information, conversation far removed from the practical daily matters of everyday life, now the normal discussion about information seems permanently linked to the URLs associated with the Web (these locators featured on billboards by the roadside, television commercials, and magazine and newspaper advertisements).

Information and its materiality, especially in the form of documents of various sorts, have long been a way of thinking about how humans create and use information or capture evidence. Thinking in this way is not unique to any facet of the still largely ill-defined world of information professions. Tom McArthur, building on the work of Karl Popper, suggests that information is the result of the interaction between material things and what has developed in our minds. His emphasis on material things, stressing writing through printing and then into electronic computation, led McArthur to believe that when writing

emerged that humans "ceased to be the slaves of transience."[2] Greg
Hunter, drawing on a variety of research and development projects,
suggests that maintaining the intellectual integrity (consisting of content,
fixity, ability to locate, provenance, and context) of new electronic
documents may be the most substantial challenge archivists and records
managers face in the digital realm (and he is right in the sense that these
records professionals continue to debate just what a record might be). [3]
And as any librarian or archivist will tell you, the problem with the
World Wide Web is that Web sites and the information and documents
they contain change frequently, often with no realization even by those
responsible about how the site has been or is being used and the
potential longer term value of the site. Julien Masanés, reflecting on
various approaches for archiving the Web, believes that "stability and
finiteness of the object itself no longer exist" on the Web; the best we
can achieve, he surmises, is that "Web archiving always means
preserving a limited and frozen version of a larger and moving
information space."[4]

    While some relate the Web to libraries and archives, there is a
fundamental difference when we consider the long-term archival
function they serve (and have served for some centuries). While a
traditional book or journal publisher may only be concerned with
immediate sales and uses, it has been understood or taken for granted
that such publications generally persist for a much longer time, residing
in libraries functioning in this sense as archives, even gathering
immense layers of dust but still being maintained (at least by most
research libraries) with the expectation of some future use or as an
essential layer in the evidence of human activity and thinking; even
when such materials are discarded, they often make their way to
remainder tables and secondhand bookstores to be generated into new
uses by scholars and leisure readers (I love remainder tables).[5] But there
are no remainder tables, it seems, in the World Wide Web, and as the
Web gobbles up more of what may have in the past been published,
new challenges in preserving a documentary heritage have appeared. As
Wendy Smith expresses it, "We have never before faced this situation –
where the constraints on creation are nugatory and the barriers to
persistence exponentially high."[6] This suggests why since its inception in
1991, the World Wide Web has been the topic of study in regards to the
durability of the information found in it[7], with every study expressing
worry about this matter, primarily because the Web sites are in the
control of their creators (rather than librarians or archivists) who can

opt at any moment to dump a site for reasons from retirement to lack of interest or lack of attention (I personally confess to all such manifestations of unenlightened self-interest myself). Even in the face of such odds of survival, we still must admit that even older, traditional forms of paper records are also often accidental survivals, and that the vicissitudes of long-term maintenance may be an inherent aspect of archival documentation.[8] As our documentary heritage spreads out from institutions such as libraries and archives into private homes with their personal and family archives, the preservation challenges grow.

Even with the immense challenges posed by maintaining anything for any length of time on the Web, cyberspace is still seen as a wonderfully dynamic place for adding to human knowledge, enabling new kinds of research or building on old forms of research or, in its most pedestrian ways, to serve merely as handy replacements for telephone directories and road maps (all the while generating concern that it might replace libraries, archives, and museums without necessarily taking into account all the priceless non-digital materials such repositories hold). Of course, it didn't take the Web to deflect some researchers from these traditional repositories, although the Web has made it much easier. As historians and other scholars interested in the past (long before the Web) turned to popular culture and public memory as subjects, they have increasingly turned to sources well outside of traditional libraries and archival repositories, even as these repositories have sought to collect such alternative materials. George Lipsitz writes that "historical memories and historical evidence can no longer be found solely in archives and libraries; they pervade popular culture and public discourse as well."[9] In the same sense, one might argue that the evidence once looked for in libraries, archives, and museums might be more readily found on various individual and organizational Web sites – but does this mean that the World Wide Web is some kind of new library, archive, records center, or museum? Many individuals also see the Web as both a publishing and archival venue, a place where they can blog with commentaries on issues of concern to them and a place where they can build virtual scrapbooks and archives documenting their lives and families.

The Value of the Archival Perspective.

Archivists (and historians and other users of archival sources) have known for a long time, of course, that records often represent less than a full accounting of the organizations and individuals creating them. This can be exaggerated in the digital environment. Seamus Ross, considering the issue of digital preservation and scholarship, states, "digital information is a cultural product. As we think of physical products of culture as artifacts, so we should also be thinking of digital and electronic products as d-facts (or e-facts). These new products form an essential fragment of our cultural record."[10] When Ross composed his assessment he was worried that what was going on the Web was mostly being lost, and that the historians and scholars of the future who need "chat-room transcripts, newsgroups, emails, webcams, and websites along side company and government records, and credit and health data sets" will walk away sadly disappointed.[11] In my opinion, this may be especially the case in the realm of personal archiving. There are other reasons, more optimistic ones, why we should be concerned with new digital preservation approaches. Ross suggests, "Digital archives combined with new technologies will liberalize scholarship. They will enable simultaneous access to a range of sources (both local and distant) and facilitate the use of research methods not possible with conventionally printed or hand written records."[12] Such perspectives indicate why archivists and records managers need to figure out just what their responsibility ought to be with regard to the World Wide Web and the range of people making use of it, and why others need to pay attention to the archival perspective, long-tested by appraisal and preservation strategies and methodologies.

Other commentators, considering the impact of very different political and cultural contexts on the maintenance of Web sites, provide similar assessments:

> Yet, however ephemeral or trivial many (or most) web pages may be, they do reflect contemporary culture and are as important in this context as printed material. Trivial and ephemeral printed materials (for example, political pamphlets and posters, theatre programs, comics, photo romances, newspaper advertisements) that have been collected over decades and centuries, provide today's social, cultural and media historians, economists, students of literary history and other scholars with invaluable raw data. Similarly, today's web pages should provide raw data for future scholars. 'Should' is the operative word, for unlike printed material, which is being collected more or less systematically by national libraries and other legal depositories in many countries, web pages are far more vulnerable to permanent and irreversible loss. Except for a minority of significant sites that may be

mirrored on more than one server, a web site normally resides on a single server. The owner of the site can at any time, at his or her sole discretion, remove the site from the web. Other parties, such as the Internet service provider, can also do this. If this happens, the loss of information is irreversible, unless it has been archived.[13]

There are obvious reasons why so many are worried about the stability of materials on the Web. And while this suggests a greater role for archivists than records managers, it is also imperative that records managers ascertain how their work in administering institutional web sites may support such broader cultural and research purposes.

Others have been skeptical of the digital record or cyberspace because of how the artifact has been seen over past centuries, seeming to denigrate the connection between documentation and its material support. David Lowenthal states, "We respond to relics as objects of interest or beauty, evidence of past events, and as talismans of continuity."[14] In other words, real things – written manuscripts or bound diaries – reassure us about their ability to last over time. Some literary theorists have also worried about the digitizing and disseminating of any version of the text of a significant literary work, including what is lost via the digitization of a formerly printed bound object, but all this may mean is that we have a new kind of text, if not artifact, to study and understand (although admittedly there are great challenges facing us on the Web in accumulating an equally informative documentary universe for such study).[15] Although many archivists continue to express their fondness for the artifacts in their repositories, they also expanded their notion of records to encompass much more than what is found in analog form or that just includes cursive writing on paper. The difficulty is trying to develop practical solutions for long-term maintenance of digital artifacts, although some would argue that the term digital artifact is an oxymoron, and extend it far beyond traditional repositories as represented by archives and libraries to the kinds of sources being maintained in our homes or by individuals in cyberspace.

Few will argue that we have that kind of connection to artifacts on the Web (where we can see representations of material things but not experience their materiality, all the while recognizing that the Web and digital recording may only provide new ways of re-imagining traditional physical means of documentation[16]), but there is also the matter of ease of access and other issues that might have us longing for more digital evidence that we can use in the convenience of our homes or anywhere we might be. I love books, and I'd rather have hundreds of printed books in my study than one handheld device with all of them in digital form. At the same time, I rather have all my copies of notes and articles for use in teaching stored in my laptop and backed up on my university personal computer than sitting in piles of deteriorating paper on bookshelves and tables or filed away in rows of drab metal file cases. Of course, if I could have both my printed collection and a virtual representation of it, available only to me for building new kinds of links and uncover new combinations of theory, research, and descriptions of practice, I would do that (and maybe I ultimately will). Such is the fate of one bridging the print and digital world (and the Web can be seen as just such a bridge between the physical world and cyberspace). We might wonder, however, whether most people today, at least those playing in the networked universe, are making such distinctions between private and public space or the physical and digital world.

There is little doubt that much of the research and other writing about the World Wide Web in the professional records community has been generated from the fears associated with a lack of control, imminent loss, legal and administrative challenges, and other similar issues. Some of these fears are also evident outside of the records community. This is a fairly normal response to new recording technologies in the records community, producing a reaction seemingly necessary to get archivists and records managers geared up to develop viable working solutions. What seems likely to change, however, are that the concerns about the Web are likely to be coming soon from the public, as personal knowledge of the potential loss of documentation increases.

Is the Web a Recordkeeping Regime?

Much of the publication about research or practical approaches for dealing with the World Wide Web does not consider cyberspace as an archival or recordkeeping domain. Of course, there is a lot on the Web that has little to nothing to do with this notion of a documentary universe, but no records professional should use this as an excuse for ignoring the Web. The Web has mostly been viewed through the lens of librarians or information technologists, and their perspectives are often very different from that of archivists and records managers (and this is not all that different from what we have seen with the work of the past decade or more with digital libraries). Still, there are many distinctive digital records forms on the Web, some purporting to be new documentary forms even though they are extensions of older forms, and considering them can be quite instructive for guiding what records professionals need to do when they confront the Web (and other emerging digital documentary systems). One documentary example distinctly tied to the Web, blogs, provides a good lesson why records professionals need to pay attention.

Web sites, blogs, YouTube, and other such elements of cyberspace can be evaluated in a variety of ways, either as the end of privacy, literacy, and community or, on the far end of the spectrum, the beginnings of a new open society and much more vibrant and interactive communities. Two historians, seeking to demolish the sense that Americans are disinterested in their past, point to a wide variety of activities, including the compilation of diaries, family trees, photo albums, and personal memories. The past is not "distant, abstract, or insignificant" they find, but, in fact, Americans, indulging in such functions, are quite concerned about "relationships, identity, immortality, and agency."[17] They find that most Americans readily talked about "documenting the past": "Almost one third wrote in diaries or journals. More than four fifths documented historical memories by taking photos or videos, and many shot their photos with a clear archival purpose."[18] Today, a decade later, we could note that much of such activity is being transferred to Web sites or other cybernetic activities like blogging. Historians, and others interested in the documentary heritage (such as archivists) may wonder about how to connect professional archivists with ordinary historical documenters,[19], but, perhaps, the issue is that the ordinary citizen is becoming a new kind of archivist (and historian); this may have many implications for just what records professionals need to do in relation to the Web.

Given the large number of Web sites that are portals to other record and information sources, linking to documentary sources not being captured in any of the more global approaches to preserving the Web (such as the Internet Archive), we also need to visualize the World Wide Web in other ways. We can think of Web sites as a kind of museum catalog or archival finding aid, except that the sites have a much greater potential for interaction and, obviously, greater potential in enhancements for linkage to other information sources. Museum catalogs can be seen as significant for adding value to an exhibition, for example, such as this description of a rare book dealer and collector visiting an exhibition at the Rosenbach Library in Philadelphia:

We have learned that regardless of how interesting we may find an exhibit or how intently we study it while we are there, it is difficult to acquire more than a superficial representation of the subject. Catalogs, which in addition to narrative text, often reproduce many of the documents, not only provide posterity to the event but also can be insightful history in their own right. In this case, we learned more about each of these subjects from the catalogs than we had learned previously in all our other research, in school, or by reading biographies.[20]

Does this not seem similar to the seemingly limitless Web sites featuring both textual descriptions and visual representations of historical documents? However, this is not the only means for thinking about the "recordness" of the Web.

Reflecting on museums (and other cultural institutions) also has another way of getting us to think about Web sites and what they represent as records or as surrogate archival repositories. Harold Skramstad once mused, "The real and authentic objects, stories, ideas, and lives that are the subject matter of museum experience have a resonance that is more powerful than all but the most compelling imaginary experience."[21] This is an argument that a focus on the authentic object may lead us astray in our concern for documenting or representing the past. In our constantly changing sense of the digital era we live in, we may be experiencing something quite new as well as quite challenging. Again, Seamus Ross believes that the

> internet has enabled an environment in which we can have new kinds of social experiences, where we can take part in new communities, and where the concepts, function and role of imagination, gender, ethnicity, identity and community are taking on new meanings and contexts. Preserving the computer boxes, screens, routers, wires, programs and applications will not make it possible for future historians to comprehend this phenomena and its transformative impact. The relationship between the function of these objects and the behavior of the user in general or within specific virtual environments is likely to remain opaque.[22]

Documenting these new worlds may not involve real objects as in the past. While in a museum exhibit seeking to convey something of the twenty-first century office we might want to have various computers and other information technologies present, the task of documenting the lives of workers, professionals, and ordinary citizens will not, as Ross indicates, mean saving hardware.

Records professionals may be creating some wiggle room for how they view records in a digital environment such as the Web. Luciana Duranti and Kenneth Thibodeau, in another report from the InterPARES project, now argue that the "fact that a system is interactive, experimental or dynamic does not entail that documents made or received in it be themselves interactive, experimental or dynamic."[23] This may seem surprising since this long-term research project has been built on a rigorous definition of records based on the diplomatics tradition. Now Duranti and her colleagues suggest that a record does not have to be absolutely fixed or unchangeable, but each document must be considered in its peculiar circumstances: "For electronic documents in general, fixed form does not mean a completely invariant form, always identical to itself."[24] This is a view that may help archivists and records managers to take a more expansive view of what the Web suggests about its role as part of a documentary heritage. Perhaps this notion also might be extended to archives as a whole, suggesting that the holdings of these repositories might reflect some degree of continuous change as they build connections with valuable documents on the Web that may shift in location from time to time. Fixity might not be the goal anymore, although just how and what this might mean to future generations and researchers is uncertain. Archives might be continuously changing, even as archivists seek to fix certain key documents; a substantial portion of future work might be the effort to identify personal and family archives (certain kinds of organizational records well) on the Web and to try to follow them as they are moved and removed. After all, when we cite Web documents we also mark when we have viewed them, knowing that by the time another examines them they may have changed, even if just slightly.

The InterPARES report may provide some hope for future initiatives in digital recordkeeping, even if there are still troubles ahead. David Bearman, in a recent assessment of the past decade of research and development concerning how archivists and records managers (but mostly archivists) perceive electronic records, sees growing consensus in many aspects of how a record is to be administered in cyberspace.[25] Bearman examines competing projects, sees their common ground, considers new and emerging projects, but laments that the archival community has given way to major research initiatives outside the records community (primarily in the library and information science discipline) that often do not fully understand the nature and elements of records and recordkeeping systems. His observations indicate that we must question just how well equipped records professionals are for working on the Web.

How Well Prepared Are Archivists and Records Managers for Handling the Web?

Some of what I have discussed above relates mainly to the cultural and historical significance of Web sites, something archivists will be interested in and records managers probably not. However, a number of records managers have also considered the records implications of the Web sites. Rick Barry, for example, contends, "Plainly stated, Web sites make records, but they do not keep records in ways that match up to sound recordkeeping requirements."[26] Barry sees how in the government sectors the expanding notion of e-government has led to an increasing use of Web sites as a mechanism for creating and accessing records. Using definitions from various sources, such as the ISO 15489 Information and Documentation: Records Management standard, Barry presses the definition of records and electronic records to encompass Web sites and their uses. Much of what Barry considers has to do with the consistent administration of Web sites, ensuring that documents are dated, kept current, and evaluated so as to remove antiquated materials. Barry notes that many Web sites are overlooked because they are not even considered to be records needing to be managed.[27] Archivists and records managers often have ignored the Web because they have so many other records to administer and because there are no readily available clear approaches for dealing with the Web sites that can be easily adapted to local conditions. We can add to this that archivists are ignoring the implications of digital personal and family records and how they will be cared for in the future.

Records managers have known for some time, of course, that there are virtual records on Web sites. As John Frost suggests, however, the challenge is in administering the "information behind virtual records."[28] Frost builds, as do most records managers, on the notion of enterprise content management, where Web code can be controlled and customized, version control handled efficiently, approval systems for posting created, and other similar functions established. Frost sees the practical advantage in such systems because they do not need to be handled by a central Webmaster, but personal observation and other professional commentaries suggest that a Webmaster, knowledgeable about records and archives management principles and objectives, could be a remarkable ally. Frost is correct, in considering such approaches as a portal whereby information, applications, and resources are linked together for the convenient use of an organizational employee or clients, that those making use of such systems often do not consider concerns such as whether a particular item is an official record or not. However, someone needs to be thinking of such matters, and if it is not the records professional with this responsibility than it ought to be someone like a Webmaster (who may be influenced and advised by the institutional archivist or records manager).

Over the past couple of decades, archivists and records managers have clung to the traditional tasks of appraising or scheduling records as a primary way of contending with electronic records. Adding to these tasks were others, such as ensuring that in the digital environment that records were being created and captured as needed (as Bearman in his recent essay sees as a element for building consensus), but records professionals still adhered to the notion of seeking to locate just what records needed to be managed as archival documentation or as organizational assets. For the records professional working as an institutional archivist or records manager, this responsibility is more clearly focused on how the institution deals with its Web sites. For the archivist, working in a repository with a mandate to acquire certain kinds of records or to document some aspect of society, this task is much more complicated. It is not a responsibility of trying to ensure the appropriate administration of what is on or taken off of a Web site; it is the much more challenging aim of trying to determine how Web sites created by others relate to their institutional mission and the means by which they might identify and maintain such sites. In other words, there may be a lot of lingering confusion out there about whose responsibility it is to identify and preserve anything on the Web, whether one is looking inwardly into an institution or looking outward from a collecting or documenting repository.

While it seems that many of the aims of archival appraisal, or records management retention scheduling for that matter, and other archival methodologies do not substantially change when applied to electronic recordkeeping systems, there are nevertheless substantial issues that will need to be addressed as the digital systems continue to evolve, such as when such records should be appraised, what exactly is being appraised, and who is responsible for appraising.[29] What archivists and records managers can surmise about the implications of electronic records is that they challenge the comfortable notion of a records life cycle, weaken the information value concept because it can become operationally vague in the midst of a deluge of records, provokes a rethinking of the physical custody of records in favor of other approaches such as distributed custody, transforms the work of the records professional into a greater advisory and policy role, and makes the distinctions between archivists and records managers seem odd and artificial. In the pre-computational era records professionals would have been more concerned with locating records long created before, but in the era of the computer there has been a shift to worrying that the records have been captured in a way that ensures that they are complete with all of their contextual links and metadata intact.[30] However, it is questionable that archivists and records managers have been able to extend effectively such concerns to what they find on the Web (with the possible exception of what they have placed there).

Records managers have tended to focus on the liabilities and other fallibilities of increasingly complex content management aspects associated with technologies such as represented by Web sites (and their approach is what we can consider to be the local approach to the Web challenge). Some have emphasized that the focus is not on the technology aspects of such systems but on the implications for people, processes, objectives, and activities that make up any organization. In fact, as Timothy P. O'Keefe and Mark Langemo argue, just figuring out the organizational needs and understanding the range of content is an immensely complicated step that must be carefully done in order to allow organizations to make the best decisions regarding how content is selected, displayed, and disseminated on a Web site.[31] Making sure that inappropriate content is not displayed, that accurate and current information is included, and that records are properly administered are all responsibilities that suggest that the relative ease of building and offering Web sites can be quite deceptive. And if this deception is occurring in situations where there are records experts, than what must be happening where individuals are using Web sites to capture and display personal and family archival materials? Such tasks naturally relate to the kinds of responsibilities records professionals have traditionally been involved in supporting, even if records managers and archivists have not been always successful in gaining full responsibility for the increasingly online functions of organizations.

What we can safely assume is that organizations will learn from legal cases and other such challenges that content management and records and archives management in the increasingly digital environment requires certain activities be in place, even if we cannot really assume that the staff carrying out such functions will be archivists and records managers as we have normally thought of them. For example, organizations need to comprehend that the challenges represented by their hosting a Web site is not merely the risk of litigation but the risk of losing corporate memory through the loss of key documents possessing ongoing administrative and memory values. Archivists can learn from records managers about how to consider administering organizational Web sites, and records managers can get some pointers from archivists about the bigger picture of how dealing with Web resources connects to the challenges of managing the documentary heritage. The more complicated challenge is how to transfer the knowledge of archivists and records to the public and how to bring the public into the mix as important and capable partners in preserving the digital documentary heritage.

Grappling with the Web: Research and Development Projects.

When one usually thinks about Web sites, the tendency is to think of the large audiences that can be reached and the relative ease of creating and maintaining such a site. However, as institutions and individuals have come to rely on Web sites for a variety of purposes, from business services to displaying family documents such as diaries and photographs, the ease of accomplishing such ends can become more complex. For some, the existence of the Internet Archive – a "non-profit that was founded to build an Internet library, with the purpose of offering permanent access for researchers, historians, and scholars to historical collections that exist in digital format"[32] – reassures them that most of what needs to be captured from the Web is taking place, although others have commented on the limitations of what has not been captured or the biases of what is archived.[33] Some of this may be, then, a false security.

A series of position papers and research reports reflect some of these concerns. John Philips, describing the enthusiasm with which organizations have embraced Web site technologies in order to enable their employees and clients to access information quickly and efficiently, makes the appropriate contrast between immediate and long-term use possibilities and probabilities. Philips thinks it is "ironic that the very business planning sentiments that insist on the 24x7x365 organizational availability equation may be ensuring that information will not be available in as little as five or more years – 24x7x365x5."[34] Phillips indicates that there needs to be careful planning to ensure that such losses do not occur, especially as there are no technological solutions or quick-fix systems or fail-safe mechanisms for preventing such information and evidence losses. Such problems exist because the nature or advantage of the Web is to build documents with multiple links and multiple formats, but such characteristics also make it extremely difficult to maintain a particular document. If a document is placed online with twenty links, what happens to the document when one or more of those links change, even disappear? It is one thing if those links are all to other sources maintained by the document's creator (although all of us have experienced frustration with broken links even in these circumstances), but imagine the complexity if each of the links is to another Web site maintained by another individual or institution.

Five years ago, Philipps noted that records professionals could not wait around for the development of "industry standards or best practices to be firmly established," but urged that the archivists and records managers needed to provide advice based on their own institution's needs and situation.[35] This entails more professional cooperation, experimentation, risk management, and reconsideration of professional and institutional objectives. For example, we know that archivists want to identify and preserve the records with continuing value to the organization and society and that records managers want to ensure that they can administer records in a fashion reducing legal liability or loss of proprietary information. The placing of documents on Web sites suggest that these records professionals need to reconcile these perspectives, especially as the formats of documents are transformed in a fashion that seem to suggest a needed convergence of professional objectives. Philipps, for example, candidly states that a "fundamental premise of records and information protection is that both information accessibility and viability must be protected over time."[36] While archivists and records managers may quibble about what documents and how long they must be kept, such differences need to be pushed aside so that collaborative efforts can be mounted to preserve records on Web sites in meaningful and useful ways. And, furthermore, knowledge needs to be built that enables records professionals to work effectively with the public in order to protect the increasing amount of personal and family archives being transferred to digital forms or being born in digital forms at the outset.

The various research projects have tackled both theoretical and practical problems relating to the management of the Web's content. Anne Kenney and Nancy McGovern describe the challenge archivists and librarians are facing with the management of digital resources since many of these resources are not owned by their repositories and given the limited time many such resources stay on the Web this poses a set of interesting questions and problems. Kenney and McGovern present three strategies – "collaborating with publishers to preserve licensed content, developing policies and guidelines for creating and maintaining Web sites, and assuming archival custody for Web resources of interest" – being used by archivists and librarians.[37] The latter two are particularly interesting to records professionals, the first helping elevate Web sites (at least some of them) to the status of a record and the second, represented by efforts such as the Internet Archive, helping to generate renewed interest in the Web as something needing archival analysis and preservation strategies. Kenney and McGovern describe in particular one effort they have been involved in, Project Prism, located at Cornell University and funded by a grant from the National Science Foundation. In this project the concept of risk management has been drawn upon to identify at what point a Web resource is threatened and the nature of the actions needing to be taken. The project builds on a "noncustodial, distributed model for archiving, in which resources are managed along a spectrum from, at the highest level, a formal repository to, at the lowest level, the unmanaged Web."[38] The project also considers a variety of ways in which Web sites can be maintained, from a site by itself with none of its context to a fully functional site with all of its hyperlinks, and how each approach might be suitable for particular kinds of sites.

Other projects have explored both technical and archival issues. The Minerva project at the Library of Congress explored issues involved in collecting and preserving selected Web sites, considering a variety of options – such as just preserving content or maintaining full functionality of a site – that combine a variety of approaches and issues.[39] The national libraries of eight European countries experimented with electronic harvesting systems to identify and capture digital publications related to the acquisition parameters of these institutions and seeking to address concerns about the growing number of digital publications.[40] Cornell's Project Prism pursued a similar risk management approach and using "Web crawlers and other automated tools and utilities ... to identify and quantify risks; to implement appropriate and effective measures to prevent, mitigate, recover from damage to and loss of Web-based assets; and to support post-event remediation. Project Prism is producing a framework for developing an ongoing comprehensive monitoring program that is scalable, extensible, and cost effective."[41] In this, we see the library as well as archival influence in managing the Web. But how long before we can discuss practically with the public the solutions to their archival issues being encountered in cyberspace?

Web Research and the Library Perspective.

Most of these kinds of projects have mostly emphasized a library approach to the World Wide Web, although some have tried to add an archival dimension to what they are seeking to accomplish. Cornell University Library's Virtual Remote Control project, as one such example, is an effort to develop the means for "monitoring websites over time—identifying and responding to detected risk as necessary, with capture as a last resort." The aim is to build a "toolbox of software for cultural heritage institutions to use in managing their portfolio of web resources." It is a project transforming certain aspects of basic archival approaches, such as that of appraisal. Appraisal, via the lens of this project, is a "stage" supporting "value assessment based on attributes such as *relevancy* to the organization's collection(s); *significance* (essential, desirable, ephemeral); *archival role* (primary archives for resource, informal agreement for full or partial capture, other); *maintenance* (rating for key indicators of good site management); *redundancy* (captured by more than one archive); *risk response* (time delay and action based on test notifications); *capture requirements* (complexity of site structure, update cycle, MIME types, dynamic content, and behavior indicators); and *size* (number of pages, depth of crawl required, etc.)."[42] Yet, it seems to be the case that in many projects the library has subsumed the archival approach to the Web, and this can present some limitations when we are thinking of the Web as a records repository (although a repository without walls).

The value of such projects, developed from or influenced by the archival perspective, is that they provide a much richer view of what Web sites represent. However, most of these approaches are from national or other high-level top-down perspectives, ones that are very different for archivists and records managers working in corporate, cultural, and other institutional realms. The National Library of

Australia's PANDORA project to harvest and archive Web sites of
interest to that country still leads to some inescapable conclusions about
the challenges of appraising and selecting such sites: ""It must also be
recognized that selective archiving as done in Australia does retain a
degree of manual intervention, specifically in the selection, quality
assurance and cataloguing processes, that requires considerable
resources in order to achieve archiving on any useful scale."[43] This
Australian effort, now with a decade of experience, has determined that
much can be achieved via cooperative approaches, although it has also
affirmed that the costs of identifying and preserving Web sites are
higher than the counterpart printed book or other traditional library
materials (although this project also demonstrates that the costs can be
built into existing budgetary constraints and restraints).[44] Of course,
these, and many other,[45] projects adopt a library collection development
project, viewing Web sites as a form of electronic publication analogous
to a printed book or magazine. When we move beyond this, considering
blogs and listserv archives and other online items as analogous to
archival materials such as diaries and letters the task looms as much
larger and much more complicated. In fact, the PANDORA project
acknowledges its own inherent conservatism, focusing on "print-like"
materials of an identifiable "quality." Its architects acknowledge its
limitations, both in its ability to maintain the materials and, more
importantly, whether its selection approach makes any sense given the
nature of the Web. Wendy Smith notes, for example, that "Current
trends in historical research and publishing indicated that this [quality]
is not necessarily what future generations will want. Such informal
documents as diaries of 'the common man', printed ephemera, family
photograph collections, and those ephemeral publications – newspapers
– are increasingly used as sources for historical scholarship, rather than
biographies of important persons and the formal records of important
events."[46]

One of the values of reading the reports on these various projects is
that they assist us to rethink how we both construct and use Web sites.
When I sit down to work on a site, for example, I may become preoccupied with constructing it, not unlike writing, editing, and publishing
an article or a book. It is easy to forget all of the various elements that
support the site. Kenney and McGovern note that a "Web site is a
collection of Web pages, but it also resides on a server within an
administrative context, all of which may be affected by the external
technical, economic, legal, organizational, and cultural environment."[47]

This could be postulated for nearly any record, but given the nature of the technology supporting a Web site such factors are both more critical and more vulnerable. Kenney and McGovern also state, "It is entirely possible that the biggest threat to the continued health of a Web site has nothing to do with how well the site is maintained or even how often it is backed up but whether the backup tapes are stored in the same room as the server – increasing the chance that a single catastrophic event … destroy them both."[48] Some of what is being considered is just trying to always have the bigger picture in mind, although there are voices in the records community that would have us focus more inwardly into the immediate and often short-term needs of particular organizations.[49] If archivists and records managers are struggling with such matters, can we expect that individuals using the Web for their personal and family archives are cognizant of these concerns? A million years ago, it seems, we could create a document – a personal letter or diary – with some reasonable expectation that it survive beyond our span of years. This is no longer the case.

What Ought to Be The Big Picture with the Web?

Records professionals, no matter what their sense of obligation to their immediate employer is, have to consider a larger context. Scientists and other researchers are particularly concerned about how quickly Web sites they cite in their research and publications may disappear. Web pages disappear on average after a hundred days and even government Web sites, providing information to citizens, change their uniform resource locators (URLs) very rapidly, creating havoc for those who cite such resources.[50] James Fallows, in one of his regular technology columns in the *Atlantic Monthly*, lamented the challenges of average citizens having to worry about what they might lose when they move from one computer system to the next one. Fallows concludes that individuals "preserving data" will face "an ongoing semi-hygienic chore, like brushing your teeth or taking out the trash." Fallows notes that "For both laptop users and mighty institutions, then, preserving digital files is an active rather passive process. You must transfer files from old tapes or disks to new ones, as storage standards change; you must import information from one program to another whenever you change software; you must rerecord backup files at least every few years, so the information doesn't just crumble away."[51] This is fine for word-processed documents and various data files, but it is not so great an option for individuals worrying about maintaining their personal Web sites and all the various links to other Web sites, personal and institutional.

While Fallows relates the challenges of electronic records to the individual's practical needs, others, such as Jeff Rothenberg, spell out all the various options for the digital documentary universe (ranging from doing nothing to relying on original software). Rothenberg is a well-known advocate for emulation, where "an emulator is a program that runs on the new computer and makes it behave like the old computer."[52] Rothenberg himself poses a number of questions about the technical and economic feasibility of emulation as a preservation approach for electronic records, but it is hard to imagine that it has much applicability for Web sites because of the hyper-linking characteristic.

Convincing all records professionals and their employers that they have a larger commitment and responsibility to society, researchers, citizens, and customers continues to prove to be a difficult task. Laurie Gingrich and Brian Morris, in an assessment indicating that records managers no longer have to try to convince others that managing electronic records is an important task, also state that "In the landscape of regulation, risk, and compliance that global companies now face, most IT managers realize the importance of keeping records as long as needed and no longer."[53] Of course, this kind of sentiment suggests that an organization removes documents from its Web site without any regard for how others on the outside may have used these sources. While we might focus, instead, on the difficulties of defining records in the online environment and the challenges of maintaining such records apart from their technology infrastructure, we can't eliminate other concerns such as our responsibilities to society, easily seen as part of our ethical responsibilities.

When records professionals indulge in debates and efforts to define records or documents, they need to do it broadly enough to encompass ethical as well as legal and administrative issues. Then they can turn their attention to the practical matters of resolving copyright issues, using the appropriate software tools, and correcting the technical glitches.[54] Indeed, now we find so much of our identity formed by how we react to the cyberspace as well as real space we reside and function in. We either face down those powerful forces and organizations seeking to control such spaces,[55] or we allow ourselves to be taken over by them. Seeking to carve out at least some sense of personal memory in cyberspace seems to be a critical and meaningful task to take on; even if the final battle results in defeat, the battle may have been what has made life worth living.

Web sites have proved to be, however, a bit more problematic to records professionals than one might readily assume. Archivists have tried to develop appraisal strategies enabling them to identify what Web sites should be preserved as part of government, university, museum, or other institutional programs. The staff of the State Historical Society of Wisconsin conducted just such a project in 2001 as this in considering what to do with one state government Web site and whether it should be considered as a group of records needing to be maintained.[56] This group of archivists assumed that traditional appraisal approaches could be used, and they considered the purpose of the Web site, the informational quality of the site, and the technical issues involved in maintaining the site. This particular project resulted in the state archival agency printing out the content of the government Web site onto paper to ensure that it would be maintained, a step that probably would not be taken today. But this is just a stop on the road of experiments, tests, and failures to find successful approaches for selecting and maintaining digital documents. These potholes and bumps have included the management of master tape files to ensure "adequate technical documentation"[57] and efforts to harness the notion of business functions with an eye on influencing the design of such systems to accommodate records with continuing value;[58] Even after more than two decades of working with electronic records, archivists by 1990 were still following a fairly traditional approach of trying to determine whether these records needed to be maintained digitally and veering away from any substantial efforts to accession them.[59]

One of the main characteristics emerging from this literature documenting professional practice in electronic records management is the focus by archival and records agencies on their responsibility, almost a kind of top-down approach to evaluating archival evidence in digital form. The rapid growth of the Web and the fostering of the cyber-community through its sites have generated as well a stronger community of interested and vested partnerships. Consider the Web-at–Risk project, funded by the National Digital Information Infrastructure and Preservation Program (NDIIPP) and involving the California Digital Library, University of North Texas, and New York University, with the aim of building "tools that will allow librarians to 'capture, curate and preserve Web–based government and political information.'"[60] Or, as Diane Zorich describes, the key to preserving the digital heritage is collaboration:

> No one can work in isolation on digital preservation and access issues because the needs and requirements are too great. We all benefit from (and generate) economies of scale, pooled expertise, larger funding, and more robust infrastructure when we collaborate. And collaboration means not just crossing over our museum/library/archives divisions, but entering whole new communities such as science, engineering, and the commercial sector.[61]

Why? Zorich continues, "We cannot preserve a digital object or a digital collection in isolation: we must preserve the entire digital ecosystem where the object or collection is found."[62] We must balance such perspectives against the needs of more local projects, including even the work of individuals, where practical decisions are made to maintain smaller pieces of the Web. It is in the local arena that we might want to measure the real successes, and where the collaboration might be better considered to be that of professional archivists assisting and guiding individuals in understanding the archival perspective in preserving Web resources.

Some records professionals hope that the large-scale Internet Archive effort will capture everything and absolve archives, libraries, and every other organization of needing to worry about Web-site preservation and the challenges of selection, technical concerns, and other matters. However, as Anne Kenney and her colleagues at Cornell surmise, this is a foolhardy attitude, noting that this kind of approach is incomplete because snapshots fail to capture changes, technology is unable to ensure a full capture of a site, a Web site may merely guide someone into a database or image or other kind of repository, the Web volume limits effective capture and access, there are problems with evolving file formats and encoding standards, and there are intellectual property problems.[63] These characteristics and challenges may suggest why we need archivists and records managers to commit to experimenting with local solutions to appraising and preserving Web content.

So, How Do We Label the Web?

Anyone choosing to wrestle with the World Wide Web soon labels it in some fashion, ranging from an archive to a library. Whatever we call it, we need to take a longer perspective about Web sites, realizing that they may be more recent manifestations of earlier documentary forms, such as scrapbooks. Susan Tucker, Katherine Ott, and Patricia P. Buckler suggest that the ephemeral nature that some attach to Web sites is nothing new: "Most scrapbooks and their ephemeral content do not last and provide only a fleeting usefulness. They disintegrate and crumble. The leaves fall out. The enclosures drop off the page. Archivists, the most conscientious embalmers of primary materials, tend to neglect them because they are conservation nightmares. None of the solutions available will correct all the problems. Sometimes an archivist must destroy a scrapbook – take it apart – to save it."[64] The point here is that the purposes of scrapbooks and Web sites have many similarities, apart from their preservation challenges. Scrapbooks possess various personal and cultural uses, such as storing official records, codifying normal routines, organizing household knowledge, building personalized narratives, assembling souvenirs, ordering relationships, creating private worlds, developing memory prompts, and providing an outlet for artistic expression – all purposes that can be assigned as well to Web sites. Scrapbooks are used to construct identity, express memories, and provide order to a chaotic existence. As Buckler writes elsewhere, the "scrapbook has been defined as a multilayered expression of individual sentiment enunciated through objects that carry an emotional association such as ornaments, fanciwork, domestic things, pictures, jewelry,"[65] the only major difference with the personal or family-oriented Web site is that in the virtual world the artifacts are digitized representations. The scrapbook captures the compiler's efforts to shape a "personal and cultural identity."[66] It is not much of a stretch to read a Web site in pretty much the same way.

Archivists and other records professionals, therefore, need to pay attention to the World Wide Web. The Web, often likened to a universal library or archive, represents a natural place for archivists, records managers, librarians, and other information professionals to ply their trade. Still, we need to be cautious about far we take the comparisons. As Jean-Noël Jeanneney, president of France's National Library, sees it, there are vast differences between the mission of Web providers such as Google and the mission of records professionals and librarians. He contrasts the long-term cultural mission of librarians and archivists with the short-term business aims of Google, arguing that there is the need for a renewed commitment to the work of librarians (and by implication, records professionals):

> The social and cultural function of librarians will be increasingly important and prestigious in the future; they will be even more useful to the public, and their profession will become more satisfying. For years, a common perception, maintained by various stereotypes, has tended to reduce the role of librarians to that of providing books, images, recordings, and other documents. In reality, librarians have always helped to organize chaos, to guide readers to the information they are seeking among the vast quality of sources and media that contain it. And now, with the irruption of digitization, this essential function will be enhanced, and librarians should benefit from renewed recognition. More than ever before, they will stand beside professors and schoolteachers as essential intermediaries of knowledge.[67]

Implying that information professionals have such a role in cyberspace also requires that these professionals stare down the Web's various challenges. As the Web gets more complicated with commercial ventures, new tools for personal archiving, and intellectual property issues, just to name a few issues, records and information professionals need to re-evaluate every opportunity with a critical eye. With Google we need to contemplate its commercial aspects, handling of censorship issues, and commitment to preservation. Will we really place our faith in preserving our documentary heritage in commercial enterprise?

From such commercial and societal changes there emerges a new mandate for professionals such as archivists and librarians. Jeanneney argues that we must educate people to have the appropriate "intellectual tools" to master the Internet. Adults, he muses, "will find our digitized collections indispensable instruments for maintaining perspective in the face of the bombardment of new information, which they themselves must place in context, classify, and weigh. Unless a culture organizes that information, society is condemned to accept the mere dissemination of information, harmful to intellectual clarity and to a rich and harmonious public life."[68] And with such notions, we return to the importance of the work of librarians, archivists, and other records professionals.

The Web site has given us an ease, perhaps a false hope, of working that generates all sorts of additional problems, and as such, it is one of the most important documentary innovations in the modern era (in

time, perhaps, it may become to be seen to be as important as the
earlier emergence of photography or moving images). For example,
imagine how easy it is to grab images off of the Web and re-use them in
your own site, publications, class lectures, and in a million other ways.
However, it is not that easy. Intellectual property has become one of the
most salient aspects of the modern Information Age. In an era when
great promises have been made for enhanced access to information,
contentious battles over who gets to use certain information or how
much they have to pay for the information threatens to erode these
promises. One commentator captures how contentious this new
environment can be for someone wanting to reuse images, no matter
how noble the purpose, indicating that "It's a world of perceived sides:
yours versus theirs, a universe of fine lines and split hairs. It is a world
that seems equitably divided between victims and bullies. One party's
gain means another one's loss. In this world, you survive by wit and
patience."[69] Another describes the challenge in this way: "Our ability to
copy and share digital information has exploded. So, however, has the
ability of corporations to regulate every use of the material they own.
Corporations can, in fact, write virtual stop signs and toll booths into
the very code of digital texts."[70] We live in a time of ownership concerns
above all else, even when we understand that the use of documents such
as photographs and reproductions of paintings and other art will
expand our sensibilities and knowledge, enhance our texts, and enliven
our discourse.

Without question archivists and librarians have worried about what
damage might be done to the documentary heritage if the World Wide
Web is not controlled. However, at the same time, archivists have long
been confident that they are documenting events primarily just through
the traditional documents they have been accustomed to working with.
If an archival repository declared that its intention was to build a strong
or substantial documentary base for understanding Virginia's four
hundred years, it probably would focus on the personal, business, and
governmental records generated over the centuries. However, we know
full well that there are some aspects of that past that will not be well
documented by such traditional documentary sources, but that must be
supplemented by archeological evidence. In one recent assessment of
the Jamestown site, we learn that the "written records pertaining to
them are scarce, ambiguous, and sometimes conflicting: maps of
questionable accuracy; a few letters and official reports; published
accounts written by interested parties..."[71] The site's physical remains

are much more important for revealing the events that shaped the settlement, putting matters in "clearer focus."[72] Artifacts, "when juxtaposed to a document" with explicit meaning, can give us a "fresh perspective on the colonists' anticipations as well as their accomplishments, leading to a more complex story than the simpler tale of poor preparation and incompetence" associated with this early settlement.[73]

The Web brings the interconnection of diverse documentary sources to a new level, enabling them to be easily assembled under one linked site. However, the question still looms as how all this will be preserved. The impact of Web sites on organizations may seem very subtle at first, but the end result may be dire. Consider that universities have run archives for many decades, but that they have not developed viable solutions for the transition from paper and print to online documents and sites. William Clark, in his study of the origins of the modern research university, relies heavily on traditional sources: "I love the smell of archives in the morning. After getting a whiff of a piping hot cup of fresh-brewed coffee and the morning paper…, nothing is quite so satisfying as nosing through a big, fat Bavarian dossier."[74] If these dossiers are now all electronic, and increasingly used via the Web, will they be maintained over the centuries ahead? And here we have the tension between a more local and global perspective.

Archivists, records managers, and other information and records professionals have mostly tended to consider the broader social and cultural implications of what is on the World Wide Web, how to select from this vast reservoir of stuff the key historical documentation, and the fear of how quickly information is lost from its millions of Web sites. This is the global perspective, stressing collaboration, funded projects, and public policy initiatives.[75] This is a perspective that can mostly overwhelm one with all of the challenges of the digital era. There is also the local perspective. Abby Smith argues that collecting, for example, is really best done on the local level: "Remembering that successful preservation is informed by a clear sense of audience, can we craft approaches that keep the compass of the relevant public small enough to make a content selection strategy feasible and sustainable?"[76] Nowhere is such an approach more relevant than in contending with the new diary form of blogging, as well as other forms of personal archiving.

Blogs and the World Wide Web.

Continuous changes in the technology of recordkeeping have kept records professionals mulling over the implications for maintaining organizational records, identifying records with continuing or archival value, and even the useful elaboration of what constitutes a record anyone should be interested in. Just less than a decade ago, someone might worry about how employees distinguish between organizational and personal records as they worked on personal computers both in the workplace and at home. As Robert Sanders opined, "there is a sense that office PCs are exactly what the name implies: personal computers. They contain records that their owners alone have created, selected, organized without collaboration or assistance. If someone decides to keep files longer than a retention schedule specifies, or to take a copy home for personal use, who is to say they are wrong?"[77] Now, it seems, individuals are creating an unlimited number of personal record forms using the Web, and they can create these records anywhere – hotel rooms, airports, workplaces, and homes. And, yes, rightly or wrongly, many of these documents also will reside in new digital personal archives.

In the brief time that has passed since Sanders considered such issues, the individual's use of the Internet has continued to evolve, where now many people are very comfortable, despite privacy and identity theft dangers, with "cyber socializing." Individuals use FaceBook, MySpace, and other sites to develop relationships and build different kinds of virtual communities. We are much more likely not even to consider the differences between home and the workplace, professional and personal activities.[78] Bruce Dearstyne recently commented on how blogs, wikis, and other such tools create the challenge of unstructured, constantly changing documents that make traditional notions of records and information management strained in their ability to capture and administer documents. Dearstyne, acknowledging that these are tools archivists and records managers might want to use, does not offer any solutions for contending with them; as many have done before, he is content at this point to point out the differences between older forms of records and these newer forms. He sees it as adding excitement to the work of the records and information manager responsibilities, although some might disagree that the excitement factor isn't really more a nightmare.[79]

Blogging is a new form of writing, but it is writing nonetheless. One definition of a blog (derived from "web log"), as useful as any, is that it is a "website where entries are written in chronological order and commonly displayed in reverse chronological order. "Blog" can also be used as a verb, meaning *to maintain or add content to a blog.*" This definition continues: "Blogs provide commentary or news on a particular subject such as food, politics, or local news; some function as more personal online diaries. A typical blog combines text, images, and links to other blogs, web pages, and other media related to its topic. The ability for readers to leave comments in an interactive format is an important part of many blogs." This definition cites a source estimating that in May 2007 there was then more than 71 million blogs."[80]

Writing, we know for sure, has had a profound influence on society and culture. As anthropologist Jack Goody suggests, "Without writing there is virtually no storage of information outside the human brain and hence no communication over great distances and long periods of times."[81] Has any such aspects of writing changed when individuals opt to write online and digitally? Not really, except for the type of storage. Instead of bound volumes we have blogging sites; instead of physical acquisition and maintenance in a physical archives we have storage online. There are, of course, different preservation challenges and different access issues – a blog ending once and for all the debate about whether diaries are intended to be private – but the matters of seeking to communicate and store still loom as primary concerns. However blogs may be used, these documents are a primary example of the challenges records professionals face as they work in cyberspace.

What Do Blogs and Bloggers Represent?

Not everyone has had a kind view of blogs or bloggers. Andrew Keen, at one time an Internet entrepreneur marketing music online, in his critique of the impact of the Internet on the value of expertise, states, "Blogging has become such a mania that a new blog is being created every second of every minute of every hour of every day. We are blogging with monkeylike shamelessness about our private lives, our sex lives, our dream lives, our lack of lives, our Second Lives. At the time of writing there are fifty-three million blogs on the Internet, and this number is doubling every six months. In the time it took you to read this paragraph, ten new blogs were launched."[82] Within a few years, by 2010, the projection is for 500 million blogs, all reflecting, along with those using the Wikipedia and YouTube, an "infinite desire for personal attention"[83]; has there ever been 500 million diarists? One question that can be asked is whether such activity on the Web will leave behind the kinds of personal, family, and institutional archives that researchers and archivists have been prone to uncover, preserve, and make available on a remarkably regular basis. For example, a project to publish selectively letters of writers and poets who published in *Poetry* became a daunting one because, as the editors state, the "riches we uncovered in the archives, particularly the correspondence files, were so abundant, the poets' first-person accounts of their lives – the private struggles, professional rivalries, backstage maneuverings, quarrels, kindnesses, and other little-known facts of poetry publishing revealed in the letters – were so fascinating, instructive, and often humorous."[84] Will we have those kinds of documents in the future?

The attitude towards bloggers and blogging derive from as much what they are as from the respective of the individual considering the blogs. One assessment indicates that bloggers write more about personal matters than anything else.[85] Some archivists may see in this characteristic an opportunity to capture the personal views of citizens to the day's major events, while records managers disparage the potential legal problems that this might pose. A political action group might see such blogs as opportunities to feature various views on political issues, while institutional managers might fear just what an employee might be revealing about their inner organizational workings. Whatever our view of blogs and blogging, we need to acknowledge that their existence is nothing more than another example of how we utilize writing in our daily lives. A recent study about how Abraham Lincoln relied on writing suggests the nature of the connection. Lincoln's life, public and private, revolved around the act of writing, and Lincoln "responded to almost every important development during his presidency, and to many that were not so important, with some act of writing." For Lincoln, "writing was often a form of refuge..., a place of intellectual retreat from the chaos and confusion of office where he could sort through conflicting options and order his thoughts with words."[86] Bloggers would probably argue that they are doing the same.

Given the rapid rise of blogging, it, like so many other digital applications, is something that is easy to take for granted, assuming that it is a logical and common form of communication and document generation. We know from looking at older office technologies, such as the personal computer and word processing, that their histories are much more complex than what they now seem to represent. Examining the notion of word processing, now so easily understood, Thomas Haigh recounts how its development was a lot more complicated than generally assumed:

> Rather than a sudden shift to the paperless automated office of the future, the result was a hybrid of old and new technologies in which documents were prepared using personal computers but usually disseminated on paper. Electronic document transmission was particularly slow to take hold. During the 1990s, it was common for documents to be prepared on a computer, then printed for fax transmittal to a recipient (a process of redigitization and reprinting) and optically scanned at the far end into another computer. As the new ease of printing sent office paper use to record levels, a joke arose that the paperless office would arrive at around the same time as the paperless toilet.[87]

This is a reminder that recordkeeping is always associated with some form of technology, suggesting that we ought to not be so concerned about changing technologies such as what the Web represents.

Records, and their nature and rate of production and subsequent preservation, have often been connected to the specifics of their technology. The richness of the American Civil War soldiers' documentary materials has to do with the development of the Federal postal service by the time of the Civil War; as Robert E. Bonner suggests, "Without such a reliable, rapid, and relatively cheap network for transmission, far fewer soldiers would have regularly committed their thoughts and experiences to paper... [The] Civil War became a written war primarily because a regular exchange of letters allowed millions of personal stories to be recorded and preserved for posterity."[88] The production of letters and other documents was affected by the ebb and flow of stationary supplies. Bonner considers how frank the letters were because there was no military censorship system in place, as there was for later wars. And there is some consideration of why individuals remembered for their Civil War letters often seem to have left little else behind; Bonner attributes this to the greater care taken with the records of the war: "As part of the normal order of things, most documents created by civilians would have seemed expendable when compared with Civil War treasures."[89]

Bonner also describes how the families of these soldiers "became unofficial archivists who were committed to preserving written relics of war and transmitting them to posterity." This historian even provides a research agenda for archivists and special collections curators who care for such documents, when he suggests that "We know less about how soldiers' letters, diaries, and sketches were saved than about how and why these items were created."[90] Given the nature of the Web technology, it is not inappropriate for us these days also to reflect on how new document forms such as blogs will be preserved as well, or, how families once again might become official archives (although, perhaps, this time around with professional experts to assist them when they need help).

Contending with blogging suggests we need to realize that the public, private citizens, and other professionals, such as writers and historians, not only have a interest in seeing documentary sources such as blogs preserved but that they may have a stronger role to play in ensuring such preservation. Some scholars, such as Penelope Papailias, studying modern Greece, have ascertained how families, local communities, and ethnic and other societal groups have contributed to a rich archival sensitivity in their nation by caring for local documentation and ensuring that that documentation is used effectively in everything from historical research to literature and popular entertainment.[91] We read, on a regular basis, accounts of researchers visiting family archives to do research, and although the archival environment may not always be up to high-level professional standards, the records are preserved.[92] The situation in present-day Greece is by no means unique. Everywhere we are seeing a renewed interest in maintaining personal and family archives, increasingly present by activities such as blogging on the Web.

As more and more people transfer their diary writing impulse to the creating and maintaining of their online blogs, one wonders how these digital diaries will be read in the long-term future. The act of creating a blog is intended to generate immediate responses, as I hope for in my own blogging efforts, as opposed to the older tradition of diary writing where a diary was intended to be read long after the writer was gone. I have been in recent months in an archives reading a diary that was closed for twenty-five years after the death of its creator, an access provision dictated as part of the gift of that individual's papers comprising the diaries. The mere fact of having closed the diaries for so long makes me anticipate that there must be detailed intimate notations on this person's life and career that will provide additional insights beyond what I learned about in his other papers (mostly correspondence, notes for and drafts of professional essays and other publications, and financial records). Having access to diaries with such private revelations often makes us wonder why we keep them for others to read at some point in the future. Bill Hayes, in his book about anatomist Henry Gray, states it this way:

> The attachment is not entirely logical; nor is sentimentality alone the motive. You come to anthropomorphize this extension of yourself. However raw the day, the diary absorbs every word, every ache or joy; its blank pages inviting ever more confession. Whether it is a gilded leather-bound volume or a simple file on your laptop, the idea of destroying the diary becomes increasingly unthinkable. It would be like throwing away pieces of flesh from your *own* body. Still, that's only half the explanation. The truth is, when you're writing a diary, a part of you hopes it will be read someday. At the very least, you are writing for the unique someone who will be the perfect reader, who will devour your sentences and *understand*: your future self.[93]

Obviously, blogging truncates the problem of access by making diary-like entries available immediately, but blogging also creates another challenge: will my blog, or anyone else's blog for that matter, be around in twenty-five years to be read?

Times are changing in terms of how we interact with documentary texts, and blogging may be as good an indicator as there is for how rapid this change may be happening. Novelist and essayist Julian Barnes in a recent essay describes this family ritual: "My brother remembers a ritual – never witnessed by me – that he calls the Reading of the Diaries. According to him, Grandma and Grandpa each kept diaries, and in the evenings would sometimes read out loud to each other what they had recorded five years earlier. The entries were apparently of stunning banality but frequent disagreement."[94] I can imagine such diary reading occurring in more than one household, but I wonder if the online quality of blogs will lend themselves to this kind of family event. Or, even that blogs will be around in five, let alone twenty-five, years? While there is a communal aspect of blogging, in that they are publicly posted for reading, there is still a solitary nature about them, as one person reads and perhaps comments on the blog's newest posting.

Blogging, for all its possibilities of individual expression and relative ease of use, brings with it other problems when viewed in the long-term issues of trying to maintain a documentary heritage. In an American archival journal, archivist Nancy Deromedi discusses a variety of issues relating to the personal web sites of university faculty. Deromedi considers efforts by the University of Michigan to investigate how these web sites are used and the archival issues they present. Scanning what faculties there do with web sites, Deromedi concludes that they serve as sites to provide information on "academic identity and achievements" and "to convey knowledge through the distribution of teaching and research materials."[95] Recognizing faculty blogs especially as mechanisms enhancing the role of faculty as public intellectuals or scholars, the University of Michigan library, along with the Bentley Library, its archival arm, started a blogging service "designed to include the option for archiving the blog" and giving the option to a faculty member to have a blog appraised by archivists when the blog is inactive.[96] This also opens the possibility of documenting more effectively what and how faculties teach in their courses and how this connects to faculty research, an aspect of university archival work that has proved to be particularly challenging to accomplish.

I am not sure how many university and college archives and records management programs focus on faculty blogs and Web sites (Deromedi suggests that faculty papers of any sort continue to be a low priority for these archival programs), but I know that little attention has been paid to these digital recordkeeping systems at my own school. This raises interesting questions regarding the future of my own blog, for example, and it obviously falls to my own resources to maintain it over time in any form. I must admit that my goals for my blog do not include its long-term preservation. I see its main value as serving as an extension of my teaching and as a means to generate additional substantive discussion about scholarly and other discourse on the nature of archives and the archival enterprise; at this early stage it may be premature to assess its value in the larger sense, although the level of conversation seems minimal (similar to other efforts I have been engaged in over the years – maybe the problem is me). As for its long-term value, I suspect that I will ultimately fold my blog postings into published essays and books, such as this one, and I see this as the final archiving of the blog (much of this own essay was previously posted in segments on my blog). Perhaps this merely places me among an older traditional generation, but until something else comes along I don't think I see the blog as anything more than a testing or drafting of ideas about societal and scholarly images of archives.

There is, of course, a personal dimension of my blog. As I write various postings, I often share something of my own life and professional experiences, as well as sharing ideas about research and writing projects. William Zinsser, in his introduction to a collection of essays on memoir writing, suggests that "This is the age of the memoir. Never have personal narratives gushed so profusely from the American soil as in the closing decade of the twentieth century. Everyone has a story to tell. And everyone is telling it."[97] In a sense, this blog joins me into this culture. We are so sensitized to this notion of sharing our private thoughts that there have even been new developments in blogging software, allowing us to share our most personal thoughts with the means to control more effectively access to the blog. That blogging is already so ingrained in our culture can be seen in that the *Economist* provided extensive coverage on Mena Trott and her Vox, the new blogging software allowing individuals to determine what aspect of their blog will be private and what part will be public.[98] Blogging, despite how some remain skeptical of it, is probably here to stay, and it may be one of the best means, as well as a serious challenge, for archivists to document a wide range of individual and family activities. I wonder if anyone in the archival community might ultimately want to archive my own blog as being important to professional discourse and development?

Diary Writing and Blogging.

Diary writing is an area of personal recordkeeping that has been the topic of sustained discussion for the past several decades, with the scholarship becoming both deeper and broader in scope. Blogging partly seems to turn upside down the notion of diary writing. Many commentators on diaries suggest that they were often compiled by individuals, such as women living on the frontier or war-time prisoners, who felt isolated and who needed to use their journals to find their voice or to communicate to other family members and intimate friends their experiences in a way that would assist others to avoid the mistakes they may have made or to solve problems they had already confronted and resolved.[99] Joanne Cooper argues that the diary or journal has been "used by women to sort their own lives. It is a way of ordering the overwhelming number of details women encounter in their often fractured lives, a way of bringing meaning to disorder."[100] Cooper continues, "Without necessarily being able to explicitly state why they keep diaries, women have done so because they have sensed the value of such record keeping, because they have experienced the pleasures and rewards of such reflection and organization." [101] We know that other forms of journal keeping, such as that required in freshman writing

classes, are used to help individuals re-evaluate their own attitudes and
perspectives.[102] For example, if as a literary scholar suggests, "Diary
writing is both rehearsal and substitution for making a death mask; it is
motivated by the desire to commemorate," how can we hold to the
same notion of the blogging surrogate, unless, of course, people really
believe that somehow the World Wide Web is really permanent and
maintainable in some fashion enabling the recreation of the blogging
environment.[103]

There is no indication that our interest in why people write diaries
is abating; indeed, there are indications, in recent scholarship, that the
interest is growing. Historian Alexandra Garbarini's study of Holocaust
diaries is an important addition to this scholarship. As this scholar notes,
her study is "an analysis of why ... people sustained such seemingly
Herculean writing efforts and of what their diaries reveal about their
perceptions of Nazi exterminatory policies in the midst of their
implementation."[104] This is also a study of how the diaries were created,
how they survived, and why they were used. The initial chapter is a
fascinating historical and theoretical investigation of the motivations for
writing diaries under such circumstances. The individuals involved in
this writing did so because they turned inward to make meaning of the
new, strange, and hostile world they found themselves living in. As
Garbarini suggests, while diarists through history compiled diaries as a
mechanism to record their experiences, these Jewish diarists also wrote
in order to live, "writing themselves into the future."[105] Indeed, these
particular diarists provide an opportunity to investigate the nature of
this record form in interesting ways, with implications for
comprehending other diarists. Garbarini comments that these "diarists
wondered if it was possible to represent their experiences in language,
and what the implications were of the representations they were in the
process of creating."[106] Furthermore, the Jewish diarists "often invested
tremendous faith in history and envisioned their diaries as evidence for
future historical writing about their plight. At the same time, they
expressed doubt that historians who had not shared their experiences
would be able to understand and accurately depict them,"
foreshadowing, as Garbarini thinks, some of the postmodernist debates
about history.[107] This study also notes how the Holocaust diaries pushed
the diary form, appearing as group efforts, series of letters, or objective
reports. Garbarini links these diaries into other studies of war diaries,
suggesting that as the diarists were written to "absent family members

and to the world at large," they became "part of this longer tradition of diary writing as public performance."[108]

This particular study divides up its analysis of the diaries according to predominant themes, such as diarists functioning as historians and interpreters of events; distributors of news (however flawed the news may be, especially as diarists tried to be more hopeful as events became worse) that became more difficult as German authorities increasingly controlled mail; correspondence writers to missing relatives to eliminate distance, provide moral advice, and give meaning for family (as families were being exterminated); and as individuals involved in a "cultural pursuit"[109] whereby they located their place in the world gone mad. Some of these ventures share great similarities with diaries written by others under normal events, but Garbarini does suggest that often there was a different psychology present with those compiling their record during the Holocaust, operating under constant fear of being caught and read by any other than those the diaries were intended for. This historian acknowledges how her study has been connected to the many recent academic theoretical discourses about history – such as the "relationship of memory to history, the concept of a fragmented self, the potential impossibility of mourning trauma, and the moral fallibility of Western science and democracy."[110] All of these relate to the issue of the limits of representation. Whatever one thinks of these conceptual discussions, one can still read *Numbered Days* and gain insights about the nature of a fundamental way of self-documentation. One could ignore all of the theoretical discourse in this volume and simply focus on the personal diary or blog or, in the case of archivists, relate it to reflecting on the nature of documents they administer.

Why Diaries and Blogs Are So Important.

For years I would debate with my wife about the work of the archivist. She would laugh, and state with a twinkle in her eye, "So, just what is the eternal significance of preserving all that old stuff?" It is, of course, a good question, if only intended to provoke me to re-evaluate just what I was doing with my life. Debates, from time to time, within the archives community about whether archival documents possess permanent or continuing value also reflect the same kind of question. While generating some interesting scholarly and professional literature, we remain far from gaining a completely satisfactory answer. Then, in a bit of reading about the vocation of the writer by the mystic Thomas

Merton, I came across this entry from his own diary, dated October 10, 1948:

> Sooner or later the world must burn, and all things in it – all the books, the cloister together with the brothel, Fra Angelico together with the Lucky Strike ads which I haven't seen for seven years because I don't remember seeing one in Louisville. Sooner or later it will all be consumed by fire and nobody will be left – for by that time the last man in the universe will have discovered the bomb capable of destroying the universe and will have been unable to resist the temptation to throw the thing and get it over with.
>
> And here I sit writing a diary.
>
> But love laughs at the end of the world because love is the door to eternity and he who loves God is playing on the doorstep of eternity, and before anything can happen love will have drawn him over the sill and closed the door and he won't bother about the world burning because he will know nothing but love."[111]

Whatever one's religious views might be, a way of reading this is to remember that there are always bigger issues than the immediate or long-term preservation of various documents. And in addition, archivists need to be in a position to at least grapple with such philosophical questions about their mission. After all, archivists are often given meager resources because of other organizational and social issues that seem to have higher priorities – and maybe they do. But one thing Merton is saying is that we also should focus on our primary responsibilities and activities with the knowledge that everything ultimately will be sorted out. However, this will only occur if archivists can look up from their own work, see beyond their daily chores, and ask and try to answer the big questions. Is this happening? I am not really sure, even as I write into my blog.

There are obvious reasons why blogging should draw more attention to the archival implications of the World Wide Web for its role in contributing to or reshaping the documentary heritage. Gayle Davis notes in one of her essays about women and diary writing that one of the obstacles to doing such research is that so many diaries are in private hands. "In family storage, loose portions or separate volumes of the diaries are commonly lost or purposely divided among the heirs, preventing or complicating their study. Some owners find the book so precious that they are reluctant to permit outsiders to read them. For others, the books are so personal that their use is allowed only after editing has protected the family's privacy."[112] We also know that many people, in their efforts to keep diaries under the most extreme circumstances such as war, also create records that are threatened repeatedly with destruction.[113] Many consider, as well, that the new online diaries are also under daily threats because of the nature of the technological infrastructure. And by necessity of various technological issues, most blogs will remain in private hands as well, the responsibility of their creators and, maybe at some point in the future, that of their descendants.

We need to balance such concerns with the notion that all recordkeeping has a strong relationship to technology and technological innovations. Molly McCarthy, considering the growth of diary writing among women in the nineteenth-century, partly attributes it to the growth in the quantity of commercially available leather bound pocket diaries in the 1850s; originally done for businessmen not women: "The pocket diary's emergence was related to improvements in printing technology and other factors contributing to the explosion of the publishing industry in the first half of the nineteenth century and reflected a continuing preoccupation in America with numeracy, calculation, and record keeping."[114] This historian describes the boom in sales of stationery for letter writing, diaries, and other record keeping purposes, and she notes that the "pocket diary, proprietors soon discovered, held strong appeal for an American clientele, for it married the features of the old almanac, such as interest tables, postal rates, and astronomical calendars, with a new section of ruled, blank pages marked off for daily journal entries."[115] In fact, we can even see the importance of the technologies associated with the quintessential manuscript diary. Lawrence Rosenwald seeks to debunk some of the myths about diary writing, such as the idea that diaries are intended to be secret documents, and suggests this about the production of a diary: "We must, then, set the diary within the local system of production and distribution, and not outside it; but that is not to say that we cannot within that system retain something of the concrete opposition between manuscript and book. In a sense, a diary is a manuscript not accidentally but essentially; if we think of a manuscript as a text in a fluid state, a diary is a manuscript by necessity. During the life of the diarist, the diary remains unfinished and open; something can always be added."[116] Or, as others argue, we must understand that the technologies supporting newer Internet forms such as the blog are just natural extensions of what we have seen in older forms such as diaries.[117]

Blogging expands, of course, on the concept of the diary. It has been well documented how family photographs create a sense of belonging and memory[118], and blogs, as well as just web sites in general, often incorporate such images as well. Andrew Hassam states this about the diary (and as you read this assessment, reflect on how it mimics what goes into making a Web site or how a blog functions): "The diary is self-referential in that the diarist employs language to construct both the space and the occasion in which to write. This act is intentional... because it marks an active, though not necessarily a conscious, choice by a historical individual; the diary is an active transformation of space in time which, reflecting the motives and viewpoint of the subject, brings that space into consciousness."[119] Weblogs, or blogs, express the same purpose and ultimate utility of diaries, such as one group of researchers found in their role as a "bridging genre":

> Our analyses revealed less evidence than expected of blogs as interlinked, interactive, and oriented towards external events; rather, most of the blogs in our corpus are individualistic, even intimate, forms of self-expression, and a surprising number of them contain few or no links. Based on the profile generated by the empirical analysis, we traced the historical antecedents of weblogs back to hand-written diaries. We also pointed out the hybrid nature of weblogs, suggesting that the technical affordances of the weblog format make it readily adaptable to multiple purposes of use. Finally, we suggested that these same affordances bridge, and ultimately blur the boundaries, between HTML documents and text-based CMC, as blogs and other interactive web-based communication systems replace some of the functions of traditional internet genres and give rise to new functions.[120]

If nothing else, records professionals should want to document this new form of diary as a means for understanding how individuals are presenting themselves in a new century.

There are other fundamental differences between traditional handwritten diaries and their online cousins, but these are differences screaming out for archivists and other records professionals to take on new and more energetic proactive roles in informing people how to maintain digital documents. Lena Karlsson, in a study of the Chinese-American community, reflects that "Internet technology has been hailed as the supreme vehicle in the imagining of diasporic communities as it enables a transcendence of physical and national borders and facilitates new spaces for the reconstruction and maintenance of ethnic and cultural identity. There is no denying that the Internet has the potential to greatly affect how diasporic identities and senses of belonging are formed: the question is how and in what specific online context."[121] Some might argue that the increasingly virtual experiences that many people are experiencing are making many individuals feel more like their natural state is diasporic. There is, however, a deep fault line in what this represents in terms of providing a stable documentary heritage for supporting such communities. Karlsson continues,

> The online diary's capacity for mutability and its rather transient quality marks a considerable discontinuity between the paper diary and the online diary. While normally diarists expect the diary to outlive them, these writers presumably expect their biological life to be longer than that of their online diaries, especially if they establish a distinction between the presentation medium (the Web) and the storage medium (a hard drive). The horizon of expectation for online self-representation is often limited to the years that the domain has been bought. Besides. the writers are able to close shop and delete archives rather immediately. However. search engines are now able to locate traces of the online journal even if the site has been erased from its former domain. Many diarists display a fraught relationship to the archive page.[122]

It is obvious that one of the future roles of archivists and records managers is to be a kind of forensic documentalist, seeking to ensure that this fragile digital evidence is maintained in some form.

But such lack of concerns about the durability of the online journal, such as in a study of LiveJournal.com, may be superseded by the immediate or short-term benefits of participating in such a virtual community. Kurt Lindermann believes that

> LiveJournal users also engage in online activities under the auspices of community and community building. The most prominent of these is the review of users' journals by other users, in which users volunteer themselves for reviews by others whose own 'success' in the review process has qualified them to function as reviewers. Audience interaction, evidenced in reviews and responses to another's journal entry, provide insight into the ways users draw on interpretive frames, how their responses reify and resist those frames, and how their responses enable and constrain the cohesive, cooperative participation

[some commentators] imply is an integral part of online communities.[123]

Laurie McNeill, while lamenting the degree of "unbridled narcissism" evident in online diaries and journals, nevertheless understands the appeal to take the diary form to cyberspace:

> For the print diarist, full participation in discourse communities will be hampered by her inability to share her text publicly, or to receive and respond to feedback on what she has written. The online diarist, on the other hand, makes this community conversation a part of the process, often incorporating readers' responses into the diary itself, thus creating a dialogue between herself and her readers. When the conversation between diarist and reader takes place on the diary site's feedback page, in the form of discussion boards, forums, or comments pages, other readers can join in, addressing their comments directly to fellow respondents. The diary then becomes a meeting place and starting point for further discourse among previously disconnected readers.[124]

What becomes clear in such descriptions of the blog as diary is that the archivist's long-term quest for acquiring manuscript diaries needs to be modified into efforts to identify and maintain blogs.

Personally, I believe the existence of blogs suggests three things about how records professionals need to contend with the World Wide Web. First, and most obvious, the existence and proliferation of blogs clearly indicates that the Web is, in part, a major recordkeeping system. Second, and maybe not as obvious, is the fact that records professionals, especially archivists, need to develop approaches for helping individuals preserve their blogs (as well as other personal digital records). Third, and finally, there is no question that records professionals need to advise their institutions about how and why blogs are being used and what they may add to the information leaking out from organizations. This latter issue is especially important for records managers who are working in organizations using proprietary and other information needing to be kept secure.

Conclusion: Basic Observations and Necessary Actions.

We need some organization or group to assume some responsibility for the trust of the World Wide Web. The directors, curators, and professional staff of many museums envision their institutions as part of a public trust. James Cuno, considering the mission of art museums, writes, "The public has entrusted in us the authority and responsibility to select, preserve, and provide its access to works of art that can enhance, even change, people's lives. And in turn, we have agreed to dedicate all of our resources – financial, physical, and intellectual – to this purpose. Art museums are a public trust." Cuno continues, "let us be reminded that we can best earn that trust simply, by remaining open as places of refuge and spiritual and cultural nourishment. In museums people can experience a sense of place and be inspired, one object at a time, to pursue the ideal of objectivity and be led from beauty to justice by a lateral distribution of caring."[125] No one has provided such a perspective for the World Wide Web; indeed, those reflecting on the mission of such cultural institutions are often able to cast their terms in comparison to what the ubiquitous Web actually represents. Philippe de Montebello notes, "But it remains vital that visitors come to see the original. This is why I continue to believe, for example, that the electronic outreach engaged by most museums on their Web sites should not ignite concern among us that the public, so glutted with images from our collections, will no longer come to museums to see original works of art. Reproductions, no matter how good, cannot and will not ever replace originals."[126] Many would debate such an assessment, of course, but that is not the point; the point here is that we need some forceful and even fanciful statements of the Web's purpose, place, and future that elevates the task of preserving its varied content into a public trust argument engaging the resources, expertise, and power of government, information professionals, the news media, researchers covering a wide spectrum, hobbyists, and individuals harnessing it for their own interests and activities that garners the resources enabling this to occur.

We need to be realistic. First, we need to have archivists and records managers move from seeing the Web as a tool to use for promoting their own resources or, mostly in the case of records managers, as another potential liability for their parent organizations to contain. Second, we need to recognize that records professionals have not been all that successful in creating sustained public support for preserving the documentary heritage, especially when that heritage includes something like the World Wide Web that might include a bottomless pit in terms of resources. It may be that the Internet Archive may be the best that it gets, although archivists and records managers need to delineate better what aspects of that initiative do not really satisfy their requirements.

There have been a number of references to the concept of risk management. David Bearman seeks to have us shift gears by looking at the critical moments in cyberspace when records are at risk, at the point of creation, when an electronic record is to be saved or received, when a record is to be archived for long-term use, and when a record is to be preserved beyond its normal range of life. Bearman also contends that there is consensus about when the moments of risk occur. Although Bearman's focus is on the transactional records of organizations, the notion of determining and then monitoring a risk cycle for Web pages is certainly a potentially useful task, with possibilities for enabling records professionals to be better prepared for the potential loss of Web-based documentation. As Bearman argues, this approach is most logically to come from the archival community, and it is a perspective that archivists can assist others with responsibilities for digital documentation to adopt and adapt as needed.[127]

We need to build more citizen archivists. We know that many scholarly disciplines are becoming more engaged by the notion of archives, much of this broadening interest due to the major research industry interested in public memory.[128] We also know that many individuals, whether they consider themselves amateurs or whether they don't even think in this fashion, are using the Web for storing and displaying personal and family archives or, in the case of blogs, creating new archival documents for the future. Perhaps the key to dealing with the Web as a documentary resource is not to try to resolve it as one endless, constantly expanding mass of stuff, but to break it into smaller chunks. Clearly, some of the projects described in this report being carried out by national libraries, state government archives, and various consortia of archives and other organizations, represent just such efforts. However, there may be quite another way to visualize this matter, and that is via equipping individuals to assume archival roles in meaningful and useful ways.

An essay in *Harper's* discusses the work of Rick Prelinger and Megan Shaw Prelinger, terming them "experimental amateur librarians," considering the Prelingers' formation of a library of cast-offs and printed ephemera, numbering about 50,000 items and located in San Francisco, considers how and why they have opted to gather this miscellany of printed stuff in the midst of all the hoopla about the demise of print and the success of the new digital library.[129] As Lewis-Kraus reports, "They think the conflict between a so-called digital culture and a so-called print culture is fake; they think we should stop celebrating, or lamenting, the discontinuous story of how the circuits will displace the shelves and start telling a continuous story about how the two might fit together."[130] Prelinger is the individual who coined the notion of the citizen archivist, and it is a concept that I believe will have more resonance and relevance in the future, especially as we deal with the reality of the breadth of challenges the World Wide Web truly represents.

The Prelinger library provides a different message in our digital age. Made up of 30,000 books and periodicals and about 20,000 pieces of ephemera, the items were "obtained from used-book stores, shrinking institutional and public libraries, periodicals brokers, private donors, and eBay."[131] What the Prelingers are seeking to do is to "preserve a space for the physical, the limited, and the fussily hand-sorted alongside the digital pile. And they think there is a way that the small private library – a phrase that, up until now, has tended to connote a marble-busted terrarium of leather-bound wealth – can be reimagined to do just that."[132] As Lewis-Kraus suggests, "every Library of Alexandria on some broad boulevard needs Prelinger libraries tucked away in the alleys behind,"[133] an idea that can be extended to archives as well. This is an interesting way of thinking about how we need to engage with Web sites. We need individuals seeking to care for institutional Web sites, their own sites such as their blogs, or to be willing to work on monitoring what is transpiring with certain kinds of documents on the Web. In other words, archivists and records managers both need allies.

Prelinger, known for his efforts on ephemeral films, orphaned works, and the Internet Archive, speaks through this essay about the promises and distractions of our modern information age. Here is how the Prelingers' work is described:

> The promise of the Internet-as-Alexandria is more than the roiling platitude of information. It's the ability of individuals to choreograph that information in idiosyncratic ways, the hope that individuals might feel invited by a gravitational pull of a broad and open commons to 'rip, mix, and burn' – to curate. This new sort of curator, in effect, is one definition of blogger: an amateur experimental librarian for the Internet, the curator of (in blogger/writer Cory Doctrow's phrase) a digital *wunderkammer*, a private informational choreographer who has made her alignments public.[134]

This is a powerful idea, one suggesting that private citizens will play an increasing role in the preservation of our documentary heritage. It is an idea worth considering and debating, especially since it is critical to contending with what the World Wide Web represents and the obstacles it presents to being tamed and maintained. Indeed, the Web's purpose suggests that its purpose is to allow everything and everyone to play equal or whatever roles they want on the Web.

In terms of the rethinking of the Web as a documentary source, we need to understand that there have been private or citizen archivists operating long before the establishment of the Web. The notion of private individuals creating and maintaining archives is nothing especially novel. In Africa, during the colonial era, tribal leaders, civil servants, writers and journalists, and ordinary inhabitants had engagement with the colonial state. As Kerin Barber reflects, "by writing directly to colonial officials, by establishing an alternative epistolary network, by using a diary to keep miscellaneous records of official information, by writing love letters with one eye on their possible future use as legal evidence, by recording their own public achievements and civic contributions (perhaps with a view to being appropriately obituarized in due course), or, by participating in the constitution of an exacting religious community, enclosed within the state but reversing some of its key values," these various individuals documented their interaction with and reaction to the colonial powers and influences.[135] What we may be seeing now is simply the same kind of efforts playing out in cyberspace.

We need to refocus the efforts of archivists and records managers. Considering the issue of citizen archivists suggests that records professionals need to redirect some of their energies to new and different roles and responsibilities. While in the past archivists have generally held to a collecting and physical custody agenda, it seems that now these professionals need to work with private individuals to instruct them about how to provide modest amount of care for personal and family archives. Some, such as myself, have argued for more than a decade that archivists need to adopt such an approach even with institutional records, both because of their increasing volume and more complex dependence on digital information technologies. So, this is not a new idea. However, the emergence and increasing growth of the scale of Web suggests not only new documentary forms but also the potential for the transference of a lot of other traditional documentary material, from photographs to scrapbooks to personal correspondence, to cyberspace. Archivists need to figure how to advise these individuals to deal with such materials that takes into account technical issues, legal issues, and privacy matters.

Records managers also need to shift their attention away from only maintenance of records according to legal, administrative, and fiscal concerns to encompass records with archival value and to consider societal interests. While the focus of records managers on their employers' needs and requirements, such as in the management of Web sites, may be important for reconsidering more of a local perspective, this perspective is not particularly useful if it does entail a full notion of the records life-cycle, meaning that records and information with archival value both to the organization and to researchers and other interested parties on the outside are understood to be included. We see this kind of schism not just with the care and feeding of Web sites, but with other areas of electronic records management such as electronic mail. Records managers ought to take leadership in instructing records professionals how Web sites in organizations ought to be managed, but so much attention has been devoted to the potential negative consequences of the use of the Web by organizations and their employees and the resultant legal implications that the other possibilities have been lost in the mix.

Let me provide a simple example of the kind of assistance that a records professional like an archivist might provide to private individuals building Web sites featuring personal or family papers, or, perhaps, volunteering at a cultural institution to assist with the construction and maintenance of a Web site. Errol Morris recently speculated about whether photographs can mean anything if they are "unaccompanied by words." What kind of evidence do they provide and can they "tell the truth"? Morris plays with this and concludes, "A captionless photograph, stripped of all context, is virtually meaningless." And this is exactly the kind of problem we often see in Web sites built by amateurs interested in historical issues or using historical documents to support sites focusing on a variety of topics. "The issue of the truth or falsity of a photograph is only meaningful with respect to statements about the photograph," writes Morris. "Truth or falsity 'adheres' not to the photograph itself but to the statements we make about a photograph. Depending on the statements, our answers change. All alone — shorn of context, without captions — a photograph is neither true nor false." In other words, photographs can be complicated historical sources. "The idea that photographs hand us an objective piece of reality," Morris continues, "that they by themselves provide us with the truth, is an idea that has been with us since the beginnings of photography. But photographs are neither true nor false in and of themselves. They are only true or false with respect to statements that we make about them or the questions that we might ask of them."[136] This is exactly the kind of assistance archivists can provide, for example, in helping to equip better the new citizen archivist.

We can amplify this example with hundreds of others, all suggesting that as the technologies make access to, reproduction of, and interpretation about historical sources something that nearly anyone with a modicum of computer literacy can do, we must also remember that these same individuals both can make simple mistakes in how they accomplish these ends and lose sight about the challenging problems in the maintenance of the Web sites. Archivists and records managers need to see this as the opportunity to expand the public understanding about the documentary heritage and how this relates to the World Wide Web. The tendency has been in the records community to sit back and allow a small number of projects, focused on mostly global solutions, engage the serious issues posed by the Web. There is, however, a role on the local level to be played out by archivists and records managers serving as resources to help private citizens, amateur historians, and the interested public solve the digital preservation problems posed by the proliferation of Web sites and the increasing digitization of documentary sources.

It is a Web of records, and it is an interesting set of questions, procedures, and techniques to be wrestled with and resolved.

Conclusion: A New Kind of Archival Future?

Introduction to the End of My Rambling.

There ought to be little doubt that personal and family archives are important *and* pose new and interesting challenges. We have generations of testimonies about the importance of such documents, as well as the problems they present in administering them. In a collaborative study of how a group of university faculty maintain their own research and teaching notes and other personal and administrative files, the authors of the study note that the "problem of personal archiving, in a nutshell, is that we collect more documents and objects than we can immediately access."[1] Replete with photographs of how some of these faculty members are managing their own records, with some of these illustrations revealing operations rivaling the finest run small professional archives, the observers conclude in this way about the significance of a personal archives: "So what is the personal archive for? To a certain extent, it is for storing and retrieving information, but more often it is about the important values, such as building a legacy, sharing information, preserving important objects, and constructing identity."[2] It is the kind of sentiment we have been seeing all along when it comes to personal and family archives.

Scholars and researchers tend to leave behind large amounts of documents relating to their work. In some cases, such as Paula Kamen discovered in her study of Iris Chang, the internationally known author of *The Rape of Nanking* who committed suicide in 2004 at 36 years of age, such records also document Chang's depression and mental illness. However, the book also is a window into the use of archival material, both by Kamen and by Chang – and again we gain a glimpse of the importance of personal records. Kamen can analyze Chang to the extent she does because Chang left behind a huge quantity of archival material. Kamen notes she was "guided throughout my quest for answers by circuitous trails of clues that Iris herself seemed to leave me – buried within her writing, correspondence, and hundreds of boxes of personal and professional papers that she had left to three major university archives."[3] As Kamen delves into Chang's personal papers, she finds that these archives revealed Chang "putting her affairs in order in the few weeks before she died."[4] Kamen also reveals that in her own personal papers she has many letters and other documents concerning Chang, and she draws on these to re-evaluate what they reveal about Chang. *Finding Iris Chang* also concerns Chang's love of research in archives, best represented in her book about Nanking but also encountered in every aspect of her life. Chang was a lover of archives, an accomplished researcher, and archives provided her life with adventure and the thrill of discovery. Chang's archival impulses prove to be infectious. Kamen notes at the end of the book, "In investigating her influence, I've also become more aware of the significance of historical documents in general to transcend speculation and rumor – and shed light on even the most convoluted and misunderstood events of the past."[5] This is a book reminding us about the power of archival documents (if not always that of their caretakers).

The absence of relevant documentation also suggests the importance of the archival impulse. William Shakespeare, who left us a substantial body of plays, is only represented in about a hundred documents. Bill Bryson remarks that "although he left nearly a million words of text, we have just fourteen words in his own hand…"[6] Bryson provides various descriptions of surviving documents, accounts of interviews with archivists about the records, tales of discovering and losing documents, and the process of analyzing documents alleged to be by Shakespeare or to have connections with him. Bryson asserts that the idea for his book is "to see how much of Shakespeare we can know, really know, from the record," indicating that this is why his book is "so slender."[7] It is amazing to imagine such an important historical figure, one who has generated a scholarly industry, leaving so little in the way of documentation. However, it is worth speculating if someone with the influence of Shakespeare in our own day might leave such a paucity of records. Given that we seem to be buried in information, this seems unlikely, except for the fact that most of this information is captured and maintained in the more volatile digital realm.

Personal and family archives are a critical aspect of our society and culture. Roger Scruton provides a sense of how culture is not some objective data repository when he writes that, "Unlike science, culture is not a repository of factual information or theoretical truth, nor is it a kind of training in skills, whether rhetorical or practical. Yet it is a source of knowledge: *emotional* knowledge, concerning what to do and what to feel."[8] We need to determine some ways of transmitting the knowledge of our culture, or as Scruton tells it, "because culture is a form of knowledge, it is a business of the teacher to look for the pupil who will pass it on."[9] In this concluding chapter, I am suggesting that archivists need to be these teachers (or at least among them), equipping individuals and families to care for their own records. Archivists have assumed their responsibility to be in providing repositories for the accumulating of such documents, just as Scruton notes:

> Of course, we have museums, universities, and archives devoted to maintaining the relics of our culture. But that does not guarantee that the culture will survive; for it survives, if at all, *in us*, the observers and users of these things. And if the relics have no effect on us, what remains in the meaning? Should we not compare them to the votive offerings of some dead religion, whose last devotees have disappeared, and whose artifacts gather dust in unvisited cellars?[10]

My point is that these archival repositories always will have a role, at least as a repository of last resort. We are beginning to see, in a promising way, some archives positioning their programs, first, to aid the average citizen, and, second, to offer their institutions as a repository (perhaps, increasingly, one of last resort).

The Digital Challenge or Promise.

I have over stated, of course, the case. Many individuals and families will not provide very good care, just like many institutions and governments provide a range of care for their records and information systems. The point is that there is now a spectrum of new information technology supporting personal and family recordkeeping that make it difficult to collect in the same way as archivists have for generations. While it is easy to drift into some variety of technological determinism and predict how the world has been transformed by such technologies, the critical thing is for us to take note that the world is in the process of changing – often in ways that defy explanation or that move beyond traditional approaches – and requiring archivists to rethink their working assumptions.

It is hard to go anywhere in the archives community and not find archivists working on some aspect of digital archives, either digitizing their holdings or contending with digitally-born materials. Archivists are aware that not everything will be digitized or that they will be able to save everything that is created digitally. However, the public, policymakers, and a lot of scholars and other researchers don't really understand such matters. Well-known historian Anthony Grafton provides a glimpse into such matters in a *New Yorker* essay, providing his perspective about the limitations of the vast Google enterprise, the challenges of intellectual property, the issues of selecting materials for digitization, and how what Google is doing is not the same as what a library does. Near the end of the article, Grafton provides a look into what archivists face: "For now and for the foreseeable future, any serious reader will have to know how to travel down two very different roads simultaneously. No one should avoid the broad, smooth, and open road that leads through the screen." Grafton also believes we need to be able to continue to examine original documents, taking what he calls the "narrow path": "The narrow path still leads, as it must, to crowded public rooms where the sunlight gleams on varnished tables, and knowledge is embodied in millions of dusty, crumbling, smelly, irreplaceable documents and books."[11]

We can catch another glimpse of this in Christine Borgman's study on the nature of the digital scholarship. Borgman is concerned, not surprisingly, about who or what will replace the traditional role of libraries and archives in bearing the "primary responsibility for access, preservation, and curation."[12] While she notes that some scholars and some research teams are assuming responsibility for their data and research publications and reports, she is worried that maintaining such material on personal Web sites is not much of a preservation system. No one involved with such efforts will disagree. I could wake up tomorrow and remove such materials from my Web site with no explanation or regrets, and I certainly understand the issues and responsibilities of preservation. Borgman notes, "Private ownership and control must be balanced with the public interest in preserving the cultural record. It is even less obvious who, if anyone, will maintain access to informal content such as discussion lists, home pages, blogs, and collections of bookmarks and links."[13] However, it is not impossible that archivists and others could develop documentation aims and processes that could work out the means to preserve such materials possessing critical importance in our society. All archivists need to do is work with those programs providing approaches to information, technology and subject expertise Borgman identifies as the solution to preserving digital scholarship and other information systems.

As part of her efforts to come to terms with maintaining the new digital scholarship, Borgman seeks to transform preservation, which she sees as a "passive process," into a process that is "active." This active process is "curation": "Digital objects, unlike printed publications, cannot be preserved through benign neglect. Curation adds value through migration to new formats, adding metadata, and ensuring trust in the integrity of the objects through technical and institutional mechanisms."[14] While this sounds all new and shiny, I am not so convinced that this is anymore than new nomenclature for an old process, a process that was certainly seeking to deal with digital formats in the manner so described. Upgrading preservation, the heart of archival work and mission, to embrace digital documents and systems only acknowledges the reality of what many preservation managers, in both libraries and archives, are already engaged in (at least partially). However, examining these efforts can result in a defeatist mentality where the immense scale of documentation and the constantly changing landscape of new technologies overwhelm archivists, their allies, and even those who rely on the evidence and information found in archival repositories.

What we know about the digital present, somewhat different from the more promising digital future, is that the growth of digital documents continues to outstrip the means to control these digital sources. Electronic records continue both to grow in scope and to replace their non-digital forbears. Study after study, report after report suggests, however, that we are a long way from being able to manage effectively these systems. The Cohasset Associates recent report, the fifth in a series going back to 1999, suggests the scope of the problem, while putting a brave face on the problem. These authors note that there have been improvements in electronic records management, suggesting that these improvements had stemmed from laws and policies, such as the Sarbanes-Oxley Act of 2002 and the Health Insurance Portability and Accountability Act (HIPPA), along with better technology solutions and an improved sense of the importance of records management. However, the various data from business and government respondents are not very reassuring. Consider some of the facts presented: While 88% have a formal records management program and 70% include electronic records in these programs, only 49% have a formal e-mail policy and only 30% have formal plans for migrating older electronic records. Williams and Ashley conclude that "most organizations have serious operational shortfalls regarding the processes by which they manage electronic records, one of their most important assets."[15] What is dismaying about the report is that it is focused on business and government institutions, and they have historically done better than most, especially cultural archives and historical records repositories and records programs.

In our era of the World Wide Web, there are many ways we can consider how to preserve and make accessible archival sources to the scholarly community and general public. Debates about whether digitization is a preservation process have simmered down.[16] We are moving into a new, more positive perspective of digitizing as a preservation mechanism. John Feather has this to say about digitization: "The websites of the world's great libraries, archives and museums ... vividly illustrate what can be achieved with imagination and resources... Digitization does not 'solve' the 'problem' of preservation but it has added another powerful weapon to the armory of solutions."[17] Marilyn Deegan, in another essay in the same volume in which Feather's essay appears, sounds a similar refrain: "Creating surrogates can never replicate or preserve everything about an original object, but creating no surrogates could mean that everything is lost in the case of fragile or compromised originals, brittle books printed on acid-based paper, older newspapers, ancient and medieval books and manuscripts, crumbling sculptures, ruined buildings, photographs on glass plates and explosive nitrate film stock."[18]

Digitalization has reached far beyond mere means for preservation or access, opening up new approaches for scholarship, as best described by Christine Borgman. Borgman resists the temptation to layout a pessimistic scenario: "We are currently in the early stages of inventing an e-Research infrastructure for scholarship in the digital age. It may take twenty, forty, or sixty years to realize the vision, by which time the technology and tools will be quite different from today."[19] Here we have the real challenge, and while we have a lot of work to do, archivists, librarians, other information professionals, and the research communities ought to feel energized to tackle these interesting issues. It may be that the kind of assistance with the public described regarding personal and family papers may take a very long time to emerge in any substantial fashion. However, there is little doubt in my mind that how we work with such personal archives today will be very different than how we work with the personal archives of tomorrow.

Archivists may always face making some decisions, determining to rescue records when destruction seems imminent by bringing them into a secure repository, about certain important individual and family papers. How do we determine those personal and family archives that are especially important that we would save when they come into harm's way – abandoned by the family or threatened by natural disaster or some other event or circumstance? For that matter, how do we determine what of these records to save now? Archival programs have usually developed appraisal approaches for such records as part of a local history agenda, topical collecting, the serendipitous fortune of discovering interesting or important materials just before they are consigned to the dumpster, or some other planned or reactive impulse. The problem has been that archivists need to develop more definable criteria and document their appraisal decisions so that they can develop a broader and more effective approach to the vast archival resources in cyberspace. The fact that the collecting of personal and family archives has been generally more of a serendipitous process will not help archivists all that much with working with this aspect of the documentary universe.

Archivists have never been in the business of saving everything, and this suggests a bit of a dilemma in a digital culture where many seem ready to accept the notion that information technologies will enable them to do just this very thing. Archivists, despite recent vigorous debate about how they appraise records, still lack clear philosophical statements about saving a representative or systematic sampling of the personal papers of everyman. There is still a sense that saving either papers of important people and families or the papers with critical insights into past events are about as far as they can go in explaining what they are doing. Archivists have no clear publicly understood statements about just what they are doing, generally giving more of a sense that they have gathered up what came their way by chance or happenstance.

Self-Help Nation – and Professional Definitions?

Perhaps the need to provide a rational description of archival work or mission may become less important as we observe more and more people create personal and family archives in a public, online venue. We are seeing an increasing quantity of publications guiding individuals in the creation of family history web sites, building on a legacy of self-help publications and sources that Americans have long relied on.[20] We can understand what such books are intending to suggest to people when we peruse the promotional materials accompanying their publication:

When people begin their genealogical adventure, they usually interview elderly members of the family and contact other family members. The next step is usually one of organization of the information collected. The third step is usually to share this information with other family members, traditionally by publishing research in a book. However, a family Web site has numerous advantages:

It is interactive so others can contribute their stories and pictures.

It will help you find long-lost relatives.

It is an ideal way to preserve research for the entire family.

It will break down the walls that have stumped you in your research.

It recognizes that family research is an ongoing process.[21]

Now, professional archivists might quibble about whether placing everything online is the best manner in which to preserve such genealogical and family history, but this genre of publications is powerful testimony to the growing strength of interest by individuals to maintain their personal and family archives. Some publications have appeared striving to help genealogists and family historians to move from their more familiar work with manuscript letters and written diaries, photographs, and other family documents to knowing how to digitize these sources so that they have easier access to the records and preserve them by creating these surrogates for consultation. The emphasis of such publications is on practical advice for these digitization projects, although the information about the challenges of generating copies that fit within any preservation paradigm is always a bit skimpy; here is a role for the archivist interested in more directly engaging the public.[22]

Do we think people who are diarists, bloggers, and scrapbookers or who are constructing online family history sites are creating, gathering, or preserving sources to put into archives? Do most people really think this way? Archivists, who have generally built a solid reputation of working with the public, community groups, and various research constituencies, need to reach out to the people and work with them in preserving materials that may come into their repositories only as a last resort (or, at least, have a carefully thought through appraisal and acquisition scheme and compelling, publicly understandable, explanation for it). While individuals involved in blogging or scrapbooking may have a stronger sense of the past and often an immense desire to save material to help keep themselves in space and time, that desire may also prompt them to want to maintain materials themselves. And archives, such as historical societies and university special collections, have a strong legacy of acquisition and may not be able to help themselves. Archives are not perfect – they have a legacy of being elitist, revealing bias to certain groups or kinds of individuals (they can seem like exclusive, gated communities to the outside world, the part of society not oriented to what archives are about through formal university education in fields dependent on the mining of archival sources). We should want to restore a kind of archival power to the people. But the "every person" will think that their effort to save old documents related to them is part of their means to mark their place in space and their passage in time. Some might want to see what is in an archives, but most probably just want to see their own intimate documents handed down and protected from generation to generation.

Something else might be going on in all this. There are other roles that archivists can play in equipping the public to handle their personal records. What should go into self-help books? What kinds of self-help books do we need? We have many examples of self-help guides purporting to aid individuals to organize and maintain their personal financial, property, medical, and other vital records; some of these records are certainly part of the personal or family archives but the aim of these texts is not really about family history. As one promotional blurb about one of these books suggests, "In just one weekend, you can enjoy the comfort of knowing that you or a relative or guardian will be able to quickly locate vital information."[23] The intelligent use of such manuals ought to be welcomed by most people, even while recognizing their limited value for more long-term advice such as could be provided by an expert archivist. In the third chapter, I made allusions to the role of ancient scribes who, while mostly in the employ of (or servititude to) the powerful and wealthy, also functioned as aides to the commoner who needed a particular document. While these scribes would only likely produce a guidebook for other scribes' use, the role that these manuals of today play are not all that unlike what these copyists of long ago would have done. Copying for security and access, procedures for preservation, examples for particular documentary genres, and other such issues are generally universal activities and spread over several thousand years.[24]

At the present, it seems that the genealogical community has stepped most strongly into the role of providing basic practical guides to gathering, organizing, and preserving personal and family historical records.[25] These guides tend to provide advice that few archivists might quibble with and that, in fact, they could refer interested parties to if archivists take on a more pro-active role of assisting the public. It is apparent in such volumes that the authors assume that their readers are intent on maintaining these materials for themselves and their families. Many of these guides have focused on how to identify, evaluate, organize, and maintain family photographs, including some guides published on such matters by archival programs.[26] Given that there is a real publishing industry on such genealogy and family history topics, archivists should take heart that this is a potentially powerful way for them to connect with the public and that they have allies to join with in promoting the preservation of our documentary heritage. Ultimately, by adopting such a public assistance role, archivists and their employing institutions might also identify more effectively critically important personal and family records needing to be preserved in their repositories (even if this means providing copies rather than originals or linking to Web-based sources).

The fact that genealogists were quick to embrace the use of the Web for building research collections, family history pages, and training guides also ought to suggest that we need guides to help people figure out how to use new and emerging software with archival implications such as MyLifeBits or FaceBook. These "cyberplaces" may face some of the same kinds of challenges, archivally-speaking, that other Internet-based systems such as e-mail and blogs also face. It is easy for archivists to try to look the other way when confronting such documentary sources as blogs, as we can see from other disciplines. Journalist Tom Goldstein contends that, "although journalists continue to see their jobs as collecting and verifying information as best they can before disseminating it, the Internet may increasingly accommodate a public demand for unverified information."[27] He drives this point home by contrasting blogging with journalistic reporting: "For bloggers, truth is created collectively, not through a hierarchy of fact seekers and verifiers. Information is not necessarily vetted before it is disseminated; instead, it is distributed via multiple and usually undifferentiated views. This is a different kind of truth than the truth that journalists have become accustomed to, arrived at by different means. Truth, in the bloggers' view, emerges from the discourse."[28] These are interesting observations, even if at times Goldstein seems to get a little curmudgeonly about the World Wide Web and its impact, and it is the kind of commentary that might make archivists at first want to dismiss blogging and bloggers as anything they need to consider; the argument, could go, that these are not the kinds of sources archivists have traditionally been focused on or should be. Of course, any form of documentation, such as the traditional manuscript diary, can present all sorts of problems in regards to veracity. Nothing really has changed all that much, except that we seem to have a lot more bloggers at work than we have ever had diarists (but that could just be the result of blogging being a much more highly visible activity).

However, as I tried to argue in the previous chapter, blogs are both pervasive and important documentary sources, and they might turn out to be the most important type of source of our present digital era. Geert Lovink argues, "blogs are the proxy of our time. It is a techno-affect that cannot be reduced to the character of the individual blogger. There are possibly as many blogs as there are voices and topics."[29] So, we should assume, archivists can't ignore the blogging phenomena if they have any interest or aim in documenting the late twentieth and early twenty-first centuries. However, such concerns might be beside the point, especially as our notion of archives and the archive expands and shifts shapes and meanings. Over the past two decades we have come to understand that the archival record is not as fixed or stable as we thought, and it is not just about the issues of technology. This has especially come to be the case, when we look at archives from a vantage point such as cultural studies. Helen Freshwater discusses the

> myth of the fixed historical record. Once removed from the world of recitation – enunction – the voices of the past preserved in the archive will be mediated by the decisions of a series of archivists, experts, and academics. The 'curators' control which voices are given the opportunity to speak again to a wider audience. As these archival researchers frequently serve as conduits between the past and the contemporary public, their attitude toward the material they study ought to be a central concern for archive theory.[30]

And, in reality, this is not a particularly new set of issues. For example, Clemens and Graham, in their wonderful introduction to the study of medieval manuscripts, note,

> It is a remarkable irony that the preservation of some manuscripts may be intimately linked with the mutilation, dismemberment, or outright destruction of others ... [O]nce a medieval scriptorium had produced a new copy of a text in up-to-date script, the other

manuscript that had served as the textual exemplar might be discarded: the production of the *new* thus led to the destruction of the old.[31]

The authors also provide discussion about how early scholars developed scrapbooks of study materials by cutting up old manuscripts for specimens for their own use. Even when not considering such practical reshufflings of documents, we realize that any efforts to define what constitutes our cultural heritage can be moving targets.[32]

The concept of the archive is pressed even more when we deal with certain kinds of documentation that are particularly associated with personal records. Let's reflect on home movies, a particularly ubiquitous form of personal documentation. Patricia Zimmerman describes how "home movies constitute an imaginary archives that is never completed, always fragmentary, vast, infinite."[33] She also adds that, "In the popular imagination, archives often are framed as the depositories of old, dead cultural artifacts. But archives are never inert, as they are always in the process of addition of new arenas and unknown objects. The archive, then is, is not simply a depository, which implies stasis, but is, rather, a retrieval machine defined by its revision, expansion, addition, and change."[34] This seems similar to Freshwater's notion that "archives are always created out of a concern for what is yet to come and that they are maintained and protected with an eye to the future."[35] Ayisha Abraham provides one example from his experience working with home movies, placing them within the context of the larger sense of the archive:

> On my journey of excavation, I have endured many excitements and disagreements. Some films survive, while others perish: often it is the preservation of home movies that is amateurish, not their aesthetic, technique, or content. Many film cans have not been opened in decades. With no ventilation, the cans trap moisture and disintegration begins. Mold and other agents of decay, such as excessive humidity, moisture, and exposure to rust, dust, and insects, destroy many collections. My archaeology of these images and their review in the present also expose the mold and decay of memory to the possibility of moving into a more public history. If the film is not projected, these memories remain hidden, removed from family and community.[36]

This sentiment suggests, of course, that a tension can exist between aiding amateurs to preserve their own archival materials and that of acquiring these sources for archives where they can be more readily used by researchers. My point is, however, that there are too many sources of personal and family archives to bring into public archives (would archivists really want all the home movies stashed in attics?) and that archivists need to work to equip a new kind of archival technician – in this case, the private citizen who can possess skills, dedication, and motivation for maintaining more of the archival universe than the archival profession can handle. Then, we can begin to sort out how to identify and acquire, perhaps, the most important cultural and historical resources that can go into these repositories (or create new kinds of repositories) when these sources might be threatened because of changing personal and family resources and interests.

There is beginning to be some research about personal archiving pointing us in the right direction. In one study examining how individuals deal with "personal digital belongings," Marshall, Bly, and Brun-Cottan conclude that "The most surprising and troubling of the observed trends is that most of our informants and members of their households had already lost valuable digital belongings such as half-finished writing projects, irreplaceable photographs, and personal records. Many also had stories about computers that they could no longer use, casualties of hardware failures, security problems, or viruses." They go on to state, "A service design will need to take into account peoples' attitudes about their digital belongings. First of all, there is a notable optimism about the incorruptibility of digital forms in spite of experience to the contrary: 'They're all digital files, why would they stop working?' Second, we encountered a considerable amount of fatalism about the reliability of digital technology; system failures are greeted by a sense that one simply needs to move on: 'I think [losing digital belongings] is like losing anything else. I mean, if your house burnt down, it would hurt, kind of, and you'd just have to let go and move on.' Finally, there is a fear about the vulnerability of networked digital storage to unknown social forces."[37] Such findings not only provide insights into how individuals are coping with their personal archives, but they also begin to show how and why archivists ought to assume a more proactive role in building and staffing sustained outreach programs for aiding individuals and families to contend with the challenges of such archiving. Neil Beagrie, in his brief review of the emergence of personal digital collections, or what he terms "digital estates," provides another glimpse into the emerging challenge:

The growth of personal digital information brings interesting issues for libraries, family and employers relating to "digital estates" following the death of individuals. This is not solely an issue of content and its value but an issue of access (although it will be interesting to see if the often very high value placed on the personal archives of correspondence and manuscripts of some creative authors will also translate to the digital world of their email and electronic documents). Most personal digital collections can only be accessed via personal passwords and authentication.[38]

In other words, all kinds of new problems, albeit interesting ones, are emerging for the digital era archivist.

Even in the strangest fictional accounts of archivists, we see that there is always a sense of the mysteries they will unravel, the discoveries they will make, and the challenges they will face.[39] One day, while browsing through the various postings on the Archives & Archivists Listserv, I happened across a message indicating that the mystery *Plum Island* by Nelson DeMille is a good read with an archivist as one of the main characters. So, I take a break one afternoon and head to a local bookstore to see what this character is about. As I approach the 1997 mystery, I am not worrying about the story or the quality of writing; I am interested in how the archivist is handled. The female archivist is introduced, a president of the local historical society, who also is a florist. The hard-boiled male detective checks her out − tall, attractive, wearing skimpy clothes, younger than expected, and listens to her explanation of the purpose of the society as being "dedicated to preserving, recording, and passing on our heritage."[40] The archivist also indicates that they have "some interesting archives" as well.[41] In her banter with the detective, the archivist suggests that she likes "archive work" and has a degree in "archival science" from Columbia University.[42] The detective is depicted as thinking, "she had a nice, soft, breathy voice which I found sexy."[43] The archivist "had a lot of gossip, a lot of insights into people, though not much of it seemed to relate to the case."[44] The archivist takes the detective on a tour of the historical society, and, along the way, the archives housed there. The detective asks her how she got into this work, and she indicates that her family was among the original settlers in the area. Here's the good part. The archivist explains, "Archive work must be a little like detective work. You know − mysteries, questions to be answered, things that need to be uncovered."[45] It seems to me that the new digital documentary universe also requires some archival detective work.

A Good Sign: Archival Self-Help.

Archives and archivists have been offering practical advice to individuals about the care and feeding of personal documentation for some time, as well as creating interesting and useful educational packets about the nature of personal documentation.[46] The Minnesota Historical Society, as part of its Conservation Outreach Program, distributes brief practical tips via online documents and workshops. For example, its "A Checklist for Preserving Your Family Letters and Paper Heirlooms" covers advice on displaying and storing such materials.[47] This organization also issued a guide to organizing family papers, concerning how to identify the papers, organize them, and the kinds of materials to store them in.[48] The National Archives of Australia provides a page on its Web site called "Looking After Your Family Archive," where one can gain advice from "specialist conservators" on how to care for paper, writing materials, photographs, scrapbooks, time capsules, as well as how to respond to disasters such as fires and floods.[49] In the United Kingdom, the Universities of Oxford and Manchester joined forces in the Personal Archives Accessible in Digital Media (PARADIGM) project, issuing guidelines with the recognition that the growing creation of personal and family documents in digital form requires that professional archivists provide some basic advice in order to ensure that there are any personal and family archives left to preserve. This project's "Guidelines for Creators of Personal Archives" is a practical tool that should be widely disseminated and used by professional archivists working with citizens. This guide first sounds an alarm about the risks associated with digital materials: "The time is near when the family photograph album, now lovingly handed down from generation to generation, is likely to exist only in digital format. Without active intervention it is unlikely to become an heirloom, or even survive the next software crash. The same is true of audio and video recordings, correspondence and personal websites." It then provides advice for naming digital files, managing e-mail, using open source software rather than proprietary software, backing up and storing files, maintaining hardware and media, being aware of how and when to use security devices, understanding intellectual property issues, and keeping everything up to date. The PARADIGM project also strongly urges consulting with archival experts when necessary.[50]

There are many other examples of such efforts by archives and archivists. The American Heritage Center at the University of

Wyoming has offered a similar guide for preserving family records in digital form. This guide offers three basic tips, including backing up digital files on a weekly basis, migrating files every time new computer or software equipment is acquired, and storing such files in places that are adequately cooled in summer months and heated in winter months. Our colleagues at this repository also recommend printing out copies on paper. Then they offer advice about digital images, arguing that these are the "most fragile photographic material that humans have ever devised" and the "best camera for a permanent record is the old-fashioned film-based camera that creates negatives to produce prints. For really long-term preservation, shoot a roll of black and white film."[51]

Some archival programs have developed innovative efforts to assist individuals care for their personal and family materials while also suggesting that they may want to consider donating these items to an established archival repository. The New Jersey Digital Highway – a collaborative effort between the New Jersey State Library, American Labor Museum, the New Jersey Department of Archives and Records Management, the New Jersey Historical Society, and Rutgers University Libraries, with funding by the Institute of Museum and Library Services – issued a brief guide to making decisions about how to care for personal and family documents and mementoes. Information is provided about storing such materials and describing them, along with a downloadable deed of gift form allowing individuals to identify items that could be copied by or donated to archives, museums, and libraries. One twist with this deed of gift is that it is designed not to focus on the physical item but to enable its digitization for extended use by others and established repositories. Posing the question about whether such material may be worth anything for others, the guide responds:

> Absolutely! You are part of history in the making. Someday, a descendant of yours will be tracing her family history and will "meet" you for the first time in a family photograph she discovers in digital space-whether the web or an entirely new technology. The ability to digitize information is getting easier and easier, and the ability to store more information digitally is getting less expensive. Libraries and archives may not have physical space to store your physical artifacts, but ultimately, they will be able to store and provide access to digital copies for future generations to study and enjoy.

The deed of gift, intended to be completed and stored with these materials at home, is explained in this way:

> You are the creator or owner of the photographs, mementos and scrapbooks in your collection. This means that you hold the rights to these materials, and only you can donate your right to copy and share this information with others. You must share this right in writing for others to be able to copy and share your information via the web or any other means of distribution.
>
> Your photographs and personal mementos are part of your estate. Be sure to let your executors and heirs know your wish to share your information with future generations. If you prepare papers for your executors, such as a will or financial documents, you can include a blanket deed of gift for all photographs and mementos or you can note that a deed of gift is included with each box or scrapbook of photographs and mementos.[52]

The PARADIGM project in the United Kingdom also suggests the same possibility for personal and family archives coming into repositories, seeking to get individuals to think about the potential societal significance of their personal and family archives:

> You may not have thought of your digital files as part of a personal archive, or as having long term historical interest, yet what seems ordinary and mundane to you now may well interest future researchers. In an archival repository, your archive will reveal a personal perspective on your life, work and environment for posterity; it will combine with the mementos of your contemporaries, forbears and successors to provide personal and historical insights into past times.[53]

In the United States, the Idaho State Historical Society provides similar advice, describing the potential dangers to personal and family records, suggesting a few commonsensical steps that can be taken to care for such materials, but mostly making a pitch for individuals to consider placing their papers in established repositories. The plea is straightforward. First, there is the danger:

> Many photographs, diaries, letters, and ephemeral materials that were produced in your great grandparents time have survived until today because they were valued and preserved. Many of the records created today will not exist 20 years from now because they are routinely disposed of through short-sighted house cleaning efforts or because they exist in formats (such as videotape, newspaper, magnetic tape,

non-archival photo albums) that self-destruct if they are not carefully preserved.

Then there is the promise of their being cared for if donated to an archival repository:

> Your family's history is important to your community! You, no matter what your occupation, education, or social standing, have shared in the heritage of a certain place and time. Your personal records document this and can be a part of your community's collective memory. Most individuals and groups lack the resources or expertise to properly preserve their own records. Fortunately, there are places that are in the business of preserving history: the archives of your local, county, and state libraries, museums, universities, and historical societies. These professional institutions are the caretakers of our documented past.[54]

Such efforts suggest an interesting new kind of partnership between professional archivists and the public, whereby citizens are equipped to deal with their personal and family archives and established archives acquire copies for the use by other researchers or the actual items as a means of last resort to protect them.[55]

When we consider the rapidly expanding digital documentary universe and the archival community's struggle to control it, we ought to realize that unless archivists can develop innovative new approaches and build stronger and more beneficial partnerships than we ought to fear for the future of understanding the past. Travis Holland, writing about the control of writers and other artists in Moscow in 1939, weaves a fictional account of Pavel Dubrov, a former literature professor, assigned to the Lubyanka prison to work with the manuscripts confiscated from Russian novelists, poets, and other writers declared to be enemies of the state and forbidden to write. Ultimately, the task of Dubrov is to destroy these manuscripts, referred to as "weeding," working from carefully prepared inventories, when instructed by Party officials to do so. There are moments when Dubrov finds himself setting aside his sinister bureaucratic tasks to read a bit and other moments when he drops his calculated cold exterior to lecture a comrade or supervisor about an aspect of literature.

Holland deftly follows Dubrov's quiet rebellion against a repressive state, and the book reminds one of Bradbury's *Fahrenheit 451* at times in its style and sentiment. This is a book for our times. Holland presents an engaging array of characters and situations, all having to do with access

CONCLUSION 307

to words and information and the consequences of their repression. As Dubrov is assigned to rearrange the archives, there are constant checks into his own personal files as the Party faithful grow increasingly suspicious of him (and nearly everyone else). Dubrov meets the writer Isaac Babel at Lubyanka (where we know he was imprisoned and later executed in 1940) and begins to read the files of Babel's confiscated manuscripts, finally resorting to smuggling some of the manuscripts out in a vain effort to save them.

Holland's account of a society fixated with repressing words but on using information collected about every citizen makes our archivist and his love for words seem both heroic and doomed. *The Archivist's Story* is a tragedy for our own so-called information age. At one moment, Holland sets a scene where "Pavel imagines a day, years from this morning, when he will return with his metal cart from the incinerator and find no more boxes waiting: no stories, no novels or plays, no poems. Just empty shelves. The end of history."[56] And that is what this novel is about, the end of history, the archivist, and archives. And the discarding of history is a breaking of his reason to live: "With every manuscript he destroys, Pavel can feel a little more of his soul being chipped away."[57] In a final defiant gesture, as he awaits his inevitable demise, Pavel disorganizes the archives, creating "chaos."[58] And we last see the archivist staring out the window into a deserted street, waiting for his keepers and executioners to arrive.

We will become like the main character, "Mr. Blank," in Paul Auster's novel *Travels in the Scriptorium.* a man with no memory who is constantly jotting down notes on a pad in a desperate effort to remember something about himself and his life. Mr. Blank can't determine if the manuscripts he reads are mere stories or reports about real events – and we share Mr. Blank's frustrations that these documents have no real ending or that Mr. Blank, in his recounting of one of them to one of his interrogators, isn't allowed to finish his own analysis of the document.[59]

Summing Up.

It is easy to speculate that the loss of documentation in the glut of the ever-changing digital universe will lead to some kind of end of history. We often forget that some of our most imaginative historians have been scholars who did not spend much time in archival reading rooms. One of the great American historians of the twentieth century eschewed the use of archival materials for his groundbreaking studies, most of which remain in print a half century after their publication. Richard Hofstader's biographer, David S. Brown, commenting on Hofstadter's classic *The Age of Reform*, considers it "at heart, a product of the mind rather than the archives. It is a richly symbolic book, the fruit of its author's imagination, his selective reading in the social sciences, and his reaction to McCarthyism."[60] Brown continues, in considering *The Age of Reform*, "His mind sparked in a spirit of expansiveness, and while he often overplayed his insights (a creative strategy he openly acknowledged), it would be difficult to overestimate his importance as an intellectual pioneer." And this is where Hofstadter's neglect of archival sources enters in: "Leaving others to mine the libraries to verify or shake his more controversial ideas, Hofstadter aroused a certain degree of jealousy among traditionalists or, as he called them, 'archive rats.'"[61] This is not, of course, an explanation or rationale for the archival community to shift away from acquiring personal and family papers. However, the increasing use by many to digitize documents or to use digital means for creating and maintaining records suggests the need for re-thinking what the archival profession has been doing, since the quantity is greater and the means of maintaining these documentary sources more complex (or more limited).

This does not mean that collecting physical items is over. While I spend more than I should on books, I am not a serious collector. I am not buying rare books, combing dealers' catalogues, or scrolling the Web in the search for the missing item in my personal collection. I buy books with a strictly utilitarian purpose – to support my research and teaching (or to indulge in my enjoyment reading in the history of baseball and golf). With minor exception, I acquire a title, read it, mark it up, reread it when necessary and make additional notes for a course lecture or an essay I am writing. While I have an extensive library, this is not a special collection but a working reference unit. While I love the physicality of the book, and certainly enjoy the feel and look of a beautifully designed and produced volume, I just as soon possess a tattered edition I can employ for my own objectives. The legal scholar Alan Dershowitz is a true collector, as he confesses in a recent book about acquiring an 1801 Jefferson letter. Dershowitz, it turns out, is an energetic collector of rare books, newspapers, manuscripts, and art – and, as it seems, just about anything striking his fancy. The first part of his book is about collecting, where he concludes, among other things, that the "joy of collecting lies generally in finding an item that appeals

to the collector's aesthetic, historical, or personal sensibilities. Finding
the object is an end unto itself... But the joy is magnified when the item
has a value beyond the intrinsic – when it teaches us something we
didn't know."[62] When in September 2006 Dershowitz discovers the
Jefferson letter in the Argosy Bookstore and purchases it, these aspects
of collecting become more evident.

Dershowitz describes the Jefferson letter as the "greatest acquisition
of my career as a collector."[63] It is why he writes both about collecting
and Jefferson's views about freedom of religion, speech, and conscience
– the topics handled by old Tom in his letter. Dershowitz provides a
detailed provenance of the letter, warming the hearts of archivists
everywhere, finding that the letter had been in one family for 205 years
until the document was sold to the bookstore. Dershowitz's book is
mostly about Jefferson's notions about such matters, but interestingly
the author writes most of his analysis in the form of a letter to Jefferson.
Finding Jefferson is, therefore, also homage to Jefferson the letter-writer.
Dershowitz notes that Jefferson wrote no books, but that it is in his
epistles that Jefferson reveals the "most important and revealing source
of his philosophy."[64] The importance of Jefferson's correspondence is
such for Dershowitz that he announces his intention to teach a seminar
for first year Harvard Law School students called "The Letters of
Thomas Jefferson." In this course, "we will read hundreds of his letters
relating to the Constitution, to law, and to political philosophy in an
effort to understand better the American legal system."[65] I am sure most
of us rather learn about the law by reading Jefferson's letters than a dry
legal text.

Now, I am not arguing that Dershowitz's personal collecting
regimen should be some kind of explanation for why our established
archival programs should continue to acquire traditional documentary
sources. However, archivists need to be mindful that the nature of
personal and family archives is transforming in ways that require some
fundamental re-imagining of archival practice. Archivists need to
expand archival documentation efforts, like the old documentation
strategy model, to include individuals and families as key players; this
requires reevaluating how rigorous archival appraisal approaches really
have been (and in the realm of personal and family papers such
approaches have been notoriously malformed, with unclear objectives
and fuzzy [if any] benchmarks). Archivists also need to utilize the World
Wide Web as a way to engage the public on personal and family
archives, since the public is increasingly using the Web for such

purposes anyway. Archivists must expand their professional mission in a way that provides a larger notion of a documentary universe, one that sees itself aiding the public in a new way to care for documents that may never come into an archival repository or that seeks to define a new type of virtual repository. Doing this will strengthen the traditional archival mission of identifying, acquiring, preserving, and enabling access to records with archival value. Both citizen archivists and professional archivists will benefit from such an effort.

In following this path, archivists have to be mindful of two issues. First, since so much of their future work with personal and family archives will be in the digital realm, archivists need to be careful not to lose or weaken their broader mission and focus. For a lesson here, we can turn to creative non-fiction writers providing some advice about their craft:

> When you look at our tendency these days to interface with technology rather than one another, perhaps the surprise is not that memoirs are flourishing but that anyone questions the trend. Neuropsychologists are discovering that the impulse for story is likely hard-wired into our brains. The less we talk to one another, the more our personal narratives – our confessions, our dark sides, our recitations of the things we do in secret – will seek other ways to emerge, finding voice in the genre of memory.[66]

This description of personal narratives sound a lot like the personal and family archives we desire to keep, in some fashion, and we need to remember that archives are stories fighting to be told. As our writers suggest, "Despite our isolation, we are drawn to story, and the more emotional the tale, the deeper the salient information lodges in our memories. We learn from personal revelations, war stories, family legends, urban myths, campfire tales, true confessions, and gossip around the water cooler."[67] Archivists have tended to isolate themselves, especially in their inward battles with digital records and descriptive standards, but now they have the opportunity to move more into the public square. And, hopefully, archivists should sound off that we also learn from the stories in their repositories and from the personal and family archives they will help a new force of citizen archivists maintain for another generation of descendants *and* researchers. "The telling of tales does more than entertain," our writing coaches argue. "It transmits important information between generations, making important events of the past relevant."[68]

Archivists, as the second factor, also need to be mindful of their own
legacy in caring for personal and family archives. As I was writing this
final chapter, I was in Williamsburg, Virginia reading the diaries of
Lester J. Cappon for a follow-up project on this important archival
leader of the mid-twentieth century.[69] On September 4, 1968, Cappon
was in Boston at the Houghton Library at Harvard University reading
the diaries of Jared Sparks of a century and a half before for a book on
historical manuscripts Cappon never finished. Cappon writes,

> Again I am impressed by the energy & industry of this man and his
> persistence in seeking out the sources for a history of the American
> Revolution, with focus on Gen. Washington. The problems of access
> to MSS in private hands, the conflicting viewpoints of public officials
> concerning the records in their custody, and the liberality of some
> persons in loaning the originals – all these problems Sparks
> encountered in varying degrees in his pioneer work of this kind, and,
> on the whole, met with great success. With letters of introduction he
> was able to meet the 'right' persons and gain admission to the 'best'
> society some of which bored him.[70]

With this entry, Cappon linked one important pioneering era of
archival acquisition with another. My own work on Cappon is intended
to link his era with my own, for Cappon's observations about the state
of archival affairs are certainly relevant to our own time. However, we
are nearing the day when most of the labor with new documentation
will be in the virtual world, necessitating new approaches Cappon could
never have imagined. What Cappon would understand is the need to
take actions to keep the archival stories coming, and his own strenuous
efforts to make archival and historical work more understandable would
certainly fit easily with the allies of citizen archivists. This is a fitting
place to end this book.

Works Cited

Note: All web links were active at the time this book manuscript went to press.

Abercrombie, Stanley. "Office Supplies: Evolving Furniture for the Evolving Workplace," in Donald Albrecht and Chrysanthe B. Broikos, eds., *On the Job: Design and the American Office* (New York: Princeton Architectural Press, 2000).

Agre, Phil. "The End of Information & the Future of Libraries," *Progressive Librarian*, (1997) at http://www.libr.org/PL/12-13_Agre.html.

Agre, Phil. "Institutional Circuitry: Thinking About the Forms and Uses of Information," *Information Technology and Libraries* 14, no. 4 (1995): 225-230, also at http://dlis.gseis.ucla.edu/people/pagre/circuitry.html.

Akenson, Donald Harman. *Some Family: The Mormons and How Humanity Keeps Track of Itself* (Montreal and Kingston: McGill-Queen's University Press, 2007).

Aly, Götz and Karl Heinz Roth. *The Nazi Census: Identification and Control in the Third Reich*, trans. Edwin Black and Assenka Oksiloff (Philadelphia: Temple University Press, 2004).

"Americans Call E-Mail Essential to Their Jobs," *Information Management Journal* 37 (March/April 2003): 16.

Anderson, Janice. "ECM:RIM – Programs that Matter. Programs that Last," *KMWorld* (October 2006): S16-17.

Andreadis, Harriette. "True Womanhood Revisited: Women's Private Writing in Nineteenth Century Texas," *Journal of the Southwest* 31 (Summer 1989): 179-204.

Angell, Roger. *Let Me Finish* (New York: Harcourt, Inc., 2006).

Appleby, Joyce. *A Restless Past: History and the American Public* (Lanham, MD: Rowman & Littlefield Publishers, Inc., 2005).

Archives Authority of New South Wales, *Steering into the Future: Electronic Recordkeeping in New South Wales* (Sydney: Archives Authority of New South Wales, 1997).

Armitage, David. *The Declaration of Independence: A Global History* (Cambridge: Harvard University Press, 2007).

Arms, William Y., et al. "Collecting and Preserving the Web: The Minerva Prototype," *RLG DigiNews* 5, no. 2 (April 15, 2001), available http://www.rlg.org/legacy/preserv/diginews/diginews5-2.html#feature1, accessed July 14, 2007.

Arms, William Y. *Web Preservation Project Final Report: A Report to the Library of Congress*, (September 3, 2001), available at http://www.loc.gov/minerva/webpresf.pdf.

Armstrong, Karen. *In the Beginning: A New Interpretation of Genesis* (New York: Alfred A. Knopf, 1996).

Association of Records Managers and Administrators, *Guideline for Managing E-Mail* (Prairie Village, Kansas: ARMA International, 2000).

Association of Records Managers and Administrators, *Requirements for Managing Electronic Messages as Records* (Prairie Village, Kansas: ARMA, 2004).

Auster, Paul. *Travels in the Scriptorium* (New York: Henry Holt and Co., 2006).

Australian Archives, *Managing Electronic Messages as Records: Policy and Guidelines* (Canberra: Australian Archives, May 1997).

Australian Council of Archives, *Corporate Memory in the Electronic Age: Statement of a Common Position on Electronic Recordkeeping* (Victoria, Australia: Australian Council of Archives, May 1996).

Baker, Nicholson. *The Size of Thoughts: Essays and Other Lumber* (New York: Vintage Books, 1997).

Balough, Ann. "Building a Knowledge Center for Records and Information Management," *Records & Information Management Report* 17 (April 2001): 1-14.

Bantock, Nick. *Griffin & Sabine: An Extraordinary Correspondence* (San Francisco: Chronicle Books, 1991).

Bantock, Nick. *Urgent 2nd Class: Creating Curious Collage, Dubious Documents, and Other Art from Ephemera* (San Francisco: Chronicle Books, 2004).

Barber, Karin, ed. *Africa's Hidden Histories: Everyday Literacy and Making the Self* (Bloomington and Indianapolis: Indiana University Press, 2006).

Barnes, Julian. "The Past Conditional: What Mother Would Have Wanted," *New Yorker* (December 25, 2006 & January 1, 2007), available at http://www.newyorker.com/archive/2006/12/25/061225fa_fact, accessed March 12, 2008.

Barry, Richard E. "Managing Distinctions: Enterprise Information, Document, Records, Knowledge, and Content Management," *Records & Information Management Report* 18 (February 2002): 1-14.

Barry, Rick. "Web Sites as Recordkeeping & 'Recordmaking' Systems," *Information Management Journal* 38 (November/December 2004): 26-30, 32.

Basbanes, Nicholas A. *A Splendor of Letters: The Permanence of Books in an Impermanent World* (New York: HarperCollins, 2003).

Beagrie, Neal. "Plenty of Room at the Bottom? Libraries and Collections," *D-Lib Magazine* 11 (June 2005), available at http://www.dlib.org/dlib/june05/beagrie/06beagrie.html, accessed August 1, 2006.

Bearman, David. "Managing Electronic Mail," *Archives and Manuscripts* 22, no. 1 (May 1994): 28-50.

Bearman, David. "Moments of Risk: Identifying Threats to Electronic Records," *Archivaria* 62 (Fall 2006): 15-46.

Beavan, Colin. *Fingerprints: The Origins of Crime Detection and the Murder Case that Launched Forensic Science* (New York: Hyperion, 2001).

Begos, Jane Dupree. "The Diaries of Adolescent girls," *Women's Studies International Forum* 10, no. 1 (1987): 69-74.

Bellafante, Gina. "Trafficking in Memories (for Fun and Profit)," *New York Times*, January 27, 2005, p. F1.

Benson, Robert. *The Game: One Man, Nine Innings, A Love Affair with Baseball* (New Yorker: Jeremy P. Tarcher/Penguin, 2004).

Berry, Wendell. *The Way of Ignorance and Other Essays* (N.p.: Shoemaker and Hoard, 2005).

Bielstein, Susan M. *Permissions, A Survival Guide: Blunt Talk About Art as Intellectual Property* (Chicago: University of Chicago Press, 2006).

Birkerts, Sven. *Reading Life: Books for the Ages* (Saint Paul, MN: Graywolf Press, 2007).

Blom, Philipp. *To Have and to Hold: An Intimate History of Collectors and Collecting* (New York: Penguin Books, 2002).

Bloom, Lynn Z. "Escaping Voices: Women's South Pacific Internment Diaries and Memoirs," *Mosaic* 23, no. 3 (1990): 101-112.

Blouin, Francis X., Jr. and William G. Rosenberg, *Archives, Documentation, and Institutions of Social Memory: Essays from the Sawyer Seminar* (Ann Arbor: University of Michigan Press, 2006).

Bonner, Robert E. *The Soldier's Pen: Firsthand Impressions of the Civil War* (New York: Hill and Wang, 2006).

Borgman, Christine. *Scholarship in the Digital Age: Information, Infrastructure, and the Internet* (Cambridge, MA: MIT Press, 2007).

Boudrez, Filip. *Filing and Archiving E-mail* (2006), available at http://www.expertisecentrumdavid.be/docs/filingArchiving_email .pdf.

Brett, Jeremy Brett, "A Case Study of the Web-Site Appraisal Process as Applied to State Government Agency Web Sites in Wisconsin," *Archival Issues* 27, no. 2 (2002): 99-110.

Brody, Florian. "The Medium is the Memory," In Peter Lunenfeld, ed., *The Digital Dialetic: New Essays on New Media* (Cambridge: MIT Press, 2000), pp. 393-417.

Brown, Bill. "The Collecting Mania," *University of Chicago Magazine* 94 (October 2001), at http://magazine.uchicago.edu/0110/features/mania.html, accessed June 27, 2007.

Brown, David S. *Richard Hofstadter: An Intellectual Biography* (Chicago: University of Chicago Press, 2006).

Brown, John Seely and Paul Duguid, *The Social Life of Information* (Boston: Harvard Business School Press, 2000).

Brown University. *Response of Brown University to the Report of the Steering Committee on Slavery and Justice* (Providence, Rhode Island: Brown University, 2007).

Bryson, Bill. *Shakespeare: The World as Stage* (New York: HarperCollins Books, 2007).

Buckland, Michael. *Information and Information Systems* (New York: Praeger, 1991).

Buckler, Patricia P., and C. Kay Leeper. "An Antebellum Woman's Scrapbook as Autobiographical Composition," *Journal of American Culture* 14, no. 1 (1991): 1-8.

Buckley, Ellie, et al. "Virtual Remote Control: Building a Preservation Risk Management Toolbox for Web Resources," *D-Lib Magazine*

10, no. 4 (Apr 2004), available at
http://www.dlib.org/dlib/april04/mcgovern/04mcgovern.html,
accessed July 14, 2007.

Bulkeley, William M. ""In the Digital Age, a Clash Over Fading
Photos," *Wall Street Journal*, April 1, 2005, reprinted in the *Arizona
Republic*, available at http://www.azcentral.com/business/articles/
0401wsj-fadingphotos01-ON.html#, accessed April 3, 2005.

Burnham, Christopher C. Burnham, "Reinvigorating a Tradition: The
Personal Development Journal," in *The Journal Book*, ed., Toby
Fulwiler (Portsmouth, NH: Boynton/Cook, 1987), pp. 148-156.

Burton, Antoinette. *Dwelling in the Archive: Women Writing House, Home, and
History in Late Colonial India* (New York: Oxford University Press,
2003).

Buss, Helen M. "Pioneer Women's Diaries and Journals: Letters
Home/Letters to the Future," *Mapping Our Selves: Canadian Women's
Autobiography in English* (Montreal and Kingston: McGill-Queen's
University Press, 1993), pp. 37-60.

Butler, Jon. *Becoming America: The Revolution before 1776* (Cambridge:
Harvard University Press, 2000).

"By the Numbers," *Newsweek Magazine* 16 (January 2001): 16.

Cameron, Fiona and Sarah Kenderdine, eds. *Theorizing Digital Cultural
Heritage: A Critical Discourse* (Cambridge, MA: MIT Press, 2007).

Cameron, Ross J. "Appraisal Strategies for Machine-Readable Case
Files," *Provenance* 1 (Spring 1983): 49-55.

Carmicheal, David W. *Rescuing Family Records: A Disaster Planning Guide*
(Iowa City, Iowa: Council of State Archivists, 2007).

Carson, Bryan. *The Law of Libraries and Archives* (Metuchen, New Jersey:
Scarecrow Press, 2007).

Carter, Kathryn Dianne. "Death and the Diary, or Tragedies in the Archive," *Journal of Canadian Studies* 40, no. 2 (2006): 42-59.

Casey, Carol. "The Cyberarchive: A Look at the Storage and Preservation of Web Sites," *College and Research Libraries* 59 (July 1998): 304-310.

Caughell, Tracy. "The Corporate Records Conundrum," *Information Management Journal* 37 (May/June 2003): 58.

Chartier, Roger. *Inscription and Erasure: Literature and Written Culture from the Eleventh to the Eighteenth Century*, trans. Arthur Goldhammer (Philadelphia: University of Pennsylvania Press, 2007).

Chosky, Carol E. B. *Domesticating Information: Managing Documents Inside the Organization* (Lanham, MD: Scarecrow Press, 2006).

Clark, Elizabeth A. *History, Theory, Text: Historians and the Linguistic Turn* (Cambridge: Harvard University Press, 2004).

Clark, William. *Academic Charisma and the Origins of the Research University* (Chicago: University of Chicago Press, 2006).

Clemens, Raymond and Timothy Graham, *Introduction to Manuscript Studies* (Ithaca: Cornell University Press, 2007).

Clemmitt, Marcia. "Cyber Socializing," *CQ Researcher* 16 (July 28, 2006): 625-647.

Clyde, Laural A. "Weblogs – Are You Serious?" *The Electronic Library* 22, no. 5 (2004): 390-392.

Cogar, Rae N. "Building an E-Mail Policy: An Organization's Electronic Mail Policy Should Protect Both the Employer and the Employee," *InfoPro* 1 (March 1999): 42

Cohen, Daniel J. and Roy Rosenzweig, *Digital History: A Guide to Gathering, Preserving, and Presenting the Past on the Web* (Philadelphia: University of Pennsylvania Press, 2005).

"Collector Systems Launches Online Art Management Solution," *Proctivity Software* 17 (March 2004): 1-2.

Comay, Rebecca, ed., *Lost in the Archives* (Toronto: Alphabet City Media, 2002).

"Company E-Mail: To Monitor or Not to Monitor," *Information Management Journal* 36 (January/February 2002): 8.

Conhaim, Wallys W. "Personal Journals: New Users for an Age-Old Practice," *Information Today* 20 (January 2003): 27.

Cook, Gareth. "Untangling the Mystery of the Inca," *Wired* (January 2007): 142-147.

Cooper, Joanne E. "Shaping Meaning: Women's Diaries, Journals, and Letters; The Old and the New," *Women's Studies International Forum* 10, no. 1 (1987): 95-99.

Council on Library and Information Resources, *The Evidence in Hand: Report of the Task Force on the Artifact in Library Collections,* November 2001.

Cox, Richard J. "Archives and Archivists in the Twenty-First Century: What Will We Become?" *Archival Issues* 20, no. 2 (1995): 97-113.

Cox, Richard J. *Documenting Localities: A Practical Model for American Archivists and Manuscripts Curators* (Metuchen: Scarecrow Press, 1996).

Cox, Richard J. *Ethics, Accountability and Recordkeeping in a Dangerous World* (London: Facet, 2006).

Cox, Richard J. *Lester J. Cappon and the Relationship of History, Archives, and Scholarship in the Golden Age of Archival Theory* (Chicago: Society of American Archivists, 2004).

Cox, Richard J. *Managing Institutional Archives: Foundational Principles and Practices* (New York: Greenwood Press, 1992).

Cox, Richard J. *Managing Records as Evidence and Information* (Westport, Connecticut: Quorum Books, 2000).

Cox, Richard J. *No Innocent Deposits: Forming Archives by Rethinking Appraisal* (Metuchen, New Jersey: Scarecrow Press, 2004).

Crease, Robert P. "The Lost Art of the Letter," *Physics Web* (January 2007) at http://physicsweb.org/articles/world/20/1/8/1, accessed January 16, 2007.

Crenshaw, Albert B. "Reality Check: E-Payments are Gaining; A Federal Reserve Study Finds that Americans are Losing Their Love for Old-Fashioned Paper," *Washington Post*, November 18, 2001, p. H02.

Cunningham, Patrick J. "IM: Invaluable New Business Tool or Records Management Nightmare?" *Information Management Journal* 37 (November/December 2003): 27-30, 32-33.

Cuno, James, ed. *Whose Muse? Art Museums and the Public Trust* (Princeton: Princeton University Press, 2004).

Dale, Denise. "Getting and Staying Organized: Focus on Personal Papers," *Feliciter* issue no. 1 (2000): 38-40.

Dale, Denise and Alexandra Bradley. *At Your Fingertips! A Household Filing System That Works for You*, 2nd ed. (Richmond, British Columbia: Streamline Information and Organizing Services, 2004).

Darnton, Robert. *The Forbidden Best-Sellers of Pre-Revolutionary France* (New York: W. W. Norton and Co., 1995).

Davenport, Liz. *Order from Chaos: A Six-Step Plan for Organizing Yourself, Your Office, and Your Life* (New York: Three Rivers Press, 2001).

Davis, Gayle. "The Diary as Historical Puzzle: Seeking the Author Behind the Words," *Kansas History* 16 (1993): 166-179.

Davis, Gayle R. "Women's Frontier Diaries: Writing for Good Reason," *Women's Studies* 14, no. 1 (1988): 5-14.

Day, Michael. "Collecting and Preserving the World Wide Web: A feasibility Study Undertaken for the JISC and Wellcome Trust" (February 25, 2003). Available at http://ww.jisc.ac.uk/uploaded_documents/archiving_feasibility.pdf

Dearstyne, Bruce W. "Blogs, Mashups, & Wikis Oh, My!" *Information Management Journal* 41 (July/August 2007): 24-28, 30, 32-33.

de Botton, Alain. *The Architecture of Happiness* (New York: Pantheon Books, 2006).

Deegan, Marilyn and Simon Tanner, eds. *Digital Preservation* (London: Facet Publishing, 2006).

"Deleted E-mails Cost Philip Morris $2.75 Million," *Information Management Journal* 38 (September/October 2004): 20.

DeMille, Nelson. *Plum Island* (New York:Warner Books, 1997).

Deromedi, Nancy. "Personal Faculty Web Sites: Exploring Archival Issues and the Digital Convergence," *Archival Issues* 29, no. 1 (2005): 9-18.

Derrida, Jacques. *Paper Machine*, trans. Rachel Bowlby (Stanford, CA: Stanford University Press, 2005).

Dershowitz, Alan. *Finding Jefferson: A Lost Letter, A Remarkable Discovery, and the First Amendment in an Age of Terrorism* (New York: John Wiley and Sons, Inc., 2008).

Dewalt, Dave. "Understanding the ERM Challenge," *KM World* (October 2006): S8.

Dickson, Paul. *The Joy of Keeping Score: How Scoring the Game Has Influenced and Enhanced the History of Baseball* (New York: Walker and Co., 2007).

Diehn, Gwen. *The Decorated Journal: Creating Beautifully Expressive Journal Pages* (New York: Lark Books, 2005).

DiGilio, John J. "Electronic Mail: From Computer to Courtroom," *Information Management Journal* 35 (April 2001): 32.

Dilworth, Leah, ed. *Acts of Possession: Collecting in America* (New Brunswick, New Jersey: Rutgers University Press, 2003).

"Does E-Mail Belong in the Courtroom?" *Information Management Journal* 36 (January/February 2002): 9.

Doig, Ivan. *Heart Earth* (Orlando, FL: Harcourt, Inc., 1993).

Do Lago, Pedro Corrêa. *True to the Letter: 800 Years of Remarkable Correspondence, Documents and Autographs* (New York: Thames and Hudson, 2004).

Dollar, Charles M. "Appraising Machine-Readable Records," *American Archivist* 41 (October 1978): 423-430.

Dornstein, Ken . *The Boy Who Fell Out of the Sky: A True Story* (New York: Vintage Books, 2007).

Douglas, Althea. *Help! I've Inherited an Attic Full of History* (Toronto: Ontario Genealogical Society, 2003).

D'Souza, Dinesh. *Letters to a Young Conservative* (New York: Basic Books, 2002).

Duranti, Luciana and Kenneth Thibodeau, "The Concept of Record in Interactive, Experiential and Dynamic Environments: The View from InterPARES," *Archival Science* 6 (2006): 13-68.

Eastwood, Terry. *Appraisal of Electronic Records: A Review of the Literature in English*, InterPARES Project, May 30, 2000.

Eggers, Ron. "Photography and the Computer: Disaster Preparedness," *Petersens's Photographic* 29 (May 2000): 50, 63.

Elkins, James, ed. *Photography Theory* (New York: Routledge, 2007).

"E-mail Archiving Market Set to Explode," *Information Management Journal* 38 (July/August 2004): 11.

"E-mail Fumbles Lead to Big Fines," *Information Management Journal* 40 (May/June 2006): 14.

"E-Mails Can and Will Be Held Against You," *Information Management Journal* 37 (March/April 2003): 12.

"E-mails Waste Businesses' Archive Space," *Information Management Journal* 38 (November/December 2004): 11.

Enneking, Nancy E. "Managing E-Mail: Working Toward an Effective Solution," *Records Management Quarterly* 32 (July 1998): 24-26, 28-32, 34, 36-38, 40-43.

Enstam, Elizabeth Y. "Using Memoirs to Write Local History," *History News* 37 (November 1982): 2.

Erdal, Jennie. *Ghosting: A Double Life* (New York: Anchor Books, 2004).

Fadiman, Anne. *At Large and at Small: Familiar Essays* (New York: Farrar, Strauss, and Giroux, 2007).

Fairclough, Graham, Rodney Harrison, John H. Jameson, Jr., and John Schofield, eds., *The Heritage Reader* (London: Routledge, 2008).

Fallows, James. "File Not Found," *Atlantic Monthly* 298 (September 2006), available at http://www.theatlantic.com/doc/200609/information-erosion, accessed March 12, 2008.

Fea, John. "Wheelock's World: Letters and the Communication of Revival in Great Awakening New England," *Proceedings of the American Antiquarian Society* 109 (2001): 99-144.

Fettig, David. "Federal Reserve Studies Confirm Electronic Payments Exceed Check Payments for the First Time," Financial Services Policy Committee, Federal reserve System, December 6, 2004, available at

http://www.federalreserve.gov/boarddocs/press/other/2004/200
41206/default.htm, accessed June 6, 2005.

Fischer, Steven Roger. *A History of Language* (London: Reaktion Books,
Ltd., 1999).

Fischer, Steven Roger. *A History of Writing* (London: Reaktion Books,
Ltd., 2001).

Fischer, Steven Roger. *A History of Reading* (London: Reaktion Books,
Ltd., 2003).

Fisher, Paul. "Electronic Records as Evidence: The Case for Canada's
New Standard," *Information Management Journal* 38 (March/April
2004): 39-42, 44-45.

Foer, Joshua. "Remember This: In the Archives of the Brain, Our Lives
Linger or Disappear," *National Geographic* 212 (November 2002),
available at http://ngm.nationalgeographic.com/ngm/2007-
11/memory/foer-text.html, accessed March 1, 2008.

Foote, George. *Shadowed Ground: America's Landscapes of Violence and
Tragedy.* (Austin: University of Texas Press, 1997).

Franks, Patricia. "The Electronic World: E-mail, the Internet, and
Other Technologies are Making Electronic Recordkeeping a Way
of Life for RIM Professionals," *InfoPro* 3 (December 2001): 50

Frazier, Ian. *Family* (New York: Picador USA, 2002).

Freeman, Frank N. *The Teaching of Handwriting* (Boston: Houghton
Mifflin Co., 1914).

Freshwater, Helen. "The Allure of the Archive," *Poetics Today* 24, no. 4
(2003): 729-758.

Freyer, John D. *All My Life for Sale* (New York: Bloomsbury, 2002).

Friedman, Lawrence M. *Law in America: A Short History* (New York:
Modern Library Chronicles Book, 2002).

Fritzsche, Peter. *Stranded in the Present: Modern Time and the Melancholy of History* (Cambridge, MA: Harvard University Press, 2004).

Frost, John P. "Web Technologies for Information Management," *Information Management Journal* 35 (October 2001): 34-37.

Gallagher, Winifred. *It's in the Bag: What Purses Reveal – and Conceal* (New York: HarperCollins Publishers, 2006).

Garbarini, Alexandra. *Numbered Days: Diaries and the Holocaust* (New Haven: Yale University Press, 2006).

Geffroy, Y. "Family Photographs: A Visual Heritage," *Visual Anthropology* 3, no. 4 (1990): 367-409.

Gelles, Edith B. *Abigail Adams: A Writing Life* (New York: Routledge, 2002).

Gemmell, Jim, Gordon Bell, and Roger Lueder, "MyLifeBits: A Personal Database for Everything," *Communications of the ACM* 49 (January 2006): 88-95.

Gilliland-Swetland, Anne J. *Policy and Politics: The Archival Implications of Digital Communications and Culture at the University of Michigan* (Chicago: Society of American Archivists, 1996).

Gingrich, Laurie L. and Brian D. Morris. "Retention and Disposition of Structured Data: The Next Frontier for Records Managers," *Information Management Journal* 40 (March/April 2006): 30-34, 36, 39.

Gitelman, Lisa and Geoffrey B. Pingree, eds. *New Media, 1740-1915* (Cambridge: MIT Press, 2003).

Glassberg, David and J. Michael Moore. "Patriotism in Orange: The Memory of World War I in a Massachusetts Town." In John Bodnar, ed., *Bonds of Affection: Americans Define Their Patriotism* (Princeton, NJ: Princeton University Press, 1996), pp. 160-190.

Gleick, James. *Faster: The Acceleration of Just About Everything* (New York: Vintage Books, 1999).

Glenn, Valerie D. "Preserving Government and Political Information: The Web–at–Risk Project," *First Monday*, volume 12, number 7 (July 2007), http://firstmonday.org/issues/issue12_7/glenn/index.html, accessed July 12, 2007.

Godbeer, Richard. *Escaping Salem: The Other Witch Hunt of 1692* (New York: Oxford University Press, 2005).

Goldstein, Tom. *Journalism and Truth: Strange Bedfellows* (Evanston, IL: Northwestern University Press, 2007).

Goldstone, Lawrence and Nancy. *Slightly Chipped: Footnotes in Booklore* (New York: St. Martin's Griffin, 2000).

Gomez, Jeff. *Print is Dead: Books in Our Digital Age* (New York: MacMillan, 2008).

Goo, Sara Kehaulani. "Privacy Advocates Criticize Plan To Embed ID Chips in Passports," *Washington Post*, April 3, 2005, p. A06; available at http://www.washingtonpost.com/wp-dyn/articles/A21858-2005Apr2.html?referrer=email, accessed April 3, 2005.

Goody, Jack. *The Power of the Written Tradition* (Washington, DC: Smithsonian Institution Press, 2000).

"Google's New E-mail Service Sparks Privacy Concerns," *Information Management Journal* 38 (July/August 2004): 6.

Gorman, G. E. and Sydney J. Shep, eds. *Preservation Management for Libraries, Archives and Museums* (London: Facet Publishing, 2006).

Grafton, Anthony. "Future Reading: Digitization and Its Discontents," *New Yorker*, November 5, 2007, pp. 50-54.

Green, Marlan, Sue Soy, Stan Gunn, and Patricia Galloway. "Coming to TERM: Designing the Texas Email Repository Model," *D-Lib*

Magazine 8, no. 9 (September 2002), available at
http://www.dlib.org/dlib/september02/galloway/09galloway.html
.

Griffith, Sally F. *Serving History in a Changing World: The Historical Society of
Pennsylvania in the Twentieth Century* (Philadelphia: Historical Society
of Pennsylvania, distributed by the University of Pennsylvania
Press, 2001).

Green, Anna and Megan Hutching, eds. *Remembering: Writing Oral History*
(Auckland, New Zealand: Auckland University Press, 2004).

Grey, Maurene Caplan. "Mitigating the Risks of Messaging," *Information
Management Journal* 40 (November/December 2006): 68.

Groebner, Valentin. *Who Are You? Identification, Deception, and Surveillance in
Early Modern Europe*, translated by Mark Kyburz and John Peck
(New York: Zone books, 2007).

Groves, Shanna. "Protecting Your Identity," *Information Management
Journal* 36 (May/June 2002): 28.

Guthrie, Kevin. *The New-York Historical Society: Lessons from One Nonprofit's
Long Struggle for Survival* (San Francisco: Jossey-Bass Publishers, 1996).

Gutkind, Lee and Hattie Fletcher, eds. *Keep It Real: Everything You Need to
Know About Researching and Writing Creative Nonfiction* (New York: W.W.
Norton & Co., 2008).

Katie Hafner. "Holding a Paper Ticket, Bracing for the Irritation," *New
York Times*, 24 March 2005,
http://www.nytimes.com/2005/03/24/technology/circuits/24tixx
.html?8cir=&adxnnl=1&emc=cir&adxnnlx=1111688590-
d7Cy1oFXXAnZaexIQEa/Og, accessed March 24, 2005.

Haigh, Susan and Roselyn Lilleniit. "A Strategy for Archiving Web
Sites at Library and Archives Canada," *Preservation of Electronic
Records: New Knowledge and Decision-Making* (Ottawa, CA: Canadian
Conservation Institute, 2004), pp. 143-148.

Haigh, Thomas. "Remembering the Office of the Future: The Origins of Word Processing and Office Automation," *IEEE Annals of the History of Computing* (October-December 2006): 6-31.

Hakala, Juha. "Collecting and Preserving the Web: Developing and Testing the NEDLIB Harvester," *RLG DigiNews* 5, no. 2 (April 15, 2001), available at http://www.rlg.org/legacy/preserv/diginews/diginews5-2.html#feature2, accessed July 14, 2007.

Hamilton, Nigel. *Biography: A Brief History* (Cambridge, MA: Harvard University Press, 2007).

Harold, Christine. *Our Space: Resisting the Corporate Control of Culture* (Minneapolis: University of Minnesota Press, 2007).

Harr, Jonathan. *The Lost Painting: The Quest for a Caravaggio Masterpiece* (New York: Random House Trade Paperbacks, 2006).

Harris, Robert. *Selling Hitler* (New York: Penguin Books, 1986).

Harris, Verne. *Archives and Justice: A South African Perspective* (Chicago: Society of American Archivists, 2007).

Hassam, Andrew. "'As I Write': Narrative Occasions and the Quest for Self-Presence in the Travel Diary," *Ariel* 21, no. 4 (1990): 33-47.

Hayden, Dolores. *The Power of Place: Urban Landscapes as Public History* (Cambridge: MIT Press, 1995).

Hayes, Bill. *The Anatomist: A True Story of Gray's Anatomy* (New York: Ballantine Books, 2008).

Hayles, N. Katherine. *My Mother Was a Computer: Digital Subjects and Literary Texts* (Chicago: University of Chicago Press, 2005).

Hedges, Chris. *Moses on the Freeway: The 10 Commandments in America* (New York: Free Press, 2005).

Henkin, David M. *City Reading: Written Words and Public Spaces in Antebellum New York* (New York: Columbia University Press, 1998).

Henkin, David M. *The Postal Age: The Emergence of Modern Communications in Nineteenth-Century America* (Chicago: University of Chicago Press, 2006).

Herring, Susan C., Lois Ann Scheidt, Elijah Wright, Sabrina Bonus. "Weblogs as a Bridging Genre," *Information Technology & People* 18, no. 2 (June 2005): 142-171.

"Highway Statistics 2003 – Section III: Driver Licensing," United States Department of Transportation – Federal Highway Administration, 2004, available at http:///www.fhwa.dot.gov/policy/ohim/hs03/dl.htm, accessed June 26, 2005.

Hipp, Deb. "The Tides of Technology," *InfoPro* 2 (June 2000): 27-28, 31-32.

Hobart, Michael E. and Zachary S. Schiffman. *Information Ages: Literacy, Numeracy, and the Computer Revolution* (Baltimore: Johns Hopkins University Press, 1998).

Hodes, Martha. *The Sea Captain's Wife: A True Story of Love, Race, and War in the Nineteenth Century* (New York: W.W. Norton & Co., 2006).

Hogan, Rebecca. "Engendered Autobiographies: The Diary as Feminine Form," in *Autobiography and Questions of Gender*. ed. Shirley Neuman (London: Cass, 1992): 95-107.

Holland, Michael E. "Adding Electronic Records to the Archival Menagerie: Appraisal Concerns and Cautions," *Provenance* 8 (Spring 1990): 27-44.

Holland, Travis. *The Archivist's Story* (New York: The Dial Press, 2007).

Horton, Forest Woody, Jr. "The Wisdom Administrator: Waiting in the Wings." *Information Outlook* 14 (September 2000): 26-30.

Howells, Cyndi. *Planting Your Family Tree Online: How to Create Your Own Family History Web Site* (Nashville: Rutledge Hill Press, 2003).

Hunt, Elaine. "Spotlight Photography," *Marketing Week* 23 (September 28, 2000): 46.

Hunter, Greg S. "The Digital Future: A Look Ahead," *Information Management Journal* 36 (January/February 2002): 70-72.

Hunter, Jane H. "Inscribing the Self in the Heart of the Family: Diaries and Girlhood in Late-Victorian America," *American Quarterly* 44, no. 1 (1992): 51-81.

Hutchings, Patricia J. *Managing Workplace Chaos: Solutions for Handling Information, Paper, Time, and Stress* (New York: AMACOM, 2002).

Hyry, Tom and Rachel Onuf. "The Personality of Electronic Records: The Impact of New Information Technology on Personal Papers," *Archival Issues* 22, no. 1 (1997): 37-44.

Inchausti, Robert, ed. *Echoing Silence: Thomas Merton on the Vocation of Writing* (Boston: New Seeds, 2007).

"In Praise of Clutter," *The Economist* (December 21,2002-January 3, 2003), p. 87-88.

Isaac, Rhys. *Landon Carter's Uneasy Kingdom: Revolution and Rebellion on a Virginia Plantation* (New York: Oxford University Press, 2004).

Ishizuka, Karen L and Patricia R. Zimmerman, eds. *Mining the Home Movie: Excavations in Histories and Memories* (Berkeley: University of California Press, 2008).

"ISPs Charge to Deliver Mass E-mails," *Information Management Journal* 40 (May/June 2006): 20.

Jardine, Lisa. *Worldly Goods* (New York: Macmillan, 1996).

Jarvis, William E. *Time Capsules: A Cultural History* (Jefferson, North Carolina: McFarland and Co., 2003).

Jeanneney, Jean-Noël. *Google and the Myth of Universal Knowledge: A View from Europe*, trans. Teresa Lavender Fagan (Chicago: University of Chicago Press, 2007).

Johnson, Dirk. "Beyond the Quilting Bee," *Newsweek* 104 (October 21, 2002): 64.

Johnson, Frances. "New Firm Puts Everything You Own on a CD DigitalSafe Records Items for Insurance," *Denver Post*, July 5, 2001, p. C2.

Johnson, Robert. "The Fax Machine: Technology That Refuses to Die," *New York Times*, March 27, 2005, available at http://www.nytimes.com/2005/03/27/business/yourmoney/27fax.html?th=&adxnnl=1&emc=th&adxnnlx=1111915090-bTj0D8FkKUloWrD7aXkx/w, accessed March 27, 2005.

Johnson, Shaun. *The Native Commissioner* (Johannesburg, South Africa: Penguin Books, South Africa, 2006).

Juhnke, Deborah H. "Electronic Discovery in 2010," *Information Management Journal* 37 (November/December 2003): 34-36, 38-40, 42.

Kahn, Randolph A. "The Risk-Cost Retention Model: A New Approach to Records Retention," *Information Management Journal* 36 (May/June 2006): 47-54.

Kahn, Randolph A. "Records Management and Compliance: Making the Connection," *Information Management Journal* 38 (May/June 2004): 28-34, 36.

Kamen, Paula. *Finding Iris Chang: Friendship, Ambition, and the Loss of an Extraordinary Mind* (Philadelphia: Da Capo Press, 2007).

Karlsson, Lena. "Consuming Lives, Creating Community: Female Chinese-American Diary Writing on the Web," *Prose Studies* 2003 26, nos. 1-2 (2003): 219-239.

Karp, Marilynn Gelfman. *In Flagrante Collecto (Caught in the Act of Collecting)* (New York: Abrams, 2006).

Kassow, Samuel D. *Who Will Write Our History? Emanuel Ringelblum, the Warsaw Ghetto, and the Oyneg Shabes Archive* (Bloomington: Indiana University Press, 2007).

Katagiri, Yasuhiro. *The Mississippi State Sovereignty Commission: Civil Rights and States' Rights* (Jackson: University Press of Mississippi, 2001).

Kaye, Joseph, Janet Vertesi, Shari Avery, Allan Dafoc, Shay David, Lisa Onaga, Ivan Roserio, and Trevor Pinch. "To Have and to Hold: Exploring the Personal Archive," *CHI 2006*, April 22-27, 2006, Montreal, Quebec, Canada, pp. 275-284.

Keen, Andrew. *The Cult of the Amateur: How Today's Internet is Killing Our Culture* (New York: Doubleday/Currency, 2007).

Kelso, William. *Jamestown: The Buried Truth* (Charlottesville, VA: University of Virginia Press, 2006).

Kenney, Anne R. et al. "Preservation Risk Management for Web Resources: Virtual Remote Control in Cornell's Project Prism," *D-Lib Magazine* 8, no. 1 (Jan 2002), available at http://www.dlib.org/dlib/january02/kenney/01kenney.html, access July 14, 2007.

Kenney, Anne R. and Nancy Y. McGovern. "Preservation Risk Management for Web Resources," *Information Management Journal* 36 (September/October 2002): 52-54, 56-61.

Kichin, Steve. "For the Record," *Forbes* 155 (June 19, 1995): 222-224.

King, Ross. *Ex-Libris* (New York: Penguin Books, 1998).

Kingson, Jennifer A. "Follow the Vanishing Check," *New York Times*, March 26, 2005, available at http://www.nytimes.com/2005/03/26/business/26check.html?th=&adxnnl=1&emc=th&adxnnlx=1111840436-gofiqGkiRFmn3ri1uGrrKQ, accessed March 26, 2005.

Koehler, Wallace. "Web Page Change and Persistence – a four-year longitudinal study," *Journal of the American Society for Information Science and Technology* 53, no. 2 (2002): 162-171.

Koeppel, Dan. *To See Every Bird on Earth: A Father, A Son, and a Lifelong Obsession* (New York: Plume, 2005).

Koerbin, Paul. "The PANDORA Digital Archiving System (PANDAS): Managing Web Archiving in Australia: A Case Study," Paper presented at the 4th International Web Archiving Workshop, September 16, 2004, Bath UK, available at http://www.nla.gov.au/nla/staffpaper/2004/koerbin2.html, accessed July 16, 2007.

Kouwenhoven, John. "American Studies: Words or Things," in Thomas J. Schlereth, *Material Culture Studies in America* (Nashville, TN: American Association for State and Local History, 1982), pp. 79-92.

Kowlowitz, Alan. *Archival Appraisal of Online Information Systems* (Pittsburgh: Archives and Museum Informatics, no. 2, Fall 1988).

Kramer, Mark and Wendy Call, eds. *Telling True Stories: A Nonfiction Writers' Guide from the Nieman Foundation at Harvard University* (New York: Plume, 2007).

Krim, Jonathan. "Net Aids Access to Sensitive ID Data: Social Security Numbers Are Widely Available," *Washington Post*, April 4, 2005, p. A01, available at http://www.washingtonpost.com/wp-dyn/articles/A23686-2005Apr3.html?referrer=email, accessed April 4, 2005.

Kriwaczek, Rohan. *An Incomplete History of the Art of Funerary Violin* (London: Duckworth Overlook, 2006).

Krugman, Paul. "The Medical Money Pit," *New York Times*, April 15, 2005, available at http://www.nytimes.com/2005/04/15/opinion/15krugman.html?th&emc=th, accessed April 15, 2005.

Kurtz, Michael L. "Oliver Stone, *JFK*, and History," in Robert Brent Toplin, ed., *Oliver Stone's USA: Film, History, and Controversy* (Lawrence: University Press of Kansas, 2000), pp. 166-177.

Kurzweil, Ray. *The Age of Spiritual Machines: When Computers Exceed Human Intelligence* (New York: Penguin, 2000).

Kushner, David. "We Put a Man on the Moon. But (d'oh!) NASA Can't Find the Videotape," *Wired* (January 2007): 166-170.

Lambert, Emily. "Thanks for the Memories," *Forbes* 147 (November 29, 2004): 79-82.

Lamott, Anne. *Bird by Bird: Some Instructions on Writing and Life* (New York: Anchor Books, 1994).

Lau, Estelle T. *Paper Families: Identity, Immigration Administration, and Chinese Exclusion* (Durham: Duke University Press, 2006).

Lee, Hermione. *Virginia Wolf's Nose: Essays on Biography* (Princeton: Princeton University Press, 2005).

Lenhart, Amanda and Susannah Fox. *Bloggers: A Portrait of the Internet's New Storytellers* (Washington, D.C.: Pew Internet & American Life Project, July 19, 2006).

Levie, Eleanor and Marc Silver. "Scrapbooking, Cyberstyle," *U.S. News & World Report* 137 (September 13, 2004): 62.

Levinson, Sanford. *Written in Stone: Public Monuments in Changing Societies* (Durham, NC: Duke University Press, 1998).

Levy, David M. "The Universe is Expanding: Reflections on the Social (and Cosmic) Significance of Documents in a Digital Age" *Bulletin of the American Society for Information Science* 4 (April/May 1999): 17-20.

Levy, Steven. *The Perfect Thing: How the iPod Shuffles Commerce, Culture, and Coolness* (New York: Simon & Schuster, 2006).

Lewis-Kraus, Gideon. "A World in Three Aisles: Browsing the Post-Digital Library," *Harper's* 314 (May 2007): 47-52, 54-57.

Lin, Maya. "Making the Memorial," *New York Review of Books* 47 (November 2, 2000): 33-35.

Linderman, Kurt. "Live(s) Online: Narrative Performance, Presence, and Community in LiveJournal.com," *Text & Performance Quarterly* 25, no. 4 (October 2005): 354-372.

Ling, Rich. *The Mobile Connection: The Cell Phone's Impact on Society* (San Francisco: Morgan Kaufmann Publishers, 2004).

Lipsitz, George. *Time Passages: Collective Memory and American Popular Culture* (Minneapolis: University of Minnesota Press, 1990).

Lloyd, Martin. *The Passport: The History of Man's Most Traveled Document* (Thrupp-Stroud-Glouchestershire: Sutton Publishing Limited, 2003).

Lor, Peter and Johannes J. Britz. "A Moral Perspective on South-North Web Archiving," *Journal of Information Science* 30, no. 6 (2004): 540-549.

Lor, Peter Johan, Johannes Britz and Henry Watermeyer. "Everything, For Ever? The Preservation of South African Websites for Future Research and Scholarship," *Journal of Information Science* 32, no. 1 (Feb 2006): 39-48.

Lott, Bret. *Before We Get Started: A Practical Memoir of the Writer's Life.* (New York: Ballantine Books, 2005).

Lovink, Geert. *Zero Comments: Blogging and Critical Internet Culture* (New York: Routledge, 2008).

Lowenthal, David. *The Past Is A Foreign Country* (Cambridge: Cambridge University Press, 1985).

Lubar, Steven and W. David Kingery, eds. *History from Things: Essays on Material Culture* (Washington, DC: Smithsonian Institution Press,

1993).

Lukesh, Susan S. "E-mail and the Potential Loss to Future Archives and Scholarship or The Dog that Didn't Bark," *First Monday: Peer-reviewed Journal on the Internet* 4 (September 1999), available at http://www.firstmonday.dk/issues/issue4_9/lukesh/index.html.

MacArthur, Tom. *Worlds of Reference: Lexicography, Learning and Language from the Clay Tablet to the Computer* (Cambridge: Cambridge University Press, 1986).

McCarthy, Molly. "A pocketful of days: Pocket Diaries and Daily Record Keeping Among Nineteenth-century New England Women," *New England Quarterly* 73, no. 2 (2000): 274-276.

Mackenzie, Maureen L. "Storage and Retrieval of E-mail in a Business Environment: An Exploratory Study," *Library & Information Science Research* 24 (2002): 357-372.

Macintyre, Ben. "History 1980-2000 has disappeared into the ether. Sorry," London *Times*, 23 March 2007, at http://www.timesonline.co.uk/tol/comment/columnists/ben_macintyre/article1555570.ec, accessed March 30, 2007.

McGee, Marianne Kolbasuk. "Computers with Patient Data Stolen on Eve of HIPAA Security Rules," *Information Week*, April 13, 2005, available at http://informationweek.com/story/showArticle.jhtml?articleID=160702270, accessed April 14, 2005.

McKay, Andrew. "Compliance and Content Governance," *KMWorld* (October 2006): S23.

McMlure, Rhonda R. *Digitizing Your Family History: Easy Methods for Preserving Your Heirloom Documents, Photos, Home Movies and More in a Digital Format* (Cincinnati, OH: Family Tree Books, 2004).

McNeill, Laurie Ann. ""Somewhere Along the Line I Lost Myself": Recreating Self in the War Diaries of Natalie Crouter and Elizabeth

Vaughan," *Legacy: A Journal of American Women Writers* 19, no. 1 (January 2002): 98-106.

McNeill, Laurie. "Teaching an Old Genre New Tricks: The Diary on the Internet," *Biography: A Multidisciplinary Quarterly* 26, no. 1 (Winter 2003): 24-47.

Madigan, Charles, ed. *-30-: The Collapse of the Great American Newspaper* (Chicago: Ivan R. Dee, 2007).

Magnuson, Doug. "Email Management Brings Harmony to Discovery, Compliance and Storage," *KMWorld* (October 2006): S25.

Mallon, Thomas. "Memories Held in Check: Pursuing a Lifetime of My Father's Expenditures," *Harper's Magazine*, October 1993, available at http://www.findarticles.com/p/articles/mi_m1111/is_n1721_v28 7/ai_13288005, accessed April 30, 2005.

Mansfield, Howard. *The Bones of the Earth* (Washington, D.C.: Shoemaker and Hoard, 2004).

Marsden, George M. *Jonathan Edwards: A Life* (New Haven: Yale University Press, 2003).

Marsh, Bill. "The Story of Government Forms: A Real Page-Turner," *New York Times*, April 10, 2005, p. 3.

Marshall, Catherine C., Sara Bly, and Francoise Brun-Cottan. "The Long Term Fate of Our Personal Digital Belongings: Toward a Service Model for Personal Archives," *Proceedings of Archiving 2006*, Society for Imaging Science and Technology, Springfield, VA, 2006, http://www.csdl.tamu.edu/~marshall/archiving2006-marshall.pdf, accessed March 7, 2008.

Martin, Henri-Jean. *The History and Power of Writing*, trans. Lydia G. Cochrane. (Chicago: University of Chicago Press, 1994).

Martin, Kristin E. "Analysis of Remote Reference Correspondence at a Large Academic Manuscripts Collection," *American Archivist* 64 (Spring/Summer 2001): 17-42.

Martinez, Katherine. "The Dickinsons of Amherst Collect: Pictures and Their Meanings in a Victorian Home," *Common-Place* volume 7, number 3, April 2007, available at http://www.common-place.org/vol-07/no-03/martinez/, accessed March 13, 2008.

Matter, Gary. "Web Portals Grease the Reality Chain," *InternetWeek*, June 5, 2000, p. 42.

Matters, Marion, ed. *Automated Records and Techniques in Archives: A Resource Directory* (Chicago: Society of American Archivists, 1990).

Max, D. T. "Final Destination: Why Do the Archives of So Many Great Writers End Up in Texas?," *New Yorker*, June 11 and 18, 2007, pp. 54, 59-60, 63-64, 66-68, 70-71.

Mehta, Nick. "Facilitate Email Records Management via Backup and Archiving," *KMWorld* (October 2006): 514-515.

Menand, Louis. "Woke Up This Morning: Why Do We Read Diaries?" *New Yorker* (December 10, 2007), pp. 106-112.

Mendelsohn, Daniel. *The Lost: A Search for Six of Six Million* (New York: HarperCollins, 2006).

Merewether, Charles, ed. *The Archive* (London: Whitechapel and Cambridge, MA: MIT Press, 2006).

"Missing E-mails Have $15 Million Price Tag," *Information Management Journal* 40 (September/October 2006): 9.

Mitchell, Domhnall. *Measures of Possibility: Emily Dickinson's Manuscripts* (Amherst: University of Massachusetts Press, 2005).

Mitchell, Grant. *Approaching Electronic Records Management at the Insurance Corporation of British Columbia: A Case Study in Organizational Dynamics and Archival Initiative* (Chicago: Society of American Archivists, 1997).

Mitchell, William J. *ME++: The Cyborg Self and the Networked City* (Cambridge: MIT Press, 2003).

Mitchell, William J. *Placing Words: Symbols, Space, and the City* (Cambridge, MA: MIT Press, 2005).

Mitchell, William J. *The Reconfigured Eye: Visual Truth in the Post-Photographic Era* (Cambridge: MIT Press, 1992).

Moerdier, Mark L. "How to Optimally Manage Email in the Enterprise," *KMWorld* (October 2006): S12.

Montaña, John C. "E-mail, Voice Mail, and Instant Messaging: A Legal Perspective," *Information Management Journal* 38 (January/February 2004): 37-38, 40-41.

Montaña, John C. "The End of the Ostrich Defense," *Information Management Journal* 39 (January/February 2005): 26-28, 30-34.

Montaña, John C. "The Information Management Implications of Public Citizen v. Carlin," *Information Management Journal* 35 (July 2001): 54, 56-57.

Montgomerie, Deborah. *Love in Time of War: Letter Writing in the Second World War* (Auckland: Auckland University Press, 2005).

Morris, Errol. "Liar, Liar, Pants on Fire," *New York Times,* July 10, 2007, available at http://morris.blogs.nytimes.com/2007/07/10/pictures-are-supposed-to-be-worth-a-thousand-words/#comment-132, accessed July 18, 2007.

Myburgh, Susan. "Knowledge and Records Management: Is There a Difference?" *Records & Information Management* 14 (September 1998): 1-14.

Nash, Gary. *First City: Philadelphia and the Forging of Historical Memory*

(Philadelphia: University of Pennsylvania Press, 2002).

National Science Foundation Cyberinfrastructure Council. *Cyberinfrastructure Vision for 21ˢᵗ Century Discovery* (Washington, D. C.: National Science Foundation, March 2007).

Neef, Sonja, José van Dijck, and Eric Ketelaar, eds. *Sign Here! Handwriting in the Age of New Media* (Amsterdam: Amsterdam University Press, 2006).

New, Jennifer. *Drawing from Life: The Journal as Art* (New York: Princeton Architectural Press, 2005).

New York State Archives and Records Administration. *Managing Records in E-Mail Systems* (Albany: The University of the State of New York, The State Education Department, 1995).

Nicholls, Catherine and John-Paul Williams. "Identifying Roadkill on the Information Highway: A Website Appraisal Case Study," *Archives and Manuscripts* 30, no. 2 (November 2002): 96-111.

Nicholson, Peter. "The Changing Nature of Intellectual Authority," paper given at the Association of Research Libraries meeting, Ottawa, Ontario, May 17-19, 2006, Held in collaboration with the Canadian Association of Research Libraries, available at http://www.arl.org/arl/proceedings/148/nicholson.html, accessed June 14, 2006.

Norman, Donald A. *The Design of Everyday Things* (New York: Doubleday Currency, 1990).

Norman, Donald A. *Turn Signals Are the Facial Expressions of Automobiles* (Reading, MA: Addison-Wesley Publishing Co., 1992)

Norman, Donald A. *Things That Make Us Smart: Defending Human Attributes in the Age of the Machine* (Reading, MA: Addison-Wesley Publishing Co., 1993).

Norman, Donald A. *The Invisible Computer: Why Good Products Can Fail, the Personal Computer Is So Complex, and Information Appliances Are the Solution* (Cambridge: The MIT Press, 1998).

Nowicke, Carole Elizabeth. "Managing Tomorrow's Records Today: An Experiment in Archival Preservation of Electronic Mail," *Midwestern Archivist* 13, no. 2 (1988): 67-75.

"Number of Anglers and Hunters Remain Steady," United States Department of the Interior – U.S. Fish and Wildlife Services, 2001, available at http://news.fws.gov/newsreleases/R9/A2D9B201-0350-4BD4-A73477A25FC69.html?CFID=764049&CFTOKEN=74280991, accessed June 26, 2005.

O'Keefe, Michael and Teri Thompson. *The Card: Collectors, Con Men, and the True Story of History's Most Desired Baseball Card* (New York: William Morrow/Harper Collins, 2007).

O'Keefe, Timothy P. and Mark Langemo. "Controlling the Risks of Content Publication," *Information Management Journal* 39 (January/February 2005): 37-40, 42-43.

"Online Today, Gone Tomorrow," *Information Management Journal* 38 (March/April 2004): 13.

Opdyke, Jeff D. "Do You Know Where Your Vital Records Are? Postattack Paper Chase Reaffirms Hard Copy's Relevance," *Wall Street Journal*, October 10, 2001, p. C1.

O'Shea, Samara. *For the Love of Letters: A 21st-Century Guide to the Art of Letter Writing* (New York: Collins, 2007).

Pagano, Rick. *For the Record: A Personal Facts and Document Organizer* (Chandler, AZ: Five Star Publications, Inc., 2007).

Papailias, Penelope. *Genres of Recollection: Archival Poetics and Modern Greece* (New York: Palgrave Macmillan, 2005).

Paquet, Lucie. "Appraisal, Acquisition and Control of Personal

Electronic Records: From Myth to Reality," *Archives and Manuscripts* 28, no. 2 (2000): 71-91.

Paretsky, Sara. *Writing in an Age of Silence* (New York: Verso, 2007).

Parisi, Joseph and Stephen Young. *Between the Lines: A History of* Poetry *in Letters; Part II: 1962-2002* (Chicago: Ivan R. Dee, 2006).

Pendergrass, Lee F. "Family History Workshops: Teaching Amateur Historians How to Investigate Their Own Past," *History News* 37 (August 1982): 30.

Pennock, Maureen. "Curating E-Mails: A Life-Cycle Approach to the Management and Preservation of E-Mail Messages," *DCC Digital Curation Manual* eds., S.Ross and M.Day (July 2006), available at http://www.dcc.ac.uk/resource/curation-manual/chapters/curating-e-mails/.

Petroski, Henry. *The Evolution of Useful Things* (New York: Vintage Books, 1994).

Petroski, Henry. *Remaking the World: Adventures in Engineering* (New York: Alfred A. Knopf, 1997).

Phillips, John T. "The Challenge of Web Site Records Preservation," *Information Management Journal* 37 (January/February 2003): 42-48.

Phillips, John T. "Start with e-Mail!" *Information Management Journal* 35 (October 2001): 56.

Phillips, Margaret E. "Selective Archiving of Web Resources: A Study of Acquisition Costs at the National Library of Australia," *RLG DigiNews* 9, no. 3 (June 15, 2005), http://www.rlg.org/en/page.php?Page_ID=20666#article0, accessed July 16, 2007.

Pols, Robert. *Family Photographs, 1860-1945: A Guide to Researching, Dating and Contextualizing Family Photographs* (Richmond, Surrey: Public Record Office, 2002).

Poster, Carol and Linda C. Mitchell, eds. *Letter-Writing Manuals and Instruction from Antiquity to the Present: Historical and Bibliographic Studies* (Columbia: University of south Carolina, 2007).

Postman, Neil. *Amusing Ourselves to Death: Public Discourse in the Age of Show Business* (New York: Penguin Books, 1986).

Presidential Doodles: Two Centuries of Scribbles, Scratches, Squiggles & Scrawls from the Oval Office (New York: Basic Books, 2006).

Prosser, Jay. *Light in the Dark Room: Photography and Loss* (Minneapolis: University of Minnesota Press, 2005).

Public Record Office. *Management, Appraisal and Preservation of Electronic Records; Vol. 1: Principles*, 2nd. ed. (Kew: Public Record Office, 1999).

Redden, Elizabeth. "Corpses in the Quad," *Inside Higher Education*, October 19, 2006, *http://insidehighered.com/news/2006/10/19/brown*.

Reed, Barbara and Frank Upward. *The APB Bank: Managing Electronic Records as an Authoritative Resource* (Chicago: Society of American Archivists, 1997).

Research Issues in Electronic Records: Report of the Working Meeting (Washington, D.C.: Published for the National Historical Publications and Records Commission by the Minnesota Historical Society, 1991).

Ridge, Pamela Sebastian. "Not-So-Safe Deposit Boxes: Retrieving Charred Memories from World Trade Vault; A Searing Oven for Days," *Wall Street Journal*, January 18, 2002, p. B1.

Rieff, David. *Swimming in a Sea of Death: A Son's Memoir* (New York: Simon and Schuster, 2008).

Romano, Carlin. "What? The Grisly Truth About Bare Facts." In Robert Karl Manoff and Michael Schudson, eds., *Reading the News: A Pantheon Guide to Popular Culture* (New York: Pantheon Books, 1987), pp. 38-78.

Romano, Jay. "A First-Time Buyer's Primer and Road Map," *New York Times*, March 3, 1996, Section 9, p. 1.

Romanowski, Joe. "Email Archiving: Analyzing the Return on Investment," *KMWorld* (February 2006): S16.

Roop, Lee. "My Folks May Hold the Record for Record-keeping," *Huntsville Times*, April 10, 2005, available at http://www.al.com/living/huntsvilletimes/lroop.ssf?/base/living/1113124509294540.xml, accessed April 11, 2005.

Rosenstone, Robert. *Visions of the Past: The Challenge of Film to Our Idea of History.* (Cambridge: Harvard University Press, 1995).

Rosenstone, Robert. "Oliver Stone As Historian," in Robert Brent Toplin, ed., *Oliver Stone's USA: Film, History, and Controversy* (Lawrence: University Press of Kansas, 2000), pp. 26-39.

Rosenwald, Lawrence. "Some Myths About Diaries," *Raritan: A Quarterly Review* 6, no. 3 (1987): 97-112.

Rosenzwig, Roy and David Thelen. *The Presence of the Past: Popular Uses of History in American Life* (New York: Columbia University Press, 1998).

Rosi, Jan. "Crashing the Inbox: Managing Email in Today's Information Age," *KMWorld* (February 2007): S8.

Ross, Seamus. *Changing Trains at Wigan: Digital Preservation and the Future of Scholarship* (London: National Preservation Office, 2000).

Ross, Seamus and Andrew McHugh. "The Role of Evidence in Establishing Trust in Repositories," *D-Lib Magazine* 12 (July/August 2006), available at http://www.dlib.org/dlib/july06/ross/07ross.html.

Rothbart, Davy. *Found: The Best Lost, Tossed, and Forgotten Items From Around the World* (New York: Simon and Schuster, 2004).

Rothenberg, Jeff. "Preservation of the Times," *Information Management*

Journal 36 (March/April 2002): 38-43.

Rule, James B. *Privacy in Peril* (New York: Oxford University Press, 2007).

Rybczynski, Witold. *City Life: Urban Expectations in a New World* (New York: Harper Collins, 1995).

Rybczynski, Witold. *Looking Around: A Journey Through Architecture* (New York: Penguin Books, 1992).

Sanders, Robert L. "Personal Business Records in an Electronic Environment," *Information Management Journal* 33 (October 1999): 60-63.

Sandweiss, Martha. *Print the Legend: Photography and the American West* (New Haven: Yale University Press, 2002).

Savage, Kirk. *Standing Soldiers, Kneeling Slaves: Race, War, and Monument in Nineteenth-Century America* (Princeton, NJ: Princeton University Press, 1995).

Schement, Jorge Reina and Terry Curtis. *Tendencies and Tensions of the Information Age: The Production and Distribution of Information in the United States* (New Brunswick, NJ: Transaction Publishers, 1995).

Schlereth, Thomas J. *Cultural History and Material Culture: Everyday Life, Landscapes, Museums* (Charlottesville: University Press of Virginia, 1992).

Schmuland, Arlene. "The Archival Image in Fiction: An Analysis and Annotated Bibliography," *American Archivist* 62 (Spring 1999): 24-73.

Scholtes, Johannes C. "Efficient and Cost-Effective Email Management with XML," *KMWorld* (February 2007): S5.

Scholtes, Johannes C. "A View on Email Management: Balancing Multiple Interests and Realities of the Workplace," *KMWorld* (February 2006): S6-7.

Schwartz, Joan and James Ryan, eds. *Picturing Place: Photography and the Geographical Imagination* (London: I. B. Taurus and Co., Ltd., 2003).

Schmandt-Besserat, Denise. *When Writing Met Art: From Symbol to Story* (Austin: University of Texas Press, 2007).

Scruton, Roger. *Culture Counts: Faith and Feeling in a World Besieged* (New York: Brief Encounters, 2007).

Schudson, Michael. *The Power of News* (Cambridge: Harvard University Press, 1995).

Schwarz, Ursula, Mark Gudrun, Michael Schwarz, and Erdmut Wizisla, eds. *Walter Benjamin's Archive: Images, Texts, Signs*, translated by Esther Leslie (New York: Verso, 2007).

Seabrook, John. "The Tree of Me," *New Yorker*, March 26, 2001, p. 58.

Seaver, Douglas F. "The New Legal Advice: Don't Press 'Delete,'" *Chronicle of Higher Education, The Chronicle Review* 53 (February 16, 2007), p. B12.

Sellen, Abigail J. and Richard H. R. Harper. *The Myth of the Paperless Office* (Cambridge: MIT, 2001).

Serfaty, Viviane. *The Mirror and the Veil: An Overview of American Online Diaries and Blogs* (Amsterdam and New York: Rodopi, 2004).

Shillingsburg, Peter L. *From Gutenberg to Google: Electronic Representations of Literary Texts* (Cambridge: Cambridge University Press, 2006).

Shimer, Preston W. "Book Review: E-mail Rules for Records Managers," *Information Management Journal* 37 (November/December 2003): 64-65.

Shipley, David and Will Schwalbe. *Send: The Essential Guide to Email for Office and Home* (New York: Alfred A. Knopf, 2007).

Shneiderman, Ben. *Leonardo's Laptop: Human Needs and the New Computing Technologies* (Cambridge: MIT, 2002).

Siegel, Lee. *Against the Machine: Being Human in the Age of the Electronic Mob* (New York: Spiegel & Grau, 2008).

Simmons, Deirde. *Keepers of the Record: The History of the Hudson's Bay Company Archives* (Montreal and Kingston: McGill-Queen's University Press, 2007).

Simon, Richard Keller. "The Formal Garden in the Age of Consumer Culture: A Reading of the Twentieth-Century Shopping Mall," in Wayne Franklin and Michael Steiner, eds., *Mapping American Culture* (Iowa City: University of Iowa Press, 1992), pp. 231-250.

Skramstad, Harold. "An Agenda for American Museums in the Twenty-First Century," *Daedalus* 128 (Summer 1999): 109-128.

Skupsky, Donald S. "Applying Records Retention to Electronic Records," *Information Management Journal* 33 (July 1999): 28, 30-35.

Smith, Abby. "The Future of Web Resources: Who Decides What Gets Saved and How Do They Do It?," Paper presented at *Archiving Web Resources: Issues for Cultural Heritage Institutions*, 9-11 November 2004, available at http://www.nla.gov.au/webarchiving/SmithAbby.rtf, accessed July 17, 2007.

Smith, Wendy. "Still Lost in Cyberspace? Preservation Challenges of Australian Internet Resources," *Australian Library Journal* 54, no. 3 (Aug 2005): 274-287.

Sorapure, Madeleine. "Screening Moments, Screening Lives: Diary Writing on the Web," *Biography: A Multidisciplinary Quarterly* 26, no. 1 (Winter 2003): 1-23.

Sprehe, J. Timothy. "A Framework for EDMS/ERMS Integration," *Information Management Journal* 38 (November/December 2004): 54-56, 58-60, 62.

"States, Localities Weak on E-Records Management," "New Rules for E-Discovery," *Information Management Journal* 40 (November/December 2006): 8.

Stewart, Robert L. "For Faster Claims Settlement Tell Your Clients to 'Go to the Videotape!" *Rough Notes* 136 (March 1993): 42-44.

Stipe, Margo. *Frank Lloyd Wright: The Interactive Portfolio; Rare Removable Treasures, Hand-Drawn Sketches, Original Letters, and More from the Official Archives* (Philadelphia: Running Press, 2004).

Struk, Janina. *Photographing the Holocaust: Interpretations of the Evidence.* London: I. B. Tauris & Co., Ltd., in association with European Jewish Publication Society, 2004).

Sturdevant, Katherine Scott. *Organizing and Preserving Your Heirloom Documents* (Cincinnati, OH: Betterway Books, 2002).

Sturken, Marita. *Tangled Memories: The Vietnam War, the AIDS Epidemic, and the Politics of Remembering* (Berkeley: University of California Press, 1997).

Sunstein, Cass R. *Republic.com 2.0* (Princeton: Princeton University Press, 2007).

"Survey: E-mail Hampers Productivity," *Information Management Journal* 40 (March/April 2004): 22.

Swartz, Nikki. "Enterprise-wide Records Training: Key to Compliance, Success," *Information Management Journal* 40 (September/October 2006): 35-36, 38-40, 42, 44.

Swartz, Nikki. "New Rules for E-Discovery," *Information Management Journal* 40 (November/December 2006): 22-24, 26.

Swartz, Nikki. "Safeguarding Corporate Secrets," *Information Management Journal* 40 (September/October 2006): 24-26, 28, 30.

Swartz, Nikki. "The Electronic Records Conundrum," *Information Management Journal* 38 (January/February 2004): 21.

Tagg, John. *The Burden of Representation: Essays on Photographies and Histories* (Minneapolis: University of Minnesota Press, 1993).

Tanselle, G. Thomas "The World as Archive," *Common Knowledge* 8, no. 2 (2002): 402-406.

Taylor, Maureen A. *Preserving Your Family Photographs: How to Organize, Present, and Restore Your Precious Family Images* (Cincinnati, OH: Betterway Books, 2001).

Tenner, Edward. "The Prestigious Inconvenience of Print," *Chronicle Review*, 53 (March 9, 2007), p. B7.

Texas State Library and Archives Commission, *Email Policy Model for State Agencies* (Austin, TX, 2002), available at http://www.tsl.state.tx.us/slrm/recordspubs/email_model.html, accessed March 11, 2007.

Thelwell, Mike and Liven Vaughan. "A Fair History of the Web? Examining Country Balance in the Internet Archive," *Library & Information Science Research* 26, no. 2 (2004): 162-176.

Thomson, R. H. *The Lost Boys: Letters from the Sons in Two Acts 1914-1923* (Toronto: Playwrights Canada Press, 2001).

Thornton, Carla. "Laptop Era Dawns," *PC World* 21 (October 2003): 22-26.

Tilsner, Julie and Amy Dunklin. "In Case of Fire or Theft – Keep a List," *Business Week*, issue 3309 (March 15, 1993): 130.

Toplin, Robert Brent. *History by Hollywood: The Use and Abuse of the American Past.* (Urbana: University of Illinois Press, 1996).

Tough, Alistair and Michael Moss, eds. *Record Keeping in a Hybrid Environment: Managing the Creation, Use, Preservation and Disposal of Unpublished Information Objects in Context* (Oxford, England: Chandos Publishing, 2006).

Trachtenberg, Alan. *Reading American Photographs: Images as History Mathew Brady to Walker Evan.* (New York: Hill and Wang, 1990).

Tucker, Susan, Katherine Ott, and Patricia P. Buckler, eds. *The Scrapbook in American Life* (Philadelphia: Temple University Press, 2006).

Turner, Fred. *From Counterculture to Cyberculture: Stewart Brand, the Whole Earth Network, and the Rise of Digital Utopianism* (Chicago: University of Chicago Press, 2006).

Ullberg, Alan D. and Robert C. Lind. "Personal Collecting: Proceed with Caution," *Museum News* 69 (September/October 1990): 33-34.

Ulrich, Laurel Thatcher. *A Midwife's Tale: The Life of Martha Ballard, Based on Her Diary, 1785- 1812* (New York: Vintage Books, 1990).

"Uncle Sam May Not Monitor E-mails," *Information Management Journal* 37 (March/April 2003): 8.

"The Universal Diarist," *Economist* (November 25, 2005, p. 68.

U.S. House of Representatives Committee on Oversight and Government Reform. *Sandy Berger's Theft of Classified Documents: Unanswered Questions* (Washington, D.C., January 9, 2007).

"2004 United States Postal Service Annual Report," available at http://www.usps.com/history/anrpt/o4/ and accessed May 28, 2005.

Updike, John. "Books Unbound, Life Unraveled," *New York Times,* 18 June 2000, 15.

Van Der Toorn, Karel. *Scribal Culture and the Making of the Hebrew Bible* (Cambridge: Harvard University Press, 2007).

Van Dijck, José. "Composing the Self: Of Diaries and Lifelogs," *Fibreculture: Internet+Theory+Culture+Research.* 3 (2004), available at http://journal.fibreculture.org/issue3/issue3_vandijck.html, accessed July 28, 2007.

"Voicemails Converted to E-mail: E-discovery Treasure Trove," *ARMA International Information Management Newswire, February 2007,*

http://www.arma.org/news/enewsletters/index.cfm?ID=1660,
accessed February 28, 2007.

Walsh, Kevin. *The Representation of the Past: Museums and Heritage in the Post-Modern World* (New York: Routledge, 1992).

Wakin, Daniel J. "When Death Means the Loss of An Archive," *New York Times*, May 18, 2005, available at
www.nytimes.com/2005/05/18/arts/dance/18will.html? and
accessed May 20, 2005.

Walker, Leslie. "Online Scrapboooks Let Globetrotters Trace Their Travels," *Washington Post*, March 27, 2005, p. F07, available at
http://www.washingtonpost.com/wp-dyn/articles/A2609-2005Mar26.html?referrer=email, accessed March 27, 2005.

Wallace, David A. "Electronic Records Management Defined by Court Case and Policy," *Information Management Journal* 35 (January 2001):
4, 6-8, 10, 12, 14-15.

Warburton, Nigel. "Is Art Sacred?" in *Is Nothing Sacred?*, ed. Ben Rogers (New York: Routledge, 2004), pp. 42-50.

Ward, Janet. "Quantity Does Matter: Records Management for Billions of Documents," *KMWorld* (October 2006): S22.

Watson, Peter and Cecilia Todeschini. *The Medici Conspiracy: The Illicit Journey of Looted Antiquities, from Italy's Tomb Raiders to the World's Greatest Museums* (New York: Public Affairs, 2006).

Weinberger, David. *Everything is Miscellaneous: The Power of the New Digital Disorder* (New York: Times Books, 2007).

Weinstein, Allen. "NARA Enters New 'ERA' of Electronic Records Management," *Information Management Journal* 39
(September/October 2005): 22-24.

Whiteley, Brian. "Stolen Data Spurs Fears for Privacy: Students Scramble to Guard Against Identity Theft, " *The Daily Californian*,
March 31, 2005, available at

http://www.dailycal.org/article.php?id=18158, accessed April 3,
2005.

Wilkinson, Alec. "Remember This? A Project to Record Everything We
Do in Life," *New Yorker*, May 28, 2007, available at
http://www.newyorker.com/reporting/2007/05/28/070528fa_fac
t_Wilkinson, accessed March 13, 2008.

Williams, Don and Louisa Jaggar. *Saving Stuff: How to Care for and Preserve
Your Collectibles, Heirlooms, and Other Prized Possessions* (New York:
Fireside Book, Simon and Schuster, 2005).

Williams, Robert F. and Lori J. Ashley. *2005 Electronic Records
Management Survey: A Renewed Call to Action* (Chicago: Cohasset
Associates, Inc., in association with ARMA and AIIM, 2005).

Williams, Robert F. and Lori J. Ashley, *Call for Collaboration: Electronic
Records Management Survey* (Chicago: Cohasset Associates in
association with ARMA International and AIIM, 2007), available at
www.MERresource.com/whitepapers/survey.htm.

Wilson, Douglas L. *Lincoln's Sword: The Presidency and the Power of Words*
(New York: Alfred A. Knopf, 2006).

Wilson, Eric. "And Give Me a Fath Archive," *New York Times*,
December 7, 2006, available at
http://www.nytimes.com/2006/12/07/fashion/07ROW.html?_r
=1&oref=slogin.

Wolf, Gary. "The New Multiple Personality Disorder," *Wired* 13 (May
2005): 36.

Wood, Denis. "The Power of Maps." *Scientific American* 268 (May 1993):
88-93, available at http://www.arts.
uwa.edu.au/HistoryWWW/mapping_conquest_htm
I/3_ThePowerofMaps.

"Work E-Mail Is Public Record," *Information Management Journal* 38
(May/June 2004): 14.

"Workplace E-mail, IM Survey Reveals Risks," *Information Management Journal* 39 (May/June 2005): 6.

Worrall, Simon. *The Poet and the Murderer: A True Story of Literary Crime and the Art of Forgery* (New York: Dutton, 2002).

Wright, Alex. *Glut: Mastering Information Through the Ages* (Washington, D.C.: Joseph Henry Press, 2007).

Wright, H. Curtis. "The Immateriality of Information," *Journal of Library History* 11 (October 1976): 297-315.

Yin, Sandra. "Picture This: A Look at Where Americans are Most Likely to Snap Up Digital Cameras," *American Demographics* 25 (July/August 2003): 18-19.

Yoshinaka, Russ. "Facing the Changes in the Federal Rules of Civil Procedure," *KMWorld* (February 2007): S7.

Zboray, Ronald J. *A Fictive People: Antebellum Economic Development and the American Reading Public* (New York: Oxford University Press, 1993).

Zinsser, William. *Inventing the Truth: The Art and Craft of Memoir*, rev. ed. (Boston: Houghton Mifflin Co., 1998).

Zorich, Diane M. "Defining Stewardship in the Digital Age," *First Monday*, volume 12, number 7 (July 2007), http://firstmonday.org/issues/issue12_7/zorich/index.html, accessed July 12, 2007.

Endnotes

Introduction

1 Christine Harold, *Our Space: Resisting the Corporate Control of Culture* (Minneapolis: University of Minnesota Press, 2007), p.134.
2 Joshua Foer, "Remember This: In the Archives of the Brain, Our Lives Linger or Disappear," *National Geographic* 212 (November 2002): 50.

Chapter 1

1 Denise Dale, "Getting and Staying Organized: Focus on Personal Papers," *Feliciter* issue no. 1 (2000): 40.
2 Richard J. Cox, *Managing Institutional Archives: Foundational Principles and Practices* (New York: Greenwood Press, 1992).
3 Richard J. Cox, *Documenting Localities: A Practical Model for American Archivists and Manuscripts Curators* (Metuchen: Scarecrow Press, 1996); *Managing Records as Evidence and Information* (Westport, Connecticut: Quorum Books, 2000); and *Ethics, Accountability and Recordkeeping in a Dangerous World* (London: Facet, 2006).
4 David Rieff, *Swimming in a Sea of Death: A Son's Memoir* (New York: Simon and Schuster, 2008), pp. 15 and 20.
5 Valentin Groebner, *Who Are You? Identification, Deception, and Surveillance in Early Modern Europe,* translated by Mark Kyburz and John Peck (New York: Zone books, 2007), p. 201.
6 See, for example, Philipp Blom, *To Have and to Hold: An Intimate History of Collectors and Collecting* (New York: Penguin Books, 2002), p. 165.
7 John D. Freyer, *All My Life for Sale* (New York: Bloomsbury, 2002), pp. vii-viii.
8 Ibid., p. 174.
9 Leah Dilworth, ed., *Acts of Possession: Collecting in America* (New Brunswick, New Jersey: Rutgers University Press, 2003), p. 7.
10 Nicholas A. Basbanes, *A Splendor of Letters: The Permanence of Books in an Impermanent World* (New York: HarperCollins, 2003), p. 5.
11 Ibid., p. 273.
12 Ibid., p. 274.
13 Ibid., p. 276.
14 Ibid., p. 218.

[15] Eric Wilson, "And Give Me a Fath Archive," *New York Times*, December 7, 2006.

[16] D. T. Max, "Final Destination: Why Do the Archives of So Many Great Writers End Up in Texas?," *New Yorker*, June 11 and 18, 2007, p. 54.

[17] Ibid., p. 59.

[18] Ibid., p. 63.

[19] Ibid., p. 63.

[20] Michael O'Keefe and Teri Thompson, *The Card: Collectors, Con Men, and the True Story of History's Most Desired Baseball Card* (New York: William Morrow/Harper Collins, 2007), p. 4.

[21] See, for example, Paul Dickson, *The Joy of Keeping Score: How Scoring the Game Has Influenced and Enhanced the History of Baseball* (New York: Walker and Co., 2007).

[22] See, for example, Peter Watson and Cecilia Todeschini, *The Medici Conspiracy: The Illicit Journey of Looted Antiquities, from Italy's Tomb Raiders to the World's Greatest Museums* (New York: Public Affairs, 2006).

[23] Marilynn Gelfman Karp has ably captured some of the aspects of collecting in her *In Flagrante Collecto (Caught in the Act of Collecting)* (New York: Abrams, 2006), p. 11.

[24] Ibid., p. 24.

[25] See Sally F. Griffith, *Serving History in a Changing World: The Historical Society of Pennsylvania in the Twentieth Century* (Philadelphia: Historical Society of Pennsylvania, distributed by the University of Pennsylvania Press, 2001). For another interesting study revealing many of the same challenges, see Kevin Guthrie, *The New-York Historical Society: Lessons from One Nonprofit's Long Struggle for Survival* (San Francisco: Jossey-Bass Publishers, 1996).

[26] Griffith, *Serving History*, p. 194.

[27] Ibid., p. 473.

[28] Ibid., pp. 390-391.

[29] Gary Nash, *First City: Philadelphia and the Forging of Historical Memory* (Philadelphia: University of Pennsylvania Press, 2002), p. 8.

[30] Ibid., p. 9.

[31] Nash makes little effort to understand the professional archival issues and standards, surprising since he is chiefly considering the role of organizations like the HSP in preserving documentation for scholars such as historians. However, Nash contrasts the efforts of the Historical Society with that of the Archives of the City of Philadelphia "which by mandate systematically preserved such invaluable sources as vagrancy

dockets, almshouse admission books and minutes, tax lists, deed and mortgage books, and probate records with inventories of personal possessions upon the death of the rich, the poor, and those in between" (p. 47). Anyone who knows the history of this and other municipal archives will be hard-pressed to find anything systematic in its work, a municipal responsibility that has been often under-funded and under-appreciated by municipal leaders. Later, Nash also displays something of a lack of appreciation for modern record-keeping when he writes, "In an era before modern record-keeping and before civil service, fragments of municipal records – even tax assessors' lists and quarter-session court records – surface in the private papers of civic leaders" (p. 71). While this is certainly true, Nash's idea that there is a clear demarcation with modern and more systematic recordkeeping is somewhat fallacious, especially as municipal records programs have been very late in developing and possess an extremely checkered success record. Compounding such problems is Nash's focus on the HSP's efforts to disperse its artifact collections while not considering whether many of the artifacts, far out of scope of any reasonable HSP mission statement or acquisition policy, should have been there in the first place. Nash mentions the work of a civic leader William Dorsey in collecting materials related to African Americans: "Unlike Historical Society leaders, Dorsey collected *everything* – news items about burglars as well as bankers, the ugly as well as the noble. Rather than shaping memory by filtering out unwanted images at the source, he collected anything relating to black life, thus allowing historians many decades later to reconstruct the lives of black Philadelphians at all levels or urban society after the Civil War" (p. 311). This assessment seems logical and warranted until one understands that Nash has made no effort to examine or understand the evolution of archival appraisal principles and approaches. We are left with the uneasy feeling that archivists should be acquiring everything so that historians and other scholars can sort out what is important to their own research. Nash celebrates the broadening of collecting by historical societies, libraries, and archives, mostly because he contrasts it to the early collecting aims of these institutions and not with the struggles of museum curators, librarians, and archivists to set realistic collecting goals and to develop professional standards. What we end with is the sense of a historian's idea of the "forging of historical memory" and not the creation of what society deems to be that memory; *First City* is an incomplete portrait of the memory, but it ought to provoke archivists and their compatriots to consider more seriously such matters.

[32] Estelle T. Lau, *Paper Families: Identity, Immigration Administration, and Chinese Exclusion* (Durham: Duke University Press, 2006), p. 47.

[33] Ibid., p. 132.

[34] George M. Marsden, *Jonathan Edwards: A Life* (New Haven: Yale University Press, 2003), p. 12.

[35] Ibid., p. 288.

[36] Ibid., p. 133.

[37] Ibid., p. 432.

[38] See, for example, Ian Frazier, *Family* (New York: Picador USA, 2002), a writer's account of his family and meaning for him, prompted by his delving into the family manuscripts.

[39] John Fea, "Wheelock's World: Letters and the Communication of Revival in Great Awakening New England," *Proceedings of the American Antiquarian Society* 109 (2001): 101-102, 104.

[40] Marsden, pp. 134, 200.

[41] Ibid., p. 136.

[42] Henry Petroski, *The Evolution of Useful Things* (New York: Vintage Books, 1994), p. 86.

[43] Marsden, p. 240.

[44] Ibid., pp. 247-248.

[45] Ibid., p. 294.

[46] Ibid., p. 483.

[47] Abigail J. Sellen and Richard H. R. Harper, *The Myth of the Paperless Office* (Cambridge: MIT, 2001).

[48] Marsden, p. xvii.

[49] Ibid., p. 448.

[50] See http://www.yale.edu/wje/html/mission.html.

[51] Jon Butler, *Becoming America: The Revolution before 1776* (Cambridge: Harvard University Press, 2000), pp. 131, 133.

[52] Stanley Abercrombie, "Office Supplies: Evolving Furniture for the Evolving Workplace," in Donald Albrecht and Chrysanthe B. Broikos, eds., *On the Job: Design and the American Office* (New York: Princeton Architectural Press, 2000), p. 82.

[53] Thomas J. Schlereth, *Cultural History and Material Culture: Everyday Life, Landscapes, Museums* (Charlottesville: University Press of Virginia, 1992), pp. 160-161. A classic example of this desk can be seen in the collections of the Kansas State Historical Society, a desk originally purchased in 1881 for use by the State Superintendent of Public Instruction in his Capitol office, at http://www.kshs.org/cool/coolwoot.htm

54 Marsden, p. 472. An illustration of the desk is on page 461.

55 Butler, p. 133.

56 Henry Petroski, *Remaking the World: Adventures in Engineering* (New York: Alfred A. Knopf, 1997), pp. 47-48.

57 Ursula Mark Gudrun Schwarz, Michael Schwarz, and Erdmut Wizisla, eds., *Walter Benjamin's Archive: Images, Texts, Signs,* translated by Esther Leslie (New York: Verso, 2007), pp. 1-2.

58 Jim Gemmell, Gordon Bell, and Roger Lueder, "MyLifeBits: A Personal Database for Everything," *Communications of the ACM* 49 (January 2006): 88-95.

59 Ibid., p. 93.

60 Ibid.

61 Alec Wilkinson, "Remember This? A Project to Record Everything We Do in Life," *New Yorker*, May 28, 2007, p. 38.

62 Ibid.

63 Ray Kurzweil, *The Age of Spiritual Machines: When Computers Exceed Human Intelligence* (New York: Penguin, 2000).

64 Council on Library and Information Resources, *The Evidence in Hand: Report of the Task Force on the Artifact in Library Collections,* November 2001, p. v.

65 Marcia Clemmitt, "Cyber Socializing," *CQ Researcher* 16 (July 28, 2006): 625-647.

66 These quotations are from Neil Beagrie, "Plenty of Room at the Bottom? Libraries and Collections," *D-Lib Magazine* 11 (June 2005), available at http://www.dlib.org/dlib/june05/beagrie/06beagrie.html, accessed August 1, 2006. Beagrie notes, as well, "It is telling that research on digital data loss has suggested that a substantial amount of personal data is not backed up and that, on average, 6% of data held on all PCs is lost each year (more for laptops and mobile devices because of the higher incidence of theft)." The work of archivists on matters like developing criteria for trustworthy digital repositories suggests how far we are from having assurances about the long-term maintenance of digital documents; see Seamus Ross and Andrew McHugh, "The Role of Evidence in Establishing Trust in Repositories," *D-Lib Magazine* 12 (July/August 2006), available at http://www.dlib.org/dlib/july06/ross/07ross.html.

67 Ben Shneiderman, *Leonardo's Laptop: Human Needs and the New Computing Technologies* (Cambridge: MIT, 2002), p. 12.

68 Ibid., pp. 26-27.

69 Ibid., p. 8.

[70] Ibid., p. 9.

[71] Ibid., p. 98.

[72] Daniel Mendelsohn, *The Lost: A Search for Six of Six Million* (New York: HarperCollins, 2006), p. 59.

[73] Ibid., p. 63.

[74] Ibid., pp. 395-396.

[75] Ibid., p. 113.

[76] Ibid., p. 237.

[77] *Presidential Doodles: Two Centuries of Scribbles, Scratches, Squiggles & Scrawls from the Oval Office* (New York: Basic Books, 2006), p. 11.

[78] Ibid., p. 24.

[79] Ibid., p. 26.

[80] Frank N. Freeman, *The Teaching of Handwriting* (Boston: Houghton Mifflin Co., 1914), p. 1.

[81] Ibid., p. 53.

[82] Samara O'Shea, *For the Love of Letters: A 21st-Century Guide to the Art of Letter Writing* (New York: Collins, 2007), p. 77.

[83] Steven Levy, *The Perfect Thing: How the iPod Shuffles Commerce, Culture, and Coolness* (New York: Simon & Schuster, 2006), p. 4.

[84] William Zinsser, *Writing with a Word Processor* (New York: Harper and Row, 1983), p. 54.

[85] Ibid., p. vii.

[86] Ibid., p. 20.

[87] Ibid., pp. 30-31.

[88] Ibid., p. 105.

[89] Davy Rothbart, *Found: The Best Lost, Tossed, and Forgotten Items From Around the World* (New York: Simon and Schuster, 2004), p. 1.

[90] Ibid., p. 2.

Chapter 2

[1] The quotation is from the inside cover of Rebecca Comay, ed., *Lost in the Archives* (Toronto: Alphabet City Media, 2002).

[2] Julia Creet, "The Archive and the Uncanny: Danilo Kis's 'Encyclopedia of the Dead' and the Fantasy of Hyperamnesia," in Comay, ed., *Lost in the Archives*, p. 268.

[3] See Charles Merewether, ed., *The Archive* (London: Whitechapel and Cambridge, MA: MIT Press, 2006) is testament to this. Part of the "Documents of Contemporary Art" series, this volume, with its no-

nonsense name, is intended to provide a "contextual introduction to the ways in which concepts of the archive have been defined, examined, contested and reinvented by artists and cultural observers from the early twentieth century to the present" (p. 10).

4 Gwen Diehn, *The Decorated Journal: Creating Beautifully Expressive Journal Pages* (New York: Lark Books, 2005).

5 Jennifer New, *Drawing from Life: The Journal as Art* (New York: Princeton Architectural Press, 2005), p. 8.

6 Ibid., p. 12.

7 Ibid., p. 13.

8 Nick Bantock, *Urgent 2nd Class: Creating Curious Collage, Dubious Documents, and Other Art from Ephemera* (San Francisco: Chronicle Books, 2004), pp. 1-2.

9 Such as his *Griffin & Sabine: An Extraordinary Correspondence* (San Francisco: Chronicle Books, 1991).

10 Bantock, *Urgent 2nd Class*, p. 3.

11 Ibid., p. 5.

12 Ibid., p. 97.

13 Ibid., p. 15.

14 See, for example, Nigel Hamilton, *Biography: A Brief History* (Cambridge, MA: Harvard University Press, 2007).

15 Anne Fadiman, *At Large and at Small: Familiar Essays* (New York: Farrar, Strauss, and Giroux, 2007), p. 120.

16 Ibid., p. 125.

17 Hermione Lee, *Virginia Wolf's Nose: Essays on Biography* (Princeton: Princeton University Press, 2005), p. 2.

18 Deborah Montgomerie, *Love in Time of War: Letter Writing in the Second World War* (Auckland: Auckland University Press, 2005), p. 65.

19 Ibid., p. 132.

20 Ibid., p. 5.

21 Ibid., p. 19.

22 Ibid., p. 39.

23 Ibid., p. 58.

24 Ibid., p. 4.

25 Ibid., p. 17.

26 Ibid., p. 68.

27 Ibid., p. 132.

28 Ibid., p. 135.

[29] Pedro Corrêa Do Lago, *True to the Letter: 800 Years of Remarkable Correspondence, Documents and Autographs* (New York: Thames and Hudson, 2004), p. 10.

[30] Ibid., p. 10.

[31] Ibid., p. 11.

[32] Ibid., p. 180.

[33] Ibid., p. 15.

[34] Anna Green and Megan Hutching, eds., *Remembering: Writing Oral History* (Auckland, New Zealand: Auckland University Press, 2004).

[35] Ibid., p. vii.

[36] Anna Green, "Oral History and History," in *Remembering*, p. 2.

[37] Danny Keenan, "The Past from the Paepae: Uses of the Past in Māori Oral History," in *Remembering*, pp. 145-146.

[38] Anna Green, "'Unpacking' the Stories," in *Remembering*, pp. 12-13.

[39] Juanita Ketchel, "'Getting Free': Oral Histories of Violence, Resilience and Recovery," in *Remembering*, p. 102.

[40] Kay Edwards, "Cast Within Alternative Realities: An Oral History of Five Actors From the Little Theatre in Te Aroha," in *Remembering*, p. 104.

[41] Anna Green, "'Unpacking' the Stories," in *Remembering*, p. 11.

[42] Mark Kramer and Wendy Call, eds., *Telling True Stories: A Nonfiction Writers' Guide from the Nieman Foundation at Harvard University* (New York: Plume, 2007) , p. 133.

[43] Ibid.

[44] Ibid., p. 135.

[45] Daniel J. Cohen and Roy Rosenzweig, *Digital History: A Guide to Gathering, Preserving, and Presenting the Past on the Web* (Philadelphia: University of Pennsylvania Press, 2005).

[46] Ibid,, p. 3.

[47] Ibid., p. 13.

[48] Ibid., p. 229.

[49] Ibid., p. 55.

[50] Ibid., pp. 48-49.

[51] Ibid., p. 84.

[52] Ibid., p. 85.

[53] Ibid., p. 111.

[54] Ibid., p. 139.

[55] Ibid., p. 161.

[56] Ibid., p. 163.

[57] Ibid., p. 182.

58 Ibid., p. 177.
59 Ibid., p. 183.
60 Ibid., p. 183.
61 Ibid., p. 203.
62 Ibid., p. 245.
63 Ibid., pp. 9-10.
64 Ibid., pp. 227-228.
65 Alex Wright, *Glut: Mastering Information Through the Ages* (Washington, D.C.: Joseph Henry Press, 2007), p. 6.

Chapter 3

1 Steven Roger Fischer, *A History of Language* (London: Reaktion Books, Ltd., 1999); *A History of Writing* (London: Reaktion Books, Ltd., 2001); *A History of Reading* (London: Reaktion Books, Ltd., 2003).
2 Fischer 1999, p. 11.
3 Ibid., p. 58.
4 Ibid., p. 87.
5 Fischer 2001, p. 35.
6 Fischer1999, p. 189.
7 Ibid., p. 88.
8 Peter Nicholson, "The Changing Nature of Intellectual Authority," paper given at the Association of Research Libraries meeting, Ottawa, Ontario, May 17-19, 2006, Held in collaboration with the Canadian Association of Research Libraries, available at http://www.arl.org/arl/proceedings/148/ nicholson.html, accessed June 14, 2006.
9 Fischer, 1999, p. 99.
10 Ibid., p. 110.
11 Ibid., p. 111.
12 Ibid., p. 205.
13 Fischer 2001, p. 12.
14 Ibid., p. 22.
15 Ibid., p. 56.
16 Ibid., pp. 44-45.
17 Ibid., p. 13.
18 Ibid., pp. 16-17.
19 Ibid., pp. 45, 50.
20 Ibid., p. 129.

[21] Ibid., p. 165.
[22] Ibid., p. 237.
[23] Ibid., p. 238.
[24] Ibid., p. 244.
[25] Ibid., pp. 264-265.
[26] Ibid., p. 66.
[27] Ibid., p. 69.
[28] Ibid., p. 106.
[29] Ibid., p. 119.
[30] Ibid., p. 147.
[31] Ibid., p. 145.
[32] Ibid., pp. 292, 293.
[33] Fischer, 2003, pp. 11, 12.
[34] Ibid., p. 27.
[35] Ibid., p. 97.
[36] Ibid., p. 7.
[37] Ibid., p. 8.
[38] Ibid., p. 20.
[39] Ibid., p. 22.
[40] Karel Van Der Toorn, *Scribal Culture and the Making of the Hebrew Bible* (Cambridge: Harvard University Press, 2007), p. 57.
[41] Fischer, 2003, p. 106.
[42] Ibid., p. 33.
[43] Ibid., p. 83.
[44] Ibid., p. 48.
[45] Ibid., p. 49.
[46] Ibid., p. 76.
[47] Ibid., p. 78.
[48] Baker's essay is available in his *The Size of Thoughts: Essays and Other Lumber* (New York: Vintage Books, 1997), pp. 182-203.
[49] See Phil Agre, "Institutional Circuitry: Thinking About the Forms and Uses of Information," *Information Technology and Libraries* 14, no. 4 (1995): 225-230, also at http://dlis.gseis.ucla.edu/ people/pagre/circuitry.html, and "The End of Information & the Future of Libraries," *Progressive Librarian*, (1997) at http://www.libr.org/PL/12-13_Agre.html.
[50] Jorge Reina Schement and Terry Curtis, *Tendencies and Tensions of the Information Age: The Production and Distribution of Information in the United States* (New Brunswick, NJ: Transaction Publishers, 1995), p. 3.
[51] Michael E. Hobart and Zachary S. Schiffman, *Information Ages: Literacy,*

Numeracy, and the Computer Revolution (Baltimore: Johns Hopkins University Press, 1998).

52 David M. Levy, "The Universe is Expanding: Reflections on the Social (and Cosmic) Significance of Documents in a Digital Age" *Bulletin of the American Society for Information Science* (April/May 1999): 18.

53 Ibid., 19.

54 Michael Buckland, *Information and Information Systems* (New York: Praeger, 1991), p. 47.

55 See Clifford Stoll, *Silicon Snake Oil: Second Thoughts on the Information Highway* (New York: Anchor Books, 1995) and *High-Tech Heretic: Reflections of a Computer Contrarian* (New York: Anchor Books, 1997).

56 John Seely Brown and Paul Duguid, *The Social Life of Information* (Boston: Harvard Business School Press, 2000), pp. 1-2.

57 Richard J. Cox, "Archives and Archivists in the Twenty-First Century: What Will We Become?" *Archival Issues* 20, no. 2 (1995): 97-113.

58 Forest Woody Horton, Jr., "The Wisdom Administrator: Waiting in the Wings." *Information Outlook* 14 (September 2000): 30.

59 Neil Postman, *Amusing Ourselves to Death: Public Discourse in the Age of Show Business* (New York: Penguin Books, 1986), p. 105.

60 Lisa Jardine, *Worldly Goods* (New York: Macmillan, 1996), p. 75.

61 Laurel Thatcher Ulrich, *A Midwife's Tale: The Life of Martha Ballard, Based on Her Diary, 1785- 1812* (New York: Vintage Books, 1990).

62 John Updike, "Books Unbound, Life Unraveled" *New York Times,* 18 June 2000, 15. There are some exceptions to this, of course. Jeff Gomez, *Print is Dead: Books in Our Digital Age* (New York: MacMillan, 2008), offers an interesting extended essay that is not the usual mix of technological futurism, basing his arguments on an insider's view of both publishing and writing as well as a levelheaded sensibility of observations about what has occurred within the music industry. Gomez does not promise dramatic, gut-wrenching societal and personal transformations. In fact, he acknowledges that the printed book will be around for a very long time. Gomez makes, instead, statements like "while print is not yet dead, it is undoubtedly sickening" (p. 3) and "books are indeed on the way out, while screens keep inching their way in" (p. 13). He turns to areas in our culture and commerce where we have seen dramatic shifts, such as the music industry, and extrapolates from there: "it is iPods – and what they've done to the music business – that may offer the best glimpse of the future of the book" (p. 15). This represents a generational shift, to a group of people who have grown up with the Internet and who are comfortable

with working and living in the digital realm. Indeed, when Gomez considers what is happening with younger generations, he seems to make sense: "And so to expect future generations to be satisfied with printed books is like expecting the Blackberry users of today to start communicating by writing letters, stuffing envelopes and licking stamps" (p. 78). Still, one might wonder about how anyone can be optimistic with all the false starts with e-books and digital rights management, but Gomez believes it is just the matter of time before we achieve the equivalent of the iPod for digital books reading.

[63] Carlin Romano, "What? The Grisly Truth About Bare Facts," in Robert Karl Manoff and Michael Schudson, eds., *Reading the News: A Pantheon Guide to Popular Culture* (New York: Pantheon Books, 1987), p. 78.

[64] See, for example, Charles Madigan, ed., *-30-: The Collapse of the Great American Newspaper* (Chicago: Ivan R. Dee, 2007). The essays in *-30-* demonstrate that the changes newspapers are going through are not just the result of sweeping trends in new information technologies; the newspaper is also being affected by market and other economic factors, the shifting of ownership from individuals and families to conglomerates and business enterprises, and changing tastes by the reading public (or, even, the decline in the reading public itself).

[65] Michael Schudson, *The Power of News* (Cambridge: Harvard University Press, 1995), pp. 26-27.

[66] Ibid., pp. 187-188.

[67] Alberto Manguel. *A History of Reading* (New York: Viking, 1996).

[68] Florian Brody. "The Medium Is the Memory," in Peter Lunenfeld, ed., *The Digital Dialectic: New Essays on New Media* (Cambridge: MIT Press, 2000), p. 136.

[69] Robert Darnton, *The Forbidden Best-Sellers of Pre-Revolutionary France* (New York: W. W. Norton and Co., 1995), p. 181.

[70] Ronald J. Zboray, *A Fictive People: Antebellum Economic Development and the American Reading Public* (New York: Oxford University Press, 1993), p. 79.

[71] Ibid., p. 119.

[72] Manguel. *A History of Reading*, p. 39.

[73] Karen Armstrong, *In the Beginning: A New Interpretation of Genesis* (New York: Alfred A. Knopf, 1996), p. 4.

[74] Ibid., p. 27.

[75] Roger Chartier, *Inscription and Erasure: Literature and Written Culture from the Eleventh to the Eighteenth Century*, trans. Arthur Goldhammer (Philadelphia: University of Pennsylvania Press, 2007), p. vii.

76 Denis Wood, "The Power of Maps" *Scientific American* 268 (May 1993): 88-93, available at http://www.arts.uwa.edu.au/HistoryWWW/ mapping_conquest_htm I/3_ThePowerofMaps.

77 Mark Monmonier, *From Squaw Tit to Whorehouse Meadow: How Maps Name, Claim, and Inflame* (Chicago: University of Chicago Press, 2006), p. ix.

78 Ibid., p. 12.

79 Ibid., pp. 34-35.

80 Alan Trachtenberg, *Reading American Photographs: Images as History Mathew Brady to Walker Evans* (New York: Hill and Wang, 1990), p. 4.

81 John Tagg, *The Burden of Representation: Essays on Photographies and Histories* (Minneapolis: University of Minnesota Press, 1993), p. 63.

82 See William J. Mitchell, *The Reconfigured Eye: Visual Truth in the Post-Photographic Era* (Cambridge: MIT Press, 1992).

83 Katherine Martinez, "The Dickinsons of Amherst Collect: Pictures and Their Meanings in a Victorian Home," *Common-Place* volume 7, number 3, April 2007, available at .

84 Henri-Jean Martin, *The History and Power of Writing*, trans. Lydia G. Cochrane. (Chicago: University of Chicago Press, 1994), p. 507.

85 Robert Brent Toplin, *History by Hollywood: The Use and Abuse of the American Past.* (Urbana: University of Illinois Press, 1996), p. 66.

86 Robert Rosenstone, *Visions of the Past: The Challenge of Film to Our Idea of History.* (Cambridge: Harvard University Press, 1995), p. 208.

87 Robert Rosenstone, "Oliver Stone As Historian" In Robert Brent Toplin, ed., *Oliver Stone's USA: Film, History, and Controversy* (Lawrence: University Press of Kansas, 2000), p. 34.

88 James Gleick, *Faster: The Acceleration of Just About Everything* (New York: Vintage Books, 1999).

89 Michael L. Kurtz, "Oliver Stone, *JFK*, and History," in Robert Brent Toplin, ed., *Oliver Stone's USA: Film, History, and Controversy* (Lawrence: University Press of Kansas, 2000), p. 174.

90 Kevin Walsh, *The Representation of the Past: Museums and Heritage in the Post-Modern World* (New York: Routledge, 1992).

91 See Steven Lubar and W. David Kingery, eds. *History from Things: Essays on Material Culture* (Washington, DC: Smithsonian Institution Press, 1993).

92 John Kouwenhoven, "American Studies: Words or Things," in Thomas J. Schlereth, *Material Culture Studies in America* (Nashville, TN: American Association for State and Local History, 1982).

[93] See Donald Norman's writings, for example: *The Design of Everyday Things* (New York: Doubleday Currency, 1990); *Turn Signals Are the Facial Expressions of Automobiles* (Reading, MA: Addison-Wesley Publishing Co., 1992); *Things That Make Us Smart: Defending Human Attributes in the Age of the Machine* (Reading, MA: Addison-Wesley Publishing Co., 1993); and *The Invisible Computer: Why Good Products Can Fail, the Personal Computer Is So Complex, and Information Appliances Are the Solution* (Cambridge: The MIT Press, 1998).

[94] Marita Sturken, *Tangled Memories: The Vietnam War, the AIDS Epidemic, and the Politics of Remembering* (Berkeley: University of California Press, 1997), p. 10.

[95] David Glassberg and J. Michael Moore, "Patriotism in Orange: The Memory of World War I in a Massachusetts Town," in John Bodnar, ed., *Bonds of Affection: Americans Define Their Patriotism* (Princeton, NJ: Princeton University Press, 1996), pp. 188-189.

[96] Maya Lin, "Making the Memorial," *New York Review of Books* 47 (November 2, 2000): 33-35.

[97] Sturken, *Tangled Memories*, p. 60.

[98] Ibid., p. 61.

[99] Kirk Savage, *Standing Soldiers, Kneeling Slaves: Race, War, and Monument in Nineteenth-Century America* (Princeton, NJ: Princeton University Press, 1995), p. 210.

[100] Sanford Levinson, *Written in Stone: Public Monuments in Changing Societies* (Durham, NC: Duke University Press, 1998).

[101] George Foote, *Shadowed Ground: America's Landscapes of Violence and Tragedy.* (Austin: University of Texas Press, 1997).

[102] Dolores Hayden, *The Power of Place: Urban Landscapes as Public History* (Cambridge: MIT Press, 1995), p. 9.

[103] David M. Henkin, *City Reading: Written Words and Public Spaces in Antebellum New York* (New York: Columbia University Press, 1998), p. 6.

[104] Ibid., p. 15.

[105] Richard Keller Simon, "The Formal Garden in the Age of Consumer Culture: A Reading of the Twentieth-Century Shopping Mall," in Wayne Franklin and Michael Steiner, eds., *Mapping American Culture* (Iowa City: University of Iowa Press, 1992), p. 236.

[106] Shopping malls have typical architectural elements as well, as described in Witold Rybczynski, *City Life: Urban Expectations in a New World* (New York: Harper Collins, 1995).

107 Witold Rybczynski, *Looking Around: A Journey Through Architecture* (New York: Penguin Books, 1992), p. xviii.

108 Alain de Botton *The Architecture of Happiness* (New York: Pantheon Books, 2006), p. 10.

109 Ibid., p. 124.

110 Ibid., p. 137.

111 Hal Varian and Peter Lyman, *How Much Information?* Berkeley: University of California, Berkeley School of Information Management and Systems, 2000, available at http://www.sims.berkeley.edu/how-much-info/index.html; Michael Bergman, *The Deep Web: Surfacing Hidden Value.* Bright Planet, July 2000, available at http://www.completeplanet.com/Tutoria Is/DeepWeb/index.asp.

112 Jeannette Walls, *Dish: The Inside Story on the World of Gossip* (New York: Avon Books, 2000).

113 Mark Caldwell, *A Short History of Rudeness: Manners, Morals, and Misbehavior in Modern America* (New York: Picador Books, 1999), p. 7.

114 Ibid., pp. 86-87.

115 "Talking to Each Other," *Economist,* 11 November 2000, pp. 8, 10.

Chapter 4

1 Sara Kehaulani Goo, "Privacy Advocates Criticize Plan To Embed ID Chips in Passports," *Washington Post,* April 3, 2005, p. A06; available at http://www.washingtonpost.com/wp-dyn/articles/A21858-2005Apr2.html?referrer=email, accessed April 3, 2005.

2 Brian Whitley, "Stolen Data Spurs Fears for Privacy: Students Scramble to Guard Against Identity Theft, " *The Daily Californian,* March 31, 2005, available at http://www.dailycal.org/article.php?id=18158, accessed April 3, 2005.

3 Jonathan Krim, "Net Aids Access to Sensitive ID Data: Social Security Numbers Are Widely Available," *Washington Post,* April 4, 2005, p. A01, available at http://www.washingtonpost.com/wp-dyn/articles/A23686-2005Apr3.html?referrer=email, accessed April 4, 2005.

4 Shanna Groves, "Protecting Your Identity," *Information Management Journal* 36 (May/June 2002): 28.

5 Marianne Kolbasuk McGee, "Computers with Patient Data Stolen on Eve of HIPAA Security Rules," *Information Week,* April 13, 2005, available at

http://informationweek.com/story/showArticle.jhtml?articleID=1607022
70, accessed April 14, 2005.
[6] Paul Krugman, "The Medical Money Pit," *New York Times*, April 15,
2005, available at
http://www.nytimes.com/2005/04/15/opinion/15krugman.html?th&em
c=th, accessed April 15, 2005.
[7] Götz Aly and Karl Heinz Roth, *The Nazi Census: Identification and Control in the Third Reich*, trans. Edwin Black and Assenka Oksiloff (Philadelphia: Temple University Press, 2004).
[8] Ibid., p. 149.
[9] James B. Rule, *Privacy in Peril* (New York: Oxford University Press, 2007), p. 113.
[10] Ibid., p. 8.
[11] Ibid., pp. 86-87. Rule examines the growth of recordkeeping legislation in the United States, including the establishment of birth and death registers, the Internal Revenue Service, the Social Security system, passports, and so forth. Rule also considers how the notion of fourth amendment protection (the main Constitutional element most frequently used in promoting personal privacy) really often only does apply to personal papers in homes, although the growth of Web sites, text messaging, and the use of cell phones has generated new concerns and debates about how the fourth amendment ought to be interpreted and applied. . As Rule concludes, "The history of privacy over the last four decades consists of one collision after another between privacy-oriented efforts to *compartmentalize* personal data and gathering pressures to share such data directly among interested parties – without consent or even knowledge of the persons concerned" (p. 36).
[12] Yasuhiro Katagiri, *The Mississippi State Sovereignty Commission: Civil Rights and States' Rights* (Jackson: University Press of Mississippi, 2001), p. xiv.
[13] Elizabeth Redden, "Corpses in the Quad," *Inside Higher Education*, October 19, 2006, *http://insidehighered.com/news/2006/10/19/brown* for analysis about the earlier report.
[14] *Response of Brown University to the Report of the Steering Committee on Slavery and Justice* (Providence, Rhode Island: Brown University, 2007), p. 1.
[15] Ibid., p. 1.
[16] Ibid., p. 6.
[17] Cass R. Sunstein, *Republic.com 2.0* (Princeton: Princeton University Press, 2007), p. 195.

18 A statement found at http://eindhoven.holiday-inn.com/location/conc2.html, accessed 29 April 2005.

19 Lee Roop, "My Folks May Hold the Record for Record-keeping," *Huntsville Times*, April 10, 2005, available at http://www.al.com/living/huntsvilletimes/lroop.ssf?/base/living/111312 4509294540.xml, accessed April 11, 2005.

20 Anne Lamott, *Bird by Bird: Some Instructions on Writing and Life* (New York: Anchor Books, 1994), p. 92.

21 Howard Mansfield, *The Bones of the Earth* (Washington, D.C.: Shoemaker and Hoard, 2004), p. 153.

22 Bill Marsh, "The Story of Government Forms: A Real Page-Turner," *New York Times*, April 10, 2005, p. 3.

23 Roxie Rodgers Dinstel, "Keeping Records Sensible to Do," *Fairbanks News-Miner*, April 12, 2005, available at http://www.news-miner.com/Stories/0,1413,113~7244~2810352,00.html, accessed April 12, 2005.

24 Peter Fritzsche, *Stranded in the Present: Modern Time and the Melancholy of History* (Cambridge, MA: Harvard University Press, 2004), p. 4.

25 Ibid., p. 40.

26 Alan D. Ullberg and Robert C. Lind, "Personal Collecting: Proceed with Caution," *Museum News* 69 (September/October 1990): 33-34.

27 William J. Mitchell, *ME++: The Cyborg Self and the Networked City* (Cambridge: MIT Press, 2003), p. 62.

28 Ibid., p. 84.

29 David Armitage, *The Declaration of Independence: A Global History* (Cambridge: Harvard University Press, 2007), pp. 21-22.

30 Ibid., p. 22.

31 R. H. Thomson, *The Lost Boys: Letters from the Sons in Two Acts 1914-1923* (Toronto: Playwrights Canada Press, 2001).

32 Ken Dornstein, *The Boy Who Fell Out of the Sky: A True Story* (New York: Vintage Books, 2007), p. 10.

33 Ibid., p. 13.

34 Ibid., p. 81.

35 Ibid., p. 54.

36 Ibid., p. 239.

37 Ibid., p. 324.

38 Albert B. Crenshaw, "Reality Check: E-Payments are Gaining; A Federal Reserve Study Finds that Americans are Losing Their Love for Old-Fashioned Paper," *Washington Post*, November 18, 2001, p. H02.

[39] David Fettig, "Federal Reserve Studies Confirm Electronic Payments Exceed Check Payments for the First Time," Financial Services Policy Committee, Federal reserve System, December 6, 2004, available at http://www.federalreserve.gov/boarddocs/press/other/2004/20041206/default.htm, accessed June 6, 2005.

[40] Thomas Mallon, "Memories Held in Check: Pursuing a Lifetime of My Father's Expenditures," *Harper's Magazine*, October 1993, available at http://www.findarticles.com/p/articles/mi_m1111/is_n1721_v287/ai_1 3288005, accessed April 30, 2005.

[41] "2004 United States Postal Service Annual Report," available at http://www.usps.com/history/anrpt/o4/ and accessed May 28, 2005.

[42] David M. Henkin, *The Postal Age: The Emergence of Modern Communications in Nineteenth-Century America* (Chicago: University of Chicago Press, 2006), p. ix.

[43] Ibid., p. x.

[44] Ibid., pp. 145-146.

[45] Ibid., p. 6.

[46] Ibid., p. 175.

[47] Carol Poster and Linda C. Mitchell, eds., *Letter-Writing Manuals and Instruction from Antiquity to the Present: Historical and Bibliographic Studies* (Columbia: University of south Carolina, 2007), p. 183.

[48] Ibid., p. 196.

[49] The estimate was made in "By the Numbers," *Newsweek Magazine* 16 (January 2001): 16.

[50] David Shipley and Will Schwalbe, *Send: The Essential Guide to Email for Office and Home* (New York: Alfred A. Knopf, 2007), p. 35.

[51] Edith B. Gelles, *Abigail Adams: A Writing Life* (New York: Routledge, 2002), pp. 26, 102.

[52] Gary Matter, "Web Portals Grease the Reality Chain," *InternetWeek*, June 5, 2000, p. 42, estimates that "there are 40 different parties involved in a real estate transaction and 128 different 'checkpoints' before a home can be sold." Jay Romano, "A First-Time Buyer's Primer and Road Map," *New York Times*, March 3, 1996, Section 9, p. 1, had one lawyer reporting that clients buying a house are told to be prepared to sign as many as 100 pieces of paper and to have 10 to 20 checks with them.

[53] Michael J. McCarthy, "Mysteries Abound for the Nancy Drew of Unclaimed Stuff – Gloria Jett Hunts for Owners of Safe-Deposit Boxes; The Comic-Book Caper," *Wall Street Journal*, October 25, 2002, p. A1,

describing the work of an individual who tracks down the lawful heirs of materials left behind in these boxes.

54 The realities of these storage containers were evident in the dramatic destruction of 1,300 safe deposit boxes at the J. P. Morgan Chase and Company's branch at 5 World Trade Center on September 11, 2001; see Pamela Sebastian Ridge, "Not-So-Safe Deposit Boxes: Retrieving Charred Memories from World Trade Vault; A Searing Oven for Days," *Wall Street Journal*, January 18, 2002, p. B1. This led some to recommend that it is better to maintain important personal and family documents at home in a fireproof container; see Jeff D. Opdyke, "Do You Know Where Your Vital Records Are? Postattack Paper Chase Reaffirms Hard Copy's Relevance," *Wall Street Journal*, October 10, 2001, p. C1.

55 Dan Koeppel, *To See Every Bird on Earth: A Father, A Son, and a Lifelong Obsession* (New York: Plume, 2005), p. xv.

56 Ibid., pp. 225-226.

57 Jennie Erdal, *Ghosting: A Double Life* (New York: Anchor Books, 2004), p. 107.

58 Robert Benson, *The Game: One Man, Nine Innings, A Love Affair with Baseball* (New Yorker: Jeremy P. Tarcher/Penguin, 2004), p. 46.

59 Ibid., pp. 53-54.

60 Ibid., p. 54.

61 Roger Angell, *Let Me Finish* (New York: Harcourt, Inc., 2006), p. 29.

62 Daniel J. Wakin, "When Death Means the Loss of An Archive," *New York Times*, May 18, 2005, available at www.nytimes.com/2005/05/18/arts/dance/18will.html? and accessed May 20, 2005.

Chapter 5

1 Dinesh D'Souza, *Letters to a Young Conservative* (New York: Basic Books, 2002), p. 82.

2 Colin Beavan, *Fingerprints: The Origins of Crime Detection and the Murder Case that Launched Forensic Science* (New York: Hyperion, 2001), p. 11.

3 Deirde Simmons, *Keepers of the Record: The History of the Hudson's Bay Company Archives* (Montreal and Kingston: McGill-Queen's University Press, 2007).

4 Alistair Tough and Michael Moss, eds., *Record Keeping in a Hybrid Environment: Managing the Creation, Use, Preservation and Disposal of Unpublished*

Information Objects in Context (Oxford, England: Chandos Publishing, 2006), p. ix.

[5] Nicholson Baker, *The Size of Thoughts: Essays and Other Lumber* (New York: Vintage Books, 1997), pp. 182-203.

[6] Nigel Warburton, "Is Art Sacred?" in *Is Nothing Sacred?*, ed. Ben Rogers (New York: Routledge, 2004), p. 46.

[7] Denise Schmandt-Besserat, *When Writing Met Art: From Symbol to Story* (Austin: University of Texas Press, 2007).

[8] James Elkins, ed., *Photography Theory* (New York: Routledge, 2007), p. 255.

[9] Ibid., p. 352.

[10] Ibid., p. 406.

[11] If you want to gain some insight into what *Wired* is part of, I recommend that you read Fred Turner's excellent *From Counterculture to Cyberculture: Stewart Brand, the Whole Earth Network, and the Rise of Digital Utopianism* (Chicago: University of Chicago Press, 2006).

[12] Gareth Cook, "Untangling the Mystery of the Inca," *Wired* (January 2007): 147.

[13] David Kushner, "We Put a Man on the Moon. But (d'oh!) NASA Can't Find the Videotape," *Wired* (January 2007): 170.

[14] Ibid., p. 170.

[15] See, for example, Winifred Gallagher's amusing and chatty little book on purses – *It's in the Bag: What Purses Reveal – and Conceal* (New York: HarperCollins Publishers, 2006).

[16] Richard Godbeer, *Escaping Salem: The Other Witch Hunt of 1692* (New York: Oxford University Press, 2005), p. 130.

[17] For an interesting account of genealogy, see Donald Harman Akenson's *Some Family: The Mormons and How Humanity Keeps Track of Itself* (Montreal and Kingston: McGill-Queen's University Press, 2007). Akenson's goal is to understand a Mormon mission, namely "to create an accurate and comprehensive genealogical tree of the entire human race" (p. 7).

[18] "Number of Anglers and Hunters Remain Steady," United States Department of the Interior – U.S. Fish and Wildlife Services, 2001, available at http://news.fws.gov/newsreleases/R9/A2D9B201-0350-4BD4-A73477A25FC69.html?CFID=764049&CFTOKEN=74280991, accessed June 26, 2005.

[19] "Highway Statistics 2003 – Section III: Driver Licensing," United States Department of Transportation – Federal Highway Administration, 2004,

ENDNOTES

375

available at http:///www.fhwa.dot.gov/policy/ohim/hs03/dl.htm, accessed June 26, 2005.

[20] Lawrence M. Friedman, *Law in America: A Short History* (New York: Modern Library Chronicles Book, 2002), p. 38.

[21] Martin Lloyd, *The Passport: The History of Man's Most Traveled Document* (Thrupp-Stroud-Glouchestershire: Sutton Publishing Limited, 2003), p. 44.

[22] Ibid., p. 258.

[23] Gary Wolf, "The New Multiple Personality Disorder," *Wired* 13 (May 2005): 36.

[24] See U.S. House of Representatives Committee on Oversight and Government Reform, *Sandy Berger's Theft of Classified Documents: Unanswered Questions*, released January 9, 2007.

[25] Rohan Kriwaczek, *An Incomplete History of the Art of Funerary Violin* (London: Duckworth Overlook, 2006), p. xii.

[26] Laurel Thatcher Ulrich, *A Midwife's Tale: The Life of Martha Ballard, Based on Her Diary, 1785-1812* (New York: Vintage Books, 1990).

[27] Robert Harris, *Selling Hitler* (New York: Penguin Books, 1986).

[28] Louis Menand, "Woke Up This Morning: Why Do We Read Diaries?" *New Yorker* (December 10, 2007), p. 107.

[29] Quoted in Bret Lott, *Before We Get Started: A Practical Memoir of the Writer's Life* (New York: Ballantine Books, 2005), p. 79.

[30] Wallys W. Conhaim, "Personal Journals: New Users for an Age-Old Practice," *Information Today* 20 (January 2003): 27.

[31] Rhys Isaac, *Landon Carter's Uneasy Kingdom: Revolution and Rebellion on a Virginia Plantation* (New York: Oxford University Press, 2004), p. 45.

[32] Viviane Serfaty, *The Mirror and the Veil: An Overview of American Online Diaries and Blogs* (Amsterdam and New York: Rodopi, 2004), p. 57.

[33] Laural A. Clyde, "Weblogs – Are You Serious?" *The Electronic Library* 22, no. 5 (2004): 390-392.

[34] John Seabrook, "The Tree of Me," *New Yorker*, March 26, 2001, p. 58.

[35] Sara Paretsky, *Writing in an Age of Silence* (New York: Verso, 2007), p. 111.

[36] Ibid., p. 18.

[37] Ibid., pp. 49-50.

[38] Ibid., p. 113.

[39] Ibid., p. 138.

[40] Joan Schwartz and James Ryan, eds., *Picturing Place: Photography and the Geographical Imagination* (London: I. B. Taurus and Co., Ltd., 2003), p. 5.

[41] Martha Sandweiss, *Print the Legend: Photography and the American West* (New Haven: Yale University Press, 2002), p. 265.

[42] Janina Struk, *Photographing the Holocaust: Interpretations of the Evidence* (London: I. B. Tauris & Co., Ltd., in association with European Jewish Publication Society, 2004), p. 15.

[43] Elaine Hunt, "Spotlight Photography," *Marketing Week* 23 (September 28, 2000): 46.

[44] Sandra Yin, "Picture This: A Look at Where Americans are Most Likely to Snap Up Digital Cameras," *American Demographics* 25 (July/August 2003): 18-19.

[45] Jay Prosser, *Light in the Dark Room: Photography and Loss* (Minneapolis: University of Minnesota Press, 2005), p. 8.

[46] Bryan Carson, *The Law of Libraries and Archives* (Metuchen, New Jersey: Scarecrow Press, 2007), p. 123.

[47] Ibid., p. 156.

[48] Ibid., p. 238.

[49] Gina Bellafante, "Trafficking in Memories (for Fun and Profit)," *New York Times*, January 27, 2005, p. F1; Emily Lambert, "Thanks for the Memories," *Forbes* 147 (November 29, 2004): 79-82.

[50] Eleanor Levie and Marc Silver, "Scrap booking, Cyberstyle," *U.S. News & World Report* 137 (September 13, 2004): 62; Dirk Johnson, "Beyond the Quilting Bee," *Newsweek* 104 (October 21, 2002): 64.

[51] Ellen Gruber Garvey's essay in Lisa Gitelman and Geoffrey B. Pingree, eds., *New Media, 1740-1915* (Cambridge: MIT Press, 2003), p. 209.

[52] Leslie Walker, "Online Scrapbooks Let Globetrotters Trace Their Travels," *Washington Post*, March 27, 2005, p. F07, available at http://www.washingtonpost.com/wp-dyn/articles/A2609-2005Mar26.html?referrer=email, accessed March 27, 2005.

Chapter 6

[1] Sven Birkerts, *Reading Life: Books for the Ages* (Saint Paul, MN: Graywolf Press, 2007), p. 22.

[2] G. Thomas Tanselle, "The World as Archive," *Common Knowledge* 8, no. 2 (2002): 403.

[3] Ross King, *Ex-Libris* (New York: Penguin Books, 1998), pp. 306-307.

[4] Shaun Johnson, *The Native Commissioner* (Johannesburg, South Africa: Penguin Books, South Africa, 2006), p. 4.

[5] Ibid., p. 46.

[6] Ibid., p. 142.

[7] Simon Worrall, *The Poet and the Murderer: A True Story of Literary Crime and the Art of Forgery* (New York: Dutton, 2002), p. 20.

[8] Carla Thornton, "Laptop Era Dawns," *PC World* 21 (October 2003): 22-26.

[9] David Weinberger, *Everything is Miscellaneous: The Power of the New Digital Disorder* (New York: Times Books, 2007), p. 99.

[10] Ibid., p. 132.

[11] Andrew Keen, *The Cult of the Amateur: How Today's Internet is Killing Our Culture* (New York: Doubleday/Currency, 2007), p. 42.

[12] Rich Ling, *The Mobile Connection: The Cell Phone's Impact on Society* (San Francisco: Morgan Kaufmann Publishers, 2004), p. 5.

[13] Katie Hafner, "Holding a Paper Ticket, Bracing for the Irritation," *New York Times*, 24 March 2005,
http://www.nytimes.com/2005/03/24/technology/circuits/24tixx.html?8cir=&adxnnl=1&emc=cir&adxnnlx=1111688590-d7Cy1oFXXAnZaexIQEa/Og, accessed March 24, 2005.

[14] Jennifer A. Kingson, "Follow the Vanishing Check," *New York Times*, March 26, 2005, available at
http://www.nytimes.com/2005/03/26/business/26check.html?th=&adxnnl=1&emc=th&adxnnlx=1111840436-gofiqGkiRFmn3ri1uGrrKQ, accessed March 26, 2005.

[15] William M. Bulkeley, ""In the digital age, a clash over fading photos," *Wall Street Journal*, April 1, 2005, reprinted in the *Arizona Republic*, available at http://www.azcentral.com/business/articles/0401wsj-fadingphotos01-ON.html#, accessed April 3, 2005.

[16] "In Praise of Clutter," *The Economist* (December 21,2002-January 3, 2003), p. 87.

[17] "In Praise of Clutter," p. 88.

[18] Robert Johnson, "The Fax Machine: Technology That Refuses to Die," *New York Times*, March 27, 2005, available at
http://www.nytimes.com/2005/03/27/business/yourmoney/27fax.html?th=&adxnnl=1&emc=th&adxnnlx=1111915090-bTj0D8FkKUloWrD7aXkx/w, accessed March 27, 2005. Other commentators report that the sales and uses of fax machines have long since peaked out, with sales of the machines declining; "Last Gasp of the Fax Machine," *Economist*, September 18, 2004, p. 14 and Bill Schweber, "When Your Time Has Come – And Gone," *EDN* 48 (November 27, 2003): 28.

[19] Domhnall Mitchell, *Measures of Possibility: Emily Dickinson's Manuscripts* (Amherst: University of Massachusetts Press, 2005), p. 3.

[20] Ibid., p. 312.

[21] Ibid., p. 19.

[22] Joyce Appleby, *A Restless Past: History and the American Public* (Lanham, MD: Rowman & Littlefield Publishers, Inc., 2005), p. 119.

[23] Ibid., pp. 119-120.

[24] Ibid., p. 129.

[25] Elizabeth A. Clark, *History, Theory, Text: Historians and the Linguistic Turn* (Cambridge: Harvard University Press, 2004), p. 117.

[26] Jacques Derrida, *Paper Machine*, trans. Rachel Bowlby (Stanford, CA: Stanford University Press, 2005), p. 16.

[27] Ibid., p. 43.

[28] Ibid., p. 58.

[29] Ibid., p. 29.

[30] William J. Mitchell, *Placing Words: Symbols, Space, and the City* (Cambridge, MA: MIT Press, 2005), p. 3. In this volume, Mitchell is exploring how the "spaces and places of twenty-first century cities provide contexts for communication – serving not only to shelter and protect their inhabitants, but also to ground and sustain meaningful interaction among them, and to construct community" (p. 3). The other volumes include *City of Bits: Space, Place, and the Infobahn* (Cambridge: MIT, 1995); *e-topia: "Urban Life, Jim – But Not as We Know It"* (Cambridge: MIT, 2000); and *Me++: The Cyborg Self and the Networked City* (Cambridge: MIT, 2004).

[31] Ibid., p. 16.

[32] Ibid., p. 78.

[33] Ibid., p. 100.

[34] Ibid., p. 102.

[35] Ibid., p. 151.

[36] Ibid., p. 9.

[37] Derrida, *Paper Machine*, pp. 7-8.

[38] N. Katherine Hayles, *My Mother Was a Computer: Digital Subjects and Literary Texts* (Chicago: University of Chicago Press, 2005), p. 89.

[39] Derrida, *Paper Machine*, p. 23.

[40] William E. Jarvis, *Time Capsules: A Cultural History* (Jefferson, North Carolina: McFarland and Co., 2003), pp. 1-2.

[41] Chris Hedges, *Moses on the Freeway: The 10 Commandments in America* (New York: Free Press, 2005), p. 41.

[42] Ivan Doig, *Heart Earth* (Orlando, FL: Harcourt, Inc., 1993), p. 4.

43 Antoinette Burton, *Dwelling in the Archive: Women Writing House, Home, and History in Late Colonial India* (New York: Oxford University Press, 2003), p. 5.

44 Ibid., p. 22.

45 Ibid., p. 139.

46 Liz Davenport, *Order from Chaos: A Six-Step Plan for Organizing Yourself, Your Office, and Your Life* (New York: Three Rivers Press, 2001), p. 3.

47 Patricia J. Hutchings, *Managing Workplace Chaos: Solutions for Handling Information, Paper, Time, and Stress* (New York: AMACOM, 2002), p. 133.

48 Davenport, *Order from Chaos*, pp. 4-5.

49 Ibid., p. 18.

50 Ibid., pp. 22-23.

51 Ibid., p. 25.

52 Ibid., p. 84.

53 Ibid., pp. 85-86.

54 Ibid., p. 122.

55 Steve Kichen, "For the Record," *Forbes* 155 (June 19, 1995): 222-224.

56 "Collector Systems Launches Online Art Management Solution," *Proctivity Software* 17 (March 2004): 1-2.

57 Julie Tilsner and Amy Dunklin, "In Case of Fire or Theft – Keep a List," *Business Week*, issue 3309 (March 15, 1993): 130. See also Ron Eggers, "Photography and the Computer: Disaster Preparedness," *Petersens's Photographic* 29 (May 2000): 50, 63.

58 Frances Johnson, "New Firm Puts Everything You Own on a CD DigitalSafe Records Items for Insurance," *Denver Post*, July 5, 2001, p. C2.

59 Robert L. Stewart, "For Faster Claims Settlement Tell Your Clients to 'Go to the Videotape!" *Rough Notes* 136 (March 1993): 42-44.

60 Lee F. Pendergrass, "Family History Workshops: Teaching Amateur Historians How to Investigate Their Own Past," *History News* 37 (August 1982): 30.

61 Elizabeth Y. Enstam, "Using Memoirs to Write Local History," *History News* 37 (November 1982): 2.

62 Wendell Berry, *The Way of Ignorance and Other Essays* (N.p.: Shoemaker and Hoard, 2005), p. 54.

63 Don Williams and Louisa Jaggar, *Saving Stuff: How to Care for and Preserve Your Collectibles, Heirlooms, and Other Prized Possessions* (New York: Fireside Book, Simon and Schuster, 2005). Williams is the Senior Conservator at the Smithsonian Institution.

[64] Denise Dale and Alexandra Bradley, *At Your Fingertips! A Household Filing System That Works for You*, 2nd ed. (Richmond, British Columbia: Streamline Information and Organizing Services, 2004), p. 2.

[65] Keen, *The Cult of the Amateur*, p. 16.

[66] Ibid. p. 55.

[67] Ibid., p. 205.

[68] Bill Brown, "The Collecting Mania," *University of Chicago Magazine* 94 (October 2001), at http://magazine.uchicago.edu/0110/features/mania.html, accessed June 27, 2007.

[69] I discussed such matters in greater detail in my *No Innocent Deposits: Forming Archives by Rethinking Appraisal* (Metuchen, New Jersey: Scarecrow Press, 2004).

[70] Lee Siegel, *Against the Machine: Being Human in the Age of the Electronic Mob* (New York: Spiegel & Grau, 2008), p. 11.

[71] See the conference description, including this definition, at http://www.pim2008.org/, accessed October 13, 2007.

[72] Samuel D. Kassow, *Who Will Write Our History? Emanuel Ringelblum, the Warsaw Ghetto, and the Oyneg Shabes Archive* (Bloomington: Indiana University Press, 2007), p. 7.

[73] Ibid., p. 211.

[74] Ibid., p. 213.

[75] Ibid., p. 211.

[76] Information about this meeting can be found at http://www3.fis.utoronto.ca/research/i-chora/home.html, accessed October 14, 2007.

[77] David W. Carmicheal, *Rescuing Family Records: A Disaster Planning Guide* (Iowa City, Iowa: Council of State Archivists, 2007).

[78] Terry Cook introduction in Verne Harris, *Archives and Justice: A South African Perspective* (Chicago: Society of American Archivists, 2007), p. xxiii.

[79] Ibid., p. xxvi.

Chapter 7

[1] "Americans Call E-Mail Essential to Their Jobs," *Information Management Journal* 37 (March/April 2003): 16.

[2] Russ Yoshinaka, "Facing the Changes in the Federal Rules of Civil Procedure," *KMWorld* (February 2007): S7.

³ "E-mail Archiving Market Set to Explode," *Information Management Journal* 38 (July/August 2004): 11.

⁴ Nancy E. Enneking, "Managing E-Mail: Working Toward an Effective Solution," *Records Management Quarterly* 32 (July 1998): 25.

⁵ Mark L. Moerdier, "How to Optimally Manage Email in the Enterprise," *KMWorld* (October 2006): S12.

⁶ Jan Rosi, "Crashing the Inbox: Managing Email in Today's Information Age," *KMWorld* (February 2007): S8.

⁷ "Google's New E-mail Service Sparks Privacy Concerns," *Information Management Journal* 38 (July/August 2004): 6.

⁸ Congress also suspended funding for Bush's Defense Department's Total Information Awareness program that wanted to monitor bank accounts, medical records, credit card purchases, and academic records. "Uncle Sam May Not Monitor E-mails," *Information Management Journal* 37 (March/April 2003): 8.

⁹ Deb Hipp, "The Tides of Technology," *InfoPro* 2 (June 2000): 27-28, 31-32.

¹⁰ "Company E-Mail: To Monitor or Not to Monitor," *Information Management Journal* 36 (January/February 2002): 8.

¹¹ "Survey: E-mail Hampers Productivity," *Information Management Journal* 40 (March/April 2004): 22.

¹² "ISPs Charge to Deliver Mass E-mails," *Information Management Journal* 40 (May/June 2006): 20.

¹³ "E-mails Waste Businesses' Archive Space," *Information Management Journal* 38 (November/December 2004): 11.

¹⁴ Nikki Swartz, "Enterprise-wide Records Training: Key to Compliance, Success," *Information Management Journal* 40 (September/October 2006): 35-36, 38-40, 42, 44.

¹⁵ Richard E. Barry, "Managing Distinctions: Enterprise Information, Document, Records, Knowledge, and Content Management," *Records & Information Management Report* 18 (February 2002): 10, 11.

¹⁶ Susan Myburgh, "Knowledge and Records Management: Is There a Difference?" *Records & Information Management* 14 (September 1998): 12, 13 and Ann Balough, "Building a Knowledge Center for Records and Information Management," *Records & Information Management Report* 17 (April 2001): 1.

¹⁷ Nancy E. Enneking, "Managing E-Mail: Working Toward an Effective Solution," *Records Management Quarterly* 32 (July 1998): 24-26, 28-32, 34, 36-38, 40-43.

[18] Ibid., p. 26

[19] Ibid., p. 36

[20] J. Timothy Sprehe, "A Framework for EDMS/ERMS Integration," *Information Management Journal* 38 (November/December 2004): 54-56, 58-60, 62.

[21] Robert F. Williams and Lori J. Ashley, *2005 Electronic Records Management Survey: A Renewed Call to Action* (Chicago: Cohasset Associates, Inc., in association with ARMA and AIIM, 2005), pp. 44-45.

[22] See, for example, Janice Anderson, "ECM:RIM – Programs that Matter. Programs that Last," *KMWorld* (October 2006): S16-17.

[23] Tracy Caughell, "The Corporate Records Conundrum," *Information Management Journal* 37 (May/June 2003): 58.

[24] Dave Dewalt, "Understanding the ERM Challenge," *KM World* (October 2006): S8.

[25] Ibid., p. S9.

[26] John T. Phillips, "Start with e-Mail!" *Information Management Journal* 35 (October 2001): 56.

[27] Maurene Caplan Grey, "Mitigating the Risks of Messaging," *Information Management Journal* 40 (November/December 2006): 68.

[28] "Workplace E-mail, IM Survey Reveals Risks," *Information Management Journal* 39 (May/June 2005): 6.

[29] Andrew McKay, "Compliance and Content Governance," *KMWorld* (October 2006): S23.

[30] Janet Ward, "Quantity Does Matter: Records Management for Billions of Documents," *KMWorld* (October 2006): S22.

[31] Doug Magnuson, "Email Management Brings Harmony to Discovery, Compliance and Storage," *KMWorld* (October 2006): S25.

[32] John J. DiGilio, "Electronic Mail: From Computer to Courtroom," *Information Management Journal* 35 (April 2001): 32.

[33] Ibid., p. 34.

[34] "Does E-Mail Belong in the Courtroom?" *Information Management Journal* 36 (January/February 2002): 9.

[35] Grey, "Mitigating the Risks of Messaging," p. 68.

[36] Ibid., pp. 68-69.

[37] "E-Mails Can and Will Be Held Against You," *Information Management Journal* 37 (March/April 2003): 12.

[38] "Deleted E-mails Cost Philip Morris $2.75 Million," *Information Management Journal* 38 (September/October 2004): 20.

39 "E-mail Fumbles Lead to Big Fines," *Information Management Journal* 40 (May/June 2006): 14.

40 "Missing E-mails Have $15 Million Price Tag," *Information Management Journal* 40 (September/October 2006): 9.

41 John C. Montaña, "The End of the Ostrich Defense," *Information Management Journal* 39 (January/February 2005): 26-28, 30-34 (quotation is on p. 34).

42 Nikki Swartz, "The Electronic Records Conundrum," *Information Management Journal* 38 (January/February 2004): 21.

43 Nikki Swartz, "New Rules for E-Discovery," *Information Management Journal* 40 (November/December 2006): 24. According to her, these "amended rules will raise the e-discovery stakes for all businesses" (p. 26).

44 John Montaña, "The Information Management Implications of Public Citizen v. Carlin," *Information Management Journal* 35 (July 2001): 54.

45 Ibid., p. 57.

46 "Work E-Mail Is Public Record," *Information Management Journal* 38 (May/June 2004): 14.

47 Paul Fisher, "Electronic Records as Evidence: The Case for Canada's New Standard," *Information Management Journal* 38 (March/April 2004): 39-42, 44-45.

48 David A. Wallace, "Electronic Records Management Defined by Court Case and Policy," *Information Management Journal* 35 (January 2001): 4, 6-8, 10, 12, 14-15.

49 See the description of the National Security Archive at its web site, http://www.gwu.edu/~nsarchiv/nsa/the_archive.html, accessed March 4, 2007.

50 Wallace, "Electronic Records Management Defined by Court Case and Policy," p. 10.

51 Donald S. Skupsky, "Applying Records Retention to Electronic Records," *Information Management Journal* 33 (July 1999): 28, 30-35.

52 Nikki Swartz, "Safeguarding Corporate Secrets," *Information Management Journal* 40 (September/October 2006): 24-26, 28, 30.

53 Preston W. Shimer, "Book Review: E-mail Rules for Records Managers," *Information Management Journal* 37 (November/December 2003): 64-65 provides a review of Nancy Flynn and Randolph Kahn, *E-Mail Rules: A Business Guide to Managing Policies, Security, and Legal Issues for E-Mail and Digital Communication* (Amacon, 2003). Shimer points to the authors' bias and corporate sponsors of the publication, advising professionals to read the publication carefully.

[54] Randolph A. Kahn, "Records Management and Compliance: Making the Connection," *Information Management Journal* 38 (May/June 2004): 30.

[55] Phillips, "Start with e-Mail!," p. 57.

[56] Ibid., p. 58.

[57] Grey, "Mitigating the Risks of Messaging," p. 70.

[58] Randolph A. Kahn, "The Risk-Cost Retention Model: A New Approach to Records Retention," *Information Management Journal* 36 (May/June 2006): 47.

[59] Ibid., p. 48.

[60] Patrick J. Cunningham, "IM: Invaluable New Business Tool or Records Management Nightmare?" *Information Management Journal* 37 (November/December 2003): 30.

[61] John C. Montaña, "E-mail, Voice Mail, and Instant Messaging: A Legal Perspective," *Information Management Journal* 38 (January/February 2004): 37-38, 40-41 (quotation, p. 41).

[62] Swartz, "The Electronic Records Conundrum," p. 24.

[63] Rae N. Cogar, "Building an E-Mail Policy: An Organization's Electronic Mail Policy Should Protect Both the Employer and the Employee," *InfoPro* 1 (March 1999): 42.

[64] The Association of Records Managers and Administrators, since the turn of the new century, has issued two guidelines for e-mail management -- *Guideline for Managing E-Mail* (Prairie Village, Kansas: ARMA International, 2000). A few years later these guidelines were generally re-issued as a new ANSI standard; *Requirements for Managing Electronic Messages as Records* (Prairie Village, Kansas: ARMA, 2004), approved as a American National Standard Institute (ANSI) Standard, October 7, 2004.

[65] "States, Localities Weak on E-Records Management," "New Rules for E-Discovery," *Information Management Journal* 40 (November/December 2006): 8.

[66] Phillips, "Start with e-Mail!" p. 58.

[67] The policy guidelines read, "If the organization has an archives program, there may be mission statements or collection policies that outline organization requirements for what may have long-term value for the organization." *Guideline for Managing E-Mail*, p. 12.

[68] Deborah H. Juhnke, "Electronic Discovery in 2010," *Information Management Journal* 37 (November/December 2003): 36.

[69] Ibid., p. 36.

[70] Ibid., p. 40.

[71] Ibid., p. 42.

72 Johannes C. Scholtes, "A View on Email Management: Balancing Multiple Interests and Realities of the Workplace," *KMWorld* (February 2006): S6-7.

73 Robert P. Crease, "The Lost Art of the Letter," *Physics Web* (January 2007) at http://physicsweb.org/articles/world/20/1/8/1, accessed January 16, 2007.

74 Susan S. Lukesh, "E-mail and the Potential Loss to Future Archives and Scholarship or The Dog that Didn't Bark," *First Monday: Peer-reviewed Journal on the Internet* 4 (September 1999), available at http://www.firstmonday.dk/issues/issue4_9/lukesh/index.html.

75 Edward Tenner, "The Prestigious Inconvenience of Print," *Chronicle Review*, 53 (March 9, 2007), p. B7, available at http://chronicle.com/weekly/v53/i27/27b00701.htm.

76 David Bearman, "Managing Electronic Mail," *Archives and Manuscripts* 22, no. 1 (May 1994), 28.

77 Filip Boudrez, *Filing and Archiving E-mail* (2006), pp. 1-2, available at http://www.expertisecentrumdavid.be/docs/filingArchiving_email.pdf. Boudrez's report considers how the "Antwerp city archives developed a custom-made records management and recordkeeping procedure for e-mails and attachments for the city administration of Antwerp," a government with about 6500 e-mail users, building on the "DAVID model" for e-mail management (p. 5). The Antwerp framework employed here takes into account the judicial or legal, archival, and other organizational requirements.

78 Allen Weinstein, "NARA Enters New 'ERA' of Electronic Records Management," *Information Management Journal* 39 (September/October 2005): 22.

79 Ibid., p. 23.

80 Kristin E. Martin, "Analysis of Remote Reference Correspondence at a Large Academic Manuscripts Collection," *American Archivist* 64 (Spring/Summer 2001): 24.

81 Ibid.,, p. 41.

82 Marion Matters, ed., *Automated Records and Techniques in Archives: A Resource Directory* (Chicago: Society of American Archivists, 1990).

83 Carole Elizabeth Nowicke, "Managing Tomorrow's Records Today: An Experiment in Archival Preservation of Electronic Mail," *Midwestern Archivist* 13, no. 2 (1988), 73.

[84] Tom Hyry and Rachel Onuf, "The Personality of Electronic Records: The Impact of New Information Technology on Personal Papers," *Archival Issues* 22, no. 1 (1997): 38.

[85] Perhaps most revealing as to where archivists were with e-mail a decade or so ago was the publication by the Society of American Archivists, with support from the National Historical Publications and Records Commission, of a series of case studies on electronic records for use in the classroom. In hindsight, the teaching tools were a failure – little used and hardly cited, but as historic documents they are revealing about what archivists thought about e-mail and other electronic records management. In every case, from businesses to universities, e-mail was acknowledged as a records generating system needing to be tamed. See, for example, Grant Mitchell, *Approaching Electronic Records Management at the Insurance Corporation of British Columbia: A Case Study in Organizational Dynamics and Archival Initiative* (Chicago: Society of American Archivists, 1997) and Anne J. Gilliland-Swetland, *Policy and Politics: The Archival Implications of Digital Communications and Culture at the University of Michigan* (Chicago: Society of American Archivists, 1996).

[86] Australian Council of Archives, *Corporate Memory in the Electronic Age: Statement of a Common Position on Electronic Recordkeeping* (Victoria, Australia: Australian Council of Archives, May 1996), p. 6.

[87] Australian Archives, *Managing Electronic Messages as Records: Policy and Guidelines* (Canberra: Australian Archives, May 1997).

[88] Archives Authority of New South Wales, *Steering into the Future: Electronic Recordkeeping in New South Wales* (Sydney: Archives Authority of New South Wales, 1997), p. 4.

[89] New York State Archives and Records Administration, *Managing Records in E-Mail Systems* (Albany: The University of the State of New York, The State Education Department, 1995), p. 4.

[90] Ibid., p. 23.

[91] Ibid., p. 25.

[92] Marlan Green, Sue Soy, Stan Gunn, and Patricia Galloway, "Coming to TERM: Designing the Texas Email Repository Model," *D-Lib Magazine* 8, no. 9 (September 2002), available at http://www.dlib.org/dlib/september02/galloway/09galloway.html.

[93] State of Texas. Texas State Library and Archives Commission, *Email Policy Model for State Agencies* (Austin, TX, 2002), available at http://www.tsl.state.tx.us/slrm/recordspubs/email_model.html, accessed March 11, 2007.

[94] Maureen Pennock, "Curating E-Mails: A Life-Cycle Approach to the Management and Preservation of E-Mail Messages," *DCC Digital Curation Manual,* eds., S. Ross and M. Day (July 2006). This is available at http://www.dcc.ac.uk/resource/curation-manual/chapters/curating-e-mails/.

[95] Ibid., p. 14.

[96] Ibid., p. 20.

[97] Ibid., pp. 24-29.

[98] Ibid., p. 34.

[99] See, for example, *Research Issues in Electronic Records: Report of the Working Meeting* (Washington, D.C.: Published for the National Historical Publications and Records Commission by the Minnesota Historical Society, 1991).

[100] Maureen L. Mackenzie, "Storage and Retrieval of E-mail in a Business Environment: An Exploratory Study," *Library & Information Science Research* 24 (2002): 365.

[101] Douglas F. Seaver, "The New Legal Advice: Don't Press 'Delete,'" *Chronicle of Higher Education, The Chronicle Review* 53 (February 16, 2007), p. B12, available at http://chronicle.com/weekly/v53/i24/24b01201.htm.

[102] Ibid.

[103] Lucie Paquet, "Appraisal, Acquisition and Control of Personal Electronic Records: From Myth to Reality," *Archives and Manuscripts* 28, no. 2 (2000): 74.

[104] Ibid., p. 75.

[105] Ibid., pp. 77-78.

[106] Ibid., p. 79.

[107] Ibid.

[108] Moerdler, "How to Optimally Manage Email in the Enterprise," *KMWorld* (October 2006), p. 513.

[109] Johannes C. Scholtes, "Efficient and Cost-Effective Email Management with XML," *KMWorld* (February 2007): S5.

[110] Nick Mehta, "Facilitate Email Records Management via Backup and Archiving," *KMWorld* (October 2006): 514-515.

[111] Joe Romanowski, "Email Archiving: Analyzing the Return on Investment," *KMWorld* (February 2006): S16.

[112] "Voicemails Converted to E-mail: E-discovery Treasure Trove," *ARMA International Information Management Newswire, February 2007,* http://www.arma.org/news/enewsletters/index.cfm?ID=1660, accessed February 28, 2007.

[113] See, for example, Boudrez, *Filing and Archiving E-mail*, p. 13.

[114] Bearman, "Managing Electronic Mail," p. 37.

[115] Ibid., p. 48.

[116] Barbara Reed and Frank Upward, *The APB Bank: Managing Electronic Records as an Authoritative Resource* (Chicago: Society of American Archivists, 1997), p. 11.

[117] Barbara Reed and Frank Upward, *The APB Bank: Managing Electronic Records as an Authoritative Resource* (Chicago: Society of American Archivists, 1997), p. 7.

[118] The great listserv debate started with a posting by Nancy Beaumont to the list on March 13, 2007 and effectively ended with a posting by SAA President Elizabeth W. Adkins to the list on March 30, 2007.

[119] Carol E. B. Chosky, *Domesticating Information: Managing Documents Inside the Organization* (Lanham, MD: Scarecrow Press, 2006).

[120] Ibid., p. 143.

[121] Patricia Franks, "The Electronic World: E-mail, the Internet, and Other Technologies are Making Electronic Recordkeeping a Way of Life for RIM Professionals," *InfoPro* 3 (December 2001): 50.

[122] Ibid.

[123] Ben Macintyre, "History 1980-2000 has disappeared into the ether. Sorry," London *Times*, 23 March 2007, at http://www.timesonline.co.uk/tol/comment/columnists/ben_macintyre/article1555570.ec, accessed March 30, 2007.

[124] National Science Foundation Cyberinfrastructure Council, *Cyberinfrastructure Vision for 21st Century Discovery* (Washington, D. C.: National Science Foundation, March 2007), p. 3.

[125] Ibid., p. 39.

Chapter 8

[1] H. Curtis Wright, "The Immateriality of Information," *Journal of Library History* 11 (October 1976): 301-302.

[2] Tom McArthur, *Worlds of Reference: Lexicography, Learning and Language from the Clay Tablet to the Computer* (Cambridge: Cambridge University Press, 1986), pp. 7, 9.

[3] Greg S. Hunter, "The Digital Future: A Look Ahead," *Information Management Journal* 36 (January/February 2002): 70-72.

[4] Julien Masanés, "Web Archiving," in Marilyn Deegan and Simon Tanner, eds., *Digital Preservation* (London: Facet Publishing, 2006), pp. 84 and 91.

[5] See, for example, Carol Casey, "The Cyberarchive: A Look at the Storage and Preservation of Web Sites," *College and Research Libraries* 59, no. 4 (Jul 1998): 304-310.

[6] Abby Smith, "The Future of Web Resources: Who Decides What Gets Saved and How Do They Do It?," Paper presented at *Archiving Web Resources: Issues for Cultural Heritage Institutions*, 9-11 November 2004, available at http://www.nla.gov.au/webarchiving/SmithAbby.rtf, accessed July 17, 2007.

[7] See, for example, Wallace Koehler, "Web Page Change and Persistence – a four-year longitudinal study," *Journal of the American Society for Information Science and Technology* 53, no. 2 (2002): 162-171.

[8] The papers of Eunice Richardson Stone Connolly (1831-1877) survive, for example, against a variety of odds, as recounted in Martha Hodes, *The Sea Captain's Wife: A True Story of Love, Race, and War in the Nineteenth Century* (New York: W.W. Norton & Co., 2006). Often utilizing inferior paper and poor ink, a member of her family saves her letters and a descendant, strapped for cash, sells the collection years later to a dealer from whom they make their way to the university where they now reside at Duke University's special collections and archives. Through her searches historian Hodes manages to connect with the individual who sold the letters in 1965 to a dealer: "I was ... astonished to realize that of all Eunice's siblings, of all the children of those siblings, and of all their children and grandchildren, the historical records had led me, with concerted, though not extraordinary, effort, to the one, great-grandchild who had once been the keeper of what were now called the Lois Wright Richardson Davis Papers" (p. 291).

[9] George Lipsitz, *Time Passages: Collective Memory and American Popular Culture* (Minneapolis: University of Minnesota Press, 1990), p. 36.

[10] Seamus Ross, *Changing Trains at Wigan: Digital Preservation and the Future of Scholarship* (London: National Preservation Office, 2000), p. 3.

[11] Ibid., p. 5.

[12] Ibid., p. 12.

[13] Peter Lor and Johannes J. Britz, "A Moral Perspective on South-North Web Archiving," *Journal of Information Science* 30, no. 6 (2004): 540.

[14] David Lowenthal, *The Past Is A Foreign Country* (Cambridge: Cambridge University Press, 1985), p. xxiii.

[15] For some instructive insight into such matters, see Peter L. Shillingsburg's *From Gutenberg to Google: Electronic Representations of Literary Texts* (Cambridge: Cambridge University Press, 2006).

[16] See, for example, Sonja Neef, José van Dijck, and Eric Ketelaar, eds., *Sign Here! Handwriting in the Age of New Media* (Amsterdam: Amsterdam University Press, 2006).

[17] Roy Rosenzwig and David Thelen, *The Presence of the Past: Popular Uses of History in American Life* (New York: Columbia University Press, 1998), p. 18.

[18] Ibid., p. 24.

[19] Ibid., p. 184.

[20] Lawrence and Nancy Goldstone, *Slightly Chipped: Footnotes in Booklore* (New York: St. Martin's Griffin, 2000), p. 124.

[21] Harold Skramstad, "An Agenda for American Museums in the Twenty-First Century," *Daedalus* 128 (Summer 1999): 123.

[22] Ross, *Changing Trains at Wigan*, p. 22.

[23] Luciana Duranti and Kenneth Thibodeau, "The Concept of Record in Interactive, Experiential and Dynamic Environments: The View from InterPARES," *Archival Science* 6 (2006): 26.

[24] Ibid., p. 46.

[25] David Bearman, "Moments of Risk: Identifying Threats to Electronic Records," *Archivaria* 62 (Fall 2006): 15-46.

[26] Rick Barry, "Web Sites as Recordkeeping & 'Recordmaking' Systems," *Information Management Journal* 38 (November/December 2004): 27.

[27] Ibid., p. 32.

[28] John P. Frost, "Web Technologies for Information Management," *Information Management Journal* 35 (October 2001): 34.

[29] See, for example, Terry Eastwood, *Appraisal of Electronic Records: A Review of the Literature in English*, InterPARES Project, May 30, 2000 for an interesting review of the relevant literature.

[30] See section 4.8, Public Record Office, *Management, Appraisal and Preservation of Electronic Records; Vol. 1: Principles*, 2nd. ed. (Kew: Public Record Office, 1999) as one example. The literature written by individuals such as Duranti, Thibodeau, and Bearman, cited above, all affirm such an objective.

[31] Timothy P. O'Keefe and Mark Langemo, "Controlling the Risks of Content Publication," *Information Management Journal* 39 (January/February 2005): 37-40, 42-43.

[32] From the Internet Archive website at http://www.archive.org/about/about.php, accessed July 20, 2007.

[33] Mike Thelwall and Liven Vaughan, "A Fair History of the Web? Examining Country Balance in the Internet Archive," *Library & Information Science Research* 26, no. 2 (2004): 162-176.

[34] John T. Phillips, "The Challenge of Web Site Records Preservation," *Information Management Journal* 37 (January/February 2003): 43.

[35] Ibid., p. 46.

[36] Ibid., p. 48.

[37] Anne R. Kenney and Nancy Y. McGovern, "Preservation Risk Management for Web Resources," *Information Management Journal* 35 (September/October 2002): 53.

[38] Ibid., p. 57.

[39] William Y. Arms... et al., "Collecting and Preserving the Web: The Minerva prototype," *RLG DigiNews* 5, no. 2 (April 15, 2001), available http://www.rlg.org/legacy/preserv/diginews/diginews5-2.html#feature1, accessed July 14, 2007. See also William Y. Arms, *Web Preservation Project Final Report: a report to the Library of Congress,* (September 3, 2001), available at http://www.loc.gov/minerva/webpresf.pdf.

[40] Juha Hakala, "Collecting and Preserving the Web: Developing and Testing the NEDLIB Harvester," *RLG DigiNews* 5, no. 2 (April 15, 2001), available at http://www.rlg.org/legacy/preserv/diginews/diginews5-2.html#feature2, accessed July 14, 2007.

[41] Anne R. Kenney... et al., "Preservation Risk Management for Web Resources: Virtual Remote Control in Cornell's Project Prism," *D-Lib Magazine* 8, no. 1 (Jan 2002), available at http://www.dlib.org/dlib/january02/kenney/01kenney.html, access July 14, 2007.

[42] Ellie Buckley... et al., "Virtual Remote Control: Building a Preservation Risk Management Toolbox for Web Resources," *D-Lib Magazine* 10, no. 4 (Apr 2004), available at http://www.dlib.org/dlib/april04/mcgovern/04mcgovern.html, accessed July 14, 2007.

[43] Paul Koerbin, "The PANDORA Digital Archiving System (PANDAS): Managing Web Archiving in Australia: A Case Study," Paper presented at the 4th International Web Archiving Workshop, September 16, 2004, Bath UK, available at http://www.nla.gov.au/nla/staffpaper/2004/koerbin2.html, accessed July 16, 2007.

[44] Margaret E. Phillips, "Selective Archiving of Web Resources: A Study of Acquisition Costs at the National Library of Australia," *RLG DigiNews* 9, no. 3 (June 15, 2005), http://www.rlg.org/en/page.php?Page_ID=20666#article0, accessed July 16, 2007.

[45] Peter Johan Lor, Johannes Britz and Henry Watermeyer, "Everything, For Ever? The Preservation of South African Websites for Future Research and Scholarship," *Journal of Information Science* 32, no. 1 (Feb 2006): 39-48.

[46] Wendy Smith, "Still Lost in Cyberspace? Preservation Challenges of Australian Internet Resources," *Australian Library Journal* 54, no. 3 (Aug 2005): 282.

[47] Ibid., p. 59.

[48] Ibid.

[49] Carol E. B. Chosky, *Domesticating Information: Managing Documents Inside the Organization* (Lanham, MD: Scarecrow Press, 2006) is a pre-eminent example of such thinking.

[50] "Online Today, Gone Tomorrow," *Information Management Journal* 38 (March/April 2004): 13.

[51] James Fallows, "File Not Found," *Atlantic Monthly* 298 (September 2006): 145,

[52] Jeff Rothenberg, "Preservation of the Times," *Information Management Journal* 36 (March/April 2002): 40.

[53] Laurie L. Gingrich and Brian D. Morris, "Retention and Disposition of Structured Data: The Next Frontier for Records Managers," *Information Management Journal* 40 (March/April 2006): 31.

[54] Susan Haigh and Roselyn Lilleniit, "A Strategy for Archiving Web Sites at Library and Archives Canada," *Preservation of Electronic Records: New Knowledge and Decision-Making* (Ottawa, CA: Canadian Conservation Institute, 2004), pp. 143-148.

[55] See, for example, Christine Harold, *Our Space: Resisting the Corporate Control of Culture* (Minneapolis: University of Minnesota Press, 2007).

[56] Jeremy Brett, "A Case Study of the Web-Site Appraisal Process as Applied to State Government Agency Web Sites in Wisconsin," *Archival Issues* 27, no. 2 (2002): 99-110.

[57] Charles M. Dollar, "Appraising Machine-Readable Records," *American Archivist* 41 (October 1978): 423-430 and Ross J. Cameron, "Appraisal Strategies for Machine-Readable Case Files," *Provenance* 1 (Spring 1983): 49-55.

[58] Alan Kowlowitz, *Archival Appraisal of Online Information Systems* (Pittsburgh: Archives and Museum Informatics, no. 2, Fall 1988).

[59] Michael E, Holland, "Adding Electronic Records to the Archival Menagerie: Appraisal Concerns and Cautions," *Provenance* 8 (Spring 1990): 27-44. The exception to this was the National Archives, this agency

having established in 1990 a Center for Electronic Records, even though it was still following a fairly standard approach of a focus on informational value in order to weed through the many thousands of databases in the federal government.

60 Valerie D. Glenn, "Preserving Government and Political Information: The Web–at–Risk Project," *First Monday*, volume 12, number 7 (July 2007), http://firstmonday.org/issues/issue12_7/glenn/index.html, accessed July 12, 2007.

61 Diane M. Zorich, "Defining Stewardship in the Digital Age," *First Monday*, volume 12, number 7 (July 2007), http://firstmonday.org/issues/issue12_7/zorich/index.html, accessed July 12, 2007.

62 Ibid.

63 Kenney... et al., "Preservation Risk Management for Web Resources."

64 Susan Tucker, Katherine Ott, and Patricia P. Buckler, eds., *The Scrapbook in American Life* (Philadelphia: Temple University Press, 2006), p. 18.

65 Patricia P. Buckler and C. Kay Leeper. "An Antebellum Woman's Scrapbook as Autobiographical Composition," *Journal of American Culture* 14, no. 1 (1991): 1.

66 Ibid., p. 2.

67 Jean-Noël Jeanneney, *Google and the Myth of Universal Knowledge: A View from Europe*, trans. Teresa Lavender Fagan (Chicago: University of Chicago Press, 2007), p. 23.

68 Ibid., p. 87.

69 Susan M. Bielstein, *Permissions, A Survival Guide: Blunt Talk About Art as Intellectual Property* (Chicago: University of Chicago Press, 2006), p. 1.

70 Harold, *Our Space*, p. 140.

71 William Kelso, *Jamestown: The Buried Truth* (Charlottesville, VA: University of Virginia Press, 2006), p. 1.

72 Ibid., p. 76.

73 Ibid., p. 169.

74 William Clark, *Academic Charisma and the Origins of the Research University* (Chicago: University of Chicago Press, 2006), p. 289.

75 See, for example, Michael Day, Collecting and Preserving the World Wide Web: A Feasibility Study Undertaken for the JISC and Wellcome Trust, (February 25, 2003), p. 2. The focus of this project is on the history and understanding of medicine, and it generally followed the guidelines of other Web "harvesting" projects such as PANDORA.

[76] Smith, "The Future of Web Resources." We can see this in the discussion of institutional projects, such as one carried out at the University of Melbourne in Australia, a project seeking to "preserve material for cultural and historical purposes," but just as much focused on the key administrative and legal needs of the university. This project discovered that some of what was thought to be obvious recordkeeping issues turned out not to be specific enough in enabling the determination of a site being archived or not. The project switched to a functional approach and sought to develop better recordkeeping and web publishing guidelines. It concluded that working with Web sites was not merely a technological issue: "The solution is more about finding a balance between the needs of the various stakeholders involved in the project … and then assessing these needs against what the technology can actually provide." Catherine Nicholls and John-Paul Williams, "Identifying Roadkill on the Information Highway: A Website Appraisal Case Study," *Archives and Manuscripts* 30, no. 2 (Nov 2002): 98, 99.

[77] Robert L. Sanders, "Personal Business Records in an Electronic Environment," *Information Management Journal* 33 (October 1999): 60.

[78] See Marcia Clemmitt, "Cyber Socializing: Are Internet Sites like MySpace Potentially Dangerous?" *CQ Researcher*, 16 (July 28, 2006): 625-648.

[79] Bruce W. Dearstyne, "Blogs, Mashups, & Wikis Oh, My!" *Information Management Journal* 41 (July/August 2007): 24-28, 30, 32-33.

[80] Available at http://en.wikipedia.org/wiki/Blog, accessed July 21, 2007.

[81] Jack Goody, *The Power of the Written Tradition* (Washington, DC: Smithsonian Institution Press, 2000), p. 27.

[82] Andrew Keen, *The Cult of the Amateur: How Today's Internet is Killing Our Culture* (New York: Doubleday/Currency, 2007), p. 3.

[83] Ibid., p. 7.

[84] Joseph Parisi and Stephen Young, *Between the Lines: A History of Poetry in Letters; Part II: 1962-2002* (Chicago: Ivan R. Dee, 2006), p. xvii.

[85] Amanda Lenhart and Susannah Fox, *Bloggers: A Portrait of the Internet's New Storytellers* (Washington, D.C.: Pew Internet & American Life Project, July 19, 2006).

[86] Douglas L. Wilson, *Lincoln's Sword: The Presidency and the Power of Words* (New York: Alfred A. Knopf, 2006), pp. 6 and 7.

[87] Thomas Haigh, "Remembering the Office of the Future: The Origins of Word Processing and Office Automation," *IEEE Annals of the History of Computing* (October-December 2006): 26.

88 Robert E. Bonner, *The Soldier's Pen: Firsthand Impressions of the Civil War* (New York: Hill and Wang, 2006), p. 19.

89 Ibid., p. 221.

90 Ibid., p. 225.

91 Penelope Papailias, *Genres of Recollection: Archival Poetics and Modern Greece* (New York: Palgrave Macmillan, 2005).

92 An example is Jonathan Harr's bestselling *The Lost Painting: The Quest for a Caravaggio Masterpiece* (New York: Random House Trade Paperbacks, 2006). Two young Italian scholars visit a family archives in Rome, and we read about decaying volumes, fading ink, brittle pages, and puzzling notarial and accountant entries and we see archivists, with light steps and a whispering voice, assisting them. We experience with the researchers their discoveries of clues "buried in the archives." We follow the researchers to another family archives outside of Rome, and we watch them work through a set of records with a jumbled organization, conducting their research while they witness the family matriarch reorganizing the archives to suit her needs. One of the researchers relates to the other that this was "like watching someone clean house by throwing things out the window – plates and silverware, pots and pans – as if that were completely normal" (p. 56). To be sure, Harr plays on popular notions of archives in order to craft a good story. *The Lost Painting* depicts archives as being in dank cellars, covered in dust, often at the mercy of strange and eccentric individuals – and it is not to argue that these circumstances and characteristics are not depicted in a faithful fashion in this book. Still, an account such as this fuels the stereotypes of archives and archivists, and those of us aware of the archival community and its practice need to be aware when such portraits of our field are painted.

93 Bill Hayes, *The Anatomist: A True Story of Gray's Anatomy* (New York: Ballantine Books, 2008), p. 71.

94 Julian Barnes, "The Past Conditional: What Mother Would Have Wanted," *New Yorker* (December 25, 2006 & January 1, 2007), p. 57.

95 Nancy Deromedi discusses a variety of issues relating to the personal web sites of university faculty, in her "Personal Faculty Web Sites: Exploring Archival Issues and the Digital Convergence," *Archival Issues* 29, no. 1 (2005): 11.

96 Ibid., p. 12.

97 William Zinsser, *Inventing the Truth: The Art and Craft of Memoir,* rev. ed. (Boston: Houghton Mifflin Co., 1998), p. 3.

98 "The Universal Diarist," *Economist* (November 25, 2005, p. 68.

[99] Harriette Andreadis, "True Womanhood Revisited: Women's Private Writing in Nineteenth Century Texas," *Journal of the Southwest* 31 (Summer 1989): 179-204; Lynn Z. Bloom, "Escaping Voices: Women's South Pacific Internment Diaries and Memoirs," *Mosaic* 23, no. 3 (1990): 101-112; Helen M. Buss, "Pioneer Women's Diaries and Journals: Letters Home/Letters to the Future," *Mapping Our Selves: Canadian Women's Autobiography in English* (Montreal and Kingston: McGill-Queen's University Press, 1993), pp. 37-60; Gayle R. Davis, "Women's Frontier Diaries: Writing for Good Reason," *Women's Studies* 14, no. 1 (1988): 5-14; Rebecca Hogan, "Engendered Autobiographies: The Diary as Feminine Form," in *Autobiography and Questions of Gender.* ed. Shirley Neuman (London: Cass, 1992): 95-107; Jane H. Hunter, "Inscribing the Self in the Heart of the Family: Diaries and Girlhood in Late-Victorian America," *American Quarterly* 44, no. 1 (1992): 51-81; Laurie Ann McNeill, ""Somewhere Along the Line I Lost Myself': Recreating Self in the War Diaries of Natalie Crouter and Elizabeth Vaughan," *Legacy: A Journal of American Women Writers* 19, no. 1 (January 2002): 98-106.

[100] Joanne E. Cooper, "Shaping Meaning: Women's Diaries, Journals, and Letters; the Old and the New," *Women's Studies International Forum* 10, no. 1 (1987): 95.

[101] Ibid., p. 96.

[102] Christopher C. Burnham, "Reinvigorating a Tradition: The Personal Development Journal," in *The Journal Book,* ed., Toby Fulwiler (Portsmouth, NH: Boynton/Cook, 1987), pp. 148-156.

[103] Kathryn Dianne Carter, "Death and the Diary, or Tragedies in the Archive," *Journal of Canadian Studies* 40, no. 2 (2006), p. 54.

[104] Alexandra Garbarini, *Numbered Days: Diaries and the Holocaust* (New Haven: Yale University Press, 2006), p. x.

[105] Ibid., p. 5.

[106] Ibid., p. 12.

[107] Ibid., p. 15.

[108] Ibid., p. 18.

[109] Ibid., p. 129.

[110] Ibid., p. 165.

[111] Robert Inchausti, ed., *Echoing Silence: Thomas Merton on the Vocation of Writing* (Boston: New Seeds, 2007), p. 13.

[112] Gayle Davis, "The Diary as Historical Puzzle: Seeking the Author Behind the Words," *Kansas History* 16 (1993): 171.

[113] Jane Dupree Begos, "The Diaries of Adolescent girls," *Women's Studies International Forum* 10, no. 1 (1987): pp. 69-74.

[114] Molly McCarthy, "A pocketful of days: Pocket Diaries and Daily Record Keeping Among Nineteenth-century New England Women," *New England Quarterly* 73, no. 2 (2000): 279.

[115] Ibid, p. 280.

[116] Lawrence Rosenwald, "Some Myths About Diaries," *Raritan: A Quarterly Review* 6, no. 3 (1987): 100.

[117] See, for example, José Van Dijck, "Composing the Self: Of Diaries and Lifelogs," *Fibreculture: Internet+Theory+Culture+Research.* 3 (2004), available at http://journal.fibreculture.org/issue3/issue3_vandijck.html, accessed July 28, 2007.

[118] Y. Geffroy, "Family Photographs: A Visual Heritage," *Visual Anthropology* 3, no. 4 (1990): 367-409.

[119] Andrew Hassam, "'As I Write': Narrative Occasions and the Quest for Self-Presence in the Travel Diary," *Ariel* 21, no. 4 (1990): 35.

[120] Susan C. Herring, Lois Ann Scheidt, Elijah Wright, Sabrina Bonus, "Weblogs as a Bridging Genre," *Information Technology & People* 18, no. 2 (June 2005): 163.

[121] Lena Karlsson, "Consuming Lives, Creating Community: Female Chinese-American Diary Writing on the Web," *Prose Studies* 2003 26, nos. 1-2 (2003): 220.

[122] Ibid., p. 228.

[123] Kurt Lindermann, "Live(s) Online: Narrative Performance, Presence, and Community in LiveJournal.com," *Text & Performance Quarterly* 25, no. 4 (October 2005): 360.

[124] Laurie McNeill, "Teaching an Old Genre New Tricks: The Diary of theInternet," *Biography: A Multidisciplinary Quarterly* 26, no. 1 (Winter 2003): 34. See also Madeleine Sorapure, "Screening Moments, Screening Lives: Diary Writing on the Web," *Biography: A Multidisciplinary Quarterly* 26, no. 1 (Winter 2003): 1-23.

[125] James Cuno, ed., *Whose Muse? Art Museums and the Public Trust* (Princeton: Princeton University Press, 2004), p. 73.

[126] Ibid., p. 153.

[127] See Bearman, "Moments of Risk."

[128] See, for example, Francis X. Blouin Jr. and William G. Rosenberg, *Archives, Documentation, and Institutions of Social Memory: Essays from the Sawyer Seminar* (Ann Arbor: University of Michigan Press, 2006).

[129] Gideon Lewis-Kraus, "A World in Three Aisles: Browsing the Post-Digital Library," *Harper's* 314 (May 2007): 47-52, 54-57.
[130] Ibid., p. 47.
[131] Ibid., p. 49.
[132] Ibid., p. 49.
[133] Ibid., p. 56.
[134] Ibid.
[135] Karin Barber, ed., *Africa's Hidden Histories: Everyday Literacy and Making the Self* (Bloomington and Indianapolis: Indiana University Press, 2006), p. 9.
[136] Errol Morris, "Liar, Liar, Pants on Fire," *New York Times*, July 10, 2007, available at http://morris.blogs.nytimes.com/2007/07/10/pictures-are-supposed-to-be-worth-a-thousand-words/#comment-132, accessed July 18, 2007.

Conclusion

[1] Joseph Kaye, Janet Vertesi, Shari Avery, Allan Dafoc, Shay David, Lisa Onaga, Ivan Roserio, and Trevor Pinch, "To Have and to Hold: Exploring the Personal Archive," *CHI 2006*, April 22-27, 2006, Montreal, Quebec, Canada, p. 275.
[2] Ibid.. p. 284.
[3] Paula Kamen, *Finding Iris Chang: Friendship, Ambition, and the Loss of an Extraordinary Mind* (Philadelphia: Da Capo Press, 2007), p. xvi.
[4] Ibid., p. 72.
[5] Ibid., p. 263.
[6] Bill Bryson, *Shakespeare: The World as Stage* (New York: HarperCollins Books, 2007), p. 8.
[7] Ibid., p. 21.
[8] Roger Scruton, *Culture Counts: Faith and Feeling in a World Besieged* (New York: Brief Encounters, 2007), p. x.
[9] Ibid., p. 30.
[10] Ibid., p. 87.
[11] Anthony Grafton, "Future Reading: Digitization and Its Discontents," *New Yorker*, November 5, 2007, p. 54.
[12] Christine Borgman, *Scholarship in the Digital Age: Information, Infrastructure, and the Internet* (Cambridge, MA: MIT Press, 2007), p. 68.
[13] Ibid., p. 97.
[14] Ibid., p. 89.

15 Robert F. Williams and Lori J. Ashley, *Call for Collaboration: Electronic Records Management Survey* (Chicago: Cohasset Associates in association with ARMA International and AIIM, 2007), available at www.MERresource.com/whitepapers/survey.htm (the quotation is on page 45).

16 For example, Fiona Cameron and Sarah Kenderdine, eds., *Theorizing Digital Cultural Heritage: A Critical Discourse* (Cambridge, MA: MIT Press, 2007) provides one clump of essays exploring the use of digitization, mostly from the vantage of museums but considering cultural heritage to span across libraries, galleries, archives, and archaeology as well. In the Cameron and Kenderdine volume there are a lot of interesting observations about digitization and the Web that will interest archivists. Peter Walsh, for example, examines how art museums have used the Web, suggesting that these institutions have not changed their approaches "towards the display and interpretation of works of art." Digital photographs are still being used in the ways photographs were used in the nineteenth century. Museum Websites "still closely resemble printed catalogs and exhibition brochures" (p. 31). Various perspectives emerge from these essays. Many of the authors remind their readers that we are still in the very early stages of digitization and the use of the Web. They ruminate about the meaning of digital versus real objects and the implications of the use of digitization for cultural repositories. The complex issues of intellectual property are also considered, as well as the means of using Web sites and digitization projects as a means to attract new audiences. We read about digital preservation, online learning, online exhibitions, and the notion of a virtual heritage. Pervading the essays are ideas about new and innovative ways to engage the public. As we consider digitization, we see entirely new ways to develop audiences and to connect with them, and these new roles may transform how we have traditionally thought of institutions like museums and archives. Harald Kraemer, in his contribution to the volume, states, "Information is the capital of the knowledge bases named museums, archives, libraries, and art trade. The boundaries between them will collapse; digital collections will combine and create information with a long time value" (p. 212). Most significantly, Kraemer believes that the "museum is transforming from a sanctuary to a production center" (p. 212). These are all attributes we can assign to archives as well.

17 G. E. Gorman and Sydney J. Shep, eds., *Preservation Management for Libraries, Archives and Museums* (London: Facet Publishing, 2006), p. 13.

[18] Ibid., p. 59.

[19] Ibid., p. 245.

[20] Elbert Hubbard's *Helpful Hints for Business Helpers*, published by the Roycrofters in 1909, provides some interesting advice offered about the production of records, in this case, business letters, that still resonate today as well as reflect how workers viewed the creation of documents. Hubbard advises workers not to write letters that "show resentment or anger," because the "letter lives long after the cause of offense if forgotten" (p. 7). How often have we encountered the same advice in modern etiquette and e-mail manuals? In Hubbard's day, advice is offered to separate personal and business matters, including the writing of personal letters, away from the business world (p. 8). Workers are instructed not to "touch pencils, pens, erasers or papers on another man's desk, unless he is there" (p. 8). The issues of economy were of concern then as they still often seem to be today: "Never use letter-paper or envelopes to figure on or for memoranda – it shows you do not realize that the first requisite in business is economy" (p. 11). And, finally, Hubbard advises workers to "date all letters, memoranda and statistics – the Dating Habit is a good one" (p. 12). In this last issue, we now think of the challenges of maintaining version control of those many word-processed drafts of a report or letter. This small publication is also filled with commentary on workers' performance reflecting both the emergence of scientific management and the tendency of the Arts and Crafts designers to cover their homes and offices in messages about life and work.

[21] Cyndi Howells, *Planting Your Family Tree Online: How to Create Your Own Family History Web Site* (Nashville: Rutledge Hill Press, 2003).

[22] Rhonda R. McMlure, *Digitizing Your Family History: Easy Methods for Preserving Your Heirloom Documents, Photos, Home Movies and More in a Digital Format* (Cincinnati, OH: Family Tree Books, 2004).

[23] Rick Pagano, *For the Record: A Personal Facts and Document Organizer* (Chandler, AZ: Five Star Publications, Inc., 2007).

[24] We can see a modern example in Raymond Clemens and Timothy Graham, *Introduction to Manuscript Studies* (Ithaca: Cornell University Press, 2007), providing "practical instruction and training in the paleography and codicology of medieval manuscripts, in particular manuscripts written in Latin" (p. xiii). We learn about scripts, dating manuscripts, provenance, writing materials, the emergence of the use of paper over other writing materials, corrections and annotations, using microfilm or online

surrogates, transcribing and editing texts, punctuation and abbreviations, forgeries, describing manuscripts, and so forth. This particular publication, although designed for students and scholars, also demonstrates the potential archivists and manuscripts experts can bring to the table in producing a guide about documentary materials. Beautifully illustrated and clearly written, this book could be profitably read by non-specialists interested in calligraphy, art, and the history of books.

25 Examples include Althea Douglas, *Help! I've Inherited an Attic Full of History* (Toronto: Ontario Genealogical Society, 2003) and Katherine Scott Sturdevant, *Organizing and Preserving Your Heirloom Documents* (Cincinnati, OH: Betterway Books, 2002).

26 The example in this genre of publishing of an established archives supporting this kind of self-help manual is Robert Pols, *Family Photographs, 1860-1945: A Guide to Researching, Dating and Contextualizing Family Photographs* (Richmond, Surrey: Public Record Office, 2002). For another example, see Maureen A. Taylor, *Preserving Your Family Photographs: How to Organize, Present, and Restore Your Precious Family Images* (Cincinnati, OH: Betterway Books, 2001).

27 Tom Goldstein, *Journalism and Truth: Strange Bedfellows* (Evanston, IL: Northwestern University Press, 2007), pp. 12-13.

28 Ibid., p. 13.

29 Geert Lovink, *Zero Comments: Blogging and Critical Internet Culture* (New York: Routledge, 2008), p. xxiii.

30 Helen Freshwater, "The Allure of the Archive," *Poetics Today* 24, no. 4 (2003), p. 734.

31 Clemens and Graham, *Introduction to Manuscript Studies*, p. 113.

32 One observer in a reader on cultural heritage provides an example, noting the "impossibility of reducing heritage to a simple formula. It is, by its very nature, an unstable and contested idea, as must be any idea that attempts to capture the things we count most valuable in our collective life. As soon as the net of definition is lifted over it, it takes flight." Graeme Davison. "Heritage: From Patrimony to Pastiche," in Graham Fairclough, Rodney Harrison, John H. Jameson, Jr., and John Schofield, eds., *The Heritage Reader* (London: Routledge, 2008), p. 40.

33 Patricia R. Zimmerman, "The Home Movie Movement: Excavations, Artifacts, Minings," in Karen L Ishizuka and Patricia R. Zimmerman, eds., *Mining the Home Movie: Excavations in Histories and Memories* (Berkeley: University of California Press, 2008), p. 18.

34 Ibid., p. 19.

[35] Freshwater, "Allure," p. 755.

[36] Ayisha Abaham, "Deteriorating Memories: Blurring Fact and Fiction in Home Movies in India," in Ishizuka and Zimmerman, *Mining the Home Movie*, p. 172.

[37] Catherine C. Marshall, Sara Bly, and Francoise Brun-Cottan, "The Long Term Fate of Our Personal Digital Belongings: Toward a Service Model for Personal Archives," *Proceedings of Archiving 2006.*, Society for Imaging Science and Technology, Springfield, VA, 2006, http://www.csdl.tamu.edu/~marshall/archiving2006-marshall.pdf, accessed March 7, 2008.

[38] Neil Beagrie, "Plenty of Room at the Bottom? Personal Digital Libraries and Collections," *D-Lib Magazine* 11, no. 6 (June 2005), http://webdoc.sub.gwdg.de/edoc/aw/d-lib/dlib/june05/beagrie/06beagrie.html, accessed March 8, 2008.

[39] For an accounting of such fiction see Arlene Schmuland, "The Archival Image in Fiction: An Analysis and Annotated Bibliography," *American Archivist* 62 (Spring 1999): 24-73.

[40] Nelson DeMille, *Plum Island* (New York:Warner Books, 1997), p. 281.

[41] Ibid.

[42] Ibid., p. 284.

[43] Ibid.

[44] Ibid., p. 291.

[45] Ibid., p. 292.

[46] Anyone wanting to consider how to issue an effective publication promoting the nature of archives might want to examine Margo Stipe, *Frank Lloyd Wright: The Interactive Portfolio; Rare Removable Treasures, Hand-Drawn Sketches, Original Letters, and More from the Official Archives* (Philadelphia: Running Press, 2004). Organized around Wright's life and some of his most important buildings (such as the Larkin Building, Fallingwater, and the Guggenheim Museum), this handsome publication includes reproductions of printed ephemera, photographs, lecture notes, architectural drawings, magazine articles, sketches, and letters that can be removed and spread out for examination. Anyone who has not been in an archives gets something of the experience of visiting one and using archival sources. The publication also includes a CD of interviews with Wright in his last years (1952-1957). The materials all come from the Frank Lloyd Wright Foundation, Taliesin West, Scottsdale, Arizona. It helps, of course, to have the records of someone as interesting as Wright, but this is a good example of how to package the archival experience in a

publication. This can double as a good teaching tool for introducing
individuals to the nature of archives. I only wish there was something
more of a discussion about how Wright preserved his papers and how this
archives came to be formed. Clearly, the goal of the Foundation was to
produce something for Wright fans, and as I am one, I am more than
happy with the effort.

47 This is available at
http://www.mnhs.org/people/mngg/stories/papers.htm, accessed March
7, 2008. Information about the workshops, focusing on "preserving
family history," can be found on the Society's website.

48 "A Checklist for Organizing Family Papers," available at
http://www.mnhs.org/people.mngg/stories/orgpapers.htm, accessed 7
March 2008.

49 This can be found at www.naa.gov.au/services/family-
historians/looking-after/index.aspx, accessed March 7, 2008.

50 This guide can be found at the PARADIGM website,
www.paradigm.ac.uk/workbook/appendices/guidelines.html, accessed
March 7, 2008.

51 University of Wyoming American Heritage Center, Brochures and
Handouts, "Preserving Family Computer Documents and Digital Images,"
http://ahc.uwyo.edu/documents/about/publications/handouts/e-
papers.pdf, accessed March 7, 2008. This institution also produced
"Preserving Family Papers and Documents" and "How to Get Started
Preserving Photographs," providing basic advice for maintaining personal
and family archives, also available on the same website.

52 This is available at
http://www.njdigitalhighway.org/personal_story_ever.php, accessed
March 7, 2008.

53 See the guide at
www.paradigm.ac.uk/workbook/appendices/guidelines.html, accessed
March 7, 2008.

54 Idaho State Historical Society, "Placing Your Personal Records in an
Archives," http://www.idahohistory.net/3Handout.pdf, accessed March
7, 2008.

55 We have earlier precedents for this in the archival community. In the
mid-1970s the Georgia Department of Archives and History launched its
Vanishing Georgia Photographic Collection, traveling around the state and
copying family and personal photographs. See

http://content.sos.state.ga.us/cdm4/vanishing.php for a description of the project, accessed March 12, 2008.

[56] Travis Holland, *The Archivist's Story* (New York: The Dial Press, 2007), p. 189.

[57] Ibid., p. 199.

[58] Ibid., p. 232.

[59] Paul Auster, *Travels in the Scriptorium* (New York: Henry Holt and Co., 2006).

[60] David S. Brown, *Richard Hofstadter: An Intellectual Biography* (Chicago: University of Chicago Press, 2006), p. 118.

[61] Ibid., p. 144. Shunning the primary sources is always a road to trouble, of course, but it is also the case that there are individuals, like Hofstadter, who can provoke new uses of such sources. In fact, according to Brown, Hofstadter worried little about the criticism concerning his slighting archival materials. Hofstadter "understood that deduction, synthesis, and irony too nourished the historical imagination. Good, exciting history, after all, was something more than a dry recitation of names, dates, and facts. He allowed to a colleague, in what stands as a succinct reply to his critics, that the historical profession needed imaginative thinking more than it needed legions of historians stumbling about in distant archives."

[62] Alan Dershowitz, *Finding Jefferson: A Lost Letter, A Remarkable Discovery, and the First Amendment in an Age of Terrorism* (New York: John Wiley and Sons, Inc., 2008), p. 18.

[63] Ibid., p. 50.

[64] Ibid., p. 82.

[65] Ibid., p. 86.

[66] Lee Gutkind and Hattie Fletcher, eds., *Keep It Real: Everything You Need to Know About Researching and Writing Creative Nonfiction* (New York: W.W. Norton & Co., 2008), pp. 98-99.

[67] Ibid., p. 111.

[68] Ibid., p. 112.

[69] Building on my earlier *Lester J. Cappon and the Relationship of History, Archives, and Scholarship in the Golden Age of Archival Theory* (Chicago: Society of American Archivists, 2004).

[70] September 4, 1968, Diary, Lester J. Cappon Papers, College of William and Mary, Lester J. Cappon Papers, Ms 90 C17.

Index

LaVergne, TN USA
07 January 2010
169180LV00001B/64/P